W9-ARG-083

HUMAN RESOURCES MANAGEMENT

IN THE HOSPITALITY INDUSTRY

Second Edition

HUMAN RESOURCES MANAGEMENT
IN THE HOSPITALITY INDUSTRY

Second Edition

DAVID K. HAYES | JACK D. NINEMEIER

WILEY

No part of this publication may be reproduced, stored in a retrieval system, or transmitted in any form or by any means, electronic, mechanical, photocopying, recording, scanning or otherwise, except as permitted under Sections 107 or 108 of the 1976 United States Copyright Act, without either the prior written permission of the Publisher, or authorization through payment of the appropriate per-copy fee to the Copyright Clearance Center, Inc., 222 Rosewood Drive, Danvers, MA 01923 (Website: www.copyright.com). Requests to the Publisher for permission should be addressed to the Permissions Department, John Wiley & Sons, Inc., 111 River Street, Hoboken, NJ 07030-5774, (201) 748-6011, fax (201) 748-6008, or online at: www.wiley.com/go/permissions.

This book was set in 10/12 Minion Pro by Laserwords Private Limited and printed and bound by RR Donnelley Kendallville.

Founded in 1807, John Wiley & Sons, Inc. has been a valued source of knowledge and understanding for more than 200 years, helping people around the world meet their needs and fulfill their aspirations. Our company is built on a foundation of principles that include responsibility to the communities we serve and where we live and work. In 2008, we launched a Corporate Citizenship Initiative, a global effort to address the environmental, social, economic, and ethical challenges we face in our business. Among the issues we are addressing are carbon impact, paper specifications and procurement, ethical conduct within our business and among our vendors, and community and charitable support. For more information, please visit our website: www.wiley.com/go/citizenship.

Copyright © 2016, 2009 John Wiley & Sons, Inc. All rights reserved.

Evaluation copies are provided to qualified academics and professionals for review purposes only, for use in their courses during the next academic year. These copies are licensed and may not be sold or transferred to a third party. Upon completion of the review period, please return the evaluation copy to Wiley. Return instructions and a free of charge return shipping label are available at: www.wiley .com/go/returnlabel. If you have chosen to adopt this textbook for use in your course, please accept this book as your complimentary desk copy. Outside of the United States, please contact your local sales representative.

Library of Congress Cataloging in Publication Data

Hayes, David K., author.
  Human resources management in the hospitality industry / David K. Hayes, Jack D. Ninemeier.—Second edition.
    pages cm
  Includes bibliographical references and index.
  ISBN 978-1-118-98850-3 (hardback)
  1. Hospitality industry—Personnel management. I. Ninemeier, Jack D., author. II. Title.
  TX911.3.P4H39 2015
  338.4'7910683—dc23

                              2014048355

Printed in the United States of America

10 9 8 7 6 5 4 3 2

CONTENTS

CHAPTER 5

EMPLOYEE ON-BOARDING: ORIENTATION AND INDUCTION   92

CHAPTER 6

PLANNING TRAINING PROGRAMS   109

CHAPTER 7

DELIVERING AND EVALUATING TRAINING PROGRAMS   135

As was true when the first edition of ***Human Resources Management in the Hospitality Industry*** was published, today's hospitality professional must be an expert at managing many functions. Ask successful hospitality managers working at all levels of the industry to identify their most daunting tasks, and you will find that these tasks frequently relate to people management. In every segment of the hospitality industry, finding, training, and retaining outstanding staff members are always challenging tasks, but every manager must master them.

Rising labor costs, increased competition for quality staff, workers' changing attitudes, evolving customer expectations, and a proliferation of new laws related to what human resources (HR) managers may and may not do legally are among the many factors that directly led to the creation of this completely updated and revised edition of ***Human Resources Management in the Hospitality Industry***.

As the text's authors, we are especially pleased with the result and believe it will again be well received by instructors, students, and those industry practitioners who are in the trenches of day-to-day hospitality operations. Some might argue that the concepts that should be taught in an HR management course are universal; thus a text useful for managers in general business, manufacturing, or other service industries would also be appropriate for students studying to enter the field of hospitality. We counter that the needs of hospitality students remain different and that teaching HR management to these students demands the availability of an excellent hospitality-specific text. We believe this to be true for three important reasons:

1. **Organizational structure of the hospitality business**—Many HR texts describe the operation of an organization's HR department. In the hospitality industry, the on-site manager typically *is* that unit's HR department in all except the largest of operations. Thus it is extremely important that hospitality managers be well versed in HR management, including employee recruitment and selection, training, compensation, performance appraisal and discipline, safety, and other key areas in which they will be personally called on to make critical decisions. Therefore this text asks the reader to assume the role of that decision maker.

2. **Diversity of employees**—The management of a hospitality unit requires managers to be adept at understanding the HR-related concerns of a wide range of employees with differing experience and skill levels. The backgrounds of workers in hospitality operations range from those who are entry level to others who are highly educated and proficient in advanced management areas such as finance, marketing, production, and revenue management. As a result, hospitality managers must be equally able to compute the overtime wages of hourly employees eligible for tip credits and to understand the different effects of the Patient Protection and Affordable Care Act on a business's full- and part-time workers. This book recognizes that diversity.

3. **Complexity**—There is no doubt that successful hospitality managers must be particularly skilled and knowledgeable. For example, they serve as both manufacturing and retail managers. A professional hospitality manager is unique because all of the functions of product sales, from item conceptualization to product delivery, are in the hands of the same individual. The result is that these managers must understand much more than how they interface with an HR department. Instead, they must realize that, in the eyes of their employees, fellow managers, company owners, and their guests, they *are* the HR department, and thus they must be aware of the legal (and many other) consequences of their decision making. As a result, the examination of complex legal implications of HR management is a dominant theme throughout this book.

❖❖ TEXT CONCEPT AND CONTENT

As we identified the content for this revision, we continually recognized the distinction between HR management and supervision. Historically, many hospitality students have been taught how to supervise employees. The reasoning was simple: Good managers become recognized as such by first being good supervisors. In today's litigious society, however, managers (and students) who do not understand the legal requirements and responsibilities that must underpin their actions are greatly disadvantaged. For example, hospitality supervisors and managers may know what they want to do to build an effective workforce; however, at the same time, they must not lack an understanding about what they are legally allowed to do, required to do, or even prohibited from doing. With the second edition of *Human Resources Management in the Hospitality Industry*, those who teach how to supervise HR now have the preferred option of teaching their students how to legally manage those resources.

With the goal of effectively aiding in the teaching of HR management, we created this edition with 12 chapters:

Chapter 1: Introduction to Human Resources in the Hospitality Industry

Chapter 2: The Legal Environment of Human Resources Management

Chapter 3: Human Resources Management: Policies and Procedures

Chapter 4: Employee On-Boarding: Recruitment and Selection

Chapter 5: Employee On-Boarding: Orientation and Induction

Chapter 6: Planning Training Programs

Chapter 7: Delivering and Evaluating Training Programs

Chapter 8: Compensation Programs

Chapter 9: Performance Management and Appraisal

Chapter 10: Employee Health and Safety

Chapter 11: Critical Issues in Human Resources Management

Chapter 12: Human Resources in Evolving Hospitality Organizations

In chapters 1–3, the three critical foundational chapters, readers will learn about the diversity of the hospitality industry's workers, important labor-related legislation they must know to manage their employees, and the key aspects of legal compliance, policy documentation, and record-keeping required of successful HR managers.

In chapters 4–7 the important topics of legally recruiting, hiring, and orienting hospitality employees are addressed. *On-boarding*, the term used to describe the socialization of new employees as they acquire the knowledge, skills, and attitudes needed for their success in an organization, is emphasized, as is the key role training plays in this process.

Because of their detailed treatment of employee training, these chapters, perhaps more than any others, illustrate the distinctive approach of this text toward HR management. Effective HR managers must understand and implement effective training principles. With the large number of unskilled positions to be filled, employee turnover rates that often approach 100 percent or more per year, a labor pool that grows increasingly diverse, and increasing job complexity, employee training is an essential key to ensuring quality products, high levels of guest service, and operational profitability in the hospitality industry.

Chapters 8–10 are important and address the philosophical and legal aspects of compensation management, including wages, salary and benefit administration, and nonfinancial employee compensation. Additional topics of importance included in these chapters are performance appraisal, discipline, and employee separation, as well as a detailed examination of the importance of employee health and physical safety. This key topic area also includes a thorough examination of harassment, a topic increasingly recognized as one important to the physical safety (as well as the physical and mental health) of employees of diverse gender, racial, religious, and sexual orientations.

Chapters 11 and 12 conclude the text and address some of the hospitality industry's most challenging HR-related issues. In chapter 11 these issues include employee unionization, managing downsizing, and the increasingly popular strategy of outsourcing key tasks. Diversity in the industry, turnover, and the manner in which a company is viewed by the community are additional important topic areas. The text's final chapter addresses organizational change and how human resource managers can best prepare for change by implementing effective mentoring, succession planning, and career development programs.

❖❖ NEW IN THE SECOND EDITION

Input from students and instructors, industry professionals, our colleagues at Wiley, and our own experiences have provided ample material for this new edition. In addition, the continually evolving legal environment in which HR managers must operate dictated specific updating and change. In this *Second Edition* readers will be pleased to find many significant text enhancements.

NEW! HR Management in Action Feature

In this exciting new feature, readers will learn about specific challenges HR managers frequently encounter at work as well as how these challenges are met. Placed near the beginning of each chapter, this new feature, developed with the assistance of HR managers currently working in the hospitality industry, helps readers better understand the things HR managers must know and do to succeed in their jobs.

NEW! HR Management Impact on New Employees Feature

This new feature addresses how the on-boarding efforts of HR managers can directly affect their new employees. As noted above, *on-boarding* is the term HR managers use to describe the wide range of activities that affect how new employees acquire the knowledge, skills, behaviors, and attitudes that lead to success in an organization.

This feature was added because turnover rates in some segments of the hospitality industry have historically been very high. These turnover rates can often be reduced when an HR manager's on-boarding efforts with new workers are highly effective. Because of this, HR Management Impact on New Employees, focusing on how HR managers' efforts specifically impact new workers, can help HR managers increase the success rates of their new employees and, as a result, the success of their own organizations.

NEW! Simplified Summary of Significant Legislation Feature

Understanding employment-related legislation is a critical part of every HR manager's job. To assist readers in recalling key features of important employment-related legislation introduced in applicable chapters, a new feature summarizing these key laws is now included in this revised edition. These easy-to-read, easy-to-understand summaries include information about the name of the law, who is affected by it, the requirements of the law, and key facts about the legislation, as well as a recommended source for acquiring more detailed information about it. These summaries serve a very valuable role in aiding reader recall as well as serving as important study and review aids.

Name of Law: Patient Protection and Affordable Care Act (ACA)
Applicable to: All US citizens and selected employers

Requirements of the Law	Key Facts About the Law
By 2014 all individuals must be enrolled in a government-approved health insurance plan or pay a fine.	The law established minimum quality standards for health insurance policies.
Each state must provide workers the option of purchasing subsidized health coverage via a state-based insurance exchange (marketplace).	The ACA requires insurers to spend at least 80 percent (85 percent for large insurers) of the health care premiums they collect for their insured's actual health claims and care costs.
Insurers are not permitted to cancel an individual's insurance coverage for health-related reasons.	The law states that selected preventive care procedures (including mammograms and domestic violence screening and counseling) must be provided without charging patients a deductible or a co-pay.
Effective for health plans offered after 2014, annual and/or lifetime limits on essential health coverage is prohibited.	The law allows those up to age 26 to stay on their parent's health insurance plans.
Firms employing 50 or more workers who do *not* provide health insurance coverage must pay a fine if the government is required to subsidize their workers' individual insurance coverage.	Health care plans may not deny or limit coverage of children younger than 19 because of pre-existing conditions.
Beginning in 2018, the law imposes a new 40 percent excise tax on the value of health coverage provided by employers that exceeds established dollar thresholds.	Effective in 2014, small-business owners are able to offer employees health plan choices through the Small Business Health Options Program (SHOP).
For detailed information on the law's requirements go to: www.healthcare.gov/law/	The law requires employers to report the cost of coverage under an employer-sponsored group health plan on an employee's Form W-2, Wage and Tax Statement.

❖❖ SPECIAL AREAS OF EMPHASIS IN THE SECOND EDITION

Our combined years of teaching hospitality management at the undergraduate, graduate, and continuing professional education levels have helped enormously to shape this textbook's original content and this revision. Specifically, the following became special areas of emphasis as we developed the second edition:

Simplification of Presentation

The readers of our text have always been our primary focus, and we are delighted to find that, again and again, creative graphics and clearly written narrative help to enhance the book's reader-friendliness and, as a result, present complex ideas in easily understandable ways. We took special care in this edition to review each paragraph and sentence to ensure the content they contain was presented in the clearest possible manner.

"For Your Consideration" Enhancements

User feedback indicates that the end-of-chapter "For Your Consideration" feature is extremely popular. This feature is frequently used for in-class assignments, class discussions, and home-work assignments. As a result of this great interest, the number of items presented in this feature has been increased in every chapter.

Targeted Utilization of Web-Based Learning Resources

The availability of Internet resources has greatly expanded the information authors are able to provide readers. Unfortunately, specific website addresses can and do change on a regular basis. For this edition, specific URLs were replaced with general instructions on how to retrieve critical information from the Web. The result is that readers will be able to easily find important websites regardless of the sites' most current Web address.

❖ TEXT FEATURES

From a reader's perspective, the features of a textbook often are as important as its content. Thoughtfully designed textbook features make the presented content easy to read, easy to understand, and easy to retain. As was true of the first edition, *Human Resources Management in the Hospitality Industry* is again especially reader-friendly. The following strategically designed features help readers learn:

- **Chapter Outline**—The two-tier chapter outline at the beginning of each chapter shows the context for each topic and provides a simple way to quickly find material within the chapter.

- **Learning Objectives**—This list of measurable learning objectives helps readers anticipate the skills or knowledge they will acquire upon completing the chapter. A unique feature of this text's design is that these learning objectives are listed a second time in their exact chapter location, allowing readers to be prepared for and excited about what they will be able to achieve when all of the chapter's material is successfully mastered.

- **Impact on HR Management**—Each chapter uses this short feature to explain, in clear terms and before any content is presented, exactly *why* the chapter's topic is important. This feature makes it easy for readers to see what the chapter is about and what information they will gain by reading it.

- **HR Terms**—As is true with many areas of specialization within hospitality management, HR managers speak their own language. In recognition of this fact, more than 300 special HR-related terms are defined within the text where they are first used. An alphabetical glossary of these terms is available on the text's website: www.wiley.com/college/hayes.

- **It's the Law**—Reinforcing its emphasis on the legal aspects of HR management, this feature is included in every chapter. It explains in detail how current or proposed legislation directly affects the topics presented and the resulting HR management–related actions that are and are not legally allowable or advisable.

- **HR Management in Action**—This new feature, included in each chapter, presents readers with brief scenarios/vignettes describing common challenges faced by HR managers, as well as how the challenge can best be addressed. For example, this new element is used when describing the practical and philosophical challenges of determining whether considering seniority when establishing worker pay is appropriate or instead whether an organization benefits most by paying its new employees the same amount it pays to longer-term workers holding the same jobs.

- **HR Management Issues**—Each chapter contains several of these real-world mini cases designed to make readers think about how they would personally use the information they have learned to respond to HR-related situations they will likely encounter in their jobs. Questions are included at the end of every case to help stimulate classroom discussion.

- **HR Management: Impact on New Employees**—This new feature appears in each chapter. Its purpose is to demonstrate clearly the impact of the various decisions HR managers must make on new employees. For example, this new element is used when describing the critical importance of an effective "employee orientation" program in easing a new employee's transition into a hospitality organization.

- **List of HR Terms**—Readers often need help in remembering key concepts that should be mastered after reading a section of a book. Thus, the HR terms introduced within each chapter are listed again at the conclusion of that chapter in the order in which they were presented to provide a helpful study aid.

- **For Your Consideration**—These end-of-chapter questions about the chapter's content are excellent for reader review. They are designed to be effective in stimulating classroom dialogue, as team activity assignments, and/or as homework assignments.

- **Case Study: Apply HR Management Principles**—The end-of-chapter case studies developed for *Human Resources Management in the Hospitality Industry* are unique. They present real-life situations and ask readers to examine that same situation from varying HR perspectives. For example, a case study examining the declining performance of an aging but long-term hospitality employee asks readers to consider the issue from three distinct perspectives: (1) the appropriateness of the employee appraisal system in use; (2) the importance to an organization of maximizing employee performance; and (3) an employer's responsibility to its long-term employees. Several questions are asked, focusing on multiple dimensions of the case study to emphasize critical thinking.

- **Internet Activities**—The importance of the Internet as a learning tool cannot be overlooked in any field of study. In this text, the Internet Activities feature that concludes each chapter not only directs students to pertinent websites but also gives readers specific instructions about what they can do, consider, and learn when they visit the sites.

We know that students learn best when concepts and practices are illustrated through many examples and features designed to engage their interest. Each of the special text features incorporated in this edition meet that criterion. The result is an effective text that is concise and informative as well as highly readable.

∴ INSTRUCTOR SUPPORT RESOURCES

Instructor support materials supplied by Wiley are among the very best available, and that is true for this text as well. The accompanying *Instructor's Manual* for this text includes teaching tips, answers to textbook exercises, and an extensive bank of examination questions and answers.

The *Instructor's Manual*, Test Bank, Respondus Test Bank, and Lecture PowerPoint slides can be found on the book's companion website: www.wiley.com/college/hayes.

∴ WILEYPLUS LEARNING SPACE

A place where students can define their strengths and nurture their skills, **WileyPLUS Learning Space** transforms course content into an online learning community. **WileyPLUS Learning Space** invites students to experience learning activities, work through self-assessment, ask questions and share insights. As students interact with the course content, each other, and their instructor, **WileyPLUS Learning Space** creates a personalized study guide for each student. Through collaboration, students make deeper connections to the subject matter and feel part of a community.

Through a flexible course design, instructors can quickly organize learning activities, manage student collaboration, and customize your course—having full control over content as well as the amount of interactivity between students.

WileyPLUS Learning Space lets the instructor:

- Assign activities and add your own materials
- Guide your students through what's important in the interactive e-textbook by easily assigning specific content
- Set up and monitor group learning
- Assess student engagement
- Gain immediate insights to help inform teaching

Defining a clear path to action, the visual reports in *WileyPLUS Learning Space* help both you and your students gauge problem areas and act on what's most important.

WileyPLUS Learning Space

An easy way to help your students **learn**, **collaborate**, and **grow**.

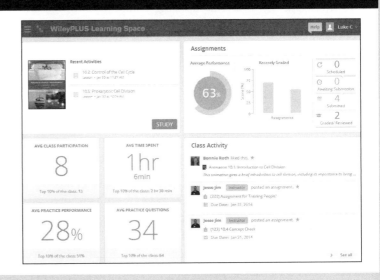

Personalized Experience

Students create their own study guide while they interact with course content and work on learning activities.

Flexible Course Design

Educators can quickly organize learning activities, manage student collaboration, and customize their course—giving them full control over content as well as the amount of interactivity among students.

Clear Path to Action

With visual reports, it's easy for both students and educators to gauge problem areas and act on what's most important.

Instructor Benefits

- Assign activities and add your own materials
- Guide students through what's important in the interactive e-textbook by easily assigning specific content
- Set up and monitor collaborative learning groups
- Assess learner engagement
- Gain immediate insights to help inform teaching

Student Benefits

- Instantly know what you need to work on
- Create a personal study plan
- Assess progress along the way
- Participate in class discussions
- Remember what you have learned because you have made deeper connections to the content

We are dedicated to supporting you from idea to outcome.

WILEY

ACKNOWLEDGMENTS AND DEDICATION

Human Resources Management in the Hospitality Industry was designed to be the most comprehensive, technically accurate, and valuable teaching resource available on the topic. We acknowledge the many individuals who assisted in its development. Special thanks go to Allisha Miller of Panda Professionals Hospitality Management and Training for her detailed manuscript review and assistance with the development of the text's student and instructor supplementary materials.

As is always true with our work, Peggy Hayes, Project Manager for Panda Professionals Hospitality Management and Training (PandaPros), and Leilani Ninemeier were instrumental in assisting with the management of this revision process. We are also extremely grateful to the many professionals in academia and industry who contributed to the original concept and idea for the book and who so freely gave of their time and advice. They include:

Michael Barnes of SUNY Delhi

David Brower of SUNY Delhi

Michelle Crabtree of Hyatt Hotels and Resorts (Area Director of Human Resources)

Misty Marie Johanson of Georgia State University

Harry Lenderman of Public Health Foundation (Consultant)

Richard Patterson of Western Kentucky University

Janet Shaffer of Lake Washington Technical College

Steve Siegel, Professor Emeritus of Niagara University

Deanne Williams of Virginia State University

Larry L. Williams of Scottsdale Community College

Allisha A. Miller of Panda Pros Hospitality, reviewer and contributor

Dr. A. J. Singh of The School of Hospitality Business, Michigan State University, contributor

As experienced authors, we know the value of a quality publisher in the development of a manuscript. We were impressed but again not surprised at the tremendous effort devoted to this project by JoAnna Turtletaub, Wiley Vice President.

Pamela Chirls, Acquisitions Editor, deserves special recognition because her efforts illustrate well the commitment of Wiley to this project. She served as our guide to reviewer input, and she scrutinized each word, concept, and even figure caption. Pamela's efforts, as much as any individual working on the project, helped ensure that this text met the high standards Wiley sets for its own publications and, by doing so, helped us contribute our best efforts as well. To the extent this text is a success, the many individuals mentioned here deserve all of the credit; for any shortcomings in the text, we willingly accept full responsibility.

Finally, we again wish to dedicate this revised text, as we did the first edition, to Professor H. B. Meek, who in 1954 founded Cornell University's School of Hotel Administration, and without whose dedication and vision the discipline of hospitality education would be greatly diminished.

Just as Professor Meek understood the uniqueness and importance of hospitality education as a separate discipline, we hope he would approve of our efforts to continue to enhance this field with this contribution to hospitality HR management. To the degree that he would approve of our efforts, we will have succeeded as much as we hope those students reading this resource succeed in their own careers.

DAVID K. HAYES, PH.D.
Managing Owner
Panda Professionals
Hospitality Management and Training
Okemos, MI

JACK D. NINEMEIER, PH.D.
Professor Emeritus
The School of Hospitality Business
Michigan State University
Hilo, HI

CHAPTER

1

INTRODUCTION TO HUMAN RESOURCES IN THE HOSPITALITY INDUSTRY

CHAPTER OUTLINE

LEARNING OBJECTIVES

When they complete this chapter, readers will be able to:

1. Describe the travel and tourism industry and the hospitality segments within it.

2. Discuss how the HR function relates to the management of hospitality organizations.

3. Identify specific HR responsibilities that are important in most hospitality organizations.

4. Describe priority challenges that impact HR activities.

5. Explain the role of ethics in HR management.

Impact on Human Resources Management

Hospitality-related organizations are an important part of the diverse travel and tourism industry, and they share some common priorities. One is the need for employees with a diverse base of knowledge, skills, and experience to produce products and services needed or desired by consumers. The industry often has been described as a "people business." The "people" referred to are the employees who produce the products and services and those who purchase and consume them. This book focuses on one of the two groups: employees.

Managers with human resources (HR) responsibilities in all types and sizes of hospitality organizations share much in common. For example, they must undertake some important HR-related activities regardless of whether they are managers of small properties or HR specialists in larger-volume organizations. These activities are affected by numerous internal and external factors that, in turn, create unique environments within which the "art" and "science" of HR management must be practiced.

A complete list of HR-related tasks can be very lengthy, and this illustrates the diversity of responsibilities that must be addressed, whether they are assumed by operating managers and/or those in specialized positions. Laws and regulations and the need to successfully address significant challenges, solve problems, and make decisions based on a solid ethical foundation are integral components of the HR process.

Professional managers are ethical managers, and they consistently use procedures that incorporate ethical considerations. The best-run organizations are influenced by a culture driven by ethical concerns, and their managers' model the practices that are appropriate for their employees. The result: Employees will likely treat guests in the same manner as they are treated, so success is better ensured when ethical concerns are at the forefront of decision making.

The HR function is complex both because it involves facilitating work performed by staff members and because of the changing environment within which HR responsibilities must be addressed. This chapter establishes a context for the study of this critical discipline by providing an overview of and a context for the use of HR principles to achieve personnel-related challenges in the hospitality industry.

❖❖ OVERVIEW OF TRAVEL, TOURISM, AND HOSPITALITY ORGANIZATIONS

LEARNING OBJECTIVE 1. Describe the travel and tourism industry and the hospitality segments within it.

Hospitality industry: The range of for-profit and not-for-profit organizations that provide lodging and/or accommodations, including food services, for people when they are away from their homes.

Human resources (HR): The staff members employed by a hospitality organization.

The **hospitality industry** is one part of the larger travel and tourism industry that, in addition to hospitality, consists of transportation services organizations and retail businesses. The for-profit and not-for-profit operations in the hospitality industry segment share a common goal: to provide lodging and/or accommodations, including food services, for people when they are away from their homes. Many people think of hotels and restaurants when they think of the hospitality industry, but it comprises many other types of organizations.

Figure 1.1 identifies three segments of the travel and tourism industry. As you review Figure 1.1, note that the travel and tourism industry can be divided into these segments: transportation services, hospitality, and destination businesses. This text concerns **human resources (HR)** and their management in the hospitality segment of the industry.

Lodging organizations within the hospitality segment include hotels, conference centers, destination resorts, campground and park facilities, and inns. The food service segment

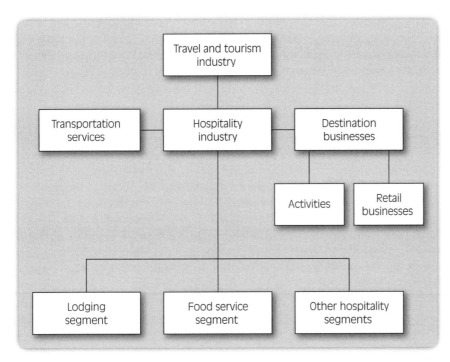

Figure 1.1   Overview of Travel and Tourism Industry

can be divided into two general components. For-profit (commercial) operations include hotels, restaurants, caterers, and retail operations such as grocery stores and service stations that provide prepackaged sandwiches, beverages, snacks, and other items. The other component, often referred to as noncommercial or on-site services, includes food services offered by educational facilities, health care institutions, the military, business/industry organizations, religious and charitable groups, correctional facilities, and transportation companies. These organizations do not exist to operate or make a profit from food services, and they may operate the program themselves or contract with a for-profit food service management company to do so.

Diverse Knowledge and Skills Are Required

A widely diverse group of employees works in the numerous types of hospitality operations, and those with HR responsibilities must interact with and facilitate the work of each of these employees. For example, a quick-service operation may be staffed with a majority of **entry-level employees** with little formal education or experience required because they can learn basic skills on the job. A restaurant with a high check average will likely require food production and service staff with a significant amount of specialized knowledge, skills, and experience.

In lodging operations, entry-level personnel may also learn necessary skills, but people with higher levels of education and experience are required, at least in large properties, to assist with technology, engineering, financial management, marketing, and other activities.

Multiunit hospitality organizations may employ specialists to assist with real estate, legal, design and layout, menu and product development, **franchisor–franchisee** relations, and other services.

HR personnel must be able to help all of their organization's employers, and doing so is an ongoing challenge because of the demographics of the hospitality workforce.

Entry-level employee: A staff member who does not have supervisory or management responsibilities.

Franchisor: The person or organization that owns a brand and sells the rights to use it within the requirements of a contractual relationship.

Franchisee: The person or organization who purchases the right to use a brand name for a specified time and cost.

Other hospitality segments include organizations such as private clubs, sports and recreational food service operations, cruise lines, casinos, vending businesses, and amusement and theme parks. Still other businesses in this segment include those providing meeting management, exhibition (trade show), and special events management services.

❖❖ MANAGING HR IN HOSPITALITY ORGANIZATIONS

LEARNING OBJECTIVE 2. Discuss how the HR function relates to the management of hospitality organizations

Labor intensive: The situation in which people, rather than technology and equipment, are used to provide products and services for an organization's customers.

Organizations in the hospitality industry tend to be **labor intensive**. Technology, including highly automated equipment, cannot provide the level of personal service sought by many hospitality industry consumers. The concept of "hospitality" refers to the friendly treatment of one's guests, and most managers would agree that this "human touch" is best provided by the organization's staff members.

HR Overview

Human resources management: Processes used by a hospitality organization to enhance its performance by effectively using all of its staff members.

Hospitality organizations require employees, and the more revenue generated and the larger the number of customers served, the more staff members are typically needed. No organization within the industry can maximize success without a full complement of staff members, ranging from owners/managers to entry-level employees, who know how to consistently meet their organization's product and service delivery standards. To attract and retain the employees it needs, an organization must place great emphasis on its **human resources management** principles and practices.

Manager: A staff member who typically directs the work of supervisors. Some people at the manager level in an organization, such as controller or director of purchasing, may not direct the work of other employees.

Most employees have the same basic wants and needs, and they typically share the same basic concerns about how they want to be treated by their employers. Their reactions, in turn, impact their work performance and length of employment. Much of employees' attitudes about work are affected by interactions with their managers. However, a wide range of HR-related concerns, including compensation and benefits, professional development opportunities, and beliefs about how they "fit into" the organization, are also important to employees.

Supervisor: A staff member who directs the work of entry-level personnel.

The staff members of every hospitality organization are its most important resource. How their work is managed (facilitated) impacts the success or failure of the organization. The basic processes used by managers are the same in almost any type of organization. These basic functions relate to the management of all an organization's resources, including its staff members. These functions, with examples of HR responsibilities applicable to each level of management, are shown in Figure 1.2.

HR department: In a large hospitality organization, the department whose employees are responsible for recruiting, screening, and developing staff members. Its employees also administer compensation and benefit programs, coordinate safety practices, implement labor law requirements, and may administer collective bargaining agreements.

When reviewing Figure 1.2, note that, while the responsibilities within each management function narrow from top-level **manager** to **supervisor**, each person with some management responsibility likely has obligations relating to each function. Top-level managers tend to have longer-term, "big picture" responsibilities; managers have more specific department-related duties; and supervisors serve as links connecting upper-level management with entry-level staff members in day-to-day operations.

HR Activities

Staff (employees): People with technical expertise in an area such as HR who provide advice to, but do not make decisions for, managers in the organization's "chain of command."

Large hospitality organizations typically have **HR departments** with **staff (employees)** whose primary responsibilities focus on HR concerns. In contrast, smaller operations typically employ managers who function as generalists and assume HR responsibilities, in addition to numerous others, as part of their jobs.

Management Function	Level of Management		
	Top-Level Manager	Mid-Level Manager	Supervisor
Planning	Analyze the number of staff needed for key management positions in the future (succession planning)	Consider estimated costs of departmental training programs for an upcoming budget period	Schedule employees for the following week
Organizing	Determine reporting relationships as a hotel front office department is reorganized	Determine tasks to be part of a specific position	Revise a work task based on work simplification tactics
Staffing	Recruit and hire employees for a health care dietary operation	Provide input about a "hire or fire" decision	Provide input to **job descriptions** used for employee recruitment
Supervising	Direct the work of managers	Direct the work of supervisors	Direct the work of entry-level employees
Controlling	Establish labor standards for a quick-service restaurant	Compare estimated and actual labor cost data and take corrective actions as necessary	Ensure that procedures used to control costs are used
Appraising	Determine the extent to which HR goals, including labor costs, professional development programs, and performance improvement, are met	Evaluate the work of department staff	Determine whether revised work procedures that address a problem have corrected it

Figure 1.2 Basic Management Functions Involve HR Responsibilities

Job description: A list of tasks that a person working within a specific position must perform.

Most organizations in the hospitality industry are small, and their managers must make HR-related decisions without the benefit of the specialized assistance received by their counterparts in larger organizations. This book is written to help all HR managers but especially to assist managers in small organizations, and it discusses basic HR concerns that these managers must address as they facilitate the work of their staff members.

Figure 1.3 reviews basic HR activities, and it indicates that external and internal influences impact these HR activities. Let's review Figure 1.3 by noting the HR activities.

◆ **Recruiting and selecting**—Using tactics and procedures to attract applicants to the organization (recruiting) and then choosing the best people from among them (selecting). This is probably among the first responsibilities that many people associate with HR management. These activities will be addressed in detail in chapter 4.

◆ **Training and development**—Preparing new staff members to do required work, updating their experienced peers, and providing opportunities for all interested employees to assume more responsible positions are important strategies to attain goals and address competitive pressures. These topics will be addressed in chapters 6 and 7.

◆ **Compensation and appraisal**—Personnel should receive pay and benefits commensurate with their contributions to the organization. Performance appraisal provides input to help employees attain on-the-job success that can yield promotions with higher compensation. These topics are examined in chapters 8 and 9.

◆◆◆◆◆◆◆◆◆◆◆◆◆◆◆

HR Is More Than Just "Filling Positions"

Corporate culture: The shared beliefs, experiences, and norms that influence how "things are done" within an organization.

Effective HR procedures must be used to recruit and select staff members. However, HR responsibilities extend beyond these and other stereotypical duties to include planning and delivering training programs, maintaining employee leave data, and providing alternative costs of benefits to management decision makers.

As you'll learn throughout this book, there are numerous personnel-related laws and regulations that must be understood and implemented in every hospitality organization. The need for compliance has a significant effect on how affected managers make personnel-related decisions and on the wasted time and financial resources that will be required if labor laws are broken.

The management of HR is of strategic importance to the organization. Goals cannot be attained without the best people in the appropriate position who consistently attain standards needed to deliver products and services of the desired quality. At the same time, those with HR responsibilities must represent and advocate for the employees. When the **corporate culture** encourages them to do so, employees working at all organizational levels can provide ideas and creative energies to yield a competitive advantage for the organization. Those with HR responsibilities help to develop, implement, communicate, interpret, and enforce policies and procedures to ensure employees are empowered to help the organization achieve its goals.

Managers with HR responsibilities also realize that labor costs must be controlled. They must help to ensure that the labor-related expenses incurred by an operation are actually value-added dollars that are worth more to the hospitality organization than what is spent for the labor that is purchased.

◆ **Protection and communication**—Safety and security concerns are important to all employees. Many laws and regulations mandate safety procedures, and there are numerous other tactics that top-level managers should do (and not do) that impact employee safety. Many legal and procedural issues with safety implications are addressed by those with HR responsibilities. These topics are addressed in chapter 10. In addition, effective communication that flows up, down, and across the organization helps to ensure that staff members know about issues that affect them. These topics are addressed in chapters 3 and 5.

External Influences on HR Activities

Managers in all types and sizes of hospitality organizations benefit from recognizing the worth of their staff members; doing so helps to develop positive relationships that are important for team efforts. These relationships are influenced by the sum of all HR-related activities. Some influences (those that are external) are beyond managers' control. Other influences (those that are internal) are not beyond their control.

Staff members with HR responsibilities must recognize and support the critical role that they play in their organization's success. They can do so by recognizing external limitations and by considering how internal influences can assist them in their efforts. Figure 1.3 indicates that the hospitality organization and the HR activities within it are impacted by several external influences. These include:

◆ **Legislation**—The impact of federal and state laws on the hiring process and their influence on management decisions affecting personnel cannot be overstated. There are numerous other laws that address the HR activities discussed above. Chapter 2 addresses the legal environment, and other legal issues are considered throughout the text.

◆ **Competition**—Competitors for the hospitality organization's employees often have an impact on HR activities. Examples include issues related to compensation (salaries, wages, and benefits), professional development opportunities, and even promotional decisions.

◆ **Consumer preferences**—What the consumer desires must be identified and delivered. Exceptions occur in some operations, including health care (hospitals and long-term care facilities), where nutritional concerns become important; in military and correctional facilities, where 100% of the dietary intake may be from the food services provided; and in religious/charitable institutions, where cost concerns are especially important. What are business/operating volumes? What products and services must be produced, and when are they needed? The answers to these and related questions drive employee recruiting/selecting, training and development, and compensation and appraisal activities, which are HR activities.

◆ **Demographics**—The characteristics of the local labor market and of present and potential guests are of concern to all hospitality organizations. For example, income levels in a community affect wage and salary rates and impact the ability and interest of consumers to purchase the organization's products and services. Young people are the foundation of employees in many organizations; are they available?

◆ **Global issues**—Many hospitality organizations exist to serve travelers. They, in turn, are dramatically affected by international and national events that encourage travel (for example, sporting events and special commemorations) and discourage travel (for example, terrorism, crime, and disease threats). Business volumes, in turn, impact HR activities.

◆ **Ethical concerns**—Issues relating to how employees are treated, how products and services are provided to guests, and how "honest" hospitality organizations are as they conduct business with suppliers are examples of ethical concerns. Do hospitality managers have an obligation of corporate social responsibility within their community? The answer to this question also has ethical implications.

◆ **Economy**—The financial well-being of world markets and those of the country, state, and community in which the hospitality operation is located have a significant impact on hospitality organizations.

◆ **Employee unions**—Staff members may belong to an **employee union** that represents their interests in all aspects of the HR activities noted in Figure 1.3.

Employee union: An organization of employees who act together to protect and promote their interests by collective bargaining with representatives of the hospitality organization.

Internal Influences on HR Activities

Figure 1.3 suggests that internal organizational influences also affect HR activities. Examples include:

◆ **Policies**—An operation's policies reveal the extent to which an organization respects its staff members. In the absence of laws that regulate specific actions, employers have significant discretion in establishing protocols that may affect the attitudes of staff members toward the organization.

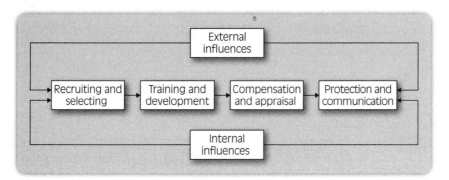

Figure 1.3 External and Internal Influences on HR Activities

❖❖❖ HR MANAGEMENT ISSUES 1.1

"This would be a great place to work if the HR department helped us," Jonathon said to Daysha, another manager at the Ocean Edge Hotel. "They send us job applicants who are not qualified, they don't do an adequate job of orienting new employees to our hotel, they have no role in training, and they issue so many policies, many of which are ridiculous, that I simply can't keep up with everything."

"You're right that communication could be better, and there is probably a need for the HR folks to learn details about what we do," replied Daysha. "Before I started here I spent five years working for a smaller property that didn't have an HR department. Each manager had to do whatever the general manager wanted. Some of the GMs we had over those years wanted a lot of responsibility for the HR function, and others wanted only a little."

"You know," said Emma, "that really wasn't a good situation either. Like everywhere else, the managers had primary responsibilities for a specific cost or revenue center, and they had to be concerned about HR details that affected their employees.

The world of HR management has many legal, technical, and other concerns far removed from preparing and serving meals and cleaning guest rooms."

"I guess I never thought about that," said Jonathon. "I've been here a long time, and it has always been a 'them versus us' relationship between operating managers and HR people. Maybe there is no ideal situation and the organization, its managers, employees, and the guests often lose!"

Case Study Questions

1. What is the primary problem at the Ocean Edge Hotel? What tactics that might address the problem can you identify?

2. What are the pros and cons of managing HR at a small property and of working at a larger property with HR specialists?

3. How can managers in small operations "keep up" with legal and other current events that impact HR?

Work Procedure: A course of action or the steps used to describe how a work-related task should be done.

Empowerment: The act of authorizing employees to make discretionary decisions within their areas of responsibility.

◆ **Work procedures**—**Work procedures** are designed with (or without) input from applicable personnel; the extent to which equipment replaces physical work tasks and the extent of employee **empowerment** impact how work is done and, in turn, the HR activities that are required.

◆ **Corporate culture**—The perceived worth of employees to the organization is an integral part of its culture. It drives the philosophies and attitudes about employees and their role in the organization and has a significant impact on many HR activities.

◆ **Long- and short-term plans**—Long-term plans such as business expansions or reductions and short-term plans such as introducing a new menu item or service impact employees and, in the process, affect recruiting, selecting, and training activities that are integral to the HR function.

◆ **Management judgment and experience**—Managers and HR specialists (in large organizations) bring their own judgment and experience to the decision-making process. This input affects the policies, procedures, and plans already discussed and influences other HR decisions.

❖❖ HR RESPONSIBILITIES

LEARNING OBJECTIVE 3. Identify specific HR responsibilities that are important in most hospitality organizations.

What tasks are involved in the management of HR in a hospitality organization? The short answer is almost everything involved in the relationship between staff members and the organization. A longer and more accurate response is found in Figure 1.4, which provides a sample job description for the director of HR in a large organization.

A wide variety of job tasks are shown in the sample job description in Figure 1.4. It is unlikely that any HR director in any hospitality organization is responsible for each of these tasks because of the diverse needs of each property. It is also possible that additional responsibilities are integral to the job descriptions of top-level HR personnel in other organizations. At the least, Figure 1.4 suggests the wide variety of activities of concern to those with HR responsibilities.

HR Management in Action

How do HR managers learn about applicable laws? The best answer is that it really depends on the specific situation.

The popular saying "Ignorance of the law is no excuse" is true. You are learning that owners/managers of small-volume operations do not typically have an HR specialist to assist with legal issues. Instead, they must rely on input from professional associations, trade magazines, and general business groups such as the local Chamber of Commerce. Other sources include government websites such as those of the US Small Business Administration and applicable state government departments. (Increasingly, these sources provide information in a form that can be easily understood without legal training.) On occasion they may also require assistance from a qualified attorney.

Small-business owners who are franchisees often have one additional source of information about legal concerns: their franchisor. Franchisors recognize that the quality of services they provide helps justify the franchisee fees they receive. "**Boiler plate**" clauses in contracts between the franchisor and franchisee attempt to excuse franchisors from their franchisees' failure to follow the law. However, franchisors also know that costs of time and money will likely be incurred to help them prove they are not legally responsible for the acts of their franchises. They also understand that the public, including those in their target markets, do not know or even care whether the local hospitality operation accused of breaking the law is a franchisee because the franchisor's name is on the sign and in the news.

Boiler plate (contracts): Clauses in contracts that are written in general terms that can be used in different contracts.

Large, multiunit organizations generally employ licensed attorneys who work full time on activities that ultimately benefit unit managers. Sometimes an employment law specialist may be retained within the corporate HR structure. It is also common for the organization to have a legal department with, for example, one or more specialists in employment law. In the former case, HR managers can receive information directly from a peer within their own HR department and share it with regional, district, and unit managers. In the latter case, the HR specialist must cooperate across department lines to determine the best way to assist unit managers.

By the time you complete this book, you will not be wondering how important legal concerns are to those with HR responsibilities. You will understand they are absolutely critical and that the legal dimension is increasing its impact on HR responsibilities in organizations of all sizes.

A quick review of Figure 1.4 may also suggest that one person cannot do all of these things. In fact, HR managers in large organizations may have one or more professional associates to whom some tasks can be delegated. However, a unit manager and his or her staff in a small hospitality organization do not typically have access to internal HR specialists. Instead, they need to rely on external specialists, and it is likely that problems can arise when there is a lack of time and/or expertise to address all of these issues.

Many hospitality organizations do not enjoy the services of full-time HR specialists, and their managers have only a few options available to them.

- ◆ The general manager must assume responsibility for some of these tasks.
- ◆ A decentralized approach in which department heads are responsible for the personnel-related issues relevant to their staff may be used.
- ◆ Basic policies and procedures are implemented, and a qualified attorney is contacted when issues arise that seem to be outside the boundaries that they impose.

Executive committee: A group composed of department heads who serve as the organization's key management team and who are responsible for the overall management of the organization.

It is hoped that a process will be in place that best ensures that all HR-related activities are done correctly. It is certainly important that managers in small operations correctly address the most important issues that are likely to cause the most significant problems.

HUMAN RESOURCES DEPARTMENT

I. Position: Director of Human Resources

II. Job Summary:

Assists department management staff with recruitment, selection, and orientation of new staff members. Administers payroll records, directs the processing of wage and salary payments, and ensures that all applicable federal, state, and local wage and hour, worker's compensation, and other labor laws are consistently complied with. Implements data collection systems and manages the organization's health, employee protection, retirement, and other benefits programs. Conducts labor analyses, staff planning, and other studies as requested. Serves on the organization's **executive committee**.

III. Job Tasks:

1. Administers employee compensation, benefits, performance management systems, and safety and recreation programs.

2. Advises managers about organizational policies; recommends necessary changes.

3. Develops and places recruitment ads; plans recruitment strategies; screens applicants and makes hiring recommendations.

4. Conducts and reviews wage and benefit surveys; proposes employee benefit modifications to the general manager.

5. Analyzes data and reports to identify and determine causes of personnel-related problems; develops recommendations for improvement.

6. Analyzes training needs and designs applicable employee development, language training, and health and safety programs.

7. Conducts exit interviews to identify reasons for employee separation of employment.

8. Maintains organization's policy manual and communicates policy changes to applicable staff members.

9. Develops, administers, and evaluates applicant tests.

10. Coordinates all employee (personnel) record-keeping functions.

11. Continually reviews the employee handbook and assists in updating it.

12. Manages the organization's group insurance, unemployment, and related benefits programs; communicates benefits information to staff.

13. Identifies staff vacancies.

14. Maintains records and compiles statistical reports concerning personnel-related data such as hires, transfers, performance appraisals, and absenteeism rates.

15. Negotiates collective bargaining agreements, helps interpret labor contracts, and administers the formal labor relations program with unionized staff.

16. Oversees the evaluation, classification, and rating of occupations and job positions.

17. Undertakes special projects relating to job description and specification updates, performance appraisal improvements, wage and salary comparison surveys, long-range staff planning, and other personnel issues.

18. Keeps abreast of laws and regulations relating to employees; ensures compliance with these laws and regulations; advises managers as necessary.

19. Advises line managers about discipline, discharge, and related employment matters.

Figure 1.4 Sample Job Description for Director of Human Resources

20. Manages educational and referral programs for alcohol and substance abuse.

21. Assists department heads in planning professional development and training programs for employees.

22. Forecasts short- and long-term staffing needs.

23. Coordinates transfer, promotion, and layoff strategies.

24. Creates and maintains organizational charts.

25. Benchmarks employee recruitment and selection processes with others in the industry; explores new strategies as appropriate.

26. Develops and maintains a library of training resources specifically designed for each position.

27. Plans and implements employee motivation and retention programs.

28. Organizes employee activities such as holiday parties and other activities as appropriate.

29. Organizes employee recognition functions.

30. Provides current and prospective employees with information about policies, job duties, working conditions, wages, opportunities for promotion, and employee benefits.

31. Provides terminated employees with outplacement or relocation assistance.

32. Serves as a link between management and employees by handling questions, interpreting and administering contracts, and helping to resolve work-related problems.

33. Analyzes and modifies compensation and benefits policies to establish competitive programs and ensure compliance with legal requirements.

34. Develops and/or administers special projects in areas such as pay equity, employee retirement alternatives, day care, and employee awards.

35. Represents organizations at personnel-related hearings and investigations.

36. Oversees all work-related injury claims to ensure integrity, ongoing case management, and reporting compliance.

37. Recruits, hires, trains, supervises, schedules, and evaluates staff members in the HR department.

38. Works with payroll personnel to ensure that all forms required of new employees are completed.

39. Conducts preliminary employment interviews with position applicants.

40. Studies legislation, arbitration decisions, and collective bargaining contracts to assess industry trends.

41. Investigates and reports on accidents for insurance carriers.

42. Meets with the employee relations committee on regular, scheduled basis.

43. Maintains Occupations Safety and Health Administration–related logs and reports.

44. Coordinates, monitors, and suggests improvements for the employee performance appraisal system.

45. Schedules and conducts employee safety meetings.

46. Recommends drug-testing procedures for employee applicants.

47. Interacts with the general manager and department heads to investigate employee violations of policies and to recommend corrective actions, if necessary.

48. Interacts with the organization's attorney relative to personnel legal issues involving concerns about the Equal Employment Opportunity Commission harassment, and lawsuits.

49. Develops personnel-related reports for the general manager or department heads.

50. Serves as a member of the organization's executive committee.

IV. Reports to: General manager

V. Supervises: HR Associates

Figure 1.4 (continued)

◆ HR MANAGEMENT ISSUES 1.2

"I don't know how you do it, Alice," said Oscar. "I manage a nutrition services department in a large hospital and receive lots of advice from our HR department about a wide variety of special concerns that otherwise I would never know about." He was speaking to a friend, Alice, who worked in the same city for a busy fast-casual restaurant.

Alice's reply was expected: "Keeping up with legal issues and finding time to address a wide variety of other HR concerns is a problem. I try to do the best possible, but there are always emergencies that must receive priority. Then, unfortunately, many 'nice to know and do' things are never done."

"How do you stay out of trouble, then, Alice?," asked Oscar. "There are always legal concerns, benefits cost issues, and compensation studies, for example, that I would assume are necessary. There also must be lots of things that your employees want and deserve that require some attention."

"Yes, Oscar, you're correct," said Alice. "As the manager of a multiunit chain property, I do get some support from corporate officials. And I belong to several professional associations and attend meetings and receive updates from those groups. I've learned some other tactics along the way, but obviously it's not possible to spend the amount of time on HR concerns that I would like."

Case Study Questions

1. What are additional ways Alice can obtain the HR-related information she needs to do her job well?

2. What information applicable to Oscar's nutrition services employees will likely be relevant to all hospital employees? What are some food service–specific HR concerns Oscar might have?

3. How might single-unit restaurant operators without corporate-level assistance cope with the readily available, but less than ideal, HR information they likely have available to them?

❖ HR CHALLENGES

LEARNING OBJECTIVE 4. Describe priority challenges that impact HR activities.

Those with HR responsibilities in today's hospitality organizations are confronted with a wide range of challenges. While their priority may vary in different organizations, the following impact most hospitality operations:

Employee turnover:
The proportion of total employees replaced during a specific time period. For example, the annual turnover rate can be calculated as the number of employees leaving during a year divided by the average number of employees in the workforce.

◆ **Recruiting and selecting qualified employees**—This topic is addressed in depth in chapter 4. However, this is an ongoing challenge that in many organizations could be minimized if current employees were retained—in other words, if **employee turnover** rates were reduced. One of the best strategies to do this occurs when managers and supervisors use effective supervisory tactics. Some of these, including appropriate recruitment, orientation, training, compensation and performance management, and appraisal, are discussed in this book. Other tactics, such as teaching those who direct the work of employees the need for respecting employees, are very helpful.

The challenge of recruiting and selecting leads directly to the second HR challenge:

◆ **Retaining and rewarding the best employees**—HR personnel have a significant impact on the extent to which the organization is an employer of choice. For example, they may be responsible for or involved in efforts to solicit employee input as visions and mission statements that shape an organization's culture are developed. HR personnel can advocate for employees as policies are written and implemented. They are often involved in developing and implementing training programs related to harassment, progressive discipline, employee incentive, and other programs that continually emphasize the worth of employees to the organization.

◆ **Leadership development**—This challenge is related to the previous one. How can the organization develop and retain good leaders? HR managers must address this question. They do so by successfully meeting the two challenges just discussed and as they promote and develop or provide professional training and education activities to prepare managers for additional responsibilities.

HR Management: Impact on New Team Members

Do HR personnel advocate for an organization's employees as their representative and also serve as communication links to upper levels of management? Or, is their role to help their organization's managers remain within the law and to plan and implement policies and procedures that reflect management's preferences?

Ideally, they do both. For example, HR personnel often have a role in implementing the organization's core values, which should include an emphasis on employees. They likely assist in the coordination of the organization's mission that suggests the role employees, including all new workers, have in their operations. They ensure that laws affecting new and long-standing staff members are followed. They may provide supervisory training activities relating to communication, motivation, discipline, and other skills that show respect for all employees.

Those with HR responsibilities work diligently to develop this cultural foundation, which is in place when new employees are hired. The recently employed staff members then benefit from an "employer of choice" culture that genuinely recognizes and supports the contribution of all of its employees, regardless of how long they have worked for the organization. This culture, in turn, encourages the respect and fairness that produces a work environment in which the organization's newest employees receive confirmation that their employment decisions were good ones.

◆ **Managing labor and benefits costs**—By definition, HR personnel are involved in the management of labor, which frequently represents the most expensive operating cost in hospitality organizations. HR personnel play an important role in selecting the best applicants, minimizing employee turnover rates, developing training programs, and developing policies and procedures to appraise performance (improve productivity).

Employee benefit costs, especially those that are related to health care, have increased dramatically during recent years. This is an area of concern to all hospitality business owners. One specific example, of great interest to HR managers, is the uncertainty about the long-term future of health care costs and how they will be affected by passage in 2010 of the Patient Protection and Affordable Care Act (PPACA), generally shortened to the Affordable Care Act (ACA) or more popularly; Obamacare.

◆ **Measuring the effectiveness of the HR function**—HR personnel have traditionally been thought of as specialists in "filling vacant positions." However, the responsibilities of the function extend significantly beyond this activity. One important challenge relates to measuring the effectiveness of the HR function on organizational success. As it does so, the HR discipline is shown to be an integral and strategic part of the organization because of its involvement with the most important resource: employees.

HR-related challenges will continue to be a priority for most hospitality and tourism operators for the foreseeable future. What can be done to meet these challenges? The organizations that successfully address this question will enjoy a competitive edge over their counterparts that do not.

❖ HR AND ETHICAL CONCERNS

LEARNING OBJECTIVE 5. Explain the role of ethics in HR management.

What Are Ethics?

The concept of **ethics** relates to a set of rules or principles that define "what is right" and "what is wrong." However, these definitions vary based on the individual making the determination.

Ethics: A set of rules or principles that define "what is right" and "what is wrong" as decisions are made.

It's the Law

Legal concerns impact almost every aspect of HR management. Some believe that this challenge largely involves understanding, remembering, and implementing legal changes and then moving on to the next challenge. However, laws and regulations can be difficult and time-consuming to understand and implement.

Consider the difference between the law requiring that customers must be 21 years of age to consume alcoholic beverages and compliance with two other laws: the Americans with Disabilities Act of 1990 (ADA) and the ACA. (Both of these laws are addressed in detail in chapter 2.) It is critical that state laws relating to alcoholic beverage consumption be consistently followed. However, doing so primarily impacts only some food and beverage personnel and involves developing procedures and training activities so employees can effectively confirm a guest's age.

In contrast, the ADA affects almost every staffing-related area of most businesses. The law applies to people with a physical or mental impairment that substantially limits one or more major life activities and to some temporary or episodic conditions such as chronic fatigue. Jobs must be examined to determine essential functions (fundamental job duties) and then to provide reasonable accommodation (any change in the work environment or in how a job is performed) unless undue hardship is created so people with a disability can enjoy equal employment opportunities.

The goal of the ACA was to expand health care coverage for insured and previously uninsured American citizens. Discussions about the business-related impacts of the ACA evolved over several years and became more focused as its regulations went into effect in January 2014. Business owners and HR specialists often were confused because the "facts" as explained by different reputable parties ranged from mostly positive to mostly negative predictions of its impact.

Large- and small-volume businesses were concerned about the potential for increased costs and decreased health care quality. With the mixed messages, many business owners and managers really didn't know the impact or how to comply with the law. This, in turn, influenced the hiring and business expansion plans of some companies. Others initially stated they planned to reduce employees' hours because part-time employees were not covered by the plan or even terminate some of their current employees to reduce health care–related costs.

What should HR specialists or business owners/managers recommend or do given the uncertainty about the ACA and its impact on health care? This question is difficult to answer, but it is clear that legal aspects of HR management can dramatically impact how a business is managed.

Business ethics: The use of ethical judgment as managers make organizational decisions.

Ethical behavior: Actions in line with generally accepted social concerns relating to how decisions and actions impact others.

Unethical behavior: Actions not in line with generally accepted social concerns relating to how decisions and actions impact others.

Through its laws, society does not become involved until something is illegal—something illegal is also unethical, but something can be legal and unethical. For example, it is legal for an HR manager to show some favoritism to a specific employee when determining who should attend a convention in a desirable out-of-town location. However, disregarding the morale and supervisory implications of this action, is it ethical?

People should make ethical personal decisions, but the practice of **business ethics** must be of professional concern to hospitality managers: They must consistently practice **ethical behavior** and avoid **unethical behavior**.

Ethical concerns have probably never been of more relevance than after recurring current news about numerous business organizations' questionable, but legal, financial dealings, political corruption, and abuses at all governmental levels.

While "ethical" conduct is required at all times, the difference between "what is right" and "what is wrong" is sometimes difficult to distinguish. Consider, for example, when top-level managers are offered significant salary increases, whereas wages for hourly paid staff are kept minimal or when selected employee benefits are increased but many full-time staff positions are eliminated because part-time workers do not receive benefits. Can these situations be addressed "ethically"? Should the social responsibilities inherent in the situations be considered? Perhaps. The "answer" depends on the individuals confronted by the situation. The availability of a code of ethics can be a guide, but sometimes ethical codes are disregarded.

Here are some ethical principles that HR managers should follow when they make decisions:

- ♦ **Honesty**—Don't mislead or deceive others.
- ♦ **Integrity**—Do what is right.
- ♦ **Trustworthiness**—Supply correct information.
- ♦ **Loyalty**—Avoid conflicts of interest and don't disclose confidential information.
- ♦ **Fairness**—Treat individuals equally; be tolerant of diversity.
- ♦ **Concern and respect**—Be considerate of those affected by decision making.
- ♦ **Commitment to excellence**—Do the best you can.
- ♦ **Leadership**—Lead by example.
- ♦ **Reputation and morale**—Work to enhance the company's reputation and employees' morale.
- ♦ **Accountability**—Accept responsibility for decisions that are made.

When decisions are made, ethical managers consider:

- ♦ **Utility**—The extent to which an act generates benefits for those affected.
- ♦ **Rights**—The extent to which the rights of people involved are considered as decisions are made.
- ♦ **Justice**—Whether a decision is fair.
- ♦ **Caring**—Whether a decision considers the responsibilities that individuals have to each other.

It is typically much easier to say that "HR managers must consistently practice ethical behavior" than it is to specifically indicate what the statement actually means in every situation. Given this limitation, most hospitality leaders claim that their organizations give priority to making ethical decisions.

An organization's culture may support and reward its members for making ethical decisions or it may provide no benefit to those who do so. In extreme instances the culture may even reward those who make unethical decisions. For example, some organizations ignore protections mandated under Equal Employment Opportunity Commission regulations, and some lodging organizations emphasize expansion in remote geographic locations without regard for affected citizens or the environmental impact of the expansion.

HR managers should recognize that their behavior often "speaks more loudly" than the philosophy expressed in their organization's mission statement. Consider managers who specify food portions that violate truth-in-menu laws and their peers who raise hotel room rates in times of emergency in states where it is legal (but perhaps not ethical) to do so.

Might employees think, "If a manager does those things to our guests, will he [or she] also do it to me?" At best, this is likely true; worse, it encourages staff members to violate commonly recognized ethical standards. These management actions may (or may not!) be effective in the short term; they will, however, likely be ineffective over longer time periods. Guests and employees desire, respectively, to purchase products and services from and be employed by hospitality organizations that are genuinely committed to doing what is right for all of their constituents.

Codes of Ethics

Many hospitality organizations develop and implement a **code of ethics** to provide broad statements to guide ethical decision making. As such, their intention is to provide a framework for decision making rather than to specify exactly what should or should not be done in a specific situation.

Code of ethics: A statement that outlines broad concepts to guide ethical decision making.

Hospitality organizations develop ethical codes for several reasons, including:

◆ to identify a foundation for acceptable behaviors.

◆ to promote standards to guide decision making.

◆ to provide a benchmark for evaluating potential decisions.

◆ to support the responsibility and obligations that decision makers have to their constituents.

Effective codes of ethics exemplify the ethical commitment of the organization and how it will interact with others as it conducts business. The best codes of ethics are developed specifically for the organization and use input from the staff members who are expected to use it. In addition, input should be solicited from investors, vendors, and perhaps other organizations in the community. Those who assist in its development should understand the organization's mission and be concerned about its commitment to a positive professional and community image.

The support of top-level leadership as codes of ethics are developed is of obvious importance. They should be reviewed by legal counsel, and formal approval from the highest levels in the organization is required.

The tactics used to implement and educate staff members about a code of ethics are important. A code displayed on the walls at the office headquarters and used as a preface for an employee handbook does little good unless the code is integrated into, and actually guides, the organization's culture. Considering enforcement concerns if the code is violated is also important. Remember also that a code of ethics is important for the continued success of any business, and its emphasis should last "forever." It is not a "program" that begins and ends at specified times. All staff members should be held accountable for behavior described in the code of ethics.

What topics might be included in a code of ethics? Figure 1.5 identifies typical concerns that are often addressed.

Following are examples of topics commonly addressed in codes of ethics:

◆ Importance of guests
◆ Respect for individual staff members
◆ Need for honesty
◆ Relations with suppliers
◆ Compliance with the law in all matters
◆ Avoiding conflicts of interest
◆ Using the organization's assets
◆ Confidentiality of proprietary information
◆ Political contributions
◆ Relations with competitors
◆ Reporting financial operating results fairly and honestly
◆ Business entertaining, gift acceptance, and bribes

Figure 1.5 Topics in Codes of Ethics

HR TERMS

The following terms were defined in this chapter:

Hospitality industry	Supervisor	Boiler plate (contracts)
Human resources (HR)	HR department	Executive committee
Entry-level employee	Staff (employees)	Employee turnover
Franchisor	Job description	Ethics
Franchisee	Corporate culture	Business ethics
Labor intensive	Employee union	Ethical behavior
Human resources management	Work procedure	Unethical behavior
Manager	Empowerment	Code of ethics

FOR YOUR CONSIDERATION

1. Review Figure 1.2 (Basic Management Functions Involve HR Responsibilities).

   a. What are additional examples of each management function applicable to HR that might be the responsibility of top-level managers, mid-level managers, and supervisors?

   b. While all of these management functions are important, which do you think are the most important? Why?

2. Review the discussion in this chapter about external and internal influences on HR activities.

   a. What are additional examples of external and internal influences on each of the basic HR activities that are identified?

   b. How might a staff HR specialist in a multiunit hospitality organization assist a unit-level property manager with each of these basic HR activities?

3. This chapter indicates that high employee turnover rates create challenges for many hospitality organizations. What role do you think HR personnel can play in reducing employee turnover?

4. How important do you think a code of ethics is for a small hospitality organization? How, if at all, is your response different for a very large hospitality organization?

5. What are examples of tactics that HR personnel and department-level managers and supervisors can use to best ensure that there are effective channels of communication between them?

CASE STUDY

Apply HR Management Principles

Mateo and Felix were good friends who worked out regularly at the Muscle Man's Gym. By coincidence, Mateo was the dining room manager in an upscale restaurant in a local hotel, and Felix was the director of housekeeping at a resort on the outskirts of the city. Both of their organizations have a similar business volume. Not surprisingly, their jobs were a frequent topic of conversation at the juice bar in the gym after their workouts.

"Felix, we've talked about this before," said Mateo. "It's hard to believe that our employers are in the same basic business and hire the same types of people, yet their HR philosophies are so different."

"I agree," said Felix. "At my resort the emphasis is on the guests first, on maximizing profit second, and on the employees third. We churn through a lot of staff members who start out

:::::::CASE STUDY (continued) :::

with a positive attitude but whose morale goes quickly downhill as they are confronted with things that shouldn't happen."

"Give me an example," replied Mateo.

"Well," responded Felix, "we use out-of-date job descriptions to recruit employees, and many times there's little resemblance between what new staff think they're going to be doing and what they actually do. Orientation sessions are done whenever there is time, training is done on the job, and if the staff members don't learn quickly, top-level managers conclude that it's because they don't care—not because they haven't been properly trained.

"A lot of supervisors have been there a long time and don't care about the organization or their staff members. They surely don't treat staff the way they would want to be treated.

"Performance appraisals focus on what staff members do wrong—not on what they can do right and how they can improve. There is an ongoing emphasis on 'job' rather then on 'career,' and many employees seem to just mark their time until there is a position vacancy at your hotel."

Mateo had heard Felix talk about these issues before. His hotel was an "employer of choice" where many people in the community wanted to work, and, subsequently, where employee turnover rates were low. In fact, Mateo had agreed long ago to let Felix know when the executive housekeeper position at the hotel became available.

Mateo wondered why Felix's employer didn't seem concerned about the problem and wasn't doing anything to address the concerns. To Mateo, they seemed like "common sense" issues with simple fixes. He realized, however, that attitudes were much more difficult to change than procedures were to revise.

After thinking about it, Mateo said, "Felix, things will have to change at the resort. You've mentioned that business is getting slower. Maybe it's because employees aren't treated well and they, in turn, are less concerned about the guests. We both know that we'll soon have another hotel in town, and the HR people there will be aggressively searching for new staff members. If things don't change at your property, things will get worse than they are."

"You're right, Mateo," said Felix. "Our highest-level managers should already know that they are hurting themselves with their current employee practices. The point will really be driven home ... and it will happen a lot sooner than they think."

Dimension: Strategic

1. How are the results of strategies used to manage HR at Felix's hotel affecting the business?
2. What are possible reasons that top-level managers at Felix's property do not recognize the problems that a lack of focus on HR concerns are creating?

Dimension: Tactical

1. What are some things that Felix, as a department head, could do within his own level of responsibility to improve the management of HR within his department?
2. What are some things that Felix might do to alert others at his resort about the HR problems that he recognizes?

Dimension: "The Friendly Competition"

1. What are some things that Mateo's hotel can do to capitalize on the HR problems accruing at Felix's resort?
2. What are some tactics that Mateo's hotel can use as it faces competition for its employees from the new hotel that soon will be opening in the community?

INTERNET ACTIVITIES

1. Assume you are the manager of a small-volume hospitality organization without access to HR staff specialists with current knowledge about employment laws that affect your operation. How would you gain access to information that will help you implement applicable laws and regulations? One way is to enter "small business administration employment and labor law" into your favorite search engine. You will reach the site of the Small Business Administration (SBA), which is part of the US Department of Labor (DOL).

You will discover a number of resources that provide information about US employment laws and regulations and

how small business owners and managers should comply with them. For example:

- ◆ www.dol.gov/elaws/ provides a wide range of "advisers" (updated information about employment laws and regulations).

- ◆ The "Employment Law Guide" classifies laws into applicable categories such as "wages and hours worked," "safety and health standards," and "health benefits, "retirement standards" and "workers' compensation."

- ◆ "Employment and Labor Laws Compliance Assistance" information helps small-business people to navigate DOL laws and regulation by topic, by audience (for example, new and small businesses, foreign workers), and by major laws.

◆ The "Labor Laws for New and Small Businesses" section provides information about compliance assistance materials, fact sheets, e-tools, and related topics.

◆ The "Summary of the Major Employment and Labor Laws" resource explains the laws enforced by the DOL, including those covering equal employment opportunities, discrimination, immigration, wage determination, and workers' compensation.

How would the above information assist you? Write a 200-word essay relating what you learned as you reviewed the above information. Comment on each of the sections that are included in each of the SBA resources.

2. Would you like to be an HR specialist? What are traits and characteristics of successful HR specialists? What exactly do they do? To answer these and related questions, enter "traits of successful HR specialists" into your favorite search engine.

a. Develop a comprehensive list of the traits you believe may be commonly shared by successful HR specialists. Do you possess many of these traits? What could you do to help you obtain or further develop these traits?

b. Would you like to be employed in an HR staff position by a large hospitality organization? Why or why not?

© sergign / Shutterstock

CHAPTER

2

THE LEGAL ENVIRONMENT OF HUMAN RESOURCES MANAGEMENT

CHAPTER OUTLINE

Employment Law

The Government's Role in the Management of HR

An HR Manager's Review of Significant Employment Legislation in the United States

    Federal Employment Legislation before 1964

    Federal Employment Legislation after 1964

The International Legal Environment

The Special Role of the Hospitality Unit Manager

HR Terms

For Your Consideration

Case Study: Apply HR Management Principles

Internet Activities

LEARNING OBJECTIVES

When they complete this chapter, readers will be able to:

1. Define and describe "employment law," legislation directly addressing employer–employee relations.

2. State the importance of the government's role in establishing legal requirements affecting HR management.

3. List and briefly describe significant labor-related legislation enacted in the United States by the federal government.

4. Identify the unique issues facing hospitality companies that operate units in countries with legal and cultural systems different from those of the United States.

5. Appraise and appreciate the unique HR-related responsibilities of a hospitality industry unit manager.

Impact on HR Management

In many cases, hospitality unit managers serve as their own on-site legal counsel. As a result, these individuals are looked to by their employers, as well as those reporting to them, to make legally appropriate decisions in a wide variety of areas. These include selecting and disciplining employees, preventing harassment in all forms, and appraising, compensating, and, when necessary, terminating staff members.

Hospitality managers responsible for HR management must understand that the wrong HR decision can subject their companies (and themselves) to significant legal liability. Multimillion-dollar jury awards levied to penalize companies found guilty of improper employment practices are common in the United States. As a result, it is critical that hospitality managers responsible for HR management recognize and follow all of the employment-related laws that directly affect their decision making.

❖❖ EMPLOYMENT LAW

LEARNING OBJECTIVE 1. Define and describe "employment law," legislation directly addressing employer–employee relations.

Hospitality managers responsible for HR activities at either the unit or company level must understand the importance of **employment law** in their daily activities and decision making.

Employment law in the United States arose in many cases as a result of the demands of workers for better working conditions and the right to organize. Whenever these worker demands were deemed reasonable by a majority of society or the courts, legislation was enacted and became part of the country's accepted employment practices.

Today, employment laws are still proposed by various segments of society in an effort to ensure fairness in the workplace. The societal view of what actually constitutes fairness in the workplace, however, is often controversial and is ever changing. For example, some employment-related legislation that would have been considered quite radical in the 1800s is today commonly accepted. The now-accepted concept that the rights of female employees should be equal to those accorded to men was certainly not the norm in the 1800s. (Recall that it was 1920 before women in the United States gained the right to vote!)

In other cases, the views of what constitutes fairness in employment may vary greatly among citizens of individual countries, states, or cities. Not surprisingly, then, various types of employment laws are likely to be enacted in those **jurisdictions**. As a result, hospitality managers must be keenly aware of the individual employment laws that directly affect them, their operations, and their employees.

In some cases the laws directly related to employment in the hospitality industry are general (e.g., the federal laws in the United States relating to the rights of workers to unionize). In other cases the laws related to employment may best be understood in the context of a particular segment of HR management. Therefore laws related specifically to employee recruiting (see chapter 4), compensation (see chapter 8), performance appraisal (see chapter 9), and employee health and safety (see chapter 10) and labor unions (chapter 11) are closely examined in those individual chapters.

Hospitality managers, even those working full time in HR management, are not expected to be attorneys. A lack of understanding about HR-related law, however, can easily produce problems that result in those managers requiring the services of a qualified attorney. Experienced managers know that lawsuits and litigation are expensive and time-consuming. Most would also agree that the negative publicity associated with highly publicized lawsuits can be a real detriment

Employment law: The body of laws, administrative rulings, and precedents that addresses the legal rights of workers and their employers.

Jurisdiction: The geographic area over which a legal authority extends.

to their business and even their careers. For these reasons, hospitality managers at all levels should take great care to ensure that their actions do not inadvertently create troublesome legal issues for themselves and their companies.

The Law and HR: Prevention Is Better Than a Cure

In medical fields it is widely agreed that preventing a serious illness beforehand is better than treating it after the fact. For example, doctors would advise that preventing a heart attack through proper diet, exercise, and stopping smoking is preferable to performing a bypass operation on a patient after a heart attack has occurred. In the case of prevention, the doctor merely advises the patient, but it is largely up to the patient to put into practice the physician's recommendations. In a similar vein, it is far better for hospitality managers to understand the laws that relate to HR management than to expose their organizations to the fines and litigation that can result from violating the law. As a result, a basic understanding of how employment law is enacted, as well as how current law affects HR management, is essential.

It's the Law

"Deb," a food and beverage server, is accused of stealing money from the purse of a colleague in the food and beverage department. Management is convinced that Deb took the cash, but she denies it. Can Deb be required by management to submit to a lie detector test? In most cases the answer is no.

Societal views about what should be legal at work change constantly. In most cases issues related to the rights of workers and employers seek to balance the best interests of each group. Sometimes the resulting legislation is a tenuous compromise at best. For example, the Employee Polygraph Protection Act of 1988 (EPPA) generally prevents employers from using lie detector tests, either for pre-employment screening or during the course of employment, with certain exemptions.

Employers generally may not require or request any employee or job applicant to take a lie detector test and may not discharge, discipline, or discriminate against an employee or job applicant for refusing to take a test or for exercising other rights under the Act. In addition, employers are required to display the EPPA poster in the workplace for their employees.

Should employers have the right to require employees to take lie detector tests? Since 1988, they have not, nor will they have it again unless the dominant societal view supports such a right. Regardless of your position on this specific issue, it is clear that employment laws will continue to directly influence what HR managers can and cannot do in all segments of the hospitality industry.*

*The EPPA prohibits most uses of lie detectors by employers on their employees and job applicants. The Employment Standards Administration's Wage and Hour Division (WHD) within the U.S. Department of Labor (DOL) enforces the EPPA. For more information, go to www.dol.gov.

∴ THE GOVERNMENT'S ROLE IN THE MANAGEMENT OF HR

LEARNING OBJECTIVE 2. State the importance of the government's role in establishing legal requirements affecting HR management.

If you manage a hospitality business in the United States, you have many partners in your HR-related activities and decision making because the hospitality industry is regulated by a variety of federal, state, and local governmental entities. They enforce the many regulations that spell out the ways you must operate your business, as well as how you are required to carry out your HR efforts.

Hospitality managers interact with governmental entities in a variety of different ways, and they must observe the procedures and regulations established by the government. Managers must fill out forms and paperwork, obtain operating licenses, maintain their property according to specified codes and standards, provide a safe working environment, and, when required, even open their facilities for periodic inspections.

It should come as no surprise that a society, working through its governmental structures, implements and often revises its rules of employee–employer conduct and responsibility. Society is in a constant state of change, which has significant implications for those working in business, especially the hospitality industry. To illustrate, consider the hospitality industry in the United States in 1850. At that time, you would certainly not find a law requiring a specific number of automobile parking spaces to be designated for a restaurant's or hotel's disabled workers and customers.

The world of the 1850s contained neither the automobile nor (importantly) the inclination of society to grant special parking privileges to those who were disabled. In today's society we have both. What changed? First, the physical world changed. We now have automobiles and need to park them. More significant, however, is the fact that society's view of how disabled individuals should be treated has changed. Parking ordinances today require designated "handicapped" parking spaces, which are generally located close to the main entrances of buildings to ensure easy access. Not only is it good business to employ those with disabilities, but current laws mandate that a hospitality manager must do so. In this case employment of the disabled (and parking requirements) grew out of a law created by the federal government: the Americans with Disabilities Act (ADA). It is mentioned here to illustrate that laws evolve just as society evolves. Knowing current law is important, but understanding that you must keep abreast of changes in the law to ensure that facilities you operate are managed legally is just as important.

Just as the federal government has played and will continue to play an important regulatory role in the hospitality industry, so too do the various state governments. Understanding that states serve both complementary and distinct regulatory roles is important. These roles are complementary in that they support and amplify efforts undertaken at the federal level, but they are distinct in that they regulate some areas for which they have sole responsibility.

Recognizing that state and local employment laws and regulations may affect the actions of hospitality managers even more often than federal regulations is important. Codes and ordinances established at the state or local level can often be strict and may be strictly enforced. The penalties for violating these laws can be just as severe as those imposed at the federal level.

In general, each state regulates significant parts of the employee–employer relationship occurring within its borders. Items such as worker-related **unemployment compensation** benefits, worker safety issues, and at-work injury compensation fall to the state entity charged with regulating the workplace.

Regardless of the state in which you work, knowing and following your state's regulations related to workplace safety and properly documenting and reporting any work-related injuries are important. In each state worker safety and **workers' compensation** are usually monitored by a workers' compensation agency, commission, or subdivision of the employment security agency.

In most communities some agency of the court system (sometimes called a "friend" of the court) has the responsibility of assisting creditors in securing payment for legally owed debts.

Unemployment compensation: A benefit paid to an employee who involuntarily loses his or her employment without just cause.

Workers' compensation: A benefit paid to an employee who suffers a work-related injury or illness.

Garnish(ment): A court-ordered method of debt collection in which a portion of a worker's income is paid directly to one or more of that worker's creditors.

These debts can include a variety of court-ordered payments, such as child support payments. In cases such as these a hospitality manager can be ordered by the court to **garnish** an employee's wages.

The importance to the hospitality industry of local and city governments can be illustrated by examining worker wage rates in San Francisco, California. In 2003 voters in San Francisco approved a local ordinance tying the minimum wage to inflation. As a result, in 2013 the city's minimum wage was set at $10.55 per hour, the highest in the nation. By contrast, the federal and California minimum wages are both lower. Regardless of the local hospitality industry's initial support of, or opposition to, this specific piece of employment legislation, its impact on the San Francisco hospitality industry is clearly significant and the law must be followed.

Employment laws in the United States may be enacted at the federal, state, or local levels. At each of these levels, the laws reflect the desires of citizens and, ultimately, their elected officials and courts. Most hospitality professionals would agree that all workers are best protected when employers, employees, and governmental entities work together to protect wages, benefits, safety, and health. In most cases that is the societal intent when passing and enforcing employment-related legislation.

Today there are literally hundreds of thousands of laws that affect the operation of a hospitality property, and the number increases annually. These laws are implemented and enforced by a variety of governmental entities. In the next sections of this chapter you will learn about some of the most significant of these many employment rules and regulations.

❖ AN HR MANAGER'S REVIEW OF SIGNIFICANT EMPLOYMENT LEGISLATION IN THE UNITED STATES

LEARNING OBJECTIVE 3. List and briefly describe the most significant labor-related legislation enacted in the United States by the federal government.

While there is a variety of ways to examine the vast amount of employment-related legislation passed by the federal government, one good way is to review significant employment legislation enacted before and after passage of the landmark Civil Rights Act of 1964.

Federal Employment Legislation before 1964

In the view of many US history scholars, the most significant employment legislation passed before 1964 related to unionized workers and took place during the 1930s. However, several important pieces of labor-related legislation were actually passed in the very early 1900s. One of the most noteworthy was the Clayton Act of 1914, which legitimized and protected workers' rights to join **labor unions**.

Labor union: An organization that acts on behalf of its members to negotiate with management about the wages, hours, and other terms and conditions of the membership's employment.

In 1926 Congress passed the Railway Labor Act, requiring employers to bargain collectively and prohibiting discrimination against unions. It applied originally to interstate railroads but in 1936 it was amended to include airlines engaged in **interstate commerce**.

The right of employees to unionize was established with the passage of the National Labor Relations Act (NLRA) of 1935, more popularly known as the Wagner Act. The NLRA was applicable to all firms and employees engaging in activities affecting interstate commerce. This law's impact included coverage of hotel and restaurant workers, and they and most other workers were guaranteed the right to organize and join labor movements, to choose representatives and bargain collectively, and to strike. It also expressly prohibited employers from:

Interstate commerce: Commercial trading or the transportation of people or property between or among states.

- ◆ interfering with the formation of a union,
- ◆ restraining employees from exercising their right to join a union,
- ◆ imposing any special conditions on employment that would discourage union membership,

Unions in the Hospitality Industry

Although the hospitality industry as a whole is not, nor has ever been, heavily unionized, the Hotel Employees and Restaurant Employees Union (HERE), a US labor union representing workers of the hospitality industry, was formed in 1891. In 2004 HERE merged with the Union of Needletrades, Industrial, and Textile Employees (UNITE) to form UNITE HERE.

UNITE HERE represents employees in the hotel, gaming, food service, manufacturing, textile, distribution, laundry, and airport industries. Major employers contracted in this union include several large casinos (e.g., Harrah's, Caesars, and Wynn Resorts); hotels (e.g., Hilton, Hyatt, and Starwood); and Walt Disney World.

◆ discharging or discriminating against employees who reported unfair labor practices, and

◆ refusing to bargain in good faith with legitimate union leadership.

Historically, the great majority of hospitality workers have not been unionized. Managers working in organizations where their employees are unionized, however, must understand the unique employer–employee relationship that exists in a unionized workplace (see chapter 11).

In 1938 Congress passed the Fair Labor Standards Act (FLSA). The main objective of this act is to eliminate labor conditions deemed "detrimental to the maintenance of the minimum standards of living necessary for health, efficiency and well-being of workers."[1] This law requires employers to pay overtime for hours worked in excess of 40 per week (defined as 7 consecutive 24-hour periods).

The FLSA also prohibits child labor in all industries engaged in producing goods for sale in interstate commerce. The act sets the minimum age at 14 for employment outside of school hours in nonmanufacturing jobs, at 16 for employment during school hours, and at 18 for hazardous occupations.

In 1963 Congress passed the Equal Pay Act. This law prohibits employers from paying women and men different wages when the work performed requires equal skill, effort, and responsibility and is performed under similar working conditions.

Federal Employment Legislation after 1964

Perhaps the single most significant piece of federal legislation affecting the workplace was passed in the aftermath of a true American tragedy. The assassination of John F. Kennedy in November 1963 resulted in the Lyndon Baines Johnson presidency. On November 27, 1963, addressing Congress and the nation for the first time as president, Johnson called for passage of a sweeping civil rights bill as a monument to the fallen Kennedy. "Let us continue," he said, promising that "the ideas and the ideals which [Kennedy] so nobly represented must and will be translated into effective action." In June 1964 Congress passed the Civil Rights Act of 1964, the most important piece of civil rights legislation in the nation's history; on July 2, 1964, President Johnson signed it into law.

THE CIVIL RIGHTS ACT OF 1964 (TITLE VII)

The Civil Rights Act of 1964 contains several important sections, but for hospitality employers, the most important of these is **Title VII**. Title VII of the Civil Rights Act of 1964 outlawed discrimination in employment in any business on the basis of race, color, religion, sex, or national origin.

In 1972 the passage of the Equal Employment Opportunity Act, an amendment to the Civil Rights Act of 1964, resulted in the formation of the **Equal Employment Opportunity Commission (EEOC)**. The EEOC enforces the antidiscrimination provisions of Title VII. The EEOC investigates, mediates, and sometimes even files lawsuits on behalf of employees. Businesses that are found to have discriminated can be ordered to compensate the employee(s) for damages in the

Title VII: The specific section of the Civil Rights Act of 1964 that outlaws discrimination in employment in any business on the basis of race, color, religion, sex, or national origin.

Equal Employment Opportunity Commission (EEOC): The entity within the federal government assigned to enforce the provisions of Title VII of the Civil Rights Act of 1964.

form of lost wages, attorney fees, and other expenses. Title VII also provides that individuals can sue their employers on their own. In most cases an individual must file a complaint of discrimination with the EEOC within 180 days of learning of the discrimination or lose the right to file a lawsuit.

In the late 1970s courts began holding that **sexual harassment** is also prohibited under the Civil Rights Act and, in 1986, the Supreme Court held in a lawsuit (*Meritor Savings Bank v. Vinson, 477 U.S. 57* [1986]) that sexual harassment is sex discrimination and thus is prohibited by Title VII.

Title VII has since been supplemented with legislation prohibiting pregnancy, age, and disability discrimination.

The Civil Rights Act of 1964 makes it illegal for employers to discriminate in hiring and in setting the terms and conditions of employment. Labor unions also are prohibited from basing membership or union classifications on race, color, religion, sex, or national origin. The law also is clear in its prohibition of employers retaliating against employees or potential employees who file charges of discrimination against them, refuse to comply with a discriminatory policy, or participate in an investigation of discrimination charges against the employer.

In later amendments the Civil Rights Act was expanded to include **affirmative action** requirements. Affirmative action constitutes a good-faith effort by employees to address past and/ or present discrimination through a variety of specific, results-oriented procedures. This is a step beyond an equal opportunity law such as Title VII that simply bans discriminatory practices. State and local governments, federal governmental agencies, and federal contractors and subcontractors with contracts of $50,000 or more, including colleges and universities, are required by federal law to implement affirmative action programs. Food service and hotel managers working in colleges, universities, hospitals, and many other settings must also implement affirmative action plans. The goal of most affirmative action programs is to broaden the pool of candidates and encourage hiring based on sound, job-related criteria. The intended result is a workforce with greater diversity and equal opportunity for all.

Sexual harassment: Unwelcome sexual advances, requests for sexual favors, and other verbal or physical conduct of a sexual nature.

Affirmative action: A federally mandated requirement that employers who meet certain criteria must actively seek to fairly employ recognized classes of workers. (Some state and local legislatures have also enacted affirmative action requirements.)

HR Management in Action

GOOD BUSINESS OR RACE DISCRIMINATION?

Danielle Hidalgo, the daughter of a Mexican citizen and an American citizen who was born and raised in the United States, applied, as did many others, for a vacant server's position at the Golden Dragon restaurant. Now she received a call from Ms. Goh, the restaurant's manager. "I'm sorry, Danielle," said Ms. Goh. "You have excellent qualifications, but people come to the Golden Dragon for an Asian dining experience, and they expect to see Asian servers. That's why I only hire a certain type person for front-of-the-house positions, but there could be a spot for you in the back of the house. Are you interested?"

Some managers might feel that Ms. Goh is simply making a good business decision by seeking to create an Asian ambience in her restaurant. Others viewing this same situation, however, may strongly feel that Ms. Goh is practicing a form of racial discrimination.

This case illustrates the fact that reasonable people can often see both sides of complex employment-related issues. In the United States, however, coworker, customer, or client discomfort or preference cannot be used as the basis for a discriminatory action. If an employer takes an action based on the discriminatory preferences of others, in nearly all cases the employer is practicing illegal discrimination. The desire to market a restaurant's image through employees' physical appearance is generally not going to satisfy the bona fide occupational qualification requirement of the EEOC.

In very few cases Title VII permits a **bona fide occupational qualification (BFOQ)** to be used to legally discriminate among workers. It is important to understand, however, that the government, through the EEOC, and not an individual hospitality business, can authorize the legal use of a BFOQ.

In addition to the Civil Rights Act of 1964, many states also have their own civil rights laws that prohibit discrimination. Sometimes state laws are more inclusive than the Civil Rights Act in that they expand protection to workers or employment candidates in categories not covered under the federal law (such as age, marital status, sexual orientation, and certain types of physical or mental disabilities). State civil rights laws may also have stricter penalties for violations, including fines and/or imprisonment. For example, in California it is illegal for an employer to discriminate against an employee because of that employee's sexual orientation or perceived sexual orientation. It is important to remember that HR managers working in the hospitality industry must be aware of all civil rights laws in effect in the location where they are working. While a state or local law is not permitted to take away employee rights granted at the federal level, they are allowed to add to them. Thus, as in this example, an employee group not protected by federal law may be granted protection by a more favorable (to the employee) local law.

Hospitality managers must understand that, in general, federal (as well as many state and local) laws are intended to define and prevent inappropriate **disparate treatment** of employees based on a non-job-related characteristic.

Disparate treatment is a basic concept in employment discrimination cases. Lawyers classify employment discrimination cases as either disparate treatment cases or **disparate (adverse) impact** cases.

In a disparate treatment case, the employee's claim is that the employer treated him or her differently than other employees who were in a similar situation. For example, both Sara and Randy are late for work one day, and their employer fires Sara but does not fire Randy. If the reason Sara was fired is that she is female, then the employer has engaged in disparate treatment because of sex, which would be a violation of Title VII. If, however, Sara had been late ten times in the last ten days and Randy had not previously been late despite having worked for the company for five years, the termination (because it was job-related, not gender-related) would be lawful.

Bona fide occupational qualification (BFOQ): A specific job requirement for a particular position that is reasonably necessary to the normal operation of a business and thus allows discrimination against a protected class (e.g., choosing a male model when photographing an advertisement for beard trimmers).

Disparate treatment: The claim that one employee was treated differently than other employees in the same situation.

Disparate (adverse) impact: The claim that an employer's action, though not intentionally discriminatory, still results in unlawful discrimination; also known as *adverse impact*.

Name of Law: The Civil Rights Act of 1964 (Title VII) as amended

Applicable to: Employers with fifteen or more employees

Requirements of the Law	Key Facts About the Law
Prohibits employers and unions from discriminating on the basis of race, national origin, religion, gender, age, or pregnancy.	The Equal Employment Opportunity Act of 1972, an amendment to the Civil Rights Act of 1964, resulted in the formation of the EEOC. The EEOC enforces the antidiscrimination provisions of Civil Rights Act of 1964.
In 2012 the EEOC ruled that employment discrimination on the basis of gender identity or transgender status is prohibited under Title VII.	The law also forbids discrimination on the basis of genetic information when it comes to any aspect of employment, including health insurance, because genetic information is not relevant to an individual's current ability to work.
Prohibits sexual harassment in the workplace.	
Employees must file charges of discrimination against an employer within 180 days of the occurrence of the discrimination.	In some employment settings the Act requires the implementation of effective affirmative action programs.
Prohibits employers from retaliating against employees or potential employees who file charges of discrimination against them.	The EEOC, as well as individual employees, may sue an employer for discriminatory practices.
For detailed information on the law's requirements go to: www.eeoc.gov/laws/statutes/titlevii.cfm/	

Disparate policies are illegal and point to the importance of HR managers carefully reviewing all employment policies to ensure they do not inadvertently lead to charges of disparate treatment or disparate impact.

THE AGE DISCRIMINATION IN EMPLOYMENT ACT OF 1967

The Age Discrimination in Employment Act of 1967 (ADEA) was initially passed to prevent the practice (widespread at that time) of requiring employees to retire at age 65. As workers' life spans increased, it made little sense for employees to be forced to retire when many could and wanted to remain on the job.

The ADEA originally gave protected-group status to those workers between the ages of 39 and 65. Since 1967, the act has been amended twice: once in 1978, when the mandatory retirement age was raised to 70, and then again in 1986, when the mandatory retirement age was removed altogether.

The ADEA makes including age preferences, limitations, or specifications in job notices or advertisements unlawful. As a narrow exception to that general rule, a job notice or advertisement may specify an age limit in the rare circumstances where age is shown to be a BFOQ that is reasonably necessary to the operation of the business. For example, airline pilots may still be required to retire at a certain age because of evidence that increasing age causes a decline in piloting abilities.

Customer preference is not a rationale that will result in the granting of a BFOQ by the EEOC. Thus, for example, a male bar owner who determines that his customers like young (and attractive) female servers better than older ones would not be allowed to hire only younger servers. He would also not be allowed to terminate servers as they became older, even if the bar owner believed it would be good for business.

The ADEA does not specifically prohibit an employer from asking an applicant's age or date of birth. In the hospitality industry, for example, establishing an applicant's age before hiring him or her to serve alcohol or to operate certain types of potentially dangerous kitchen equipment may be legally necessary. Because such inquiries may deter older workers from applying for employment or may otherwise indicate possible intent to discriminate based on age, however, requests for age information are closely scrutinized by the EEOC to make sure that the inquiry was made for a lawful purpose, rather than for a prohibited purpose.

Name of Law: The Age Discrimination in Employment Act

Applicable to: Employers with 20 or more employees

Requirements of the Law	Key Facts About the Law
Prohibits employers and unions from discriminating on the basis of age with respect to any term, condition, or privilege of employment, including hiring, firing, promotion, layoff, compensation, benefits, job assignments, and training.	The ADEA now protects individuals who are 40 years of age or older from employment discrimination based on age.
Makes it unlawful to retaliate against an individual for opposing employment practices that discriminate based on age or for filing an age discrimination charge, testifying, or participating in any way in an investigation, proceeding, or litigation under the ADEA.	It is also unlawful for a labor organization to exclude, or to expel from its membership, any individual because of his or her age.
For detailed information on the law's requirements go to:	The ADEA's protections apply to both employees and job applicants.
http://www.eeoc.gov/laws/statutes/adea.cfm/	The EEOC is responsible for enforcing this law.

The Older Workers Benefit Protection Act of 1990 amended the ADEA to specifically prohibit employers from denying benefits to older employees. This law was passed to prevent the practice of reducing employment benefits such as medical insurance based on an employee's age.

THE PREGNANCY DISCRIMINATION ACT OF 1978

The Pregnancy Discrimination Act of 1978 is actually an amendment to Title VII of the Civil Rights Act of 1964. The Pregnancy Discrimination Act made discrimination on the basis of pregnancy, childbirth, or related medical conditions unlawful sex discrimination under Title VII.

The law requires that women affected by pregnancy or related conditions must be treated in the same way as other applicants or employees with similar abilities or limitations. An employer cannot refuse to hire a woman because of her pregnancy-related condition as long as she is able to perform the major functions of her job. Also, an employer cannot refuse to hire her because of prejudices against pregnant workers or the prejudices of coworkers, clients, or customers.

Pregnant employees must be permitted to work as long as they are able to perform their jobs and must be allowed to take a "reasonable" amount of unpaid leave after a baby's birth. Although the law does not specifically establish a definition for "reasonable" time off after a baby's birth, many organizations consider six weeks to be reasonable, and that time frame has been supported by the EEOC.

The Pregnancy Discrimination Act also requires that pregnancy-related benefits cannot be limited only to married employees. If an employer provides any benefits to workers on leave, the employer must provide the same benefits for those on leave for pregnancy-related conditions. When a specific benefit is not offered to all employees, the employer is not required by this law to provide the benefit for those who are or become pregnant. The law simply states that, when employee benefits are *already* offered, they must be uniformly offered to those employees who are or become pregnant.

Name of Law: The Pregnancy Discrimination Act

Applicable to: Employers with 15 or more employees

Requirements of the Law	Key Facts About the Law
An employer cannot refuse to hire a pregnant woman because of her pregnancy, because of a pregnancy-related condition, or because of the prejudices of coworkers, clients, or customers.	The Pregnancy Discrimination Act amended Title VII of the Civil Rights Act of 1964.
Employers must hold open a job for a pregnancy-related absence the same length of time jobs are held open for employees on sick or disability leave.	If an employee is temporarily unable to perform her job because of a pregnancy, the employer must treat her the same as any other temporarily disabled employee. For example, if the employer allows temporarily disabled employees to modify tasks, perform alternative assignments, or take disability leave or leave without pay, the employer also must allow an employee who is temporarily disabled because of pregnancy to do the same.
It is unlawful to retaliate against an individual for opposing employment practices that discriminate based on pregnancy or for filing a discrimination charge, testifying, or participating in any way in an investigation, proceeding, or litigation under Title VII.	
For detailed information on the law's requirements go to: http://www.eeoc.gov/laws/statutes/ pregnancy.cfm	Employers must allow an employee a "reasonable" amount of time off after having a baby. Also, pregnancy-related benefits cannot be limited to married employees. Employers must provide the same level of health benefits for spouses of male employees as they do for spouses of female employees.

"I don't get it," said Tonya Zollars, the new HR director for Clubs International, a company that specializes in the operation of golf, city, and other private clubs. Tonya had just finished reading the annual evaluation for Naomi Yip, the sous chef at one of the private city clubs managed by her company. Naomi had been with the organization for five years and was considered one of the company's best and brightest culinary artists. Every evaluation she received since joining the company was excellent. However, her current supervisor did not, at the end of the evaluation, check the box "Ready for Promotion" that each of her previous supervising chefs had checked.

"Well," said Thomas Hayhoe, the executive chef who completed the evaluation, "you know Naomi's gonna have a baby. She's due in five months. I like Naomi a lot, but maybe it would be better for her right now not to take on the added responsibilities a promotion would require. She told me she's looking forward to spending as much time as possible with her baby, and you know as well as I do that at the next level, 60-plus hours weekly for the executive chef's job are the norm around here."

Clubs International was recently awarded a contract to operate a new and lucrative account, the Hawk Hollow Golf Club. Assume that, prior to Chef Hayhoe's evaluation, Naomi would likely have been asked to fill the job of Executive Chef at the new account. Assume further that Tonya is now advising the company's vice president of operations about filling the new (and vacant) executive chef's position at Hawk Hollow.

Case Study Questions

1. Should Tonya recommend the company offer Naomi the promotion to executive chef at Hawk Hollow?

2. Based on Chef Hayhoe's evaluation, what would you advise Tonya to do if her own boss opposed her recommendation to promote Naomi?

3. Do you feel it would be appropriate to inform the new client (Hawk Hollow) of Naomi's condition so their input could be considered?

THE AMERICANS WITH DISABILITIES ACT (ADA) OF 1990

The Americans with Disabilities Act (ADA) was enacted in July 1990. The ADA prohibits discrimination against people with disabilities. The ADA is a five-part piece of legislation, but Title I of the Act focuses primarily on employment.

Three different groups of individuals are protected under the ADA:

1. An individual with a physical or mental impairment that substantially limits a major life activity. Some examples of what constitutes a "major life activity" under the Act are seeing, hearing, talking, walking, reading, learning, breathing, taking care of oneself, lifting, sitting, and standing.

2. A person who has a record of a disability

3. A person who is "regarded as" having a disability

Reasonable accommodation: Any modification or adjustment to a job or the work environment that enables a qualified applicant or employee with a disability to participate in the application process or to perform the job's essential functions.

Employers cannot reduce an employee's pay simply because he or she is disabled, nor can they refuse to hire a disabled candidate if, with **reasonable accommodation**, it is possible for the candidate to perform the job.

Not surprisingly, one of the significant issues regarding ADA is the practical application of the word *reasonable* when considering how to best accommodate a disabled job candidate or employee. Therefore a basic understanding of the US court system's continuous defining and refining of the term is critical for hospitality managers.

For example, the courts have held that restructuring a job to shift a minor (nonessential) responsibility for a task from a disabled to a nondisabled employee is a reasonable accommodation. In addition, allowing disabled workers extra unpaid leave when it does not present a hardship to the business is considered a reasonable accommodation. An employer is not, however, required to provide a disabled worker with more paid leave than the employer provides its nondisabled workers.

Certain things are not considered reasonable accommodations and are therefore not required. For example, an employer does not have to eliminate a primary job responsibility to accommodate a disabled employee. In addition, an employer is not required to lower productivity standards that are applied to all employees, but the employer may be required to provide reasonable accommodation to enable an employee with a disability to meet the productivity standard. An employer is also not required to provide a disabled worker with personal-use items such as a prosthetic limb, a wheelchair, eyeglasses, hearing aids, or similar devices. In other words, an employer is not required to make a reasonable accommodation when that accommodation would cause an undue hardship on the employer.

In general, an undue hardship occurs when the expense of accommodating the worker is excessive or when it would disrupt the natural work environment. Unfortunately, the law in this area is vague. Therefore, any employer who maintains that accommodating a worker with a disability would impose an undue hardship should be prepared to document such an assertion. After investigation, the EEOC ultimately issues a "right to sue" letter to an employee if it determines an employer is in violation of the ADA.

An employee's request for a reasonable accommodation or the granting of a reasonable accommodation is typically a matter to be discussed only between the employer and the employee. An employer may not disclose that a disabled employee is receiving a reasonable accommodation because this usually amounts to a disclosure that the individual has a disability. (The ADA specifically prohibits the disclosure of an employee's medical information except in very limited situations, which never includes disclosure to coworkers.)

As a hospitality employer, you may be faced with questions from your nondisabled employees about why a coworker is receiving what is perceived as different or special treatment. The best response to questions of this type is to emphasize that all employees' special needs are accommodated when it is possible to do so. Pointing out that many of the workplace issues encountered by employees are personal and that, in these circumstances, it is your company's policy to respect employee privacy may also be helpful. You may be able to make this point even more effectively by reassuring the employee asking the question that his or her privacy would similarly be respected if it was necessary for him or her to request some type of workplace change for strictly personal reasons. There may not be any pressure from the employer to do so, but employees with a disability may voluntarily choose to disclose to coworkers that they are receiving a reasonable accommodation.

Even with the passage of the ADA, an employer does not have to hire a disabled applicant who is not qualified to do a job. The employer can still select the most qualified candidate, provided that no applicant was eliminated from consideration because of a qualified disability.

Although the law in this area is changing rapidly, the following conditions currently meet the criteria for a qualified disability and are protected under the ADA:

◆ AIDS
◆ Cancer
◆ Cerebral palsy
◆ Tuberculosis
◆ Heart disease
◆ Hearing or visual impairments
◆ Alcoholism

Passage of the ADA changed the way employers may select employees. For example, questions that should not be asked on job applications or during interviews because they likely violate the ADA include:

1. Have you ever been hospitalized?
2. Are you taking prescription drugs?
3. Have you ever been treated for drug addiction or alcoholism?
4. Have you ever filed a workers' compensation insurance claim?
5. Do you have any physical defects, disabilities, or impairments that may affect your performance in the position for which you are applying?

Accommodating Disabled Employees

To reduce the risk of an ADA noncompliance charge related to reasonable accommodation, the following steps can be of great assistance.

Steps for ADA Reasonable Accommodation

1. Can the applicant perform the essential functions of the job with or without reasonable accommodation? (You can ask the applicant this question.)

   If "no," then the applicant is not qualified and is not protected by the ADA.

   If "yes," then go to question 2.

2. Is the necessary accommodation reasonable? To answer this question, ask yourself the following: Will this accommodation create an undue financial or administrative hardship on the business?

   If "yes," you do not have to provide unreasonable accommodations.

   If "no," then go to question 3.

3. Will this accommodation or hiring the person with the disability create a direct threat to the health or safety of other employees or guests in the workplace?

   If "yes," you are not required to make the accommodation and have fulfilled your obligation under the ADA.

Accommodating Disabled Guests

In their role as HR specialists, hospitality managers are, of course, primarily concerned about the impact of ADA regulations on hiring and employment. But the ADA also affects an operation's treatment of its guests. The provision of handicap parking spaces in restaurant parking lots is one such common accommodation.

In 2010 new regulations were issued that directly affect the reasonable accommodations many hospitality operations must make for their customers. These regulations expanded the responsibilities of hotels and restaurants for their disabled guests in a variety of important areas including:

Hotel guest room layout

Exercise machines and equipment access

Swimming pools and spa access

Restroom layouts

These changes impact HR managers because, in many cases, the changes affect the training programs HR managers have in place for their own service-oriented employees. To review all of the changes made by the 2010 expansion of the ADA and to consider how they can impact employee training programs in the hospitality industry go to www.ada.gov/regs2010/factsheets/2010_Standards_factsheet.html/.

Name of Law: The Americans with Disabilities Act (ADA)

Applicable to: Employers with 15 or more employees

Requirements of the Law	Key Facts About the Law
An employer cannot refuse to hire or continue to employ a disabled worker if, with reasonable accommodation, the worker can adequately perform the job.	The ADA applies to private employers, state and local governments, employment agencies, and labor unions.
Modified or part-time schedules are considered reasonable accommodations. A modified schedule may involve adjusting arrival or departure times, providing periodic breaks, altering when certain job tasks are performed, allowing an employee to use accrued paid leave, or providing additional unpaid leave.	Employers are not required to eliminate a primary job responsibility to accommodate a disabled employee. The law addresses many disabilities, but among those conditions it does not consider disability are: ◆ Kleptomania ◆ Disorders caused by the use of illegal drugs ◆ Compulsive gambling ◆ Sexual behavior disorders ◆ Migraine headaches ◆ Short-term conditions such as a broken limb
An employer is not required to make a reasonable accommodation when that accommodation would cause an undue hardship on the employer.	
Employers are required to post notices of the ADA and its provisions in a location where they can be seen by all employees.	Each year, the US Secretary of Health and Human Services publishes a list of communicable diseases that, if spread through the handling of food, could put a food service operation's guests at risk. Under the ADA, employers have the right not to assign or hire an individual carrying one of these identified diseases to a position that involves the handling of food, but only if there is no reasonable accommodation that could be made to eliminate such a risk.
The ADA addresses reasonable accommodation for a business's disabled employees and customers.	
Provisions of the ADA are enforced by the Civil Rights Division of the US Department of Justice.	
For detailed information on the law's requirements go to: www.ada.gov/	

THE FAMILY MEDICAL LEAVE ACT OF 1993

The Family and Medical Leave Act (FMLA) was enacted in February 1993. This law allows an employee to take unpaid leave because of pregnancy or illness or to care for a sick family member. The FMLA currently requires employers of 50 or more employees (and all public agencies) to provide workers up to 12 weeks of unpaid, job-protected leave in a 12-month period:

- ✓ for the birth and care of a child;
- ✓ for placement with the employee of a child for adoption or foster care;
- ✓ to care for a serious illness of the employee or an immediate family member; or
- ✓ for a serious health condition that makes the employee unable to perform the essential functions of his or her job.

Under the FMLA, employers can require that a request for leave be certified as necessary by the health care provider of the eligible employee or of the child, spouse, or parent of the employee, as appropriate. When the employer requests it, the employee is required to provide, in a timely manner, a copy of the certification to the employer.

In most cases (there are some limited exceptions for extremely critical or key positions) an employer must allow the employee to return to the same position he or she held when the leave commenced, to an equivalent position, or to one virtually identical to the employee's former position in terms of pay and working conditions, including status and benefits. Also, the fact that the employee took leave may not be held against the employee in other ways, including when determining pay increases or during the employee's performance reviews.

Name of Law: The Family Medical Leave Act (FMLA)
Applicable to: Employers with 50 or more employees

Requirements of the Law	Key Facts About the Law
The FMLA allows eligible employees to take up to 12 workweeks of unpaid leave a year and requires group health benefits to be maintained during the leave as if employees continued to work instead of taking leave. To be eligible for the benefits provided under the FMLA an employee must: ◆ work for a covered employer. ◆ have worked 1,250 hours during the 12 months prior to the start of leave. ◆ work at a location where the employer has 50 or more workers within 75 miles. ◆ have worked for the employer for 12 months. The 12 months of employment are not required to be consecutive for the employee to qualify for FMLA leave. Special rules apply to those workers whose employment is interrupted due to the employee's fulfillment of military obligations. For detailed information on the law's requirements go to: www.dol.gov/whd/fmla	Employees may elect (and employers can require) that any paid leave accumulated by employees (e.g., vacation or sick time) be used before the employee begins unpaid leave. Employees are required under the FMLA to make a reasonable effort to schedule any medical treatment so as not to disrupt their employer's business. They must also, when possible, give their employer 30 days' notice of their intent to take FMLA-mandated time off. For purposes of this law an "immediate family member" is defined as a spouse, child, or parent of the employee. According to recent data from the US Department of Labor, 42 percent of workers who have taken unpaid time off under the FMLA have done so to care for their own serious illness; 26 percent have done so to care for a new child or for maternity disability reasons; 13 percent to care for a seriously ill parent; 12 percent to care for a seriously ill child; and 6 percent to care for a seriously ill spouse.

THE LILLY LEDBETTER FAIR PAY ACT OF 2009

Lilly Ledbetter was a salaried worker employed by the Goodyear Tire and Rubber company. In 1998 Ledbetter filed a formal EEOC charge against Goodyear alleging sex discrimination in her pay. Essentially, Ledbetter charged that for many years her male counterparts, doing identical work at the company, were paid more money than she.

Name of Law: Lily Ledbetter Fair Pay Act
Applicable to: Employers covered by the Civil Rights Act

Requirements of the Law	Key Facts About the Law
Changes the statute of limitations on charges of equal-pay violations from 180 days of the first occurrence (per the Civil Rights Act) to 180 days from the issuance of each worker paycheck resulting from the discriminatory act. The Act has a retroactive effective date of May 28, 2007, and applies to all claims of discriminatory compensation pending on or after that date. For detailed information on the law's requirements go to: www.eeoc.gov/laws/statutes/ epa_ledbetter.cfm/	The Act was the direct result of a 5–4 Supreme Court ruling dismissing Ledbetter's original charge of discrimination, which she filed against the Goodyear Tire and Rubber Company. The Act restored the pre-*Ledbetter* position of the EEOC that each paycheck that delivers discriminatory compensation is a wrong that is actionable under the federal EEO statutes. This was the first act signed by President Barack Obama after he took office in 2009.

Ledbetter's charge was upheld in District Court and she was granted compensatory back pay for the previous years in which she was discriminated against. However, Goodyear appealed the decision stating that, according to the Civil Rights Act, only pay discrimination that occurred 180 days before Ledbetter's complaint filing should be subject to repayment.

While not directly addressing the facts of her allegation, in 2007 the United States Supreme Court ruled Ledbetter could not file charges of pay discrimination under Title VII of the Civil Rights Act because she was time-barred. That is, the discrimination occurred more than 180 days before Ledbetter filed her charges, and thus the **statute of limitations** for her complaint had expired.

Immediately following the Supreme Court's decision Congress introduced legislation to state that if an act of discrimination is ongoing, claims about it can be made beyond the 180-days' statute of limitations that normally apply to an employee's EEOC complaint. The legislation was passed into law and signed by the president in 2009.

Statute of limitations: A legal concept that establishes the specific time period after an event happens during which legal proceedings related to that event can be undertaken.

THE PATIENT PROTECTION AND AFFORDABLE CARE ACT OF 2010

Understanding the Patient Protection and Affordable Care Act (ACA) is especially important for food service professionals for two reasons: (1) the actual content and impact of the law; and (2) the history of the ACA provides managers with a recent (and continuing) example of how employment laws in the United States are proposed, debated in the public arena, and, in many cases, enacted in one form or another.

The US Congress passed the ACA by the narrowest of margins in early 2010 and President Obama immediately signed it into law, thereby gaining the law the nickname "ObamaCare." The constitutionality of the law was challenged by the National Federation of Independent Businesses but, in 2012, the US Supreme Court upheld the constitutionality of most of the law's provisions.

The intent of the ACA was to expand the availability of affordable health care coverage to Americans and to reduce the cost of health care. The law has passionate supporters and it has those who just as passionately oppose it.

Provisions of the ACA take effect over a period of years (see www.healthcare.gov/law/timeline). The law contains a variety of key provisions that directly affect workers and companies in the hospitality industry, including:

✓ Guaranteeing the ability of all individuals to obtain health care coverage regardless of their preexisting health conditions

✓ Mandating that all employees who are not covered by a health insurance plan at work must purchase individual health care coverage

✓ Providing health insurance cost subsidies for low-income individuals and families

✓ Banning annual and lifetime caps on insurance coverage for all individuals

✓ Providing tax incentives for small businesses that provide health coverage for their workers and pay at least 50 percent of the cost of the coverage

✓ Fining affected employers who do not provide adequate health coverage to their full-time employees, defined as those who work over 30 hours per week or 130 hours per month

Opposition to the ACA continues from those groups concerned about the law's costs to businesses and individuals, concerns about the potential for the law to result in increases in actual health care costs, issues related to civil liberties, and, in some cases, concerns about religious freedom. Proponents of the law, however, cite the fact that Americans spend nearly 2.5 times the amount per person on health care costs compared with other developed countries.[2] These supporters maintain the ACA will reduce long-term health costs and provide better health care coverage for all—especially for those who did not have, or in many cases could not obtain, health insurance before the law's passage.

For HR managers, the implications of the ACA are many, but two of the most significant relate to coverage mandates and penalties.

Coverage Mandates

One of the most controversial components of the ACA is the requirement that all citizens purchase insurance unless it is provided by their employers. The provisions of the **individual coverage mandate** established under the ACA affects small and large employers differently.

Individual coverage mandate: The provision of the ACA that imposes a fine on individuals who do not maintain minimum essential health coverage for themselves and their dependents. Exceptions to the mandate include undocumented immigrants, members of Native American tribes, members of religious orders, and those who cannot afford insurance.

EMPLOYERS WITH FEWER THAN 50 EMPLOYEES   The ACA does not require businesses with fewer than 50 full-time employees to provide these employees with health care insurance. Those employers with fewer than 25 employees who do choose to provide coverage, however, receive a tax credit (up to 50 percent of their actual cost) to help offset the costs associated with providing the health coverage.

Effective in 2014, individual employees of businesses who employ fewer than 50 workers and who do not receive health care insurance from their employers are eligible to purchase their own coverage through the **health insurance exchanges** that are operated within each state.

Health insurance exchange: The series of government-regulated and approved individual health care plans that qualify those who are enrolled in them for government subsidies. US citizens residing in all states must have access to such plans. Also referred to as the "Health Insurance Marketplace."

EMPLOYERS WITH MORE THAN 50 EMPLOYEES   Businesses employing more than 50 full-time workers as defined by the ACA are required to provide health care coverage to their employees. Those who do not provide this coverage face significant and escalating fines and penalties. However, effective in 2017, the law allows states to permit companies employing more than 100 workers to purchase health care coverage in the state-based health insurance exchanges.

Penalties

Failure on the part of individuals or businesses to comply with the coverage mandates of the ACA subjects these individuals and business to fines. Enforcement of the parts of the ACA related to employers and their compliance with the health care mandate is assigned to the Internal Revenue Service (IRS). The IRS is authorized to impose a penalty on affected employers if:

1. the employer does not offer employee health insurance, or
2. the employer requires an employee to contribute (pay) too much to his or her own insurance costs and, as a result, the employee qualifies for a government subsidy for health coverage.

It's the Law

Controversy surrounded the ACA both before and after its passage. As of June 2014, the US House of Representatives had voted to delay or repeal all or parts of the ACA over 50 times. Americans, on the whole, remain sharply divided about the law. Most of those who were unable to obtain health insurance before the law's passage are in favor of it. A large number of people who already had coverage before passage of the law worry that it will increase their costs or reduce their own health-related, decision-making options. Still others oppose the law because they feel it did not go far enough in providing subsidized government health insurance to all Americans.

Some specific features of the law, such as the one preventing insurers from refusing to insure people with preexisting conditions and the provision allowing young people up to age 26 to stay on their parent's insurance policies, are widely popular. Other features of the law, such as the individual mandate requiring everyone to purchase insurance and the requirement that all employers include contraceptive care for women in the insurance policies they offer employees, are much less popular.

The ACA is an excellent example of the means by which a democratic society determines what is deemed lawful and unlawful. Most experts expect that changes and modifications to the ACA will occur in the near future. The result is that HR managers should continue to monitor the evolving manner in which the provisions of the ACA and other laws will be applied to their own businesses to best ensure their full compliance with them.

Name of Law: Patient Protection and Affordable Care Act (ACA)
Applicable to: All US citizens and selected employers

Requirements of the Law	Key Facts About the Law
By 2014 all individuals must be enrolled in a government-approved health insurance plan or pay a fine.	The law established minimum quality standards for health insurance policies.
Each state must provide workers the option of purchasing subsidized health coverage via a state-based insurance exchange (marketplace).	The ACA requires insurers to spend at least 80 percent (85 percent for large insurers) of the health care premiums they collect for their insured's actual health claims and care costs.
Insurers are not permitted to cancel an individual's insurance coverage for health-related reasons.	The law states that selected preventive care procedures (including mammograms and domestic violence screening and counseling) must be provided without charging patients a deductible or a co-pay.
Effective for health plans offered after 2014, annual and/or lifetime limits on essential health coverage is prohibited.	
	The law allows those up to age 26 to stay on their parent's health insurance plans.
Firms employing 50 or more workers who do *not* provide health insurance coverage must pay a fine if the government is required to subsidize their workers' individual insurance coverage.	Health care plans may not deny or limit coverage of children younger than 19 because of pre-existing conditions.
Beginning in 2018, the law imposes a new 40 percent excise tax on the value of health coverage provided by employers that exceeds established dollar thresholds.	Effective in 2014, small-business owners are able to offer employees health plan choices through the Small Business Health Options Program (SHOP).
For detailed information on the law's requirements go to: www.healthcare.gov/law/	The law requires employers to report the cost of coverage under an employer-sponsored group health plan on an employee's Form W-2, Wage and Tax Statement.

Regardless of an HR manager's personal position on the value the ACA does, or does not, bring to workers and to businesses, the dialogue on the law and other issues related to health care and the public interest will no doubt continue. The outcomes of these dialogues will ultimately shape changes in existing employment law, and these will directly affect what HR managers in the hospitality industry can or must do as they operate their facilities.

In subsequent chapters you will learn about more laws that affect the HR-related decisions of hospitality managers. As the workplace continues to evolve, legislation affecting it will also likely continue to evolve at the federal, state, and local levels. Therefore hospitality managers with HR responsibilities must stay informed about pending legislation and actively take part in the public opinion debates that help shape governmental policies. It is for those reasons (obtaining information and making their voices heard) that many hospitality managers become active in one or more professional trade associations.

The US federal government has passed a large number of significant pieces of legislation directly affecting employers and their relationships with employees. Some of the most significant of these for HR managers are summarized in Figure 2.1.

Effect of the Legislation	Law	Enacted
Protected workers' right to join labor unions	Clayton Act	1914
Prohibited employment discrimination against union members	Railway Labor Act (RLA)	1926
Gave unionized workers the right to collective bargaining and the right to strike	National Labor Relations Act (Wagner Act)	1935
Established overtime pay requirements and child labor laws	Fair Labor Standards Act (FLSA)	1938
Mandated equal pay to men and women for equal jobs	Equal Pay Act	1963
Prohibited employment discrimination on the basis of race, color, religion, sex, or national origin; later revisions (in 1972) established the EEOC	Civil Rights Act (Title VII)	1964
Prohibited employment discrimination on the basis of age	Age Discrimination in Employment Act	1967
Prohibited employment discrimination on the basis of pregnancy	The Pregnancy Discrimination Act	1978
Prohibited discrimination based on workers' disabilities	Americans with Disabilities Act (ADA)	1990
Allowed affected workers unpaid leave for selected medical and family health-related issues	Family and Medical Leave Act (FMLA)	1993
Extended the time allowed to file a lawsuit alleging pay discrimination	Lilly Ledbetter Fair Pay Act	2009
Mandated minimum levels of health care insurance coverage for all US citizens	Patient Protection and Affordable Care Act (ACA)	2010

Figure 2.1 Selected Labor Legislation Enacted by the US Federal Government

❖❖ THE INTERNATIONAL LEGAL ENVIRONMENT

LEARNING OBJECTIVE 4. Identify the unique issues facing hospitality companies that operate units in countries with legal and cultural systems different from those of the United States.

As a hospitality organization grows from one that operates within a single country (and therefore within a single legal environment) to one that operates internationally, the HR management function must also grow to consider a new and broader perspective. As a hospitality company expands, first with single operations (and, perhaps, franchise partners) to multiunit management on multiple continents, the legal environment in which that company must operate becomes increasingly complex.

The rise of global expansion should be no surprise to hospitality managers because travel, tourism, and an interest in international cuisines have historically been integral parts of the industry. As cooking methods and menu items that are popular in one culture are introduced to another, their popularity often expands. Examples in the US food service industry include Coca-Cola, the Atlanta, Georgia–based soft drink company, and McDonald's, the Oak Brook, Illinois–based franchisor and restaurant operator. In the hotel segment, companies such as Hilton and Marriott have long operated hotels internationally.

To more closely examine just one international success story, consider Ray Kroc, who opened the first McDonald's restaurant in Des Plaines, Illinois, in 1955. Today, McDonald's restaurants are operated in 115 countries worldwide and serve more than 50 million customers per day. McDonald's operates or franchises more than 13,500 restaurants in the United States, but an even larger number of stores now exist *outside* the United States.

Clearly, the HR function at McDonald's, as well as many other hospitality companies, has significant international dimensions. As the US hospitality business continues to grow, it is natural that more companies will look beyond their own country's borders for expansion and growth. This trend is certainly likely to continue in the areas of restaurants, hotels, and contract and health care food services.

Many hospitality professionals work at some point in their careers with a company that does business internationally. There are a variety of reasons why you might be assigned the responsibility of HR management in your company's international operations. These include:

◆ Your education and work history give you the experience you need to succeed in the job.

◆ No local staff (in the foreign country) is currently qualified to assume the responsibility.

◆ Your responsibilities include the training of local HR staff.

◆ Local people are being trained for positions that will ultimately replace the need for your assistance, but they are not yet qualified to assume 100 percent responsibility.

◆ Your employer wants you and other managers to gain a global perspective.

◆ It is in the company's best long-term interest to improve the cultural understanding between managers and employees in the company's various international components.

◆ An international assignment is considered an integral part of your professional development process.

◆ There is an interest in obtaining tighter administrative control over a foreign division or addressing and correcting a significant problem.

◆ There are HR operating or public relations issues that require long-term, on-site management direction to properly address the issues.

How different are HR-related issues (and their management) in other countries? Consider an item as straightforward as paid vacation and holiday time off. In this area, the expectations management may have for its workers and the expectations these workers have for management can differ widely. Historically, American workers have tended to value higher pay to a greater degree than they value additional paid time off from work. While this view is one commonly shared by workers in the United States, is not necessarily shared by workers worldwide. To illustrate, Figure 2.2 details the amount of mandatory paid time off earned by employees who have worked

Country	Annual Minimum Paid Time Off (days)
Germany	34
Italy	31
France	31
Ireland	29
United Kingdom	28
Norway	27
Greece	26
Switzerland	20
Canada	19
Japan	10
United States	0 (10 days is common; but not mandatory)

Figure 2.2 Statutory Minimum Paid Time Off by Selected Country[3]

at least one year in several different countries in which US companies typically do business, as well as the amount typical in the United States.

The quality of training and the availability of qualified numbers of employees can be problematic HR issues in many areas of the world. Also, employee and management attitudes toward gender equality, appropriate dress, work ethic, religious tolerance, and minorities' rights are additional areas that can present significant challenges to international HR managers. As you have learned, individual societies create laws that reflect their cultures and values and, because cultures vary, HR-related laws in different cultures are also different.

It is also important to understand that the introduction of US cultural values that are highly prized by US citizens does not ensure that individuals working in other countries will readily embrace those values. Some people believe that the expansion of US companies such as Coca-Cola, McDonald's, KFC, Pizza Hut, and others to foreign countries has had an overall negative effect on the local culture of the areas in which they are located. Others, however, believe that the impact of international expansion and development in terms of economic benefits (job creation and the expansion of local entrepreneurship) is extremely positive.

Both groups would likely agree, however, that the past need not dictate the future. International companies may or may not have done all they should have in the past to ensure a positive impact on their host countries. All should agree that these companies, through enlightened HR practices, can shape the future through positive activities to improve their own profitability and the quality of life in the communities where they are located. But to do so, **expatriate managers** often must seriously reexamine their personal views of fairness and even morality.

Expatriate manager: A citizen of one country who is a working manager in another country.

For example, assume that you, as a restaurant manager in a foreign country, pay wages that are considered to be very good in that country but are significantly less (in US dollars

Impact on HR Management

NEW TEAM MEMBERS

Understanding that new employees who have been selected to work in hospitality operations located in foreign countries face their own very unique challenges is important. These employees must carefully navigate three cultures that are likely quite unique. The first culture, of course, is their own. Workers in foreign countries will come to their jobs with their own expectations and definitions of important and complex business concepts such as pay fairness, gender-related equality of opportunity, and obedience to authority.

The second culture that must be well understood and assimilated by new workers is the one belonging to their unit managers. It is not surprising that foreign workers' cultural beliefs and values will vary significantly from those of their expatriate managers. One popular example is that of punctuality. In many countries punctuality is a highly prized worker characteristic. In other countries, adherence to a strict time schedule is not considered as critical.

Finally, in addition to adapting their own cultural norms to those of their managers, new employees have a third culture-related challenge. That challenge exists because the specific business operation in which the new worker is employed likely has its own unique business culture. In each business culture concepts such as product quality, service excellence, pace of work, and customer care can vary, and these cultural values likely are highly integrated. In some cases the culture of a business may include attitudes and beliefs that new workers do not automatically share.

Effective HR managers responsible for orienting and assimilating new workers in foreign countries do best when they recognize the uniqueness of these three culture-related challenges and take steps to help their new workers successfully adapt to each of them.

paid per hour) than those granted to US workers who are doing the same job. Some observers would say your restaurant is providing valuable local jobs at fair wages. Others might accuse you and your company of injustice because of the disparity in wage rates paid to your US workers versus those paid to your foreign workers. Add to this challenge the fact that in many cultures it is traditional to pay men more than women for doing identical work, and you can easily see the type of HR difficulties you may face. It is beyond the scope of this text to address and comment on all of the legal issues of wage and gender inequities and business variations due to the cultures that are routinely experienced by expatriate managers. It is important to remember, however, that those expatriate managers who most succeed do so by demonstrating a genuine knowledge, respect, and understanding of the legal and cultural norms of their host countries.

Those working in HR must understand that US-based employers who employ US citizens in locations outside of the country are still subject to the majority of employment laws designed to protect those workers. The antidiscrimination (and many other) laws of the United States do not, however, apply to noncitizens of the United States who work in facilities operated outside of the United States. Of course, companies may choose to voluntarily prohibit discrimination anywhere they operate a business.

Conversely, multinational companies based outside of the United States with properties inside the United States are subject to the same US employment laws as are US employers. As a result, in many cases a significant HR role to be played by US managers is that of teaching internationally trained expatriate managers working *in* the United States about the important components of US employment law.

❖❖ THE SPECIAL ROLE OF THE HOSPITALITY UNIT MANAGER

LEARNING OBJECTIVE 5. Appraise and appreciate the unique HR-related responsibilities of a hospitality industry unit manager.

Regardless of whether a hospitality manager's assignment is within his or her own country or outside its borders, **unit managers** are perhaps the single most important factor affecting an operation's short- and long-term profitability and success. These managers are generally the on-site leaders of their operating units and are held directly responsible for the actions of the employees and supervisors who report to them. In fact, the unit manager's job in the hospitality industry is so important that a primary focus of this text is the HR-related information that must be known and applied by the individuals holding these key positions.

Unit manager: The individual with the final on-site decision-making authority at an individual hospitality operation.

Hospitality management has always been a challenging profession. Whether in a casino, a school lunch program, a five-star hotel, a sports stadium concession program, or a myriad of other environments, hospitality managers are required to have a breadth of skill not found in many other areas of management. Hospitality managers are in charge of securing raw materials, producing a product or service, and selling it—all under the same roof. This makes them very different from their manufacturing counterparts (who are in charge of product production only) and their retail counterparts (who sell, but do not manufacture, a product). Perhaps most important, hospitality managers have direct contact with guests, the ultimate end user of the products and services supplied by these managers' operational teams.

The hospitality industry is also unique because the first industry job for many managers was often an entry-level, hourly paid position rather than a salaried management assignment. For example, in the table service restaurant segment, nine out of ten salaried managers started as hourly employees. Hospitality unit managers are also a diverse group. According to the US Department of Labor, "eating-and-drinking" places employ more minority managers than any other industry. As a result, a diverse group of unit managers are responsible for ensuring their operations consistently adhere to their company's policies and prevailing employment laws.

In this chapter you have learned how evolving employment legislation reflects an American society that has changed the way in which employers manage employees. The often mentioned "social contract" between employer and employee is—most hospitality industry professionals would agree—exactly that: a contract. Like all contracts, it spells out the obligations undertaken by all contractual parties. Hospitality personnel at the unit management level represent their company in this contract, and they must understand it. Because contracts are legal documents, violations typically result in repercussions for one side or the other. In the business world this can mean loss of job for an offending employee. For employers, violations can create adverse publicity, the loss of significant time and money to address legal issues, or, in egregious cases, the closure of their businesses. A major goal of this text is to provide unit managers with up-to-date information they need to responsibly fulfill their HR-related obligations to their employers, employees, society, and, most important, to themselves.

Historically, most students of hospitality management have been taught how to supervise employees. The rationale was that by better understanding and motivating staff members, a better workforce would emerge. The reasoning is that good managers become recognized as such by first being good supervisors. It is true that some concepts, including communications, motivational theory, and team building, that have traditionally been addressed using this supervisory approach to HR management have value. However, those unit managers and others who do not understand the legal requirements and responsibilities that underpin these concepts are at a huge disadvantage to their peers who recognize these and related legal issues. For example, managers may know exactly what they want to do to build an effective workforce, but they may lack an understanding about what they are legally allowed to do, required to do, or even prohibited from doing. The result can be that well-intentioned unit managers unwittingly create difficulties for their organizations and themselves because they do not understand the ever-changing terms of the employment contract.

Written company policies can be fairly easily relayed to unit managers, but it is simply not possible for you as a unit manager to know every governmental regulation that could affect your segment of the hospitality industry, and some laws change regularly. Changes in major federal laws are typically well publicized, but you cannot be sure that the policies of all federal agencies, state regulators, and local governments will be readily known. As a result, hospitality industry journals and publications (many of them delivered online) can be of real assistance in helping you follow legislation at the national level. Regularly reading about changes directly affecting the hospitality industry will not only make you a better unit manager but also let you keep up with evolving legal requirements. For those managers employed by a national chain or management company, the company itself will be an excellent source of information on changing regulations. For example, one valuable service provided by many franchisors to franchisees is regular updates on regulatory agencies and their work.

As a hospitality manager, it is important for you to stay involved in the hospitality trade association that most closely represents your industry segment. The National Restaurant Association (NRA), the American Hotel & Lodging Association (AH&LA), the Club Managers Association of America (CMAA), and the Academy of Nutrition and Dietetics (formerly the American Dietetics Association), as well as others like them, regularly provide their membership with legislative updates. Many of these organizations have state, regional, or local chapters that can be invaluable sources of information. On a local level, chambers of commerce, business trade associations, and personal relationships with local police, fire, and building officials can help a unit manager keep up to date with changes in municipal regulations.

As a professional hospitality manager, it is also critical that you take an active role in *shaping* the regulations that affect your industry. As you have learned in this chapter, societies, through their governments, pass regulations that they believe are in the best interests of the communities they represent. Problems can arise, however, when those who do not truly understand the hospitality industry propose legislation that will result in excessive costs or infringement upon individual rights that far exceed the societal value of implementing the proposed regulation. In these cases, all hospitality professionals must make their own views known.

HR MANAGEMENT ISSUES 2.2

"You've got to get down there and straighten them out," said Anita Ponseca, owner of the GastroPub. Anita was the most successful real estate developer in town, as well as the owner and the sole investor in the popular GastroPub. The GastroPub specializes in upscale menu items served with on-premise microbrewed beers.

Anita was talking to Oscar, the GastroPub's manager, about the local city council's recently announced new initiative to increase the minimum wage in town to two dollars more than the federal minimum wage. Oscar had mentioned to Anita that the newspaper reported the city council and mayor would be accepting input on the proposal from local residents and businesses for the next 60 days.

"That increase would just kill our business," said Anita. "We would have to raise our prices, and that means fewer customers. And fewer customers mean we would need fewer workers. Increasing the minimum wage wouldn't help low-wage workers in this town, it would hurt them! You need to let them know this is a really bad idea."

Case Study Questions

1. Assume Oscar agreed with his boss that the proposed increase in the locally mandated minimum wage would not be in the long-term best interest of their business or its workers. What specific steps would you advise him to take to make his voice known?

2. Assume Oscar did not agree with his boss that the proposed increase in the locally mandated minimum wage would negatively affect their business and its workers. In fact, Oscar would support such an increase. What advice would you now give Oscar? Explain your answer.

HR TERMS

The following terms were defined in this chapter:

Employment law

Jurisdiction

Unemployment compensation

Workers' compensation

Garnish(ment)

Labor union

Interstate commerce

Title VII

Equal Employment Opportunity
Commission (EEOC)

Sexual harassment

Affirmative action

Bona fide occupational qualification
(BFOQ)

Disparate treatment

Disparate (adverse) impact

Reasonable accommodation

Statute of limitations

Individual coverage mandate

Health insurance exchange

Expatriate manager

Unit manager

FOR YOUR CONSIDERATION

1. Some businesspeople believe that the government is too intrusive in the operation of business. Consider the employment-related laws presented in this chapter. Are there any that you believe should not have been passed? Is so, what legislation? Is there any employment-related legislation you believe should be passed? If so, identify it and explain the reason for your support.

2. Hospitality trade associations often lobby to influence proposed labor-related legislation. Given the diversity of opinion that often accompanies proposed legislation that may be controversial, do you think lobbying is a good use of these associations' resources? Why?

3. Discrimination based on physical appearance is not expressly prohibited by the Civil Rights Act. As a result, some hospitality organizations hire only "attractive" staff members for many of their front-of-house and service positions. Do you think doing so is good for business? Do you think doing so is legal? Do you think it is ethical? Explain your answers.

4. The Patient Protection and Affordable Care Act (ACA) was controversial at the time of its passage and remains so today. Do you think its passage was good for business? For hospitality industry workers? Explain your answers.

5. In some cases Americans working internationally have been seen as not having respect for local laws and customs of their host countries, including those related to employer–employee relations. Assume you are an international manager and you encounter an employment practice that would be illegal and discriminatory in the United States but is commonly accepted where you are working. How should you respond to it?

CASE STUDY

Apply HR Management Principles

Donna Moreau was employed for nine years as a room attendant for the Windjammer Hotel. Her work and attendance during that period were considered excellent. The hotel was moderately busy during the week and then typically filled with tourists on the weekends.

In accordance with a hotel policy requiring two weeks' notification, on May 1 Donna submitted a "day off" request for time off on Saturday, May 15, to attend the 1:00 p.m. high school graduation ceremony of her only daughter. The hotel was expected to be extremely short of staff on the weekend of

May 15 because of some staff resignations and terminations, as well as a forecasted sell-out of guest rooms.

Donna's supervisor, Tara Roach, denied Donna's request for the day off, stating the housekeeping department needed her to work that entire weekend. Donna was visibly upset when the schedule was posted and she learned that her request had been denied. She confronted Tara and stated, "I *will* be attending my daughter's graduation. I've been a single parent to my daughter for 17 years, and there's no way I am going to miss that day!" Tara replied that she was very sorry, but all employee requests for that weekend off had been denied, and Donna was to report to work as scheduled.

On the Saturday of the graduation, Donna, in accordance with written hotel policy, called in "sick" four hours before her shift was to begin. The hotel was extremely busy and, in part because of Donna's absence, each room attendant who did show up at work was assigned a heavier than average workload, causing a great deal of departmental tension.

Tara, who was angry at what she saw as willful disregard for supervisory authority, and recalling the earlier conversation with Donna, recorded the employee's call-in as an "unacceptable excuse" and completed a form stating that Donna had, in fact, quit her job voluntarily by refusing to work her assigned shift. Tara referred to the portion of the employee manual that Donna signed when joining the hotel. The manual read, in part:

"Employees shall be considered to have voluntarily quit or abandoned their employment upon any of the following occurrences;

1. *Absence from work for one (1) or more consecutive days without excuse acceptable to the company*
2. *Habitual tardiness*
3. *Failure to report to work within 24 hours of a request to report"*

Donna returned to work the next day to find that she had been removed from the schedule. She was also informed that she was no longer an employee of the hotel. Donna filed for unemployment compensation. In her state, workers who voluntarily quit their jobs were not typically eligible for unemployment compensation. Those who are terminated do typically receive the benefit (which is ultimately paid for by the hotel).

Dimension: Societal Reaction

Review the actions described in the case:

1. What do you think those outside the hospitality industry would think about Tara's decision to terminate Donna?

2. Assume that accurate information regarding this situation were to become well-known in the local community surrounding this hotel. Would this information likely increase or decrease the interest of other professional housekeepers in working at the Windjammer in the future?

3. The concept of "unacceptable excuse" can be difficult to define. Despite that, define it in terms you believe Donna and other employees would use. Define the term in a manner that Tara and other supervisors would likely use.

Dimension: Company Procedure and Decision Making

Review the actions described in the case.

1. What do you think of the "time off" request system in use at the Windjammer?

2. If you were the hotel's general manager, would you support the actions of your housekeeping supervisor?

   a. If your answer is yes, how would you respond to Donna if she maintains (accurately) that she has not called in "sick" in the past 15 months and in fact has frequently been called in to work on her days off because other employees call in sick fairly often?

   b. If your answer is no, how would you respond to Tara if she maintains (accurately) that allowing employees to set their own schedule in her department would lead to severe difficulties that would result in poorly cleaned guest rooms and, ultimately, unhappy guests who were likely to complain to the general manager or even directly to the hotel's owners? In addition, Tara is adamant that if you do not support her decision on this issue, her credibility as a departmental supervisor will be severely diminished.

   c. Were Tara's actions in the best interests of the hotel? Explain your answer.

Dimension: The Unemployment Compensation Hearing

Assume you were called to an administrative court hearing to defend the Windjammer's contention that Donna was not fired but that she quit (and thus is not eligible for unemployment compensation). Review the actions described in the case.

1. If you were an Unemployment Compensation administrative hearing judge in this case, would you initially be more likely to side with the employee or the hotel?

2. How would you likely answer the following specific questions asked by the administrative hearing judge?

   a. Is there a distributed list of "unacceptable" reasons for calling in sick? Who decides what is "unacceptable"?

   b. In the past six months have all employees who followed the hotel's policy of calling in sick four hours before their shift ultimately been documented as "resigned" from their job?

   c. Assuming the answer to the above question is no, what was the hotel's basis for treating Donna differently from:

   - Males in the hotel?
   - Those of a different ethnic background (the hearing officer explains that this is asked simply to ensure that the hotel is not guilty of a civil rights violation)?

3. How important would it be to be very familiar with the state's unemployment compensation laws if you were:

   - The person representing the hotel at the administrative hearing?
   - The hotel's general manager?
   - Tara?

INTERNET ACTIVITIES

1. In many cases you simply will not know some of the applicable employment laws of a state until you are actually assigned to work there. Identify a state (or one of the states) in which you are most likely to work when you graduate. To practice using the Internet to find specific employment-related information, go to your favorite search engine and enter the name of that state in which you are located and the words *worker unemployment claims*. Select the agency that is responsible for processing unemployment claims and determine the following:

   a. The number of weeks for which employees in that state are typically eligible for unemployment compensation and the maximum amount of weekly compensation allowable to them

   b. Specific reasons for which unemployment compensation is denied to workers in that state

2. If you are responsible for the management of a hospitality operation in another country, you will likely have access to a variety of resources that will help you familiarize yourself with that country's specific labor-related laws. However, you may be responsible for finding your own learning aids. For this exercise, go to the Amazon website, then choose "Books" and type "International Management" into the search bar.

   a. What is your initial assessment of the variety of resources available to managers seeking to know more about international management?

   b. What criteria would you use to determine which of these resources would be of most value to you?

ENDNOTES

1. "The Fair Labor Standards Act of 1938, As Amended." U.S. Wage and Hour Division. WH Publication 1318. Revised May 2011. Accessed October 15, 2014. http://www.dol.gov/whd/regs/statutes/FairLaborStandAct.pdf.

2. Jason Kane. Health Costs: How the U.S. Compares with Other Countries. October 22, 2012. Accessed September 1, 2013. http://www.pbs.org/newshour/rundown/2012/10/health-costs-how-the-us-compares-with-other-countries.html.

3. Rebecca Ray, Milla Sanes, and John Schmitt. "No-Vacation Nation Revisited." Center for Economic Policy and Research. May 2013. Accessed June 18, 2013. http://www.cepr.net/documents/publications/no-vacation-update-2013-05.pdf.

© bikeriderlondon / Shutterstock

HUMAN RESOURCES MANAGEMENT: POLICIES AND PROCEDURES

CHAPTER OUTLINE

LEARNING OBJECTIVES

When they complete this chapter, readers will be able to:

1. Explain the difference between HR policies and HR procedures.

2. Identify the steps managers use to develop HR policies and procedures.

3. State the importance of conducting a legal review before implementing HR policies and procedures.

4. Assess the impact of advanced technology on HR-related policy and procedure development.

5. Explain why HR managers must develop, implement, and maintain effective recordkeeping systems.

◆◆◆◆◆◆◆◆◆◆◆◆◆◆

Impact on HR Management

Just as chefs in the hospitality industry know that standardized recipes help produce a high-quality menu item every time the recipes are followed, managers working in the HR field recognize that consistency in their own policy-related actions is critical to the smooth operation of their units.

Employees and managers alike want to know that all policies and procedures will be equally applied to each of their coworkers. If they do not believe this is true, charges of bias, favoritism, sexism, and even racism can result. Therefore, experienced HR managers know they must (1) carefully design and implement their operating policies and (2) maintain evidence that their policies are applied fairly and consistently.

∴ HR POLICIES AND PROCEDURES

LEARNING OBJECTIVE 1. Explain the difference between HR policies and HR procedures.

Policy and Procedure Development

As you have learned, the responsibilities for HR management issues may lie with unit-level managers (in smaller properties) or full-time specialists (in larger hospitality organizations). Assume you have taken a position in which you are ultimately responsible for the HR management issues related to the operation of a newly constructed, 45,000-square-foot casino with an attached 400-room hotel and supporting food service operations. The facility will ultimately employ more than four hundred full- and part-time staff members. Also assume that the facility has yet to open. In such a situation you will soon be required to make decisions about many employee-related issues and policies. The policies you develop must address many topics. A few examples include:

1. Employee selection criteria
2. Accumulation and use of employees' vacation time
3. Required dress and uniform codes
4. Attendance and tardiness
5. Performance evaluation
6. Termination

The actual procedures used to address these issues are also important. In this example the procedures must address a variety of issues related to the policies you have developed, such as:

1. Who is responsible for selecting employees?
2. How will employee vacation time be accrued and recorded?
3. What will be the penalties for dress code violations?
4. Who will record employee absences and tardiness?
5. How frequently will employee performance reviews be conducted? Who will do them?
6. What written documentation will be required in cases of employee termination?

HR policy(ies): A detailed course of action designed to guide future decision making and achieve stated objectives.

HR procedure(s): A technique used to develop and apply HR policies.

Note that there is an important relationship between what your business will do (its **HR policies**) and exactly how you will do it (its **HR procedures**).

Policies: What We Will Do	Procedures: How We Will Do It
1. Select employees.	1. Use standardized application forms.
2. Grant employees paid vacation.	2. Record accumulated vacation time biweekly.
3. Implement employee dress codes.	3. Impose consistent penalties for policy noncompliance.
4. Monitor attendance and tardiness.	4. Record employee arrival and departure times daily.
5. Conduct performance evaluations.	5. Schedule annual employee reviews and designate the reviewers.
6. Terminate employees.	6. Develop standards for documenting (in writing) the reason for an employee's termination.

Figure 3.1   HR Policy and Procedure Relationship

Consider the HR policy and procedure examples presented in the casino scenario. Figure 3.1 shows some ways in which these example policies and procedures are related to each other. For purposes of this chapter, the term *policy* is used to refer to *what* a business operation has determined it should do, whereas the term *procedure* refers to *how* it will do it. These procedures may spell out rewards for policy compliance, penalties for noncompliance, and steps required for policy implementation. In many cases a single policy will require multiple supporting procedures.

In some cases, the line between what businesses will do and how they will do it can be a fine one. However, it is important to remember that to be effective HR policies must be supported by procedures that, when followed, ensure the fair and consistent application of the policy.

HR Management in Action

ATTENDANCE OR AGE?

Lucinda was a 53-year-old hotel concierge. She was terminated for leaving her shift two hours early and without her supervisor's permission. The hotel's position is that Lucinda was fired for violating its attendance policy. Although Lucinda admitted to leaving early, she claims she had arranged for another concierge to complete her shift and that such arrangements were common in the hotel. But when the replacement failed to report for duty, both Lucinda and her replacement were fired. Lucinda, who had been employed at the hotel for 15 years, alleged in federal court that she was the victim of age discrimination. Her suit sought damages for lost wages, pain and suffering, mental anguish, medical expenses, and attorney's fees.

Employers certainly have the right to develop and enforce reasonable employment policies. They may, however, still be required to prove to the courts that they have not practiced illegal discrimination. Discrimination on the basis of "age" is clearly prohibited by Title VII of the Civil Rights Act of 1964 (see chapter 2).

In Lucinda's case it will be important that the hotel has maintained written records to demonstrate that their attendance policy and its enforcement has been fairly and consistently applied to her and to all others in similar situations. In this example it is clear that both the hotel's policy and its procedures for enforcing it will now be subject to intense judicial scrutiny.

It's the Law

In chapter 2 you learned about employment laws that affect some of the policies that businesses are, and are not, allowed to implement. Can a business organization that has developed and implemented a perfectly legal employment policy still be sued because of the policy and ultimately lose the case? Absolutely. It happens all the time when the procedures the managers used to support the policy were flawed, deficient, or both.

A policy or action that is perfectly legal must still be applied in a legally coherent (fair) manner, or the courts simply will not support its use. For example, can a hotel, restaurant, casino, or other hospitality operation lay off or terminate employees because of declining sales? In most situations, clearly, it can. However, consider the real case of an organization that elected to lay off six employees, of whom five were African-American women and one was a Caucasian man.

The women were called into the manager's office and informed they were being laid off effective immediately. They were told to collect their belongings and leave within 30 minutes. In full view of their coworkers, managers monitored them as they cleaned out their lockers. The monitoring was such that their coworkers assumed they had been caught stealing. They did not have an opportunity to say goodbye to their coworkers, some of whom cried because they would miss them and felt badly for them.

This was in stark contrast to the treatment the white male received upon his termination. He was given a month's advance notice of his layoff. He was allowed to come to the operation at his convenience to receive his termination notice. He was not monitored as he cleaned out his work area, and he was permitted to walk around the building freely to say goodbye to his coworkers. In this case, the Court of Appeals held that the *manner* in which the layoff was conducted was discriminatory, and the women won their case.

Despite some popular misconceptions, employers in the United States still enjoy a tremendous amount of freedom (more than in many other economically advanced countries) regarding how they operate their businesses. Can employees be laid off or terminated when business warrants it? Yes, they can. Can an employer (as in this case) do it so poorly that the courts will refuse to support it and, in fact, punish the employer? Yes. Terminations and layoffs are emotional situations in the best of times. HR managers must conduct them professionally and with respect. The number 1 rule to prevent claims of discrimination related to terminations and layoffs is simple: Be fair and be consistent! That rule is a good one to apply to all HR policies and procedures.

Areas of Policy and Procedure Development

Not all of a hospitality operation's policies and procedures relate to HR. To continue our example of the HR manager of a casino, many issues would not be under your control. How frequently the casino's floors are vacuumed, the proper number of cloth napkins to be available for restaurant use, and establishing the ideal selling price of guest rooms on a given weekend are not decisions made by the HR manager. HR policy and procedure development does, however, have a direct effect on all areas of the operation. As experienced managers know, identifying all of the subjects within every hospitality operation that require written policies and procedures is not possible. Clearly, the policy and procedure needs of a large, multinational hospitality organization are very different from the needs of a small, independently owned sandwich shop.

Despite differences in size and need, however, all hospitality organizations undertake HR-related activities that can be readily identified. There are a variety of ways to classify these activities and the policy- and procedure-making related to them. Figure 3.2 lists one way to

Assigned Area/Activity	Requires Policies and Procedures Related to
Staffing the organization	Operational planning and needs analysis Recruiting Interviewing Selecting
Developing staff	Employee orientation Training Employee development and career planning Managing and implementing organizational change
Motivating staff	Job design Employee evaluation Compensation Employee benefits Employee recognition
Maintaining staff	Employee health Employee safety Employee-related organizational communications

Figure 3.2 HR Policy and Procedure Development Areas and Activities

categorize the areas of policy and procedure responsibility commonly assigned to the HR function. It categorizes the areas of HR policy and procedure development as related to

◆ staffing the organization;

◆ developing staff;

◆ motivating staff; and

◆ maintaining staff.

As you read about the following tasks normally assigned to those responsible for HR management, consider the policies and procedures development and implementation efforts needed to address each of these tasks.

STAFFING THE ORGANIZATION

The recruitment and selection of employees is probably the area that most hospitality managers think of first when they consider the work of the HR department or the HR manager. Before recruiting and selecting employees, however, the HR manager must carefully assess the operation's needs. If, for example, the executive chef of a large convention hotel informs the HR department that an additional chef is needed, the specific skills of the necessary individual must be identified. Clearly, if the skills of a *garde-manger* (pantry chef responsible for cold food production) are sought by the executive chef, the recruitment and selection of a *patissier* (pastry chef responsible for baked items) or *saucier* (sauté station chef), regardless of their ability and skill level, is inappropriate.

In all hospitality operations, before employees can be recruited, their skill requirements must be established. As a result, even at the smallest of local restaurants, the manager of the operation must identify the specific skills, knowledge, and abilities of the employees needed by the operation. In addition, it is important to recall that the specific requirements of current labor law mandate that managers thoroughly understand the specific skills required for the jobs they advertise. Identifying and documenting those specific skill sets effectively helps limit the potential legal liability that could be incurred if particular groups of employees are excluded from the search process.

Excluding potential employees on the basis of identified and legitimately required job skills is legal. Excluding potential candidates for non-job-related reasons is typically illegal.

When the critical characteristics related to a job's successful candidates have been carefully identified (see chapter 4), the two most important staffing-related tasks facing the HR manager are

1. ensuring an adequate pool of qualified applicants to maximize the operation's chances to hire an outstanding candidate; and

2. providing sufficient job information to discourage unqualified job applicants to help prevent the organization from wasting time and resources in the interviewing process.

The policies and procedures related to employee recruitment and selection are among some of the most important to any organization. In chapter 4 you will learn how hospitality managers develop policies that help ensure fair hiring practices.

After an adequate number of qualified candidates have been identified, it is the HR manager's job to refer those candidates to the individual who will make the hiring decision (typically in large organizations) or to make the actual selection (in many smaller organizations). In both situations candidate testing and/or other assessment steps may precede the actual job offer.

Identifying qualified candidates and offering positions to them is only a part of the professional HR manager's job because, in a tight labor market, qualified and talented applicants are likely to be sought by a variety of organizations. Therefore the HR manager must also encourage the desired candidate to ultimately accept the position. To do this the HR manager typically provides the candidate with a good deal of job-related and organization-related information. Topics such as organizational culture, growth plans, and performance expectations are all notable areas that could influence an individual's acceptance decision, and these should be fully discussed with the candidate. Information related to these subjects should be accurate and help the candidate make an appropriate career decision that is best for the candidate and the hospitality organization.

HR Management: Impact on New Employees

In nearly all cases workers who accept a new position with an organization do so with the hope that they will like their work and the organization that employs them. HR managers can help employees make the right job choice when they are honest and realistic about each new employee's job and the employee's future potential with the company. Establishing unrealistic expectations of the employee benefits neither the new employee nor the organization.

There are some questions nearly every new employee would like to have honestly addressed by their employer before they accept a job. These include:

◆ How secure is my position?

◆ What will be the financial and nonfinancial benefits associated with performing my job well?

◆ Are there realistic possibilities for promotion? What are they?

◆ Who should I talk to during my first few weeks of employment if I am having trouble adjusting to the new job?

It's certainly in the short-term best interest of HR managers to fill their vacant positions. But, in the long run, it's in their best interests to fill vacant positions with employees who have a realistic understanding of the limitations and potential available to them in their new jobs. Doing so helps reduce employee turnover and enhances their employees' job satisfaction. This requires HR managers to be both informative and honest as they describe positions in their organizations to all potential employees.

DEVELOPING STAFF

After new employees are selected, orienting them to the organization becomes an important HR function. Even experienced employees who need little or virtually no skill training will still need to learn much about their new employer. Information about items such as organizational rules, regulations, and goals of the organization, department, and work unit need to be communicated. Procedurally, questions of who will do the orientation, when it will occur, and what specific topics will be addressed are all HR policy and/or procedure issues.

In some cases employees may be qualified for the job they have secured but will require facility-specific skill training. For example, even housekeepers with many years of experience cleaning rooms will likely still need to be shown "how we do it here" when they begin work with a new employer. Minor variations in housekeeping procedures, such as the preferred manner of folding guest room towels, hand towels, washcloths, and the like must be taught. Similarly, even experienced service staff, if newly hired, will likely need to be instructed on a restaurant's specific table settings, order taking, guest check recording, order pickup, food delivery, and check presentation procedures.

As an employee's career within an organization progresses, that employee may need to acquire new skills. In many cases changes in the employee's work unit or in the goals and needs of the organization may dictate that additional training is needed. It is also important to remember that many employees hope to advance within their employing organization. The HR manager should provide those employees, to the greatest degree possible, with opportunities to do so. This may take the form of providing employees with advanced skills training related to their present jobs, training in jobs they may hold in the future, or cross-training employees in new skills to prepare them for different jobs.

The best HR managers—whether serving the dual role of unit manager and HR manager, or heading a large HR department on a full-time basis—know that planning for the future staffing needs of their organization is an ongoing process. The competitive nature of the hospitality industry requires that most organizations have the ability to rapidly add products or services that will directly impact the organization's employees. Newly added menu items, for example, will likely require additional food production skills training. Adding the service of free wireless Internet access to a hotel's guest rooms may require that one or more hotel employees receive additional training in computer-related technology. Regardless of the individual within the organization who actually does the training, it remains the HR manager's role to ensure that proper training is provided.

MOTIVATING STAFF

The task of motivating employees to do their best is one of the most studied, talked about, and debated of all HR-related topics. The question of how to motivate employees to do their best (or even if it is possible for management to do so) will continue to be discussed. However, one helpful way to consider the role of HR managers in policy and procedure development related to employee motivation is to consider two factors that are commonly agreed to affect worker motivation. These are an employee's

◆ ability to do a job; and
◆ willingness to do a job.

The ability of an employee to effectively do the job is affected by the employee's skill level, the availability of effective training, and the worker's access to the tools or information needed to properly complete assigned tasks.

The willingness of employees to work efficiently has long been the subject of study by motivational theorists. Figure 3.3 briefly summarizes five of the most popular and widely discussed theories of employee motivation. Interested managers will be able to readily find additional information about each of these views of employee motivation via a basic Internet search (e.g., www.google.com or www.bing.com). Regardless of the motivational philosophy adopted by a manager or a hospitality organization, adequate policies and procedures related to its implementation are crucial to motivating employees.

Motivational Theorist	Motivational Theory	Theory Overview
1. Abraham Maslow	Needs Hierarchy	Assumes needs are arranged in a hierarchy and that some needs are more powerful than others. Workers seek to satisfy their needs in the following order: 1. Physiological (first) 2. Safety 3. Love/belonging 4. Esteem 5. Actualization (last) The first four layers of Maslow's "pyramid" are called "deficiency needs," or "D-needs," because the individual does not feel anything if they are met but feels anxious if they are not met.
2. Douglas McGregor	Theory X and Theory Y	States that managers tend to hold and act on one of two basic views (theories) about workers. Theory X assumptions: 1. The average person dislikes work and will avoid it if he or she can. 2. Most people must be forced with the threat of punishment to work toward an organization's objectives. 3. The average person prefers to be directed, to avoid responsibility, is relatively unambitious, and wants security above all else. Theory Y assumptions: 1. Effort in work is as natural as effort in play. 2. People will apply self-control and self-direction in the pursuit of organizational objectives, without external control or the threat of punishment. 3. Commitment to objectives is a function of the rewards associated with their achievement.
3. Frederick Herzberg	Motivation/Hygiene Theory	Identifies two separate groups of factors affecting motivation. "Hygiene factors" cause feelings of dissatisfaction among employees. They include working conditions, pay, and job security. These do not motivate, but their absence adversely affects job performance. "Motivation factors," including concerns such as achievement, learning, and advancement, play a major role in positively influencing performance. Workforce motivation is not possible if hygiene factors are deficient.

Figure 3.3   Motivational Theorists, Theories, and Theory Overview

4. David McClelland	Three-Need (achievement, affiliation, and power) Theory	States that workers have needs for achievement, affiliation, and power, each of which must be satisfied if they are to be motivated. The theory suggests that these three needs are found to varying degrees in all workers and managers. It also indicates that this mix of motivational needs characterizes an individual's management style in terms of being motivated, as well as in the management and motivation of others.
5. Victor Vroom	Expectancy Theory	Proposes that a worker's motivation is primarily influenced by the "expectation" that additional effort will lead to additional organizational rewards. If this expectation is not met, influencing an employee's motivation in a positive way will not be possible.

Figure 3.3 (continued)

MAINTAINING STAFF

Even the best of work teams require regular maintenance and care. Policies and procedures related to the maintenance of employees include those that help encourage quality workers to stay with the organization. Major areas of concern include worker health and safety, as well as the development and implementation of **Employee Assistance Programs (EAPs)**.

Additional areas of staff maintenance relate to communication efforts designed to keep employees informed about the work-related issues that are important to them. Other policies may identify opportunities for employees to have their voices heard by management. Staff meetings, bulletin boards, newsletters, and suggestion boxes are common examples of devices employers routinely use to encourage information exchange.

Now that you are familiar with many common areas in which HR managers develop policies and procedures, it is important for you to know the process managers use to properly develop and implement them.

Employee Assistance Program (EAPs): The term used to describe a variety of employer-initiated efforts to assist employees in the areas of family concerns, legal issues, financial matters, and health maintenance.

❖ STEPS IN HR POLICY AND PROCEDURE DEVELOPMENT

LEARNING OBJECTIVE 2. Identify the steps managers use to develop HR policies and procedures.

In general, making HR-related decisions based on momentary operational needs is a poor practice. Consider the case of the dining room manager who, because he was rushed and harried during a busy dinner period, "fires" an employee (busser) who (the manager feels) violated the dress code because the busser's shirt was untucked while clearing tables. In this case, the busser's shirt was indeed untucked. Therefore the dining room manager's actions might seem reasonable. Experienced managers advising this dining room manager, however, would likely first ask a few relevant questions.

1. Was the employee ever informed of the restaurant's "no untucked shirts" policy? Is that requirement specifically listed within the restaurant's dress code?

2. Is there written evidence that the employee received and understood (in his own native language) this specific policy?

3. How long has the employee been with the organization?

4. Is this the employee's first dress code policy violation?

5. Was the employee given a reasonable chance to explain the circumstances leading to his violation of the policy?

6. In the past have all employees found to be in similar violation of this same policy been fired immediately? If not, what was the rationale for the firing of this specific employee?

7. Under the laws of the state in which the restaurant is located, will the employee likely qualify to receive unemployment compensation in this case?

8. Are the restaurant's employees unionized? If so, is the termination allowed under the terms of the union contract?

9. Is the restaurant part of a chain? If so, was the termination consistent with the action that has, in the past, been taken by other dining room managers working within the chain?

10. In the past has this manager been rightly, or wrongly, accused of discrimination in the hiring or firing of the restaurant's employees?

11. Given the circumstances of this incident, what message did the dining room manager seek to send to the restaurant's remaining employees? Does the manager feel that the message sent will help or harm the restaurant's long-term HR efforts?

As you can readily see from these questions, management is, in many cases, generally given broad powers to hire and terminate employees. However, today's legal environment, as well as the basic concept of fairness and quality employee relations, mandates that operators should carefully follow policies that they have thoughtfully developed when managing HR issues.

To help minimize the negative consequences that can be associated with improperly developing or applying HR policies, experienced managers should establish a basic policy and procedure development process. While this process varies based on the size and type of hospitality operation involved, most follow a series of important steps designed to ensure that only an appropriate development approach is used. These steps are shown in Figure 3.4.

Step	Rationale
1. Identify the HR issue to be addressed.	Policies and procedures typically are developed to address an important issue, establish a standard, or solve an identifiable problem.
2. Consider on-site factors affecting implementation.	Internal factors directly affecting the development of policy or procedures are considered. Examples include items such as the existence of a union contract, the objectives management seeks to achieve, and the time frame required for implementation.
3. Consider off-site factors affecting implementation.	Off-site factors that may need to be considered in the policy and procedure development process include overriding chain or franchise policies; local, state, and/or national labor-related legislation; and competitors' policies.
4. Draft policy and procedures and submit them for (legal) review.	After a policy and the procedures required to implement it have been drafted, it is always a good idea to have the draft examined by a qualified legal expert. This step is important in helping to reduce potential litigation directly related to the policy.
5. Develop related documentation and recordkeeping requirements.	After a legal review has been completed, managers develop the recordkeeping procedures needed to ensure the consistent application of the policy, as well as the ability to prove it has indeed been applied consistently.
6. Communicate finalized policy and procedures to affected parties.	HR policies and procedures that have not been adequately communicated to those affected are difficult or perhaps impossible to enforce. The final step in policy development and implementation is the policy's clear and timely communication to all affected parties, as well as the documentation of that communication.

Figure 3.4 Six-Step Policy and Procedure Development Process

In some cases HR managers can save time by purchasing prewritten policies and procedures that can be used as is or modified to properly apply to their own operations. To see examples of such product offerings, type "policies and procedures manuals" into your favorite search engine and view the results.

❖❖ REVIEW FOR LEGAL COMPLIANCE

LEARNING OBJECTIVE 3. State the importance of conducting a legal review before implementing HR policies and procedures.

Earlier in this chapter you learned that a legal review is an important step in the policy and procedure development process. The reason why this step is critical for managers is readily apparent when you consider that developing procedures to support an illegal policy makes no sense. While experienced HR managers understand that the manner in which a policy is implemented can be flawed, a policy that is already flawed or illegal from the outset simply should not be implemented. In most cases a legal review of a policy proposed by experienced managers does not indicate that the proposed policy is illegal. Rather, the legal review more likely indicates potentially troublesome procedural areas to which HR managers should pay close attention.

To see how a legal policy that is improperly applied could create difficulties and, as a result, to illustrate the importance of a thorough legal review, consider the case of Latisha. She is the food service director at a local hospital. Latisha's operation prepares and serves more than 500 meals per day. Latisha knows that the law allows her a good deal of discretion in setting appearance standards for her staff, and she wishes to do so by creating and implementing a department-wide dress code.

In nearly all cases, hospitality managers such as Latisha can (and often do) legally impose rules and guidelines that have a basis in social norms, such as those prohibiting visible tattoos, body piercings, or earrings for men. While tattoos and piercings may be examples of employee self-expression, they generally are not recognized as signs of religious or racial expression (and thus are not typically protected under federal discrimination laws). For example, in *Cloutier v. Costco Wholesale Corp.* (390 F.3d 126 [1st Cir. 2004]), the First Circuit Court considered whether an employer was required to exempt a cashier from its dress code policy prohibiting facial jewelry (except earrings) and allow her to wear facial piercings as a reasonable religious accommodation. The employee claimed that her religious practice as a member of the Church of Body Modification required she wear the piercings uncovered at all times.

This court accepted that the cashier was protected by Title VII of the Civil Rights Act, without specifically discussing the sincerity of her beliefs, and ruled only on whether her requested exemption from the dress code would impose an undue hardship on the employer. The court found that exempting the employee from the policy would in fact create an undue hardship for the employer because it would "adversely affect the employer's public image," and the employer had a legitimate business interest in cultivating a professional image. The employee's case was dismissed. Certainly, hospitality employers such as Latisha have the same legitimate business interest.

In most cases a carefully drafted dress code that is applied consistently does not violate discrimination laws. Despite the wide latitude given to hospitality employers, all or part of an implemented dress code may be found to be discriminatory. It is not uncommon for hospitality employees to challenge even well-designed dress codes on the basis of purported discrimination related to their sex, race, or religion.

Sex discrimination claims related to dress codes are not usually successful unless the dress policy has no basis in social customs, differentiates markedly between men and women, or imposes a burden on women that is not imposed on men. For example, a policy that requires female managers to wear uniforms while male managers are allowed to wear "professional attire," such as their choice of suit and tie, is likely discriminatory. However, dress requirements that reflect current social norms generally are upheld, even when they affect only one sex. For example, in a decision by the Eleventh Circuit Court of Appeals in

Harper v. Blockbuster Entertainment Corp. (139 F.3d 1385 [11th Cir. 1998]), the court upheld an employer's policy that required only male employees to cut their long hair.

In most cases, race discrimination claims would be difficult for an employee to prove because the employee must show that the employer's dress code has a disparate (and unfair) impact on a protected class of employees. One limited area where race claims have had some success is in challenges to "no beard" policies. A few courts have determined that a policy that requires all male employees to be clean-shaven may discriminate if it does not accommodate individuals with pseudofolliculitis barbae, a skin condition aggravated by shaving that occurs almost exclusively among African-American men.

Employees have had the most success challenging dress codes on the basis that they violate religious discrimination laws. These charges occur most frequently when an employer is unwilling to allow an employee's religious dress or appearance. For example, a policy may be discriminatory if it does not accommodate an employee's religious need to cover his head or wear a beard. However, if an employer can show that the accommodation would be an undue hardship, such as if the employee's dress or grooming created a safety concern, it likely would not be required to vary its policy. Interestingly, dress code claims also may be filed under the National Labor Relations Act (NLRA). For example, to comply with the NLRA, employers, even in nonunion workplaces, generally may not ban the wearing of union insignia.

As you have now learned, even in an area such as dress codes—where employers such as Latisha have wide latitude to manage their businesses as they see fit—the potential for legal difficulties can still exist. Virtually any of the areas in which policies and procedures are developed may be the source of litigation, but managers must be most careful in areas related to the control of employee dress, expression of opinion, and behavior away from the worksite. As a result, experienced HR managers know that a periodic legal review of an organization's overall policy and procedures manual, as well as a specific review each time it is significantly modified or revised, conducted by a qualified legal professional, is a wise use of organizational resources in nearly all cases.

It's the Law

Posting on and communicating with others via Facebook, Twitter, Tumblr, and similar social media sites is extremely popular. Most posts and tweets are of a personal nature, but some inevitably have to do with work. Just as inevitably, the comments workers make about their workplace or their managers are sometimes less than complimentary. It may be tempting for managers who become aware of derogatory comments to punish those who made them (especially if the statements are unfair or one-sided). But these managers need to tread carefully.

As a result of "lawful conduct" statutes, employees generally have rights to engage in lawful activities during nonwork hours. Communicating electronically is certainly not illegal. In fact, the NLRA grants employees free speech rights that include criticism of their companies and their managers. Furthermore, the NLRA generally protects from retaliation measures those workers who (even publicly) are critical of management.

It is just as important to note, however, that not all work-related speech is protected by the NLRA or laws related to free speech. Reckless or malicious lies, disclosure of confidential company information, and threatening and harassing statements are not typically protected forms of free speech.

Savvy HR managers recognize they must carefully navigate the sometimes very fine line between their companies' rights and the free speech rights of their employees. A legal review of any policies addressing employee's rights to communicate freely in social media and other electronic platforms is certainly beneficial.

❖ APPLYING ADVANCED TECHNOLOGY TO HR POLICIES AND PROCEDURES

LEARNING OBJECTIVE 4. Assess the impact of advanced technology on HR-related policy and procedure development.

Some managers in the hospitality industry view the application of technology to operational issues as a problem, rather than an opportunity. It is true that the technological systems implemented in restaurants, bars, clubs, hotels, and other hospitality operations are far more advanced and complicated today than those used only a short time ago, and these systems continue to advance rapidly. Rather than viewing technology applications as conveying impersonal attributes used only for cost-savings, HR managers will find that advances in technology have made it easier than ever to do their jobs. In most cases, two extremely important functions of HR and, as a result, two areas where HR-related technology can be effectively utilized, include information dissemination and information storage.

Information Dissemination

Consider the challenges and opportunities facing the management team of a ski resort that elects to implement a new HR policy about the specific procedures to request time off under the Family Medical Leave Act (FMLA; see chapter 2). For the managers involved in this policy and procedure development process, one major hurdle they must overcome relates to informing the proper individuals about the new policy and any new procedures associated with it. In the recent past, the managers would have had limited options for disseminating the new information and, just as important, their options for documenting that dissemination would have been limited as well. As a result, changes in policies and procedures were typically accompanied by a written document (hard copy) detailing the new policy and procedures. This hard copy would typically be distributed and signed by employees, and then a copy of the document with the confirming signature would be placed in the employee's **personal file**. In other cases, the information might be added to an existing **employee handbook (employee manual)**, which, after management had updated all of the affected sections, would be redistributed to employees.

It is important for managers to understand that the courts generally allow employers wide latitude to enforce a variety of job-related policies and procedures. In most cases, however, those employers must first conclusively show that their employees were, in fact, informed about the policies and procedures. Therefore, documenting an employee's actual receipt of important policy and procedure information is imperative.

Personal file: A record of information about a single employee's employment. Typically, this file includes information about the employee's personal status, application, performance evaluations, and disciplinary warnings; also known as a personnel file.

Employee handbook (employee manual): A permanent reference guide for employers and employees that contains information about a company, its goals, and its current employment policies and procedures; also often referred to as the employee manual.

HR MANAGEMENT ISSUES 3.1

"But that's nearly impossible!" said Trisha Sangus, general manager of the Plaza Intercontinental Hotel, the 750-room convention hotel located in the heart of downtown and adjacent to the city's convention center. "How can we do that?"

"I don't know, but that's what the e-mail from corporate says," replied Pam Cummings, the director of human resources.

"So let me get this straight," said Trisha. "We have to certify, in writing, that each of our employees has received and understands the information in our corporate employee handbook."

"That's right," said Pamela. "I've had my staff do some checking. With our current 430 employees, we would need a total of about 16 translations. You know, Russian, Portuguese, Korean, Polish, Croatian, and others. Plus Spanish, but

corporate already has that translation, so I guess we really only need 15 more."

Case Study Questions

1. Do you believe it is the right of all employees to receive a copy of their work-related policies and procedures rules written in their native language?

2. What, if any, accommodation do you believe should be made for those employees who are not capable of reading any language?

3. What specific advice might you give Trisha and Pamela as they seek to comply with this directive from their corporate HR office?

In many hospitality operations, the initial dissemination of and documentation that essential employment policies and procedures were received occurs when employees are hired and given an updated copy of the employee handbook. Documentation most often involves placing in the employee's personal file a signed document (or photocopy) with the employee's signature stating he or she did receive a copy of the manual. Figure 3.5 is an example of a document that can be used to verify an employee's receipt of an operation's employee handbook and its important policies and procedures.

Increasingly, because of advances in communications technology, the options available for information dissemination are numerous. HR managers can select from a wide variety of communication devices and approaches both for the initial dissemination of important policies and procedures information and for their later modification, additions, and deletions. Returning to the example of the ski resort managers seeking to implement new procedures for requesting time off under the FMLA, Figure 3.6 summarizes some of the more popular information-related options available to these managers.

ACKNOWLEDGMENT OF RECEIPT OF EMPLOYEE HANDBOOK

The Employee Handbook contains important information about *<insert company name>*. I understand that I should ask my supervisor, manager, or the HR administrator about any questions I have that have not been answered in the handbook. I have entered into my employment relationship with the company voluntarily and understand that there is no specified length of my employment. Either the company or I can terminate the relationship at will, at any time, with or without cause, and with or without advance notice.

Because the information, policies, procedures, and benefits described in this manual are subject to change at any time, I acknowledge that revisions to the handbook may occur. All such changes will be communicated through an official notice, and I understand that revised information may add to, modify, or eliminate the company's existing policies.

Also, I understand that this handbook is neither a contract of employment nor a legally binding agreement. I have been given the time needed to read the handbook, and I agree to accept the terms in it. I also understand that it is my responsibility to comply with the policies contained in this handbook and any revisions made to it.

I understand that I am expected to read the entire handbook. After I have done so, I will sign two original copies of this Acknowledgment of Receipt, retain one copy for myself, and return one copy to the company's representative listed below. I understand that this form will be retained in my personal file.

_____   _____

Employee's Signature   Date

_____

Employee's Name (printed)

_____   _____

Company Representative   Date

Figure 3.5 Sample Employee Handbook Signature Page

Communication Device	Dissemination Characteristics	Documentation Characteristics
E-mail with attachment	Fast, inexpensive	Recipients can be asked to confirm e-mail receipt before opening
Website posting	Permanent accessibility, but website modifications may be costly	Employees may be asked to sign in via an individually issued code before gaining access to protected Web pages
Hard copy	Inexpensive to produce and revise	Documents may be easily maintained and filed
Toll-free number; telephone voice recording	Employees may access information via a numerically initiated options menu. Recordings may be made available in multiple languages	Employees may be asked to verify, via their signature, receipt of the toll-free number allowing their access to the policy and procedure information
Electronic news postings/blog	Inexpensive and instantaneous updates	Employees may be asked to verify, via their signature, receipt of the address of the site/blog

Figure 3.6 Managers' Options for the Initial Dissemination and Documentation of Policies and Procedures

It is important to recognize that many employees in the hospitality industry have neither the language skills nor the computer skills and access required to take advantage of some of the communication options available today. Enlightened managers know that, ultimately, it is their responsibility—not that of their employees—to ensure and document that required policy and procedure information has been provided to those who need it.

Information Storage

In addition to expanding the number of information dissemination options available to managers, advances in technology have increased the number of available **information storage** options.

In the fairly recent past, most HR-related records in the hospitality and tourism industry simply consisted of hard-copy (paper) files stored in the appropriate employee personal file or in a file developed specifically for recordkeeping purposes. For example, information related to employees' requests for time off or paid vacation might be kept in the individual employee's file or in files designed to track and record these types of employee requests. Obviously, in very large hospitality operations with hundreds of employees, such a paper-based system could easily become unwieldy and cumbersome. Increasingly, even smaller restaurants, hotels, clubs, and other operations find that management of today's HR-related records and information requires the application of advanced technology hardware and software, in part because of the increases in recordkeeping requirements, as well as the challenges of maintaining the accessibility (and security) of HR-related information.

Many HR managers actually find that information storage is one of their greatest challenges. To understand why this is so, consider the following areas for which data storage is of significant concern:

◆ Employment applications
◆ Resumes
◆ Performance evaluations
◆ Disciplinary records
◆ Medical files
◆ Insurance-related records and correspondence
◆ Training records and documentation
◆ Certificates, transcripts, diplomas
◆ Military records
◆ Governmental entity inquiry records
◆ Lawsuit-related information
◆ Other employee or employment-related correspondence

Information storage: The processes, equipment, and documents that make up a company's records retention effort.

Hospitality managers who are responsible for designing effective recordkeeping systems also face a conflicting challenge. Stored records must be easily available for viewing, but they also must be kept secure and inaccessible to viewers who would compromise the confidentiality of the records. Fortunately, although the recordkeeping requirements facing HR managers are greater than ever, the tools available to HR managers also provide more options.

In addition to paper documents, HR managers can choose from a variety of advanced technology recordkeeping and retrieval systems. These systems often include the following components:

- ◆ **Security features**—In many cases, HR managers develop information storage systems that allow for multiple levels of security to protect sensitive documents and files from unauthorized viewers. Each user has a security access level, and each document has a sensitivity level. Depending on the access level granted to the users, they see only the lists of documents that are appropriate for their security access level. Such documents may be kept on site or posted on the cloud—the common name given to files and a number of computers connected via the Internet.

- ◆ **Records-specific servers**—A dedicated server can be designed to provide restricted viewing access to important HR-related data. Dedicated servers perform no other tasks besides their server tasks.

- ◆ **Document archival features**—These components allow information or documents to be downloaded to another computer or to another data storage device to ensure back-up copies of needed documents are readily available.

- ◆ **High-speed image printing**—This component of a recordkeeping and retrieval system is used to create hard copies of electronically stored information.

Regardless of the sophistication level of the information storage and retrieval system they develop, HR managers must comply with the documentation and recordkeeping requirements imposed on them by their own companies as well as by governmental entities that mandate and monitor their compliance.

⬩⬩ HR POLICIES AND PROCEDURES DOCUMENTATION AND RECORD KEEPING

LEARNING OBJECTIVE 5. Explain why HR managers must develop, implement, and maintain effective recordkeeping systems.

Regardless of the level of technology they apply to the process, all HR managers must follow specific laws and regulations that address employment-related documentation and recordkeeping issues. In addition, businesses often develop some of their own in-house procedures for policy and procedures documentation and record keeping. As a result, HR managers must make decisions regarding their own record retention policies and procedures. For example, most HR managers agree that keeping a copy of all applications and resumes received when they advertise to fill an employment vacancy is a good idea. The reasons for retaining these documents are many but include the ability to monitor the quality of the available workforce, to help ensure that advertisements by the organization appeal to the broadest labor pool possible, and to help judge the workforce demand for the employer's position. Consider, however, the HR manager who must answer the following specific questions:

- ◆ Are all individuals who submit resumes via the Internet considered applicants for recordkeeping and reporting purposes?
  - • If so, how will these records be stored and for how long?
- ◆ What if the candidates are clearly unqualified for the position?

Questions such as these may be difficult to address, but HR managers must still do so thoughtfully. Other examples of records-related questions that require policy and procedures decisions include the following:

- ◆ How do regulations related to specific laws, such as the ADA, FMLA, and FLSA (see chapter 2), affect the length of time records should be kept?

- ◆ Should employees have access to their discipline records? Can they make copies?

- ◆ How long should a terminated employee's files be kept?

- ◆ Which personnel management–related documents should require actual (not electronic) signatures?

Regardless of how questions such as these are answered, HR managers must make significant decisions regarding the employment records that must be retained and the length of time to retain them. In some cases, employment-related legislation dictates the full or partial answers to questions of this type.

Figure 3.7 lists selected recordkeeping requirements enforced by the U.S. government. Other requirements may be imposed at the state or local level.

To further illustrate the practical importance of proper documentation and record keeping, consider the case of Andrea Walker, the director of food services at a large corporate dining facility. The facility is operated under contract by a nationally recognized food service management company that has employed Andrea for the past 15 years. Her operation serves more than 1,000 persons per day. Approximately 200 of her diners are salaried managers who eat in the executive dining room, whereas 800 are hourly workers who eat in a separate, larger dining area.

Andrea is an excellent manager, so she was surprised when Becka Larsen, the company's vice president of human resources, arrived at her operation to announce that the company had received a letter from the EEOC stating that an ex-employee had charged Andrea's operation with discrimination and **constructive discharge**.

Essentially, explained Becka, the EEOC's letter was sent to officially notify Andrea's company of the charges initiated by the former employee. The letter also included an official **Request for Information (RFI)**, which was the reason for Becka coming to see Andrea.

When questioned, Andrea explained to Becka that the employee making the charges was a dining room attendant who had, in fact, complained once about the sexually oriented nature of comments made by a fellow worker. That same employee had also complained once about some comments made by one of the diners in the executive dining room.

Andrea also explained that she, as the facility manager, had personally addressed both situations and, to further assist the employee, had reassigned her from the executive dining room to the regular employees' dining area. Andrea finished by stating that two or three weeks after the second complaint was addressed, the employee resigned because she had accepted a higher-paying job across town. Although this occurred more than five months ago, as Andrea now recalled the situation, no mention was made of any unhappiness at the time the employee resigned.

Cases such as this one are most often very complex. However, from the few details presented it should be apparent that if Andrea's employer is to successfully defend itself—and if Andrea is to continue to be perceived as an effective manager—Andrea's HR policies, procedures, and documentation systems should conclusively show the following:

1. An effective sexual harassment policy was clearly stated in the employee manual that Andrea issued to each employee when hired.

2. The employee making the charges in this case was given a copy of the manual as well as the opportunity to have it explained by management if any parts of it were unclear.

3. The existence or absence of other, similar charges filed by Andrea's current or former employees have been documented.

4. Andrea responded to this ex-employee's complaints in a timely manner.

5. Andrea (or members of her management team) properly followed the specific investigation procedures proscribed in the sexual harassment complaint portion of the employee manual.

Constructive discharge: An employee-initiated termination of employment brought about by conditions that make the employee's work situation so intolerable that a reasonable person would feel compelled to quit; also known as constructive wrongful discharge.

Request for Information (RFI): An official EEOC form requiring the accused party to submit all requested copies of personnel policies, the accuser's personal files, the personnel files of selected other individuals, and any other information deemed relevant by the EEOC.

HIRING AND EMPLOYMENT ACTIONS*

Employee Record	FLSA, EPA	FMLA	ADEA	IRCA	Title VII, ADA	OSHA	Tax Laws
Employee name, address, Social Security number, gender, date of birth	Three years from last entry	Three years from last entry	Three years from last entry	Three years from hire or one year after termination	One year after record created or personnel action taken	One year after termination	Four years after tax due or paid
Position, job category	Two years after created	—	Three years from last entry	—	—	—	Four years after tax due or paid
Applications, resumes, recruitment notices, job orders, employment tests	—	One year after related personnel action	—	—	One year after record created or personnel action taken	—	—
Date of hire	—	—	—	—	One year after record created	—	—
I-9 form	—	—	—	Later of three years after hire or one year after termination	—	—	—
Work permits/age certificates for minors	While employed	—	—	—	—	—	—
Dates and reasons for promotion, demotion, transfer, layoff, rehire, and termination	—	One year after related personnel action	—	—	One year after personnel action	—	—
Performance evaluations	Two years after created	—	—	One year after record created or personnel action taken	—	—	—
Training opportunities, agreements	Duration of training	—	—	One year after related personnel action	—	One year after personnel action	One year after termination

Key Terms

FLSA, EPA	Fair Labor Standards Act, Equal Pay Act
FMLA	Family & Medical Leave Act
ADEA	Age Discrimination in Employment Act
IRCA	Immigration Reform & Control Act
Title IV, ADA	Civil Rights Act, Americans with Disabilities Act
OSHA	Occupational Safety & Health Act

Figure 3.7 Selected Federal-Level Hiring and Employment Actions: Recordkeeping Requirements

6. The measures Andrea took in response to the allegations were not only proper but also were fully documented, with precise detail about items including time, date, actions taken, and persons involved.

7. Relevant information related to those individuals accused of harassment by the ex-employee was recorded and is now available for review.

8. Management's resolutions of the complaints were fully explained to the ex-employee in a timely manner.

9. No changes in the former employee's employment status, work assignment, or employment conditions occurred that could be used to support or justify the constructive discharge allegation.

10. Andrea clearly followed her own company's internally mandated policies and procedures, as well as all applicable federal and state laws, when responding to the former employee's harassment charges.

The absence of records such as those indicated in the list does not definitively mean that Andrea's employer will be unable to defend itself against the ex-employee's charges. However, the ability of Andrea's employer to successfully mount a valid defense to the ex-employee's charges will be greatly reduced, as will Andrea's ability to support her own managerial action (or inaction), if any of these records are unavailable.

While this is just one example of the importance of proper record keeping, it is critical to understand that a large number of similar examples could be shown. Experienced HR managers agree that determining exactly which employment-related records to keep, and for how long, is one of their most essential tasks. Most hospitality managers would also agree that having well-documented employee-related policies and procedures in place, despite the enormity of the task, is critical for large, multiunit operators. Even for managers of small hospitality operations, while the effort required to address the task may be lessened, in today's litigious society its successful completion is no less critical.

HR MANAGEMENT ISSUES 3.2

"But Larry, I just can't work on Sunday," said Shingi, a room attendant at the 800-room Courtplace Hotel.

Larry, the executive housekeeper, had just told Shingi that a storm in the area had delayed flights out of the regional airport and that a group that had been scheduled to leave the hotel on Sunday morning was now staying until Monday morning. The result was an additional 110 stayover rooms to clean Sunday, and Larry was hurriedly attempting to add eight housekeepers to the employee schedule.

"Why can't you work on Sunday?" Larry asked. Then, before Shingi could answer, he added, "You know when we hired you, we told you that our business can be unpredictable and that all employees' work schedules are subject to change."

"I know," replied Shingi, "and I'd work if I could, Larry, because I really need this job. However, after you posted the schedule last week and I saw I was off Sunday, I told my boss it was okay to schedule me at my other job. They always work around my schedule here, but I know I'll get fired if I don't go in, and I need that job too. I'm sorry, I just can't work Sunday."

Case Study Questions

1. Many employees in the hospitality industry hold more than one job. What are some reasons why they do so?

2. How can Larry determine whether this situation warrants the future development of a "second job" (or moonlighting) policy?

3. As an HR specialist, what specific issues would you advise Larry to think about as he considers developing and implementing his new policy?

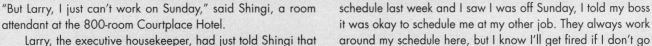

HR TERMS

The following terms were defined in this chapter:

HR policy(ies)

HR procedure(s)

Employee Assistance Program (EAP)

Personal file

Employee handbook (employee manual)

Information storage

Constructive discharge

Request for Information (RFI)

FOR YOUR CONSIDERATION

1. The debate about which theory of motivation is true is a long-standing one. Review the various theories presented in Figure 3.3. Which theory most closely represents your own view of motivation? Identify one event that helped shape the way you feel about this topic.

2. Employee Assistance Programs (EAPs) are increasing in popularity. Identify two specific EAP components that you, as a manager, believe employees would find to be important. Do you think these would be the same two components your employers would consider most important? Explain your answer.

3. Many managers are surprised to hear that they can be held personally responsible for damages resulting from HR-related events that happen in their workplace. What specific steps would you recommend individual hospitality managers take to minimize this liability?

4. HR recordkeeping activities must be well planned, detailed, and implemented consistently. What are some specific personality characteristics of individuals who may excel at these tasks? Do you think most hospitality managers have (or could acquire) these traits?

5. Increasingly, multiunit companies turn to the Internet "cloud" when developing their HR recordkeeping systems. The cloud allows these companies to move critical HR data from the company's individual units to a common storage site. What information-related security concerns might this approach generate? How can hospitality managers best address these concerns?

CASE STUDY

Apply HR Management Principles

"This is a pain," said Sara. "And it doesn't make any sense."

"What doesn't make sense?" replied Dave Berger, the owner of the Golden Rose, the restaurant where Sara had begun working full time, splitting her duties between that of part-time accounting clerk and part-time HR assistant.

In her accounting role, Sara's job is to prepare the checks needed to pay the restaurant's bills, verify credit card receipts, and make cash deposits. In her role as HR assistant, her job is to total employee time cards and prepare the biweekly payroll, as well as to keep track of each employee's use of sick time,

holiday, and vacation pay. Even though she is new, Sara is very good, very bright, and cares deeply about the restaurant and its employees. Because of that, Dave increasingly has come to value the talent she brings to her position, as well as the insightful opinions she is certainly not afraid to share.

"Full-time employees accrue two weeks of vacation per year, and part-time employees accrue about one week. Is that right?" asked Sara.

"That's right," said Dave. "I have always thought that part-timers who work regularly and who stay with the company should earn some vacation time also. It's in the manual."

"Right," said Sara. "It's right here. It says:

'A regular employee who works one-half time or more but less than full-time shall accrue vacation/annual leave prorated on the basis of their actual number of hours worked. An employee who is employed less than ten hours per week shall not be eligible to accrue vacation/annual leave.'"

"So, if I work 20 hours per week, I earn one week a year. And I use it or lose it. That is, employees are not allowed to carry vacation forward to the next year. Right?" asked Sara.

"That's right," said Dave. "When I started the restaurant I decided that would be our policy because the idea is that an employee's vacation should be a time to relax and refresh. So it just makes sense to me that if we are going to give employees vacation time, they should take it every year."

"So, does the part-time person earn one week of 40 hours' pay, or one week of 20 hours' pay?" asked Sara.

"Well, they should be getting one of their regular weeks in my opinion. That is, if they only work 20 hours per week, they should only get paid for a 20-hour vacation week. If they average 30 hours, they should get a 30-hour paid vacation."

"That would make sense," replied Sara, "but your old accounting clerk wasn't doing that. She was recording 3.07 hours for each full-timer per pay period worked and 1.54 hours for each part-time employee."

"3.07 hours and 1.54 hours? Why?" asked Dave.

"Well," replied Sara, "with 26 pay periods per year and 10 days—or 80 hours—of vacation accrued, it works out to 3.07 hours per pay period. One week a year is half that— 1.535 technically. But rounding to 1.54 is darn close."

"Sounds like she took a shortcut and treated all of the part-timers the same," replied Dave. "We should be able to fix that."

"You could, but that's the problem," said Sara. "You have 52 full-time employees and 38 part-timers. Not all part-timers work every week, and not all of them work 20 hours. You want them to accrue time based on the hours actually worked, but your current record keeping doesn't match the policy. Your current system treats all part-timers as if they worked the same amount of time. To calculate each employee's actual time each week would be insane. Even worse, if they work less than 10 hours one week but 20 the next, you have a whole different problem. That's probably why the old accounting clerk did it this way."

"Well," replied Dave, "let's just change the way we record it. Make it more accurate."

"Dave," said Sara, "it already will take me nearly two hours every pay period just to update the vacation records on our 90 employees. That's 52 hours, or more than a week per year, just to have me track employee vacation time the way you

do it now. Tracking it even more accurately would likely double the time, not to mention the time it already takes to record the employee's sick days earned and used and their paid holidays. There's got to be a more efficient way to do this!"

Dimension: Workforce Enhancement

Consider the vacation policy Dave has implemented at the Golden Rose.

1. How do you think the restaurant's policy affects each of the following HR functional areas?
   a. Staffing the operation
   b. Developing staff
   c. Motivating staff
   d. Maintaining staff
2. Why do you think paid vacations are so frequently used by many businesses in an effort to motivate employees?
3. The hospitality industry employs a large number of part-time workers. Most do not accrue paid vacation time. Why do you think the industry has been reluctant to grant paid vacations to this large segment of its workforce?

Dimension: Record Keeping and Documentation

Consider the recordkeeping system put in place by the former HR assistant.

1. Would you change the recordkeeping system that has been used?
2. What alternatives could Sara suggest to Dave that could help the restaurant save time and money in maintaining these records?
3. What role could advanced technology play in helping solve this problem? (*Hint*: Google "vacation records software: employees" and record your findings.)

Dimension: Policy Development

Assume you were considering the development of vacation policies and procedures for an operation of your own.

1. Draft a two-paragraph statement explaining your policy for use in your employee handbook.
2. Draft a two-paragraph statement explaining the policy and procedure employees would use when requesting the use of their paid vacation time, which will also be included in the handbook.
3. Draft a procedures summary that details how your operation will document granting employee vacation time requests in a manner designed to minimize any charges of bias or unfairness by your employees.

INTERNET ACTIVITIES

1. One of the most difficult areas of employee policies and procedure management relates to the amount of time you must spend creating and maintaining employee records. Fortunately, there are resources to assist you in determining which records you must keep and for how long. Type "maintain employee records" into your favorite search engine and select one or two sites for review. After your review consider the following:

   a. Are there readily available records-related materials and products you think would be applicable to the hospitality industry?

   b. How could a hospitality manager evaluate the cost-effectiveness of materials such as these?

2. One challenge faced by HR managers is that of staying up to date with changes in labor law. A variety of websites have been developed to help HR managers do just that. Type "labor law updates" into your favorite search engine and select one or two sites for review. After your review consider the following:

   a. Do you think websites such as these would be helpful to HR managers in the hospitality industry? How could HR managers best utilize them?

   b. This chapter presents an argument for performing a legal review of all significant HR policies and procedures. If you secured information from these sites would you still seek a legal review of it before applying it in your operation? Why or why not?

© Geri Lavrov / Getty Images

CHAPTER

4

EMPLOYEE ON-BOARDING: RECRUITMENT AND SELECTION

LEARNING OBJECTIVES

When they complete this chapter, readers will be able to:

1. Explain the concept of employee on-boarding.

2. Identify the factors that HR managers must consider when planning and implementing their organization's employee recruitment efforts.

3. Explain the importance of and procedures to effectively use job applications, interviews, testing, background checks, and reference checks—the five major activities used to screen employees for possible selection.

4. Explain the potential legal liability related to negligent hiring.

5. Explain the purpose of a job offer and describe the legal differences between a conditional job offer and a final job offer.

Impact on HR Management

Competitive edge: Factors such as something a business does well, a popular history, or an enjoyable location that persuade customers to purchase from it rather than from other businesses.

Exceptional hospitality management leaders often say that "our people are our greatest asset," and they know this is true. There are few, if any, "trade secrets" or entry barriers in the hospitality industry that would stop new businesses from successfully developing and competing for customers. An organization's employees, then, who deliver the desired products and services to the customers at price levels representing value represent a **competitive edge** over other organizations that do not.

One characteristic that has historically distinguished the hospitality industry from others is the ability of a single, innovative entrepreneur to make a remarkable impact. Examples such as Ray Kroc (McDonald's), Howard Schultz (Starbucks), Steve Ells (Chipotle), Kemmons Wilson (Holiday Inns), and Horst Schulze (Ritz Carlton) are powerful reminders that a single individual (and often one whose first entry-level job in the industry was modest indeed) can have an incredible impact on the industry.

Many successful hospitality industry leaders state that they have little personal interest in making their companies the biggest or even the most profitable. They know that if they focus on providing outstanding guest service, growth and profits are the inevitable results.

With success and more customers, however, comes the need to identify, train, and retain talented people who must be kept satisfied, focused on excellence, and committed to the organization's goals. This is why employee recruitment and selection efforts are so critical to the long-term success of every hospitality business. These activities are part of an overall commitment to initiate and continue a spirit of hospitality that forms the employees' first favorable impressions of the organization.

❖ THE ON-BOARDING PHILOSOPHY

LEARNING OBJECTIVE 1. Explain the concept of employee on-boarding.

On-boarding: The process by which a new employee is welcomed and integrated into a hospitality organization.

Recruitment: The process of identifying candidates for current or future position vacancies.

Selection: The process of choosing an individual for a current or future position vacancy.

"**On-boarding**" refers to the process by which a new employee is welcomed and integrated into a hospitality organization. According to some observers, the process begins with the first contacts a person seeking employment has with the organization during **recruitment**. Depending on the organization, the on-boarding process then continues for 30–90 or more days after the employee's first day on the job. In contrast, some managers believe that the on-boarding process does not really begin until after the **selection** process is completed and the new employee completes orientation.

Many people form impressions of an organization before they begin to work in it. Consider, for example, an "employer of choice" for whom many within the community want to work, and the application rate is high when there are openings. In contrast, think about an "employer of last resort" for whom people work only until they can find preferred employment. Recruitment and selection best practices, including using appropriate interviewing skills and honest answers to job applicants' questions, are needed so people are not "turned off" before they accept a position.

Below are listed some best practices HR managers can use to assist in their organizations' on-boarding efforts:

◆ **Be truthful**—Ensure that job descriptions accurately identify the tasks an employee in the position must perform. Minimize statements such as "Other miscellaneous tasks as required by the supervisor" and explain the most commonly performed "other miscellaneous tasks" (there should not be many). Misrepresenting the position breeds mistrust that cannot be overcome with orientation.

HR Management: Impact on New Team Members

HR managers must be experts at "back door marketing." If you are not familiar with the term, think about who comes in the back door (employees) and the focus of marketing (the guests). In other words, HR managers should treat employees the same way they treat guests: with a spirit of hospitality.

Hospitality managers want every moment of truth—each opportunity a guest has to form an impression of the operation—to be favorable. In the same way, shouldn't the employees' impressions of the hospitality organization also be favorable?

There is an old saying that "first impressions are lasting impressions," and it is applicable here. If you had some early disappointing experiences with a potential employer, would you want to work for him or her? Conversely, if your recruitment and selection experiences were enjoyable, wouldn't that make you pleased to receive a job offer, prompt you to accept it, and make you look forward to your first day of work and ongoing experiences with the operation?

Your answer was probably "no" to the first question and "yes" to the next three questions. If so, your responses represent those of most applicants and support the need for an effective, positive, and welcoming on-boarding philosophy during the recruitment and selection processes.

◆ **Pay attention to the applicant**—Don't allow interruptions such as phone calls, e-mails, or text messages that may suggest the person or the position is unimportant. Focus on the individual as though he or she is important, because that is true.

◆ **Make introductions, if appropriate**—If you see employees while completing recruitment or selection activities with an applicant, provide introductions. This is evidence that the manager cares about team members.

◆ **Lay the groundwork**—Begin to describe the organization's core values and culture that emphasizes communication with and respect for the employees. Explain the emphasis on training to provide necessary knowledge and skills and ongoing opportunities to prepare for more responsible positions.

Numerous additional examples of welcoming activities are described in this chapter on recruitment and selection and in the next chapter, which addresses the employee's first day, as well as orientation and induction activities.

∴ EMPLOYEE RECRUITMENT PROCEDURES

LEARNING OBJECTIVE 2. Identify the factors that HR managers must consider when planning and implementing their organization's employee recruitment efforts.

Employee recruiting is the first step taken to identify and select the best employees to serve the customers.

Factors Affecting Recruiting Efforts

Numerous factors affect recruiting activities in the hospitality industry. Examples include the following:

◆ **Legal constraints**—As you learned in chapter 2, local, state, and federal laws significantly affect recruiting activities. Potential employers cannot seek out individuals based

What About Job Analysis?

Job analysis: A process to determine the specific tasks that must be done, as well as the knowledge and skills workers must have to complete those tasks.

Job specification: The knowledge, skills, and other requirements necessary to perform the tasks described in a job description.

Job analysis involves determining the specific tasks that must be done, as well as the knowledge and skills workers must have to complete those tasks. HR managers must know these tasks so they can develop the job descriptions and **job specifications** that are critical for the recruitment process. A detailed examination of job analysis is presented in chapter 6. The reality for most hospitality unit managers is that even the most experienced employees will require training about how specific tasks are to be done in the new operation.

Consider an excellent server with ten years' experience working in a family style table-service restaurant. This employee will still need operation-specific training to work in a fine dining establishment. As well, people with no previous job experience hired to be dishwashers will need to learn a specific set of "new" job skills. In both cases the employees will not have the knowledge and skills needed when they are hired. Instead, managers provide to new employees the necessary skills training—driven by position analysis results—to ensure they are able to meet job performance standards.

What the best new employees can bring to the operation is a sincere commitment to serve guests, a willingness to learn, and the work ethic needed to perform as a valued employee. With these characteristics present, an "unskilled" employee will be selected, but he or she will be an excellent addition to the staff. Many managers "hire for attitude" because they can teach knowledge and skills. Position analysis can be thought of as a prerequisite for the training that occurs after recruitment and selection.

on non-job-related factors such as age, gender, or physical attractiveness; if they do, significant legal problems are likely to result. For example, some hospitality managers have historically viewed some positions as being best suited for men or women. Today, people of both genders can and do wait on tables, perform housekeeping tasks, and serve as unit general managers and in much more responsible positions in multiunit organizations.

Historically, the hospitality industry has provided tremendous opportunities for employees of all backgrounds. It will continue to do so, not only because it is the legal thing to do but also because it is the right thing to do.

Compensation: The amount of money and other items of value (e.g., benefits, bonuses, perks) given in exchange for work performed.

◆   **Economic constraints**—Economic constraints affect both the hospitality organization and the applicants. The **compensation** paid to employees is typically directly determined by an operation's profitability. All organizations face economic restraints, and this challenge is one that must be addressed by all hospitality managers.

Most applicants are attracted to or deterred from positions in part, at least, because of the compensation offered. The best interests of the employer and employee are served when pay ranges for positions are reasonable and competitive. Note that pay rates are only one of several critical factors (see chapter 8) that good employees consider when applying for positions.

◆   **Industry constraints**—Some people incorrectly view the hospitality industry as one with few advancement opportunities and low compensation. In fact, significant personal and financial rewards can be earned by employees with a variety of education and experience backgrounds. While an HR manager is unlikely to change every applicant's perceptions, recruitment efforts should, when necessary, directly address potential candidate biases.

One way to do so is to focus on a position's varied and positive characteristics that include employment stability, work variety, an opportunity to use personal creativity in a team environment, the rewards of serving others, and a pleasant work atmosphere.

Each hospitality position has its own positive features, and specific industry segments have their own unique and positive attributes. The attractive features of available positions should be publicized to better educate those who do not fully understand the advantages of a career in the hospitality industry.

◆ **Organizational constraints**—Some applicants may react to the specific organization offering a position. For example, managers operating school food service units may find their positions are favorably perceived because applicants know these jobs will have traditional hours, may offer above-average benefits, and may provide time off during summer months. Alternatively, managers operating high-energy nightclubs will likely find their best potential applicants are drawn to the excitement of the operation despite working during nontraditional (extremely late night) hours.

HR managers should truthfully identify the employment advantages offered by their organizations. As noted earlier, those with excellent reputations will have larger pools of potential employees than their counterparts with less favored reputations.

◆ **Position constraints**—Some hospitality jobs are perceived as glamorous, whereas others are not; recruiting a large and qualified pool of applicants for the latter may be challenging. Many managers have difficulty filling manual labor positions such as dishwashers, janitors, landscaping and grounds care, room attendants, and others. In job markets with a low **unemployment rate** a worker shortage may exist. Then, qualified applicants may be hard to find, and managers must work diligently and creatively to identify potential applicants.

> **Unemployment rate:** The number of unemployed people in a community or other designated area who are seeking work; expressed as a percentage of the area's entire labor force.

The Search for Qualified Employees

Managers in most hospitality organizations must actively recruit employees. From company presidents to the lowest skilled entry-level position, candidate recruitment is often an ongoing activity. One way to discuss the employee search process is to think about internal, external, and outsourced searches.

INTERNAL SEARCH

An **internal search** is used when the best candidates for positions are believed to be currently employed by the organization.

Done properly, this approach can be very effective when, for example, an executive housekeeper needs a rooms inspector and thinks the best job candidates are among the hotel's current room attendants.

Current employees may be informed about pending job openings in conversations with their supervisors or through the posting of the information on employee bulletin boards, websites, newsletters, or other media.

> **Internal search:** A promote-from-within recruitment approach used to seek qualified job applicants.

Advantages of using internal searches include that they

◆ build employee morale;

◆ can be initiated quickly;

◆ improve the probability of making a good selection because much is already known about the individual who will be selected;

◆ are less costly than initiating external or outsourced searches;

◆ result in reduced training time and fewer training costs because the individual selected need not learn about organizational topics with which he/she is already familiar;

◆ encourage talented individuals to stay with the organization; and

◆ are looked upon favorably by the Equal Employment Opportunity Commission (EEOC).

Possible disadvantages to the use of internal searches include the following:

◆ **Inbreeding**—Employees selected from outside the organization may broaden current views and bring needed knowledge, enthusiasm, and skills to the job. The negative effects of inbreeding can be reduced when managers are committed to the continued training and upgrading of current employee skills at all levels.

◆ **Resentment among managers**—While most supervisors and managers would welcome the promotion of their employees, sometimes an internal promotion is subtly or even openly opposed. Consider Craig, an outstanding full-time auditor at an all-suites hotel. He has been in his position for five years and reports to the hotel's front office manager (FOM). The hotel has a vacant assistant controller position and, because much of the controller's work relates to the night audit process, Craig is an ideal candidate for the position, and it would give him more traditional working hours as well as a significant pay increase. However, Peggy, the FOM, opposes the promotion because it will create a crucial night auditor vacancy in her department. Note that Peggy's own interests cannot be placed above those of the hotel. Likewise, a promote-from-within policy allowing managers to block transfers of their employees to other departments is not useful if managers are allowed to prioritize what is "best" for their departments over their organization's needs.

◆ **Employee resentment**—When several employees have been considered for internal advancement and only one is chosen, those who were not chosen may feel resentment, and decreased morale can result.

◆ **Recruitment and selection are still needed**—When one position is filled internally, the position vacated must also be filled. Sometimes it may even be more difficult to attract qualified candidates for the newly created vacancy than to select an outsider for the original vacancy.

◆ **Increased use of training resources**—When two positions are filled with new employees (the original position and the now-vacant position), training efforts to address both of their needs may be greater than if an external applicant was chosen for the original position.

Despite these potential disadvantages, most HR managers believe the advantages of an internal search outweigh them. Most hospitality employees want to do a good job and improve themselves and their families through hard work and employer loyalty. Employers can reward them in a visible manner by considering, when possible, current workers for higher-level job openings.

While not really an internal search system, some HR managers use **employee referral** systems to discover potential applicants recommended by employees.

Employee referral systems often work well because employees rarely recommend someone unless they feel he or she could do a good job and fit well in the organization. Also, existing employees tend to have an accurate view of the job and the organization's culture, and this information reduces unrealistic expectations and can help reduce new employee turnover. In some operations a financial bonus is paid to a staff member who recommends a person who is hired by and remains with the organization for a specified time.

Lower-level and supervisory jobs can often be filled with applicants recommended by current employees. Upper-level positions such as unit or district manager or higher are more likely to be referred by a professional acquaintance than by a close friend. That is why many managers are active and visible in professional hospitality industry associations.

Employee referral: A recommendation about a potential applicant provided by a current employee.

Treat All Applicants the Same

HR managers must treat employees who have been referred internally the same as nonreferred employees for hiring purposes. To minimize potential charges of bias or discrimination, job application, evaluation, interview, and selection procedures used for internally referred individuals should exactly match the procedures used for nonreferred employees.

There are potential challenges with employee referral systems, including that recommenders may suggest friends or relatives regardless of their qualifications. For this reason the same standards of employment consideration that apply to other individuals being considered for a position should be used for referred candidates.

Nepotism, the hiring of relatives, may also be a problem with employee referral systems. Consider, for example, the opportunities for theft by collusion that can arise when two persons, such as a bartender and a beverage server, are related or are very good friends. Some operations, therefore, prohibit the hiring of a current employee's close relatives.

Nepotism: Favoritism in employment based on kinship.

EXTERNAL SEARCH

Many managers use an **external search** to help identify a pool of qualified job applicants. Traditional strategies for external searches include:

External search: An approach to seeking job applicants that focuses on candidates not currently employed by the organization.

- **Traditional advertisements**—These can range from simple "help wanted" postings in newspapers or on public bulletin boards to signs in a property's window and on tray liners in quick-service restaurants. The best locations are those where targeted job applicants will see them. Some organizations provide their names in advertisements, and others place blind ads that do not identify the potential employer. These are sometimes used when an organization wishes to replace a current employee but does not want the current employee to know about the replacement search. They are also used when the employer does not want the public to know about a large number of vacancies. Note that some people may not respond to blind ads because they fear the ads were placed by their current employer.

   Some venues for placing ads are free or low cost, including social media sites and bulletin boards at apartment complexes, child care centers, supermarkets, libraries, community centers, and school newspapers. Employers seeking candidates for whom English is not their primary language may place ads in foreign-language newspapers and newsletters.

- **Public employment agencies**—These organizations help the state's citizens find jobs. Their function is usually related to unemployment benefits (see chapter 2) provided to those registered with the state employment agency. Since many of these people have limited skills and training, they may be excellent candidates for entry-level positions. Public employment assistance agencies do not charge employers or potential employees for their services, and many managers find this source to be an effective way to communicate with potential job candidates.

- **Private employment assistance agencies**—These organizations charge for the services they provide and may be used as a source for some higher-level position vacancies. They may also provide employers with additional services such as advertising jobs, screening applicants, and even providing "money back" guarantees if the applicant provided does not meet the employer's expectations. The fees charged may be absorbed by the employer, the employee, or split between both.

- **Educational institutions**—Most educational institutions provide services to assist their graduates in finding jobs. Whether the job to be filled requires a high-school diploma, specific vocational training, or an associate's, bachelor's, or advanced degree, educational institutions are a source of qualified job candidates that should not be overlooked. Colleges and universities, technical schools, and secondary (high) schools in an employer's area typically offer employers the chance, at little or no cost, to assess the quality of their students.

- **Unsolicited applications**—Employers often receive unsolicited applications or requests to be considered for job openings. These may arrive in the manager's office by letter, fax, or e-mail or may be delivered in person. Even if there are no current vacancies, these applications may be kept on file. Note that unsolicited applications submitted to hospitality organizations generally have a relatively short life span because those who are searching for jobs typically continue their search until it ends successfully. Therefore many managers review all unsolicited applications submitted each day, and some even arrange to conduct on-the-spot interviews if good candidates are scarce.

OUTSOURCED SEARCH

Outsourced search: A search for job candidates performed by a professional company specializing in employee searches.

In some cases, HR managers use an **outsourced search** to find candidates, usually for executive positions.

Executive search firms typically charge the employer a fee ranging from one-third to one-half of the annual wages that will be paid to the employee who will be hired. These firms monitor executive-level talent so that they can advise clients about the best candidates available.

The search firm usually identifies potential candidates from their lists of contacts and performs preliminary screening. The best firms are able to identify executives with the proper skills who will fit into the organization's culture if they are hired.

Technology and Employee Recruitment

Not surprisingly, technology has significantly changed how hospitality (and most other) organizations recruit employees. Increasingly, electronic networking, including instant messaging and e-mail, are used to communicate with applicants about vacancies, questions, and other information.

Many hospitality organizations feature general "Career Opportunity" information on their websites along with more specific information about current position vacancies. Career-related information on well-developed company websites may include:

- ◆ Organization overview, including press releases, current news stories, awards, and anecdotes that emphasize employee careers.

- ◆ Corporate culture, including information about the organization's values, vision, and mission.

- ◆ General information about the organization's history and operating statistics, as well as employee testimonials.

- ◆ Internships and possible career tracks.

- ◆ Compensation, including a description of benefits.

Websites may also include application forms and e-mail or other addresses for additional information. This is particularly useful for attracting younger workers, who often prefer online applications.

Many hospitality organizations have Facebook pages, which position them within their communities and offer information about employment opportunities. Twitter allows HR managers to announce position vacancies and receive inquiries from those who are potentially interested in the positions.

Numerous employment websites exist. These include general business sites such as Monster.com and hospitality-specific websites such as Hcareers.com, a site that provides a huge database of hospitality industry–related employment opportunities. Both of these websites provide a great deal of information that can be of assistance to job seekers and those who are posting their open positions. Similarly, a recruiter who uses LinkedIn may discover potential applicants for management and leadership positions. Those in his or her network might be asked for referrals and to alert others about position vacancies.

❖❖ EMPLOYEE SELECTION PROCEDURES

LEARNING OBJECTIVE 3. Explain the importance of and procedures to effectively use job applications, interviews, testing, background checks, and reference checks—the five major activities used to screen employees for possible selection.

Major Selection Tools

After HR managers have identified a pool of qualified candidates, they must select the best applicant, and they generally use some or all of the five major selection tools to do so: applications, interviews, pre-employment testing, and background and reference checks.

APPLICATIONS

An employment application should be completed by all candidates for employment, and it does not need to be complex. Its purpose is to learn information necessary to determine whether the applicant can, with training, perform the job's essential functions. The requirements for a legitimate, legally sound application are many but, in general, the questions asked should focus exclusively on job qualifications. It is wise to have the proposed employment application reviewed by an attorney who specializes in employment law before use.

Each candidate for a specific position should fill out an identical application, and the application for the candidate selected should be kept on file. It is a good practice for the application to clearly state the "**at-will**" nature of the employment relationship.

Many applicants for jobs in the hospitality industry have limited skills in speaking, reading, or writing English. These limitations should not necessarily disqualify an applicant from being selected and doing an excellent job. Knowing this, many HR managers provide assistance to applicants who need help when filling out their employment applications.

Figure 4.1 is an example of an employment application that is legally sound. Note specifically how questions are related only to the ability to work, work history, and job qualifications.

At-will employment: An employment relationship in which either party (the employer or employee) can, at any time, terminate the relationship without liability.

INTERVIEWS

Some candidates who have submitted employment applications will be selected for one or more interviews. However, the types of questions that can be asked in the interview are restricted. If interviews are improperly performed, significant legal liability can result and, if a candidate is not hired based on his/her answer to, or refusal to answer, an inappropriate question, that candidate may have the right to file a lawsuit.

The EEOC suggests an employer consider three issues when deciding whether to include a particular question on an employment application or in a job interview:

1. Does this question tend to screen out minorities or women?

2. Is the answer needed to judge this individual's competence for job performance?

3. Are there alternative, nondiscriminatory ways to judge the person's qualifications?

Applicants, Applications, and the Internet

Most HR managers use a single, uniform application form for all job candidates to help show who is considered an "applicant," an important determination in complying with the federal government's record retention and reporting requirements. For example, Title VII of the Civil Rights Act requires covered employers to retain "applications" for employment and other documents pertaining to hiring for one year from the date the records were made or the last action was taken. Does that mean an HR manager who receives an unsolicited resume from a job seeker must keep it for one year? What if dozens or even hundreds of such e-mails are received? Are they all really applicants?

The EEOC and the Office of Federal Contract Compliance Programs broadly define *applicant* to include any person who has indicated an interest in being considered for hiring, promotion, or other employment opportunities. This interest might be expressed by completing an application form or in writing or verbally, depending on the employer's practice.

Fortunately, the EEOC has issued opinions to clarify recordkeeping requirements for applicants using the Internet and related cyber technologies. The EEOC's guidance limits the definition of *applicant*, in the context of the Internet and related technologies, to those people who have indicated an interest in a specific position that the employer has acted to fill and who have followed the employer's *standard procedures* for submitting an application. For this reason, many employers require that *all* job applicants, including those with resumes, submit a completed job application to be considered for employment, and these completed applications are retained.

LIGHTHOUSE RESTAURANT

Application for Employment

It is the policy of the Lighthouse Restaurant to provide equal employment opportunity to all qualified persons without regard to race, creed, color, religious belief, sex, age, national origin, ancestry, physical or mental handicap, or veteran status.

Name: Last_____ First_____ Middle_____

Street Address

_____

City_____ State_____ Zip _____

Telephone (   )_____ Social Security #_____

Position applied for

_____

How did you hear of this opening?

_____

When can you start?_____ Desired wage per hour_____

Are you a US citizen or otherwise authorized to work in the US? Yes_____ No_____

Are you capable of performing the essential functions of the job you are applying for with or without reasonable accommodation? Yes_____ No_____

If under 18, indicate date of birth:_____

If applying for a job involving the service of alcoholic beverages, are you over 21?
Yes_____ No_____

Are you looking for full-time employment? Yes_____ No_____

If no, what days and hours are you available? (please list all that apply)

	Sun.	Mon.	Tues.	Wed.	Thurs.	Fri.	Sat.
From	___	___	___	___	___	___	___
To	___	___	___	___	___	___	___

Do you have dependable means of transportation to and from work?
Yes_____ No _____

Do you have any criminal charges pending against you?
Yes_____ No _____

Have you been convicted of a felony in the past seven years?* Yes_____ No_____

If yes, please fully describe the charges and disposition of the case:

_____

_____

*Conviction of a felony will not necessarily disqualify you from employment.

Education: School Name; Location; Year Completed; Major/Degree

High School _____

Technical School _____

Figure 4.1   Employment Application

College _____

Other _____

In addition to your work history, are there other certifications, skills, qualifications, or experience we should know about?

_____

Employment History: (Start with most recent employer.)

Company name _____ Location_____

Date Started _____ Starting Wage _____ Starting Position_____

Date Ended _____ Ending Wage_____ Ending Position _____

Name of Supervisor _____ May we contact? Yes _____ No _____

Responsibilities _____

Reason for leaving

_____

Company name _____ Location _____

Date Started _____ Starting Wage _____ Starting Position _____

Date Ended _____ Ending Wage _____ Ending Position _____

Name of Supervisor _____ May we contact? Yes_____ No _____

Responsibilities _____

Reason for leaving

_____

Company name _____ Location _____

Date Started _____ Starting Wage_____ Starting Position _____

Date Ended _____ Ending Wage _____ Ending Position _____

Name of Supervisor_____ May we contact? Yes _____ No _____

Responsibilities _____

Reason for leaving

_____

I state that the facts written on this application are true and complete to the best of my knowledge. I understand that if I am employed, false statements on this application can be considered cause for dismissal. The company is hereby authorized to make any investigations of my prior educational and employment history. I understand that employment at this company is "at will," which means that I or the company can terminate the employment relationship at any time, with or without prior notice. I understand that no supervisor, manager, or executive of this company, other than its owner, has the authority to alter the at-will status of my employment.

I authorize you to make such legal investigations and inquiries into my personal employment, criminal history, driving record, and other job-related matters as may be necessary in determining an employment decision.

Signature _____ Date _____

Confidential Material/Property of Lighthouse Restaurant LLC.

Figure 4.1 (continued)

It's the Law

The Americans with Disabilities Act (ADA) provides a good example of how HR managers' jobs and those of an organization's employees are directly affected by employment-related legislation. The actions to be taken begin even before an employee is hired because some special provisions may be necessary for employment interviewing. These may include the following:

◆ Scheduling an on-site interview with a qualified candidate with a hearing loss rather than requiring the person to first pass a telephone screening interview.

◆ Modifying the job application process so a person with a disability can apply. Examples include providing large print, audiotape, or Braille versions of the application or allowing a person to apply with a paper application when an online application is normally required (or the reverse).

◆ Providing a sign language interpreter or a reader during the interview process.

◆ Conducting interviews in a first-floor office when an elevator is unavailable and ensuring all areas required for the application process are accessible.

◆ Altering the format or the time allotted for a required test unless the test is measuring a skill that is essential to job function.

◆ Providing or modifying equipment or tools needed to perform an essential function of the job when the function is tested or assessed as part of the job application process.

Medical exams as part of the employee selection process are also addressed by the ADA: They are prohibited before a job offer is made. After a job has been offered and before employment begins, a medical examination may be required, and the job offer may be a condition of the exam results. Note that an examination must be required of every applicant in the same job category.

If the employment offer is withdrawn because of medical findings, the employer must show the rejection was job related because of a business necessity and there was no reasonable accommodation that would enable the individual to perform that job's essential functions.

The ADA does not generally allow employers to require medical examinations of employees except

◆ to determine whether the employee can do the essential job functions after a leave for illness or injury or if the employee's fitness for duty is questioned;

◆ after an employee requests an accommodation to determine whether the employee has an ADA-related disability and what reasonable accommodations may be required;

◆ if required for employer-provided health or life insurance or for voluntary participation in an employer-sponsored health program; or

◆ if it is required by some federal law or regulation.

HR managers must carefully select questions to ask in an interview. In all cases it is important to remember that the job itself dictates whether questions are allowable. The questions to be asked of all applicants should be written down in advance and carefully followed. In addition, supervisors, coworkers, and others who may participate in the interview process should be trained to avoid asking inappropriate questions that could increase the operation's liability.

In general, age is considered irrelevant in most hiring decisions, and questions about date of birth are improper. However, age can be a sensitive pre-employment question because the Age Discrimination in Employment Act protects employees 40 years old and above. Asking applicants to state their age if they are younger than 18 years old is permissible because they are permitted to work only a limited number of hours each week. It may also be important when hiring bartenders and other servers of alcohol to confirm that their ages are at or above the state's minimum age for serving alcohol.

It's the Law

In 2013, San Francisco officials passed an ordinance prohibiting city contractors from inquiring about the criminal backgrounds of many job applicants. This is part of a national trend to improve job prospects in times of increased incarceration.

Some say that after a person has paid his or her debt to society, the job "playing field" should be fair. Others think the law potentially endangers employers who have an obligation to protect customers and employees.

In 2012, Newark, New Jersey, began to forbid private employers and the city government from asking about an applicant's criminal history until after a conditional employment offer is made, and employers can consider only certain offenses committed within the past five to eight years. Note that murder, voluntary manslaughter, and sex offenses can be inquired about with no time limitations. Also, some applicable laws do not apply to those seeking sensitive positions, such as those that involve working with children.

Questions about race, religion, and national origin are always inappropriate, as is the practice of requiring that photographs of the candidate be submitted before or after an interview. Questions about physical traits such as height and weight violate the law because they may eliminate a disproportionate number of female, Asian-American, and Spanish-surnamed applicants, who are statistically "shorter" than white males.

If a job does not require a particular level of education, asking questions about educational background may be improper. Applicants can be asked about their education and credentials if these are bona fide occupational qualifications. For example, asking a candidate for a hotel controller's position if he/she has a degree in accounting and which school granted that degree is allowable.

Asking an applicant if he or she uses illegal drugs or smokes is permissible because either of these traits can be legally used to disqualify applicants. Asking candidates if they are willing to submit to a voluntary drug test as a condition of employment is also allowable.

Safe questions can be asked about a candidate's present employment, former employment, and job references. Questions asked on the application and during the interview should focus on the applicant's job skills and nothing else. Figure 4.2 contains one state's recommended guidelines for asking appropriate interview questions.

PRE-EMPLOYMENT TESTING

Pre-employment testing can improve the employee screening process because, for example, test results can measure the relative strengths of two candidates. In the hospitality industry, pre-employment testing is generally of three types: skill, psychological, and drug screening.

Skills tests can include activities such as typing tests for office workers, computer application tests for those involved in using word processing or spreadsheet tools, and, for chefs and cooks, food production tasks. Psychological testing can include personality tests and others designed to predict performance or mental ability. For skill and psychological tests, it is critical to remember that, if the test does not have documented **validity** and **reliability**, the results should not be used for hiring decisions.

Pre-employment drug testing is allowable in most states and can be an effective tool for reducing insurance rates and potential worker liability issues. Many HR managers feel a drug-free environment attracts better applicants, with the resulting effect of a higher-quality workforce.

If pre-employment drug testing is used, care is needed to ensure the accuracy of results. In some cases, applicants whose erroneous test results have cost them a job have successfully sued the employer.

The laws surrounding mandatory drug testing are complex. HR managers who elect to implement a voluntary or mandatory pre- or postemployment drug testing program should first seek advice from an attorney who specializes in labor employment law in the jurisdiction.

Validity: The ability of a measuring tool to evaluate only what it is supposed to evaluate.

Reliability: The ability of a measuring tool to yield consistent results.

Introduction

In Michigan, the Elliott-Larsen Civil Rights Act (ELCRA) MCL §37.2206, and the Persons with Disabilities Civil Rights Act (PWDCRA) MCL §37.1206 provide significant guidance to employers in the hiring process. In addition, this guide includes the requirements of Title VII of the Civil Rights Act of 1964, 42 USC §§ 2000(e) et seq.; Title I of the Americans with Disabilities Act, 42 USC §§12101 et seq.; the Age Discrimination in Employment Act, 29 USC §§ 621 et seq.; and the Immigration Reform and Control Act of 1986, 8 USC §§ 1324a et seq.

Recruitment

The referenced federal and state laws make it unlawful for an employer to print, circulate, post, mail or otherwise cause to be published a statement, advertisement, notice or sign which indicates a preference, limitation and/or specification based on religion, race, color, national origin, age, sex, height, weight, marital status or disability. Employers are not prohibited from including statements that affirm equal employment opportunity.

Pre-Employment Inquiries

Except as permitted by the Michigan Civil Rights Commission (MCRC) Rules or by federal law, these statutes make it unlawful for an employer or employment agency to ask questions, orally or in writing, that elicit information, try to elicit information, or express a preference on the basis of race, color, religion, national origin, age, sex, height, weight, marital status, or disability of a prospective employee. These laws are not intended to interfere with an employer's right to hire qualified persons; rather, they prevent characteristics which are not job-related (such as race, sex, marital status, etc.) from influencing the selection process.

Job Description

One way to ensure sound hiring procedures and avoid unlawful discrimination is for employers to write job descriptions outlining the required skills and abilities for each position. Focusing on the individual's skills and specific job requirements helps employers select the most qualified candidate.

Requests for information that are unlawful pre-employment may be legal once the applicant is hired, such as information needed for payroll and benefit processing (marital status, number of dependents, etc.). However, the information should not be requested on the employment application or during the interview.

Arrest Records

Under Michigan law, employers **may not** ask an applicant about a misdemeanor arrest that did not result in a conviction. Employers **may** ask about felony or misdemeanor convictions or felony arrests which did not result in a conviction. Some employers are required to conduct criminal history background checks on potential hires. However, unless required by law, it is a violation of Title VII of the US Civil Rights Act for employers to have a blanket policy of not hiring or accepting applications from anyone with a criminal conviction.

Data Collection

Under limited circumstances, employers may be required to gather information that might otherwise be unlawful under the ELCRA and the PWDCRA. Documentation required by the Immigration Reform and Control Act, 8 USCA §§ 1324a et seq, and criminal history background checks required for applicants in certain occupations all require gathering otherwise prohibited data. Employers must use care to gather **ONLY** the information required by the controlling statute or

Figure 4.2   State of Michigan Pre-Employment Inquiry Guide

BACKGROUND CHECKS

Hospitality employers increasingly use background checks before hiring workers for selected positions in response to the large number of resumes and employment applications that are, at least partially, falsified.

While many types of background checks are available, not all are advisable. Background checks should be specifically tailored to obtain only information relating directly to each applicant's employment suitability.

Review the following commonly used background checks.

◆   **Criminal history**—As a general rule, criminal conviction records should be checked when there is a possibility that the person could create significant safety or security risks for coworkers, guests, or others. Examples include employees who will have close contact with minors, the elderly, the disabled, or patients and those who will have access to weapons, drugs, chemicals, or other potentially dangerous materials. Other examples include applicants who will work in or deliver goods to customers' homes and those who will handle money or other valuables or have access to financial information or

Pre-Employment Inquiry Guide

regulation, restrict access to this information, and require collection only after the employer has made a conditional offer of employment.

Bona Fide Occupational Qualification
Employers can request an exemption from Michigan civil rights law if they can show that religion, national origin, age, height, weight or sex is a bona fide occupational qualification (BFOQ) that is **necessary** to normal business operations. Employers can ask the MCRC for a BFOQ before posting a position. If a BFOQ is not requested and the employer is later charged with discrimination, the employer can raise BFOQ business necessity as a defense to the charge. For example, a juvenile detention facility concerned with the privacy of the youth may request hiring one person per shift of the same sex as the facility residents.

EEO/Workforce Diversity Plans
Equal Employment Opportunity (EEO) and workforce diversity plans are permitted to require the aggregate collection of data on race, religion, color, national origin, sex or disability of applicants and employees as long as the data is separated from hiring or promotional processes.

To file a complaint, or to ask questions contact 1/800.482.3604 or TTY 1/877.878.8464. You can also file online:
www.michigan.gov/mdcr

Revised 6/2012 – web only

What can employers ask before hiring someone in Michigan?

What is illegal?

MICHIGAN DEPARTMENT OF

Only Fair Is Fair.

Figure 4.2 *(continued)*

employees' personal information. In addition, some states require a check for criminal convictions before hiring individuals as employees of health care facilities (including food services), financial institutions, or public schools.

◆ **Credit reports**—Credit reports typically include financial information such as payment history, delinquencies, amounts owed, liens, and judgments relating to an applicant's credit standing. Arbitrary reliance on the results of these checks, however, has sometimes been found to result in adverse impact discrimination against women and minorities. Accordingly, use of credit reports should be limited to situations where there is a legitimate business justification, such as for jobs that entail monetary responsibilities, the use of financial discretion, or similar security risks.

◆ **Driving records**—Motor vehicle records (MVRs) are available from state motor vehicle departments. They usually contain information about traffic violations, license status, and expiration date. MVRs should be checked for any employee who will drive a company or personal vehicle for the employer's business.

◆ **Academic credentials and licenses**—Academic information such as schools attended, degrees awarded, and transcripts should be verified when a specified level or type of education is necessary for a particular job. Similarly, proof of licenses and their current status, expiration dates, and any past or pending disciplinary actions should be obtained if a license is required for the position in question.

Pre-Employment Inquiry Guide

Subject	Lawful Pre-Employment Inquiries	Unlawful Pre-Employment Inquiries
Address	Applicant's current and prior addresses	
Age	Are you 18 or older?	Applicant's age or date of birth
Arrests	Have you ever been convicted of a crime? Have you ever been arrested for a felony?	Misdemeanor arrests which did not result in conviction[i] **unless** applicant is seeking a position with a law enforcement agency
Birthplace		Birthplace of applicant and applicant's relatives; birth certificate, naturalization and baptismal records, unless required by federal law[ii]
Citizenship	Are you legally authorized to work in the United States?	These questions are unlawful **unless** asked as part of the Federal I-9 process[iii] a.) Of what country are you a citizen? b.) Are you a naturalized or native-born citizen? c.) Are your parents or spouse naturalized or native-born citizens?
Disability	Ability to perform the essential functions of the job with or without accommodation[iv]	Physical or mental conditions which are not directly related to the requirements of a specific job
Education	Applicant's academic, vocational or professional education and schools attended	
Genetic Testing		Applicant's genetic information; requiring applicant to undergo genetic testing[i]
Height or Weight		Applicant's height or weight[i]
Marital Status		Marital status or children; titles such as Mr., Mrs., or Ms.[i]
Name	Applicant's name; other names used by applicant	Applicant's maiden name[i]
National Origin	Languages spoken and written by applicant	Applicant's lineage, ancestry, national origin or nationality (see note ii below)
Notice in Case of Emergency	Name, address and phone number of person to be notified in case of accident or emergency	Name, address and phone number of **relative** to be notified in case of accident or emergency
Organizations	The organizations and clubs to which applicant belongs except as noted in the column to the right	Names of organizations to which an applicant belongs **IF** information would reveal the race, color, religion, national origin or ancestry of the members of the organization
Photograph		Applicant's photograph **prior to hire**
Race or Color		Applicant's race, national origin or color
Religion		Religious denomination or affiliation; religious holidays observed
Sex		Applicant's gender; ability or desire to have children; child care arrangements

[i] Unlawful under Michigan law only, not covered by federal law
[ii] Documents required by the Immigration Reform and Control Act (IRCA), 8 USCA §§ 1234a et seq., may only be collected after a conditional offer of employment has been made
[iii] The IRCA mandates that employers verify citizenship and work authorization, but only after a conditional offer of employment
[iv] This question is only lawful if applicant has been informed of the essential job functions

Figure 4.2 *(continued)*

Using background checks as a screening device does involve some risk to and responsibility for employers. Seeking only information with a direct bearing on the position for which a candidate is applying is important. If an applicant is denied employment based on a background check, the employer should give the candidate a copy of that report. Sometimes candidates can help verify or explain the results of background checks. Also, reporting agencies can make mistakes, and if false information influences a hiring decision, the hospitality organization may be put at legal risk.

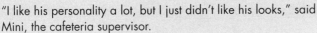

HR MANAGEMENT ISSUES 4.1

"I like his personality a lot, but I just didn't like his looks," said Mini, the cafeteria supervisor.

"What was wrong?" asked Teri, the dietitian for the hospital food service where Mini worked.

Mini and Terri were discussing Josh, a 23-year-old man who had interviewed for a job bussing tables in the hospital's "open to the public" dining room.

"It was his neck," replied Mini, "he had these black tattoos on his neck! I don't understand these young people...."

"I don't know Mini, I'm not sure they are much different than we were at that age," replied Terri.

Case Study Questions

1. Do you think Mini's reaction to Josh's tattoos is representative of the general public?

2. While it may be legal to reject an applicant with a tattoo because those with them are not legally defined as members of a protected class, do you personally think visible tattoos should be grounds for rejecting an otherwise qualified job applicant? Why or why not?

3. As an HR specialist, what policies, if any, would you develop for employee body adornment including makeup, visible tattoos, and body piercings? What factors might influence your decisions?

HR Management in Action

Hospitality employees are young and old and every age in between, and tactics to manage generational differences begin during employee recruitment.

As you'll learn in chapter 12, HR managers often interact with young employees from minors aged 14 to their upper teens to senior citizens aged 65 and older. Not surprisingly, there are numerous differences in how people of different ages think and act and how they react to tactics used to recruit and retain them in hospitality operations.

For example, HR managers note that some older job applicants resist and may not even apply for positions when the completion of an online application form is required. In contrast, some younger applicants prefer electronic employment application forms and have never completed a hard copy version. Older workers often learn of position vacancies in newspaper advertisements or from bulletin board placements in locations throughout their communities, but young people almost never use these sources. Instead, Craigslist and social media tools such as Twitter and Facebook are among the preferred venues to communicate with younger job applicants.

Not surprisingly, age difference perceptions often affect HR personnel in much the same way they impact the perceptions of managers in operating departments. For example, consider older HR managers interviewing young employees. These HR managers are surprised that younger applicants often focus on "what's in it for me now," and many seem less concerned about long-term careers, job benefits, and their futures than do their older job applicant counterparts. Other physical differences, including dress, jewelry, and even hairstyles and colors, seem out of character to the "dress for success" suggestions of traditional "how to get a job" recommendations.

The reverse is also true. Young unit managers with HR responsibilities may find it difficult to identify with some of the concerns of older workers who are interested in job conditions and responsibilities, employee benefits, and long-term opportunities with the employer. Other questions may generally relate to the concern of "How can I [the job applicant] help you [the potential employer]?"

Generational differences represent a very interesting aspect of employment in the hospitality industry, and they begin at the time of recruitment and selection.

More About Applicant Background Checks

Four key principles should always be addressed to ensure that background checks are completed legally and effectively.

Principle 1: Always obtain written consent before conducting any background check. This helps protect against invasion of privacy, defamation, and other wrongful act claims. It is also a good idea to expand the waiver language on consent forms to include the employer and those who assist with background checks, such as HR staff, former employers, and screening firms.

Principle 2: Evaluate results fairly and consistently. Avoid hasty rejections when negative information surfaces during a background check. Consider the negative information in the context of the job to be performed. For example, to reject an otherwise qualified front desk agent because of a poor driving record is unwise if the job requires no business driving. However, it may be a sensible action for a hotel van driver.

Principle 3: Restrict access to information obtained in background checks. This information should be kept in secure, confidential files and disclosed only on a strict "need to know" basis. Access to records relating to criminal or financial history should be limited as narrowly as possible.

Principle 4: Do background checks as one of the last steps in the selection process. There is no need to spend the time and money for background checks on a candidate until the decision has been made to offer the candidate a position.

REFERENCES

Employment references have historically been a popular screening tool. In today's litigious society, however, information of this type is often more difficult to obtain because employers may be held liable for inaccurate comments made about past employees. This concern is increased because job seekers can employ the services of companies that specialize in providing job seekers with a confidential and comprehensive verification of the employment references given by former employers. Therefore the information provided is generally limited to the employer's name, employee's name, date(s) of employment, job title, and the name and title of the person supplying the information.

If references from past employers will be sought, secure the applicant's permission in writing before contacting a former employer to help minimize the risk of litigation related to the reference checks.

Defamation: False statements that cause someone to be held in contempt, lowered in the estimation of the community, lose employment status or earnings, or otherwise suffer a damaged reputation.

HR managers must be cautious in both giving and receiving reference information. Employers are usually protected if they give a truthful reference; however, they may still incur the time and expense to defend a **defamation** case brought by a former employee.

If, for example, an employer giving a reference states that a former employee was terminated because he or she "didn't get along" with coworkers, the employer may need to prove that statement is true and that all of the difficulties were caused by the former employee.

To minimize risk of a lawsuit, never reply to a request for information about a former employee without a copy of that employee's signed release authorizing the reference check. The amount of information disclosed is determined by the HR manager, but answers should be honest and defendable. It is best to not disclose personal information such as marital or financial problems because this could result in an invasion of privacy lawsuit.

If a prospective employee provides letters of reference, always call the authors of the reference letters to ensure that they did in fact write them. When possible, put any reference information request in writing and ask that the response also be in written form. If only an oral response is possible, document the conversation with as much dialogue as possible, including the name of the person interviewed and the date and time the contact occurred.

Employment Status Verification

HR managers must understand their responsibilities for determining the legal status of potential workers.

All newly hired employees are required to fill out an Employment Eligibility Verification form (commonly known as an I-9 form) stating that they are authorized to work in the United States. US Citizenship and Immigration Service (USCIS) regulations allow an individual 72 hours from time of hire in which to complete Form I-9.

To see a current copy of the form, enter the following in your favorite search engine:

http://www.uscis.gov/sites/default/files/files/form/i-9.pdf

The form requires potential employees to verify both their citizenship status and legal eligibility to work. There are numerous documents that an employee can use to provide this information, including a US passport, driver's license, Social Security card, and school identification card.

Under current law, employers are not required to verify the authenticity of the identification documents they are presented, but they must keep a copy of them on file. The documents must pass a good-faith test ("Do they look real?"); if they do, the applicant may be hired. If an employee is later found to be unauthorized, the employer must terminate employment. Employers who do not end employment of unauthorized workers or who knowingly hire unauthorized workers face significant fines.

The USCIS has developed an Internet-based system called "E-Verify," which allows businesses to determine the eligibility of their employees to work in the United States. E-Verify is fast, free, and easy to use—and it's the best way employers can ensure a legal workforce. (To learn more about the system, enter "uscis e-verify" into your favorite search engine.)

HR managers should never knowingly break the law. They should also continue to monitor this important area of employment law to ensure their compliance with it.

Technology and Employee Selection

Technology is available to help HR managers to match the right applicant to the position vacancy. This is critical because employee retention rates, individual productivity, and competitiveness require that this activity be done effectively.

Larger-volume properties in the hospitality industry often implement technology-based solutions before their smaller-volume counterparts. Examples include point-of-sale systems in food and beverage operations and the use of self-check-in kiosks to register guests in hotel lobbies.

Below are some examples of how employee selection procedures might be assisted by the use of technology. Some of these applications are now used by multiunit organizations, and others might become more commonplace in the future. Many are most applicable to the selection of management personnel.

APPLICANT PRE-SCREENING

How can a large pool of job applicants be narrowed to focus on the best candidates? There are two possibilities.

- ◆ **Weighted application forms**—Specific application form items can be assigned a value and then scored. Screening questionnaires can also be designed for a specific job. These tools can be completed online and scored in real time. Differential weights are applied to candidate responses to create a weighted score. Elimination factors can be identified, if desired.

◆ **Profile matching**—This tactic attempts to match information provided by a candidate with position requirements determined by the employer. Characteristics that might be addressed relate to background requirements, job specifics such as compensation and required travel, and personality, experience, and competency requirements. Note that profile matching might be done as a later step in the selection process because of the time required to complete it.

PRE-EMPLOYMENT

Tests. Pre-employment ability and personality tests are widely used and can be nonproctored and Web-based. However, concerns about validity and reliability are ever present and must be considered as decisions about their use are made.

EMPLOYMENT INTERVIEWS

The use of computer-assisted interviews provides an assurance that the same questions are asked of each applicant. The questions used should be related to competency requirements so they will be job related. Technology also enables online interviewer training and can provide a management process to manage the entire interview process.

❖ NEGLIGENT HIRING

LEARNING OBJECTIVE 4. Explain the potential legal liability related to negligent hiring.

Negligent hiring: Failure of an employer to exercise reasonable care in the selection of employees.

Negligent retention: Retaining an employee after the employer becomes aware of an employee's unsuitability for a job by failing to act on that knowledge.

You've learned that providing references for past employees can subject HR managers to litigation if the comments made are challenged, if the information secured is false, or if it is improperly disclosed to third parties and violates the employee's right to privacy. However, failure to conduct background checks on applicants to some positions can subject HR managers to even more legal difficulty under the doctrines of **negligent hiring** and **negligent retention**.

Negligent hiring liability usually occurs when an employee who caused injury or harm had a reputation or record that showed his or her propensity to do so and this record would have been easily discoverable if reasonable care (a diligent search) had been shown. Similarly, negligent retention may be charged if an employer hires an employee and then discovers disqualifying information but does not remove the employee from the job.

How can HR managers show that reasonable care was used when hiring? The best tactic is to thoroughly verify all pertinent information about each candidate before making a job offer. For example, it would be difficult to argue that the employer knew or should have known about false

---

HR MANAGEMENT ISSUES 4.2

Holly is the HR manager of a country club and interacts with the club's athletic director to select swimming pool lifeguards, who are required by local statute.

Each lifeguard must be certified in cardiopulmonary resuscitation (CPR), and Holly has interviewed a candidate who lists the successful completion of a CPR course in his resume. However, Holly did not verify the accuracy of this statement as part of the selection process.

Assume that a child dies because the candidate was selected and he could not render the appropriate aid because he lacked knowledge of proper CPR procedures.

Case Study Questions

1. Do you think Holly could be guilty of negligent hiring?
2. Do you think a jury of average citizens would find Holly and/or her club guilty of negligent hiring?
3. As an HR specialist, how would you determine which positions at the club could subject you and/or your club to potential charges of negligent hiring?

information if multiple references were contacted and if all relevant credentials of the applicant were verified to the best of an employer's ability. It would also be difficult (but not, unfortunately, impossible) for a judge or jury to find that an employer had been negligent in its hiring processes if this standard of care was exercised prior to every hiring decision.

⁂ JOB OFFERS

LEARNING OBJECTIVE 5. Explain the purpose of a job offer and describe the legal differences between a conditional job offer and a final job offer.

A final step in the selection process is to clarify the conditions of the **employment agreement** with the employee.

All employers and employees have employment agreements with each other. They can be as simple as agreeing to a specific hourly wage rate and at-will employment for both parties. This can be true even if nothing is in writing or if work conditions have not been discussed in detail. Employment agreements may be individual, covering only one employee, or, as in a unionized operation, they may involve groups of employees. In general, hospitality industry employment agreements are established orally or with a **job offer letter**.

Properly composed job offer letters help prevent legal difficulties caused by employee or employer misunderstandings because they detail specific terms of the offer made by the employer to the employee. Some employers believe job offer letters should be used only for managerial positions, but to avoid difficulties all employees should have signed job offer letters in their personal files. Components of a sound job offer letter include:

- Position being offered
- Compensation, including benefits
- Evaluation period and compensation review schedule
- Start date
- Location of employment
- Special conditions such as the at-will relationship
- Reference to the employee handbook (see chapter 5) as a source of information about employer policies governing the workplace
- Lines for the employer and employee signatures
- Date of the signatures

A job offer letter may be conditional or final. With a conditional offer letter, the employer tentatively (conditionally) offers the job subject to "conditions" that must be met before the job offer is finalized, such as passing drug tests or background checks. When a conditional job offer letter is used, the legally binding employment agreement is not in effect until the employee accepts the terms of the job offer letter and fulfills the requirements it identifies. In contrast, a final job offer letter contains no conditions to be met before acceptance. An enforceable employment contract is in effect when the final job offer letter is legally accepted by the job applicant.

To illustrate the difference between a conditional and final job offer, consider Antonio, who applies for the maintenance manager position at a hotel. He is selected and given a conditional job offer letter, which specifies the employment condition that he must pass a drug test. While Antonio can sign the letter when it is received, his employment will not be finalized until he passes the drug test.

Employee agreement: The terms of the employment relationship between an employer and employee that specifies the rights and obligations of each party.

Job offer letter: A proposal by an employer to a prospective employee that specifies employment terms. A legally valid acceptance of the offer creates a binding employment agreement.

HR TERMS

The following terms were defined in this chapter:

Competitive edge	Unemployment rate	Validity
On-boarding	Internal search	Reliability
Recruitment	Employee referral (system)	Defamation
Selection	Nepotism	Negligent hiring
Job analysis	External search	Negligent retention
Job specification	Outsourced search	Employment agreement
Compensation	At-will employment	Job offer letter

FOR YOUR CONSIDERATION

1. Talk to your classmates and employee peers (if you are working) about how hospitality managers do and should recruit applicants for entry-level positions. Which recruitment venues are best? Which are least effective? Explain your response.

2. Discuss two situations in which you as a manager would recruit from within for a current position vacancy and two situations when you would be better served utilizing external recruitment tools.

3. Some HR managers emphasize skills and experience when hiring new employees, whereas others choose employees based on the candidates' personality and attitude. While choosing employees with all these traits would likely be best, if you had to select a new staff member based on fewer than all of these traits, which do you feel are most important? Explain your answer.

4. In some lodging operations physical attractiveness is important when selecting employees for front desk clerks, and in some restaurants that factor is important when selecting a bartender or beverage server. What is your opinion of the legality and ethics of utilizing such a hiring factor? Explain your answer.

5. Many employers refuse to answer any questions about the prior employment status of individuals who previously worked for them. What, if any, legal or ethical responsibility does a past employer have to provide information about a previous employee? Defend your position.

CASE STUDY

Apply HR Management Principles

"Tell me again," said Tammy, the executive housekeeper at the Plaza Hotel. "What did she write?"

"I told you," said Mike, the hotel's HR director, "Under the 'Have You Ever Been Convicted of a Crime' section, the applicant put 'yes.' Under the 'Explanation' section she put 'Drug Possession, 20xx. Served 3 months in county jail.'"

Tammy and Mark were discussing Stephanie, who had applied for a job as a room attendant.

"This was over ten years ago," said Tammy.

"Right," replied Mike, "but does it concern you that she served three months' jail time? It must have been serious."

"We don't know the specific circumstances," replied Tammy. "The question is, does this keep me from considering her for the job? I really liked her, and we are short of room attendants right now."

CASE STUDY (continued)

Dimension: Societal Responsibility

Review the conversation described in the case.

1. Do you think Stephanie should be considered a viable candidate for the vacant housekeeping position? Why or why not?

2. Assume you were the on-site food services director in a large elementary school. Would you consider hiring Stephanie for your kitchen operation? Why or why not?

3. How, if at all, would your responses to the above two questions be different if Stephanie had been convicted of drug distribution?

4. Some companies ask applicants to list only recent criminal activity (typically within the previous seven years) when completing job applications. Do you agree or disagree with such an approach? Explain.

Dimension: Company Procedures and Decision Making

Review the conversation described in the case.

1. What crimes, if any, do you feel would automatically disqualify an applicant from job consideration?

2. What types of criminal activity, if any, do you feel would not automatically disqualify an employee from job consideration?

3. What personal factors do you believe would influence your or any other hospitality manager's responses to the two questions above?

Dimension: Negligent Hiring

Review the conversation described in the case. Assume that the decision was made to hire Stephanie. Assume also that nine months later she was involved in a physical altercation (shoving match) with a fellow employee in which both were slightly injured. During the investigation of the incident, and in keeping with company policy, both employees were required to undergo drug/alcohol testing on the day of the incident. Stephanie tested negative for alcohol and positive for trace cocaine. The other employee tested negative for alcohol and positive for trace marijuana.

1. What, if any, actions would you take as Stephanie's supervisor? How would the absence or presence of a company-established Employee Assistance Program (EAP) affect your decisions?

2. Assume Stephanie's fellow employee was seriously injured in their shoving match, and the attorney representing that employee charged your company with knowingly hiring a person who could reasonably have been expected to pose a risk to others (negligent hiring). How would you respond?

INTERNET ACTIVITIES

1. The Internet has made just as large an impact on employee recruiting as it has on most other parts of business. Enter the phrase "hospitality industry careers" into your favorite search engine. Select three sites and answer the following questions for each.

   a. What site did you select?

   b. What are your impressions about the variety of positions available on the site?

   c. Did you find the site easy to navigate?

   d. If you were searching for a hospitality position, would you use the site? Why or why not?

2. Executive search firms help HR managers fill top-level management positions. Enter the phrase "hospitality management executive search firms" into your favorite search engine. Review three sites, select one, and then answer the following questions.

   a. What site did you select?

   b. Would you use this site if you were an HR manager looking for a candidate? Why or why not? Explain your response.

   c. Would you use the site if you were searching for an executive position? Why or why not? Explain your response.

© Tim Pannell / Corbis

CHAPTER

5

EMPLOYEE ON-BOARDING: ORIENTATION AND INDUCTION

CHAPTER OUTLINE

LEARNING OBJECTIVES

When they complete this chapter, readers will be able to:

1. Explain some useful tactics for a new employee's first day on the job.

2. Analyze the basic concerns of new employees as they begin to work in and adapt to the hospitality organization.

3. Explain important processes that should be used as employee orientation programs and procedures are developed and implemented.

4. Describe two final orientation-related activities: departmental induction and orientation follow-up.

5. State the importance of employee handbooks, and list policy and procedure topics typically included in them.

Impact on HR Management

You've probably heard the expression, "You only have one opportunity to make a good first impression!" This commonsense observation sets the scene as we address a new employee's first on-job activities.

As new employees participate in initial work experiences, they are looking for reinforcement that their decision to join the hospitality organization was a good one. What managers do (and don't do) likely makes a significant and lasting impact on their perceptions. Therefore, the on-boarding process that began during recruitment and selection (see the previous chapter) should continue as the new employee begins work.

Several activities should occur on the employee's first day of work, and managers should consider their own initial work experiences on previous jobs and the impressions that were created during those times.

Background information about the process by which new staff members adapt to the work situation establishes the context within which orientation programs are planned and implemented. A well-planned and consistently implemented orientation program can help ensure that new employees have favorable rather than unfavorable first impressions of their employer, workplace, managers, and team. Another planned activity, departmental induction, can continue the HR manager's emphasis on using the most hospitable procedures to introduce the new employee to his or her mangers, peers, and the work environment itself.

Employee handbooks provide a wealth of helpful information as managers make decisions affecting employees. Handbooks also assist staff members when they want to know about work requirements that affect them. Managers and supervisors must be "fair," and equitable treatment of employees is most assured when the same requirements apply to all employees all of the time. These requirements should be addressed in a current and well-organized employee handbook provided to new employees during their orientation process.

❖ THE NEW EMPLOYEE'S FIRST DAY

LEARNING OBJECTIVE 1. Explain some useful tactics for a new employee's first day on the job.

"What have I gotten myself into?" might be the thought of a new employee walking into a hospitality operation on his or her first day. The staff members making initial contact ("Hello, we've been expecting you, and we're so glad you're here!") should be organized because first-day activities will have already been planned. The employees will not be surprised nor will they have forgotten about this important experience for the new staff member. Note that the enthusiasm shown for the new employee should not conclude at the end of his or her first day. In fact, hopefully, it will continue beyond the first 30, 60, or 90 days of on-boarding for as long as the new staff member is part of the hospitality team.

Typically, the first day's activities should be limited to what a new employee can reasonably be expected to learn and do on a first shift. The actual orientation process may or may not begin on the first day; however, it is important that the new employee be made to feel genuinely comfortable and happy about the employment decision.

Below are examples of activities that may be planned for the employee's first day on the job. Each incorporates the on-boarding philosophy that welcomes a new staff member and differs from an attitude expressed by some managers whose actions suggest the new employee is just an interruption of ongoing work.

- ◆ Provide staff members with the new employee's résumé or discuss his or her experience before the new employee begins work. Encourage current staff to genuinely welcome the new employee, explain how their roles interact with that of the new hire, and discuss how they might work together.

- ◆ Assign an experienced employee to serve as a short-term mentor to support and advise the new hire. The mentor can then be an immediate resource for questions and provide useful information as the new employee becomes acclimated to the job and organization.

- ◆ Set up the new employee's workstation, if applicable, and ensure his or her assigned employee locker has been cleaned out (and is clean!) and is readily accessible. Note that when these types of basic tasks have been overlooked, the new employee may consider the lack of planning and preparation to be an early sign of an uncaring manager.

- ◆ If employment-related forms must be reviewed and/or signed, they should be available, ideally in an organized packet of information.

- ◆ It will be much more than a "nice touch" if the senior manager of the unit personally meets and greets the new employee on his or her first day. Even if a peer supporter is assigned, the employee's supervisor should attempt to visit informally with the employee. Note that short discussions or conversations are fine.

- ◆ Remember that the new employee is experiencing the organization's culture for the first time. Hopefully, that experience will be exactly as was expressed during the earlier recruitment and selection processes. The new employee (and all of his or her peers) wants to be respected. It is the sum of many seemingly little things that indicates whether the organization's culture is one that emphasizes a respectful relationship between managers and employees.

- ◆ Think beyond the on-boarding process, regardless of its duration, in the specific operation. If the employee discovers that there really is a continuously supporting and caring organizational culture, one of the primary causes of employee turnover will not exist, and all of the operation's stakeholders will benefit.

❖ THE NEW EMPLOYEE ADAPTATION PROCESS

LEARNING OBJECTIVE 2. Analyze the basic concerns of new employees as they begin to work in and adapt to the hospitality organization.

Managers have an important responsibility to help their new employees learn about and become comfortable working in the hospitality operation. Whether it is planned or just "happens," all newly employed staff go through an **adaptation** process as they learn about the values of the organization and "what it's like" to work for it.

Adaptation (to an organization): The process by which new employees learn the values of and "what it is like" to work for a hospitality organization during their initial job experiences.

Effective managers realize that their efforts to meet employees' needs and to reduce turnover rates begin the moment new employees are selected. They understand that new staff members are anxious and perhaps even stressed because they do not fully understand specific job expectations or how their performance will be judged. They are uncertain about relationships with supervisors and peers, about whether there will be unexpected work tasks, and if there will be unanticipated physical and/or mental challenges. These are among the concerns that managers should address in their earliest interactions with new staff members.

Employee Adaptation Concerns

For employees to work effectively, they must know what to do and must perform job tasks properly. These concerns should be addressed in training programs that begin after orientation concludes. However, new staff members will see, hear, and experience things as they begin work that set the context for more formal experiences that follow. Contrast, for example, two greetings that might accompany the introduction of a new employee to an experienced peer: "So glad you're here; welcome to the team," and "Hey, we really need help; hope you stay here longer than the last guy." While a manager cannot write the script for what a current employee says to a new employee, the manager's history of actions that impact the work environment will be easily and quickly seen as the new staff member begins work.

The cleanliness of work stations, conversations of employees between themselves and guests, and behaviors of employees that represent their work attitudes are observed by and influence the attitudes and behaviors of new staff members.

New employees want to be accepted by their peers and to quickly become contributing members of their work teams. While the socialization process takes time, it begins as workers are initially put at ease and as they are involved in hospitable interactions with their peers. Managers know that employees want to "fit in" with their peers and become effective team members, rather than advocates of the "them versus me" culture that exists in some operations. Managers have a significant influence over the attitudes and actions of staff members. The precedence they have set with their employers and their ongoing interactions impact staff members' interactions with new employees.

Experienced hospitality managers know that new staff members adjust to new employment situations in similar ways; this is the topic of the next section.

Steps in the Adaptation Process

Several steps are typically involved in the process by which new employees adapt to their organization and the employees within it. Figure 5.1 provides an overview of the new employee adaptation process.

Let's review the steps in the new employee adaptation process shown in Figure 5.1.

◆ **Step 1**—When new employees are selected, they have basic perceptions and attitudes about the work and the organization. These are probably based on factors including (1) information learned during the employment interview, (2) advertising messages (if the new employee has experienced the company's advertising messages), (3) previous experience, if any, as a guest in the operation, and (4) feedback about the property from others in the community, including family and friends, as well as current or former employees.

HR MANAGEMENT ISSUES 5.1

Cindy had been working as a bartender at the Harbor View Hotel for about two months. She liked her job (great tips!), and she appreciated the way her supervisor, Florence, respected and treated her on the job.

One night while closing, Cindy saw Florence leave carrying a canvas bag that appeared to contain several bottles of liquor. She saw tops of the bottles, could hear the sound of the bottles striking each other as the bag moved, and could tell that the bag was heavy.

"Just a little something for a late-night party," said Florence, when she noticed Cindy watching her. "I'll stop at the liquor store on the way in tomorrow to replace them."

While Cindy never had any problems with Florence's leadership style, she had noticed that Florence had her "favorites." (Cindy was glad she was one of them.) However, Florence also had other "direct reports" she treated much less fairly and sometimes disrespectfully. Cindy also remembered times when Florence had spoken inappropriately about top-level managers, some of the regular hotel and lounge guests, and even the hotel and the entire hospitality industry.

While Cindy had overlooked these conversations and Florence's philosophy because they didn't directly affect her, she began to think, "Why is Florence nice to me? Is this really a good place to work? I have lots of other options and really desire a career in the hospitality industry. Is it better to stay here and learn what not to do or take another job to learn things that will help me in my career?"

Case Study Questions

1. If you were Cindy, what would you do about the immediate issue of Florence taking alcoholic beverages from the property?

2. How might Florence be affecting the corporate culture of her department?

3. How is the corporate culture affecting Cindy?

4. If you were Cindy, what would you do as you considered your relationship with the hotel, your interest in remaining an employee at the property, and your desire to learn as much as possible about the hospitality industry early in your career?

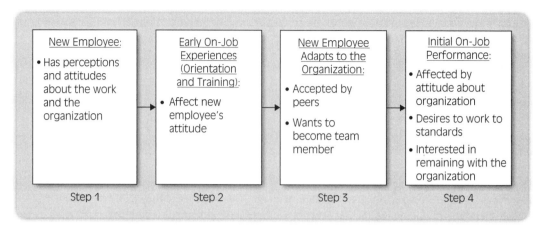

Figure 5.1　The New Employee Adaptation Process

◆ **Step 2**—Early on-job experiences including orientation and training may reinforce initial perceptions (step 1), or they may prove them to be less than accurate. Some apprehension is typical, however, if there is a significant difference between what new employees perceived (step 1) and what they actually experience (step 2). New staff members must either make significant changes in perceptions and expectations or, perhaps more frequently, new employees are likely to become discontented and become additional turnover statistics. This is especially so when the new employee desires to work for an organization in a position that meets initial expectations (step 1) and/or when the staff member has other employment opportunities.

◆ **Step 3**—Employees who begin to recognize and accept the culture of the organization and who want to become cooperating members of work teams will likely be accepted by their peers. They then want to become contributing members of the organization.

◆ **Step 4**—At this point, perhaps the most difficult challenge has been accomplished. The new staff member has a positive attitude about the organization and is willing to learn about and contribute to it. The initial orientation and training activities enable new employees to perform work meeting quality and quantity standards. Successful performance reinforces the employee's attitude about the organization, and they begin to experience and relate to cultural norms, encouraging retention rather than turnover.

Many tactics required to successfully assist new employees as they adapt to the organization relate to on-job leadership and supervisory concerns that extend beyond the scope of this book. However, they also suggest that it is a combination of "big picture" HR strategies and effective "on-the-firing line" supervisory procedures that yield a workforce committed to partnering with the organization.

In large organizations HR managers and their line department counterparts must work together closely to best ensure that the work environment is favorable to staff members. In smaller organizations without HR specialists, managers have the increased responsibility to plan, implement, and maintain work environments that encourage employee retention. This should be of obvious concern. However, hospitality managers are very busy and, unfortunately, may spend significant time addressing short-term challenges rather than longer-term actions that can positively influence employee relationships.

❖❖ ORIENTATION PROGRAMS AND PROCEDURES

LEARNING OBJECTIVE 3. Explain important processes that should be used as employee orientation programs and procedures are developed and implemented.

Orientation is the process of providing basic information about the hospitality organization that must be known by all staff members in every department. Implemented effectively, orientation efforts provide initial on-job experiences that help new staff members learn about the organization and its purposes, become comfortable with the work environment, and learn where they fit into it.

In other words, orientation assists with the new employee adaptation process addressed in the previous section. As well, discussions about basic policies and procedures help new staff members learn about matters of personal importance such as their employer's expectations and job-related benefits for which they qualify. In effect, then, orientation and other initial work-related experiences help the new employee learn how the organizational culture views its staff members. It is critical that an effective orientation program be planned and implemented because it significantly affects the initial and ongoing relationship between the organization and its newly hired staff members.

Orientation: The process of providing basic information about the hospitality organization that must be known by all staff members in every department.

Goals of Orientation Programs

Orientation has numerous goals.

- **It provides an overview of the organization**—Many newly employed staff members want to know their employer's history, size (number of locations and staff members, for example), and the products and services it provides. They should learn about the results their new organization is attempting to achieve. Trainees may want to know how their organization adds value for its guests, to themselves, and to the organization's owners. Hopefully, there is a **mission statement** explaining what the organization wants to accomplish and how it intends to do so. Hopefully, the mission statement serves as a guide for decision making, as well, and is used every day and not just as an introductory page in an employee handbook or as a slogan on the managers' business cards.

Mission statement: A strategic statement that indicates what the hospitality organization wants to accomplish and how it intends to do so.

- **It indicates the new staff member's role**—If you were a new staff member, would you like to see an organizational chart showing all positions, including yours, and the reporting relationships between them? Would you like to learn where you fit in and about promotion tracks if you perform well? You probably would, and new staff members would like to learn this information as well.

- **It explains policies, rules, and other information**—Staff members want to know general guidelines, including their days and hours of work, uniform requirements, break times, auto parking, and other similar information to help them feel more comfortable.

- **It outlines specific expectations**—Topics including responsibilities of the employer to the employees and, in turn, their responsibilities to the employer should be addressed.

- **It provides details about employee benefits**—Staff members want information about nonsalary/nonwage compensation and the requirements to receive these benefits.

- **It motivates new staff members**—The enthusiasm and excitement exhibited by those providing orientation experiences are important. Orientation helps to establish a solid foundation for a positive relationship between the organization, its managers and supervisors, and the new staff member.

Taken together, the benefits of effective orientation programs can eliminate confusion, heighten a new staff member's enthusiasm, create favorable attitudes, and, in general, make a positive first impression. Would you like to receive a proper orientation to your new organization? Your answer is likely yes, and this is the probable response of almost every new staff member in every organization.

Properly conducted orientation sessions address many concerns of new staff members. Managers should encourage questions and recognize their role as they provide an appropriate "welcome" to the organization.

It's the Law

Employers are required by law to obtain and retain some information from new employees, and this may be done during orientation. Examples include federal, state, and/or community withholding tax information, immigration and naturalization documentation, and age verification (for minors) if this was not provided (finalized) during the selection process.

As well, potential legal challenges might be avoided if some information is provided to employees during orientation or at another early time in their employment. Examples include information about the employer's sexual harassment complaint procedures and about Americans with Disabilities Act (ADA) concerns. Also, many hospitality operations that sell or provide alcoholic beverages begin their emphasis on responsible service during their orientation programs. Note that this issue relates beyond food and beverage personnel to others who come into contact with guests in a property that offers alcoholic beverage service. The provision of this information helps establish a priority for concern, and it establishes a record of consistent and ongoing emphasis that could be of significant help in defending the organization if alcoholic beverage service–related lawsuits arise.

HR Management: Impact on New Employees

The priority goal of an orientation program is to help new employees feel comfortable in their new position and to provide helpful information that enables them to maximize their contribution to the organization. It is also planned to reduce their possible anxiety and stress by addressing the types of questions and concerns they might typically have as they begin their new jobs. Examples of questions and concerns include:

- ◆ Where do I fit in to the organization?
- ◆ Where and how can I contribute my time and talents?
- ◆ What are my duties?
- ◆ What are my rights?
- ◆ What are my limits?
- ◆ How can I advance (and to what positions) within my new organization?

Orientation programs are effective when they help to establish a relationship between the new staff member and the organization that is based on both parties helping each other to attain important goals.

Orientation is the first step in training, and it must be well planned and organized. In smaller organizations, orientation may be the responsibility of the new staff member's immediate supervisor. In large hospitality organizations, there will hopefully be a cooperative effort between staff (HR) personnel and line department supervisors or others. The new employee's supervisor, for example, can assist in the orientation program as he/she reviews the organization chart and position description and previews the training program(s) in which the new staff member will participate. Regardless of property size, the basic concerns to be addressed by orientation are the same because the basic needs and concerns of a new staff member do not differ when they are employed by large or small organizations.

HR Management in Action

LET'S GET THIS OVER AND GET TO WORK!

Some hospitality organizations lose opportunities to help their new employees confirm their employment decision was a good one. Have you ever participated in a several-hour (or less) orientation basically focused on policies and rules, "dos and don'ts," and the completion of paperwork? How about an orientation session in which it was very obvious the facilitator had done this many times before and would likely be doing it many times in the future?

These types of orientation sessions are missing the critical "we're glad you're here!" exuberance of a hospitable greeting. Isn't it just as important to meet and greet new employees as it is to do this for guests? If employees model behavior—and they do—what does this "let's get this over and get to work" attitude reflect when it is demonstrated by the HR managers themselves?

Contrast these experiences with others where orientation is an integral part of the on-boarding process. The emphasis is on all of the departments, subsystems, and functions that team members fulfill as they assist each other and the guests. The focus is not just on a specific job but, rather, on the beginning of a rewarding career. Promotion tracks can be discussed during orientation. As well, new employees can learn how HR managers can help them become proficient in their current position and how they can help to plan and implement activities to enhance their own career advancement.

While the above examples may not seem significant, in fact, they are. Each provides a little more evidence about the welcoming culture of the hospitality organization, and new employees can begin to envision an enjoyable and rewarding future within it. The organization benefits as well because, with each successful orientation, it is closer to or becoming more embodied as an employer of choice within the community.

Use an Orientation Checklist

Careful planning of an orientation program is important. Figure 5.2 illustrates a checklist that identifies many concepts that can be addressed in an effective orientation program.

It is important to assemble all needed materials required before the orientation session begins. Some hospitality operations include these in an **orientation kit**. Examples of items that can be included in an orientation kit include a copy of the current organization chart and employee handbook and copies of employee performance appraisal forms and procedures. Other examples include federal, state, and local tax materials; a diagram of the property layout (if it is large); and accident prevention and emergency procedures guidelines.

Orientation kit: A package of written materials given to new employees to supplement the oral information provided during the orientation session.

When Does Orientation End?

Typical staff member orientation sessions require several (or fewer) hours or perhaps a half day (or longer). However, they generally conclude without follow-up sessions. Some hospitality organizations schedule additional orientation sessions several weeks or even longer after the initial session(s). By this time, staff members are familiar with their organization, department, and position. Based on their on-job experiences, they can ask additional questions, participate in discussions, and learn about topics including guest service and teamwork that can be better addressed and understood with personal knowledge of the organization.

ORGANIZATION INTRODUCTION
Welcome new staff member(s)
Present/explain mission statement
Discuss history of organization
Review types of guests served (if applicable)
Note products and services provided
Review current organization chart

STAFF MEMBER – RELATED POLICIES

☐ **APPEARANCE**
___ Hygiene standards
___ Name tag
___ Uniform including shoes
___ Jewelry

☐ **CONDUCT**
___ Attendance
___ Drug-free workplace information
___ Respectful behavior required
___ Harassment policy and discussion

☐ **JOB PERFORMANCE**
___ Position description
___ Work schedules
___ Training programs
___ Breaks
___ Performance evaluation system
___ Probationary period

☐ **EMPLOYEE BENEFITS**
___ Vacation
___ Leaves (personal, military, jury duty, emergency, other)
___ Sick leave
___ Education incentives
___ Insurance programs (medical, dentist, life, disability, other)
___ Workers' compensation
___ Meals/uniform allowances
___ Other: _____
_____
_____

☐ **COMPENSATION INFORMATION**
___ Salary/wage
___ Pay periods; pay day

___ Procedures for checking in and out of work shifts
___ Holiday pay
___ Overtime policies
___ How and when pay is received
___ Compensation increase policies

☐ **SAFETY CONCERNS**
___ Safety training
___ Emergency situations
___ Fire prevention, control, and evacuation
___ Food safety training (general; if applicable)
___ Reporting hazards
___ Reporting injuries

☐ **OTHER ORIENTATION INFORMATION**
___ Smoking
___ Access to facility during nonworking time
___ Personal time
___ Work permits (minors and non-United States citizens)
___ Use of alcohol and drugs on the job

☐ **PHYSICAL FACILITIES**
___ General tour
___ Employee restrooms/lockers
___ Employee dining area
___ First aid
___ Employee entrance
___ Other: _____
_____
_____

☐ **OTHER ORIENTATION ACTIVITIES**
___ Provide employee handbook
___ Answer questions
___ Preview departmental induction and training programs
Other:
_____
_____
_____

Figure 5.2   Sample Orientation Checklist

*Note: if the employees are represented by one or more unions, an overview of union relations information should be provided to applicable employees (see Chapter 12).

HR MANAGEMENT ISSUES 5.2

"I wonder what I'm getting into now," thought Daren, as he parked his car and walked through the parking lot. He had accepted a position as a cook in the food services department of a large hospital.

"I've cooked at several restaurants, and I have learned one thing: I like to cook, to be creative, and to work with a great team that feels like I do," were his next thoughts as he neared the entrance closest to the parking lot.

"However, I've never worked for a health care facility. While it sounds good (great working hours, higher pay, and better benefits), I don't know about the environment with a lot of patients who are going to be depending on me."

As he walked closer to the building, he saw a sign reading, "Patient Entrance–Straight Ahead; Visitors' Entrance–Turn Left; Vendors Proceed to Purchasing Office."

"Well, what do I do now?" thought Daren. "I'm not a patient, I'm not a visitor, and I'm not selling anything. I guess employees know where to go, and they don't need a sign. So what should I do now?"

Case Study Questions

1. What would you do now if you were Daren? Why?

2. What are examples of special orientation tactics that can best help Daren and others without previous health care experience adapt to the unique environment?

3. Should an initial tour of the hospital include all areas or just those in which Daren will be working? Why?

4. Assume the hospital's orientation process is excellent except for the "glitch" about not telling new employees where to report to work. What do you think will be the major differences between this orientation program and a similar (excellent) one in a restaurant?

❖ OTHER EARLY EMPLOYMENT ACTIVITIES

LEARNING OBJECTIVE 4. Describe two final orientation-related activities: departmental induction and orientation follow-up.

A hospitality organization's emphasis on on-boarding continues after the initial orientation process is completed. Two additional processes include those for departmental induction and postorientation follow-up.

Departmental Induction Procedures

Induction relates to the process of providing new employees with basic information that everyone in their department must know and that is unique to their department. For example, everyone in the hospitality operation must know about compensation policies and procedures and the importance of guest service. This information should be part of the orientation program. However, perhaps only food production personnel must know about kitchen workflow concerns and, in a hotel, only front office personnel may need to know about the different classifications of hotel guests.

Hopefully, new employees arrive at their department when there is time for an organized and orderly induction. Contrast this with the unfortunate situation that often arises when a new employee begins work during a busy shift and is expected to become an immediate productive member of the team. Our earlier discussion about the new employee adaptation process addressed the impact of initial on-job experiences. An unplanned induction program can quickly destroy the benefits gained from an effective orientation program.

What are examples of concerns that can be addressed in an induction program? Figure 5.3 presents a checklist of possible activities.

Induction: The process of providing new employees with basic information that everyone in their department must know and that is unique to their department.

Orientation Follow-Up

Use of orientation and departmental induction procedures such as those explained above will take more time and effort than is spent by some hospitality organizations. However, a comprehensive program helps to implement an effective employee adaptation process that produces committed staff members.

DEPARTMENT INDUCTION CHECKLIST

☐ Department introduction
☐ Department mission statement
☐ Review of departmental organization (positions/current incumbents of management/
    supervisory positions)
☐ How department impacts other departments

☐ Position duties/responsibilities
    — Provide/review current job description
    — Explain importance of position and its impact on other department positions
    — Review performance standards and evaluate methods
    — Work schedules (days/hours)
    — Overtime needs (if any)
    — When/how to request assistance

☐ Policies and procedures
    — Emergencies
    — Safety precautions/accident prevention
    — Reporting hazards
    — Sanitation concerns (if applicable)
    — Smoking/eating policies
    — Recording time/attendance
    — Breaks
    — Personal telephone calls
    — Performance appraisal procedures
    — Other: _____
             _____
             _____

☐ Department tour
    — Fire alarms
    — First aid kits
    — Restrooms/lockers
    — Bulletin board
    — Shift check-in procedures
    — Employee entrances
    — Smoking areas
    — Explain work flow (workstation layout)
    — Locations of major equipment
    — Other: _____
             _____
             _____

☐ Introduction to department employees
    — On-job managers/supervisors
    — Other on-duty employees

Figure 5.3   Sample Department Induction Activities Checklist

Basic Orientation Principles Are Useful in All Hospitality Segments

The most important orientation principles are universal because "people are people," and they have the same basic concerns and react in much the same way in similar situations.

Here are some principles that should be incorporated into all orientation programs:

◆ Carefully plan them to ensure they are organized and provide consistent information each time a new employee participates in them.

◆ Be sure the new employee is able to meet other employees.

◆ Alert current coworkers that the new employee will be beginning work.

◆ Make new staff members feel comfortable by informing them about the "basics" before they arrive for the first day. Examples may include where to park, which entry door to use, and who and where they meet their on-job contact.

◆ When possible, use multiple orientation presenters.

◆ If possible, provide material that new employees can take off-site to read at their own pace and determine whether they have questions.

◆ Solicit feedback about orientation sessions so they can be continually improved.

Note that none of the principles listed above have any economic cost, and each can help new employees feel welcome to the hospitality organization and pleased about their employment decision.

Orientation follow-up activities are also important. It is not sufficient to say, "If you have any questions, just ask someone," or "Just assume you're doing okay unless someone tells you differently." New staff members should understand they will be participating in a well-organized training program designed to help them perform job tasks that meet quality and quantity standards.

The trainer may or may not be the same staff member who provided orientation and induction information. If so (as is typical in a small operation), this provides an opportunity for continuity as the orientation/induction/training processes evolve. When different staff members are involved (as is more likely in a large organization), those involved in orientation and induction can still offer genuine enthusiasm and provide follow-up assistance as requested. They can regularly check back with the new staff member and answer questions that arise after the orientation and induction procedures have concluded.

You've learned that these early on-job experiences are important for the employee and the organization. Therefore they should be evaluated to determine whether they are cost-effective (worth more than what they cost) and whether improvements are possible.

Feedback from new staff members several months (or longer) after they have completed these initial on-job activities can help. Perhaps they can complete anonymous surveys or participate in interviews conducted for that purpose or as part of more general efforts to receive employee input about operational improvements. Exit interviews of departing employees may also be helpful.

Employees will, one way or another, learn about organization, their position, and their employer's expectations. It is better for them to acquire this information through a formal, planned, organized, and hospitable orientation effort than to "pick it up" in casual conversations with and by watching their peers on the job.

∴ EMPLOYEE HANDBOOKS

LEARNING OBJECTIVE 5. State the importance of employee handbooks, and list policy and procedure topics typically included in them.

Employee handbooks are personnel management tools used in hospitality organizations of all sizes.

Employee Handbooks Are Necessary

An employee handbook is a centralized source of information detailing an employer's policies, benefits, and employment practices. It is typically distributed and discussed as part of the general orientation process for new employees. This enables staff members to review information presented during the orientation, and it provides other information that, because of time limitations, may be best delivered in this manner.

Employee handbooks must be current, and plans and processes must be place to provide updated material as well. These resources must be professionally presented; clean and current copies make a better statement about the hospitality organization and the importance it attaches to providing employee information than do their counterparts that appear to be "thrown together" haphazardly. Note that some organizations make their employee handbook available on the company's intranet. This makes it readily available (copies will not be "lost") and easy to update.

Employee handbooks tell new and all other staff members about the organization. They detail all policies/procedures to which the employer/employee agree, and they can be referenced by courts seeking to define terms of the employment agreement if disputes arise.

Typically, employee handbooks should indicate that the hospitality operation has the right to modify, alter, or eliminate any/all contents at any time. Further, it is important for the handbook to indicate that it is not a contract. The organization's attorney should be consulted as the employee handbook is developed and, most certainly, before it is circulated.

Important Policies and Procedures Are Identified

Figure 5.4 lists a wide range of topics that might be applicable to hospitality organizations and that could be addressed in an employee handbook. However, not all topics are relevant or useful for all properties.

Managers can use a questioning approach to help determine useful topics. Do new or longer-tenured staff members have questions about issues related to the topic? Is there an inconsistent understanding about how, if at all, an issue is managed from the perspective of subordinate staff? When answered affirmatively, these and related questions may determine the need for new or revised policies and procedures.

It's the Law

Can policies contained in employee handbooks be considered a contract that must be followed without exception? Or, alternatively, are they guidelines that generally explain requirements and how staff members are normally treated?

Employee handbooks or policies in them might be considered a binding part of the employee relationship if the policy language is such that an employee could reasonably believe a contractual offer was being made. Careful wording is required to help ensure that employees will not construe policies to be contractual promises.

One of the most significant legal concerns relates to the at-will employment relationship that exists when employers can hire any employee they wish and dismiss that staff member with or without cause at any time. Note that at-will employment also permits employees to terminate their work relationships anytime they decide to do so. Mixed messages can be created when, for example, handbook policies specify detailed discipline and discharge procedures that must be followed before termination. As well, if statements such as "our employees are our family" or similar messages are made, readers can perceive them to supersede at-will disclaimers.

Absenteeism	Drug Testing	Leave of Absence
Accessibility for Disabled	Drug Use	Leaves
Accidents	Drug-Free Awareness Program	Leaving Department
Accrual of Vacation	Drug-Free Workplace	Leaving Employment
Advancement	Drugs	Lockers
Alcohol Testing	Educational Assistance	Lost Time Claims
Americans with Disabilities Act	Educational Leave	Meal Allowance/ Periods
Announcements of Openings	Emergency Plans/ Preparedness	Medical Claims
Appearance and Grooming	Employee Assistance Program	Military Leave
Appraisal	Employee Badges	Modified Duty
Attendance	Employee File	Multiple Employment
Awards	Employee Identification Program	New Jobs
Badges (name tags)		On-Call Pay
Benefits	Employee of the Month/ Year	Orientation Period
Bereavement Leaves		Overtime
Bids	Employee Performance Appraisal	Overtime Pay
Breaks		Paid Holidays
Call-Back Pay	Employee-at-Will	Parking
Call-Out Pay	Equal Employment	Pay and Pay Periods
Changing Departments	Ethics	Payroll Deductions
Child Care Leave	Evaluation	Pension
Code of Ethics	Exit Interview	Personal Business
Commendations	Expenses, Noneducational	Personal Code of Conduct
Commercial Driver's License	Extended Sick Pay	
Compensation	Family Medical Leave Act	Personal Holidays
Competence	Fitness for Duty	Personal Leave
Complaints	Funeral Leave	Personal Records
Compilance	Gifts/Gratuities	Posting
Computer Use (Personal)	Grant Employees	Probationary Employees/ Periods
Concerns	Grants	
Conferences	Grievance/Complaint Procedures	Problems
Confidentiality		Professional Dues
Conflicts of Interest	Harassment	Professionalism
Consultants (Use of)	Health Insurance	Qualifications
Continuing Education	Hiring	Qualifying Periods
Controlled Substances	Hiring of Family Members	Recall
Conventional Standards of Workplace Behavior	Holidays	Recording Work Time
	Hourly Associate Forum	Recruiting
Corporate Compliance	Hours of Work	Reference Checks
Counseling	Identification	Relationships (on-job)
Criminal Convictions	Industrial Injury	Resignation
Customer Service	Integrity	Retirement Programs
Dental Insurance	Investigation	Return of Organization's Property
Department Transfer Questionnaire	Job Evaluation	
	Job Opportunities	Return to Work
Differentials	Job Postings	Safety/Security
Disability Insurance	Job Qualifications	Salary
Disciplinary Process	Job Rotation	Schedule Posting
Discrimination Claims	Job Vacancies	Scheduling Vacation
Displacements	Jury Duty	Seniority
Dress Code	Layoffs	Seniority Calculation

Figure 5.4   Sample Employee Handbook Topics

Service Awards Recognition Program	Termination	Vacation Accrual
Severance Pay	Time Off without Pay	Vacation Pay
Sexual Harassment	Training	Vacation Scheduling
Sick Pay	Transfers	Vacations
Sick Time Accumulation	Transportation Allowance	Violence
Sick Time Buy-Back	Transportation Work Program	Voluntary Time Off
Smoking	Travel	Wages
Staff Reductions	Tuition	Weapons
Suggestions	Tuition Grant	Weather (Inclement)
Tax-Sheltered Annuity	Tuition Reimbursement	Work Rules
Telephone Calls (Personal)	Uniforms	Work Time
	Vacancies	Workers' Compensation

Figure 5.4   *(continued)*

Keep Employee Handbooks Current

To be useful, employee handbooks must be kept current. While this seems obvious, busy hospitality managers sometimes replace written policies and procedures recorded in an employee handbook with "understandings" based on "how we've done things lately."

Changes typically begin with small breaks in or small discrepancies with procedures that go unchallenged. For example, a restaurant's uniform code requires solid-toed shoes for kitchen workers to prevent punctures from dropped knives or burns from spilled hot liquids. However, a cook occasionally, then frequently, and then always, arrives at work in canvas tennis shoes. "Bending the rules" the first time may have no immediate consequences. However, it may establish the precedent that the policy is not always necessary, it is not important, and applies to only some employees.

Small lapses in policies and procedures can lead to larger ones. They can send the message that these management and communication tools can be disregarded when it is convenient to do so and that they involve personal interpretation.

Policies and procedures should be designed for a specific purpose and, if they are not necessary, should be discarded or revised. They should, therefore, be consistently followed. To help prevent the inconsistent application of policies and procedures, several tactics can be used.

- ◆ Standards should be respected. Policies and procedures should be followed all the time, and their expectations should be consistently met.
- ◆ Managers, supervisors, and employees should model examples for their peers.
- ◆ Inform staff members about the reasons for the policies and procedures.
- ◆ Information about the most important policies and procedures should be presented during orientation. Other policies can be discussed on an ongoing basis as part of in-service or other training programs.
- ◆ Staff members should recognize that compliance with reasonable policies and procedures is part of the agreement with, and relationship between, their employers and themselves.

HR TERMS

The following terms were defined in this chapter:

Adaptation (to organization)   Mission statement   Induction

Orientation   Orientation kit

FOR YOUR CONSIDERATION

1. What is the impact of one's orientation experiences on his/her ability to perform work that meets required standards?

2. What are some early job experiences that you liked in previous positions you have held? Some that you disliked? How did each of these experiences impact your attitude about the organization, your manager/supervisor, and your position? What suggestions would you make to correct the things that you disliked about your early job experiences?

3. A. What are some first-day-on-the-job experiences that would make you feel good about your employment decision and your new employer? Why would they make you feel good?

B. What are some first-day-on-the-job experiences that would make you feel bad about your employment decision and your new employer? Why would they make you feel bad?

4. Assume you are the HR manager responsible for keeping your organization's employee handbook updated. What process would you use to do so? How would you provide employees with the updated information?

5. Assume you are a department manager in a hospitality organization, and you are facilitating a staff meeting. Two new employees will begin work in your department next week. Develop an outline about what you would say as you announced that these two new staff members will be joining your department.

:::::: CASE STUDY :::

Apply HR Management Principles

"I guess there are advantages and disadvantages to being hired at the height of the busy season at a ski resort," said Sergio as he sat in the employee lounge with Patty during a well-deserved break.

"I like my job in the maintenance department, especially the gang I work with, and it's great to have all of the tools and supplies needed for routine maintenance. That has not been the case in some of my previous positions, and it really caused me to stress out!"

"We're all glad you're here," replied Patty, a housekeeping supervisor. "I didn't know what you would say now after I heard you talk earlier about your initial experiences with our resort that were less than perfect. I remember you telling me that you didn't know the location of the work sites for many of the maintenance tasks because the property is so large. I also remember you telling me how silly you must have looked to your peers because you didn't know specific maintenance

tasks or the required tools for servicing some of our specialized equipment. In fact, you said you had been here two weeks before you even met the department head.

"You're right," said Sergio. "The initial orientation process could have been much more organized and better delivered. If it was, I wouldn't have felt so awkward, and I could have better helped the resort by doing things right the first time without the need for lots of rework. I remember thinking a couple of times that they weren't treating me very well, and the fact that everyone appeared to be so busy, and weren't doing it intentionally, didn't really soften my feelings.

"Since then, I guess I've become more 'neutral,' where I could 'take the job or leave it,' to my present attitude that it's getting to be a better place to work."

"I don't think things would be very different in my housekeeping department if you started in the middle of the season," commented Patty. "I've always thought, incorrectly, that the excuse of 'being busy' was accepted by new staff members. But now I see that managers owe their staff members more than promises that 'things will get better.'

"I'm going to make some changes and suggest to other department supervisors that they consider the need for changes in their departments as well. Thanks for the education, Sergio."

Dimension: Employer-of-Choice Concerns

1. How do you think most potential job applicants would react to the resort's reputation of "rough starts, but it gets better after you've been working there for a while"?

2. Many restaurant guests say almost nothing to friends if they have a good dining experience, but they say many things to contacts when they have a poor dining experience. Do you think the tendency to say a few nice things and many bad things is also true about one's experience with an employer? Why or why not?

Dimension: HR Issues

1. Since the ski resort is large, it likely has an HR department. Is it possible that these specialists are not aware of their property's problems with orientation programs? If they are, what are reasons they might not be more proactive in addressing issues? If they are not, what changes in the property's communication network might be appropriate?

2. What, if any, role should HR personnel play in advising (improving) the orientation program? What should be the role, if any, of top-level managers?

Dimension: Employee Retention Issues

1. What impact, if any, do you think inadequate orientation programs have on employee retention rates?

2. How might you, as a department manager, better determine how the quality of new employee orientation affects the property's turnover rates?

3. Assume you could prove a positive relationship between effective orientation programs and improved employee retention and that it was cost-effective to improve the orientation program. What are potential responses of higher-level officials at this resort to this information?

INTERNET ACTIVITIES

1. General business and management resources contain information applicable to the development and implementation of orientation programs for personnel in the hospitality industry. Enter the search term "planning employee orientation programs" into your favorite search engine. Develop a list of 10–15 tactics noted during your Internet search and then rank them from 1 to the end of the list in terms of those that you feel would be most appreciated by new entry-level employees.

2. HR managers can obtain much online assistance as they develop employee handbooks. They can, for example, review sample handbooks, analyze and/or purchase hard copy and software guides to develop handbooks, and review sample handbook topics. They can also review websites of organizations that sell handbook development resources and provide customized services.

Enter the phrase "developing employee handbooks" into your favorite search engine. Review several websites and then write a list of the best principles that should be used when developing this important HR tool.

© Martin Barraud / Getty Images

CHAPTER

6

PLANNING TRAINING PROGRAMS

CHAPTER OUTLINE

LEARNING OBJECTIVES

When they complete this chapter, readers will be able to:

1. Describe the benefits of performance-based training and discuss common obstacles to and myths about training.

2. Apply basic principles to perform a position analysis.

3. Apply basic principles when training programs are planned and implemented.

4. List characteristics important for an effective trainer.

5. Explain procedures used to plan for training activities.

Impact on HR Management

Effective training is the best way to ensure that staff members make maximum contributions to an organization's success. This is critical because, in the labor-intensive hospitality industry, employees are an organization's most important asset.

HR managers know there are numerous benefits to training. Unfortunately, these are sometimes overlooked because of training obstacles and myths that speak against an emphasis on training. The best HR managers know about these challenges and are spokespersons for the importance of training in their operations.

Before one can train, it is necessary to know how the tasks for which the training is provided should be performed. A position analysis can be used for this purpose; this involves developing task lists and job breakdowns that incorporate the operation's performance standards. The process ends with this information summarized in job descriptions.

The best training is not possible unless basic principles are used to plan training activities. Also, the best trainers must be selected and taught how to train.

A six-step process can be used to plan for training, and it involves defining training needs, which in turn drive the training objectives. Then broad training plans and more specific training lessons can be prepared. These materials can be compiled into a training handbook for future use, and, finally, the trainees must be prepared for the activities they will experience.

While the process as explained above may seem complex, it really isn't. This chapter addresses these concepts in a way that highlights their practical application in any hospitality operation.

❖❖ TRAINING OVERVIEW

LEARNING OBJECTIVE 1. Describe the benefits of performance-based training and discuss common obstacles to and myths about training.

Hospitality operations are labor-intensive. While technology has reduced the need for staff in departments such as accounting and the front office, it generally has not affected the number of employees required to produce and deliver most of the products and services guests desire. Recently employed staff must acquire the knowledge and skills needed to become proficient in their positions. Their more experienced peers must obtain new knowledge and skills to keep up with an ever-changing workplace. Effective **training** is critical to attaining these goals.

Performance-Based Training Is Needed

Numerous responsibilities and tasks demand the ongoing attention of those responsible for training, and they are confronted with a challenge of determining whether "nice-to-know" or, alternatively, only "need-to-know" information and skills should be emphasized. In fact, training must be **cost-effective**: It must provide time and money benefits that outweigh its costs. To do so, training must be **performance-based**. It should be planned and delivered in a systematic way to help trainees become better able to perform the tasks that are essential for their job. The success of training can then be demonstrated by considering the extent to which knowledge and skills improve as a result of the training.

Training: The process of developing a staff member's knowledge, skills, and attitudes necessary to perform tasks required for a position.

Cost-effective: A term that indicates that an item or activity, such as training, is worth more than it costs to provide it.

Performance-based (training): A systematic way of organizing training to help trainees learn the tasks considered essential for effective on-job performance.

Does Training Affect Attitudes?

We have defined *training* as "the process of developing a staff member's knowledge, skills, and attitudes necessary to perform tasks required for a position." Can a good trainer modify an employee's attitude with training? Maybe so—but maybe not! The **morale** of staff members generally improves when they are impressed with an employer's ongoing commitment to provide training that allows advancement to more responsible, higher-paying positions. In this example, training can have a positive impact on attitudes.

However, assume a training program has the goal of ensuring that food safety concerns are a priority for food production personnel. The training provides important information about this topic. If a cook has a positive attitude and wants to use the safe food-handling practices he or she has learned, the training is successful. If the trainee is not motivated to follow safe food-handling practices, the training will not be successful even though the "why" and "how" aspects of training were learned.

Morale: The total of one's feelings about his or her employer, work environment, peers, and other aspects of the job.

Performance-based training is typically best delivered at the job site during one-on-one interactions between the trainer and trainee. Conceptually, this is much better than group training. Why? The trainer can focus on what the individual must learn, **feedback** can be immediate, and training can be delivered at the best pace for the individual trainee.

Feedback: Response provided to a question or larger-scale inquiry such as a customer survey.

Training Benefits

There are numerous benefits to the hospitality organization when effective training programs are in place.

- **Improved performance**—Trainees learn knowledge and skills to perform required tasks more effectively, and their on-job performance improves.

- **Reduced operating costs**—Improved job performance helps to reduce errors and rework, and associated costs are reduced. Workers performing their jobs correctly will be more productive, and fewer labor hours will be needed.

Performance-Based Training

The need for training to be performance-based can create a significant hurdle because the following are required to do so:

- All **tasks** in a position must be identified.
- The specific knowledge and skills required to perform each task must be known.
- Training that addresses all of the knowledge and skills required for each task must be developed.
- Competencies (standards of knowledge, skills, and abilities required for successful performance) must be identified. These should be shared with the trainees to help them understand what the training program will accomplish.
- A formalized evaluation process is needed. The worth of training represents the difference between what trainees know and can do before and after the training.

Task: A specific and observable work activity that is one component of a position and that has a definite beginning and end. For example, one task performed by a cook may be to prepare a Béarnaise sauce using a standardized recipe.

◆ **More satisfied guests**—Training can yield more service-oriented employees who know how to please guests.

◆ **Fewer operating problems**—Busy managers can focus on priority concerns and will not need to address routine operating problems caused by inappropriate training.

◆ **Lower employee turnover rates**—Fewer new staff members become necessary as turnover rates decrease. Those who are properly trained and rewarded for successful performance are less likely to leave, and managers have less need to recruit new employees.

◆ **Higher levels of work quality**—Effective training identifies quality standards that define acceptable product and service outputs. Trained employees are more interested in operating equipment correctly, in preparing the "right" products, and in properly interacting with guests.

◆ **Easier to recruit new staff**—Satisfied staff members tell their family and friends about their positive work experiences, and their contacts may become candidates for position vacancies that arise. Hospitality operations that emphasize training can evolve into "employers of choice" that provide "first choice" rather than "last choice" employment opportunities.

◆ **Greater profits**—If guests are more satisfied and revenues increase, and if labor and other operating costs are reduced, there is significant potential for increased profits. In the long run, training must be "value-added" and should be measured by the difference between the increased profits and the added training costs. While this measurement is not easy to make, most industry observers believe that, if done correctly, training will always "win" in the comparison.

◆ **More professional staff**—Professionals want to do their job as best they can, and this is only possible with appropriate training.

HR Management: Impact on New Team Members

New employees typically begin training when they complete orientation and induction programs. Therefore early training activities may still be considered part of the on-boarding experiences addressed in the previous two chapters.

Properly planned and implemented training further confirms the new staff members' employer-of-choice perceptions. Great training experiences will help them "feel good" about themselves and their employer. These positive attitudes can have a significant influence on one's overall perceptions of the workplace.

There are additional ways that well-designed training programs impact new employees:

◆ **Reduced stress**—Those who can correctly perform required tasks will feel better about doing their jobs. Stress created by interactions with supervisors who are upset about improper work outputs, from peers who must do rework because of the new employees' errors, and/or from frustrated guests about service and/or quality defects will be reduced.

◆ **Increased opportunities for job advancement**—Who is most likely to be promoted: a competent or an incompetent employee? Training can assist new staff in attaining their long-term promotion goals.

◆ **Improved staff relationships**—Those who can properly do their jobs are more likely to be part of a team effort, and this acceptance will make new employees feel more comfortable on the job.

Training Obstacles

In spite of the above benefits, training does not always receive the proper priority. Obstacles to effective training can include:

◆ **Insufficient time** for managers, supervisors, and/or trainers to plan for and deliver training.

◆ **Too much time** required for trainees to be away from their positions when participating in the training.

◆ **Lack of financial** resources to compensate for the trainer's and trainees' time and to acquire necessary training resources.

◆ **Trainers' insufficient knowledge and skills**—People must be taught how to train just as they must be taught to perform any other unfamiliar task. Formal "train-the-trainer" programs are not provided by many hospitality organizations.

◆ **Lack of quality resources available for training**—Managers and supervisors do not have the time, knowledge, or ability to develop training videos and/or to prepare extensive or sophisticated training resources or training evaluation tools. If these items can't be developed in house, are they available **off-the-shelf**? Resources addressing generic topics such as a supervision tactics, sanitation, and safety can be purchased for a modest cost. However, excellent trainers are creative, and they would never elect to "not train" simply because supplemental resources are unavailable. The alternative: Take time to develop several basic training tools, including those described later in this chapter.

◆ **Scheduling conflicts**—When can front desk agents meet to learn a new way to perform a task? Managers must schedule training sessions while at the same time scheduling other employees to perform required work tasks.

◆ **Turnover**—In many hospitality operations some staff members leave within a few months (or less) of initial employment. Managers may think, "Why train employees if they don't remain on the job long enough to use what they have learned?" In fact, as noted above, effective training can reduce turnover rates, and property managers who do not train employees are likely contributing to their unacceptably high turnover rate.

◆ **Insufficient lead time** between one's first day on the job and the time when he or she must begin performing work tasks. Hopefully, a **warm body syndrome** is never used as a selection tactic.

◆ **Difficulty in maintaining training consistency**—When individual trainers plan and deliver training activities based on what they think staff must know, the "what" and "how" of training will likely be inconsistent. Then those who train may begin to think that, "We tried to train, and it hasn't worked very well. There must be a better problem resolution alternative than training. What else can we do?"

◆ **Trainer apathy**—There should be reasons for trainers to want to train. Benefits for successful training duties can include special privileges, compensation increases, promotion consideration, educational opportunities, and/or recognition. By contrast, when trainers must assume these duties in addition to other tasks, if they do not receive train-the-trainer training, and/or if there is little (or no) support for training, why should trainers want to do so?

Off-the-shelf (training materials): Generic training materials typically addressing general topics of interest to many trainers that can be used if company-specific resources are not available.

Warm body syndrome: A selection error that involves hiring the first person who applies for a vacant position.

Training Myths

Myths (untruths) about training can create obstacles:

◆ **Training is easy**—In fact, when training involves only a trainee "tagging along" with a more experienced staff member, it is easy. However, the lack of planning and the increased possibility that basic training principles will be disregarded increases the likelihood that this form of training will be ineffective.

◆ **Training costs too much**—Hospitality operations with a history of inadequate training yielding unsatisfactory results may not invest in the resources to plan and deliver more effective training. "Been there, done that" is a philosophy that can easily evolve.

A "Picture" of Training

When you consider the training obstacles and myths noted in this chapter, a "picture" of training in many hospitality properties begins to emerge. Top-level managers may not commit resources to training because they are unaware of its benefits and/or because of previous negative training experiences. Lack of resources, training knowledge, and training plans work against training priorities and/or minimize effectiveness when training is offered.

Employee resistance can also arise when training must compete with the limited time in which to perform required work. This is especially so if staff members have not experienced positive results from previous training and/or if they are "turned off" by poorly designed and delivered or inadequate training efforts.

Professional development program: Planned educational and/or training activities to prepare an employee for successively more responsible positions in an organization or industry.

◆ **Training is a staff function**—Staff positions are manned by technical specialists who provide advice to but do not make decisions for people in "chain of command" line positions. Training is a line function that is too important to delegate to staff HR personnel, if they are available.

◆ **Only new staff need training**—New employees do need training, but so do their more experienced peers when, for example, operating procedures are revised or new equipment is purchased. As well, experienced employees may want to participate in **professional development programs**.

◆ **There is no time for training**—Many priorities compete for hospitality managers' time. In this context, training is often deemphasized, and available time is allocated to other tasks.

✖ POSITION ANALYSIS

Position analysis: A process that identifies each task in a position and explains how it should be done, with a focus on knowledge and skills.

LEARNING OBJECTIVE 2. Apply basic principles to perform a position analysis.

A **position analysis** identifies each task in a position and explains how it should be done, with a focus on knowledge and skills. As such, it becomes the foundation for developing

✖ HR MANAGEMENT ISSUES 6.1

"I don't understand," said Ralph. "What's the big deal about training? Maybe you and I are smarter than the kids coming to work today. However, I remember watching and listening, and following people who taught me everything I needed to know about my job."

Ralph and Lorine were supervisors talking about the hotel's department staff meeting they had just attended. The department head had announced that all staff were to participate in two training programs: guest service and technology updates.

"You're right about the past, Ralph," said Lorine. "However, you and I can cite lots of problems at our hotel. Will proper training reduce them? Do things need to change to remain competitive and to keep our good employees?"

"It's easy to keep good employees; just pay them more," replied Ralph. "You and I are good employees, and we learned by watching. That's good enough today because it was good enough yesterday."

Case Study Questions

1. What are your reactions to Ralph's thoughts about training?

2. How can effective training help a hospitality organization remain competitive and retain its best employees?

3. What do you think of Ralph's comments about compensation and employee turnover?

Which Comes First?

A position analysis identifies tasks that are included in job descriptions, which in turn are used for recruitment. Therefore one can argue that a position analysis should be developed before the job description. Likewise, since a position analysis identifies tasks and how they should be done, it is required before training programs can be planned.

In practice, basic tasks in most job descriptions do not change frequently, nor do the procedures to do them correctly. Therefore, once developed, position analysis information needs to be modified only as position responsibilities change (tasks are reassigned) or when new products, services, equipment, or other changes that directly affect tasks in a job or the procedures required to perform them well are made.

training programs that provide basic information about a position to new employees. Position analysis can also be done to study specific tasks that require revision because of, for example, changes created by technology and other tasks that create operating or guest service–related problems.

There are four basic steps in the position analysis process: prepare a **task list**, develop a **task breakdown**, consider **performance standards**, and write a job description.

The sequence of these four steps is shown in Figure 6.1.

Step 1: Prepare a Task List

A task list indicates all tasks included in a position and focuses on "how-to" activities that a successful employee must learn and do. Staff members in each position must perform several tasks that typically require numerous **steps**.

Consider a dishwasher who performs numerous tasks that include operating the dishwashing machine. To successfully wash dishes, the employee must complete several steps, including rinsing soiled plates, properly placing dishes in a rack, and removing and placing clean dishes in mobile carts after washing.

Task list: A list of all tasks in a position.

Task breakdown: A description of how one task in a task list should be performed.

Performance standards: Measurable quality and/or quantity indicators that identify when a staff member is performing a task correctly.

Step: One element in a task. For example, to prepare sandwiches (a task), a cook must know how to portion ingredients using portion control tools (one step).

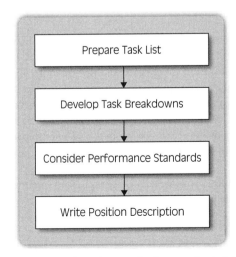

Figure 6.1 Four Steps in the Position Analysis Process

What is the complete list of tasks the dishwasher must perform? The answer to this question is indicated in a detailed task list. Procedures to develop a task list include some or all of the following activities:

◆ Obtain input from the supervisors of and several experienced workers in the position being analyzed. Good interview questions are open-ended (e.g., "Describe what you do in a normal work shift from when you begin work until you complete your shift"). Detailed interviews can include questions about the time spent on specific tasks, position responsibilities, instances of interaction with other staff, and the importance, frequency, and difficulty of performing specific tasks.

◆ Use available written information, such as job descriptions, that provides a summary of tasks, existing task lists, and training materials currently used to teach new staff about their jobs.

◆ Use a simple questionnaire that asks, "What do you and others in your position do as part of your job?"

◆ Observe staff members as they work in their positions; compare what they actually do with the tasks they identified when questioned about their responsibilities.

◆ If practical, work for a period of time in the position(s) for which a task list is being developed.

After input and analysis of the above information, an extensive list of tasks can be identified. Then a validation process can help to (1) condense/combine similar tasks, (2) clarify tasks, and (3) note factors such as work shift or production volume that impact task responsibilities. A format for a task list is shown in Figure 6.2.

Once developed, the scope of training requirements for a specific position is known. New trainees must be taught how to correctly perform each task in their new position. The definition of "correct performance" is addressed in the task breakdown.

Step 2: Develop Task Breakdowns

A task breakdown indicates how each task in the task list should be performed by specifying the series of steps necessary for completion. For example, one task for a dishwasher may be "to properly operate a dishwashing machine." The task involves several steps, including loading the machine, monitoring its operation, and adding additional detergent, wetting agents, and/or other chemicals.

There are various benefits of task breakdowns:

◆ They indicate how a task should be done to best ensure performance standards are attained.

◆ Trainees benefit from written instructions. A trainer can review a task breakdown with a trainee, who can then demonstrate it using the task breakdown as a guide. Another benefit: Trainees can practice each step and then compare procedures used with those noted in the task breakdown.

Even uncomplicated task steps can usually be done more than one way. For example, a room service attendant could push or pull a food cart from a hotel elevator. Which way is the best (safest)? Why? Written communication in a task breakdown is more precise than spoken words. Properly done, there is less chance that information will be misinterpreted.

Task breakdowns can be written using the same basic process that yielded the task list. Experienced staff can be interviewed, available information (existing task breakdowns and/or existing training documents, for example) can be studied, and/or employees can be asked to write, in sequence, the steps needed to perform a task. They can also be observed, and brainstorming sessions can be used.

Writing a task breakdown does not need to be complicated or time-consuming and can be cost-effective. Consider a simple process such as when a manager or trainer:

◆ watches an experienced staff member perform a task.

◆ records each activity (step) in sequence.

◆ asks the experienced staff member to review the information to confirm its accuracy.

Position: _____

Staff working in this position must be able to perform the following tasks:

1.

2.

3.

4.

5.

6.

7.

8.

9.

10.

11.

12.

13.

14.

15.

Notes:

Date of last review:

Task list approved by:

Figure 6.2 Task List

- ◆ shares the task analysis information with other experienced staff members and their supervisors.
- ◆ makes modifications, if necessary, to yield the agreed-upon work method.
- ◆ reviews the task worksheet with the staff member's supervisor and the employee.
- ◆ validates the agreed-upon task breakdown by observing an experienced person performing the task using the identified procedures.

Figure 6.3 illustrates the format for a task breakdown worksheet.

Step 3: Consider Performance Standards

Performance standards specify required **quality** and quantity outputs for each task. For example, the proper quality of a restaurant's dessert is that which is expected when the applicable standard recipe is followed. The quantity of work output expected of a front desk agent in a hotel considers the number of guests to be checked in during a shift. Quality requirements cannot be sacrificed as quantity requirements are attained.

It is important that proper performance be clearly defined so employees know what is expected of them and managers know when performance is acceptable. A training goal is to teach

Quality: The essential characteristics consistently required for a product or service to meet the appropriate standard(s).

Position: _____

Task: _____

Date of Observation: _____

Employee Name: _____

Observer: _____

Task Step	What Is Done	Tools/Equipment	Comments

General Comments:

Figure 6.3 Task Breakdown Worksheet

HR MANAGEMENT ISSUES 6.2

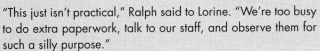

"This just isn't practical," Ralph said to Lorine. "We're too busy to do extra paperwork, talk to our staff, and observe them for such a silly purpose."

Ralph was referring to his department head's request that supervisors help to develop new job descriptions because the current ones had not been revised for years. The recommended approach was to ask employees in selected positions and their supervisors to list the tasks the employees normally perform. Two supervisors and two employees would then review the list and develop a final document. "I wish I knew what was going on around here," said Ralph. "When are we supposed to get our regular work done?"

"You're right," said Lorine. "I'm not sure what's going on."

Case Study Questions

1. What is the "communication problem" that seems to be causing Ralph and Lorine to feel as they do?

2. If you were Ralph's and Lorine's manager, how would you seek their cooperation in revising job descriptions?

3. What suggestions can you make to ensure the job description revision process is "practical"?

a trainee how to correctly perform a task, and the definition of correct refers to both quality and quantity dimensions.

Task performance standards should be reasonable (challenging but achievable). Staff should be trained in procedures specified by task breakdowns, and they must be given the tools and equipment needed to attain the performance standards.

Performance standards must also be specific so they can be measured. Which standard is better stated: "The front desk agent should be able to check in guests as quickly as possible" or "The front desk agent should be able to check in guests using the procedures specified in the task breakdown"? The latter standard is best because it can be objectively measured.

Step 4: Write a Job Description

A job description lists the major tasks that comprise a position. You've learned about the role of job descriptions in recruitment and training. They also assist with supervision; staff members should normally perform only those tasks noted in them. As well, they can be used for performance evaluation activities that consider the extent to which staff adequately perform the tasks in their position.

✷ TRAINING PRINCIPLES

LEARNING OBJECTIVE 3. Apply basic principles when training programs are planned and implemented.

There is a saying that "an organization pays for training even if it doesn't offer it." This recognizes that developing and delivering training takes time and money to do well. In the absence of training, however, time and money are wasted because of errors and rework, and guests are less likely to receive the proper quality of offered products and services.

If one accepts the idea that managers will, one way or another, pay for training, it makes good business sense to implement effective training that returns benefits exceeding costs. A first step is to incorporate several basic principles that should be included in the training process. The following apply to the largest and smallest hospitality operations regardless of location, type of guests served, or financial objectives being pursued.

◆ **Training Principle 1**—*Trainers Must Know How to Train.* In many hospitality properties, the supervisor and/or a peer of a new staff member serves as the trainer. In the former case, the supervisor may have been a "good" employee who is promoted and now performs tasks, including training, that were not part of their previous position. One does not become an effective trainer by "magic" or by default. Instead, he or she must be taught how to train, and "train-the-trainer" programs are needed to provide necessary knowledge and skills.

This principle also applies to a new employee's peer who will conduct training. If training fails because the trainer doesn't know how to do it properly, the problem rests with the manager, not with the trainer. Effective training requires more than just one's willingness to do it.

◆   **Training Principle 2**—*Trainees Must Want to Learn and Need Motivation to Do So.* The old expression "You can lead a horse to water, but you can't make it drink" applies here. Trainees must want to learn and they must recognize its worth. "Because the boss says it is necessary" is not a meaningful reason from the perspective of most staff. By contrast, the reason "This training is a step in a career-long professional development program to help you become eligible for promotion" may be of interest to many trainees.

◆   **Training Principle 3**—*Training Must Focus on Real Problems.* Problems are frequently encountered for which training is believed to be a resolution tactic. It would seem, then, that this principle is frequently used. However, think about the content of some training programs, such as detailed motivational theories in a supervisory session that must be interpreted and then applied to the job. Effective trainers must constantly consider whether training should address "nice-to-know" or "need-to-know" issues in the context of the specific training program being planned.

◆   **Training Principle 4**—*Training Must Emphasize Application.* Most people learn best by doing, and "hands-on" training using an individualized training program is typically the best way to teach many tasks to entry-level employees.

You've learned that training should be performance-based. However, training can also present information that extends beyond one's position or department. For example, shouldn't all staff members learn about their organization's values, vision, and mission? What should every staff member in every department know about what their employer intends to do, how it adds value, and how it intends to act? How much, if any, of the organization's long-range plan should be explained? What about the organization's philosophy and policies relative to guest service?

Perhaps these topics are addressed during orientation, but ongoing formal and informal training opportunities may also be planned for more experienced staff. Fortunately, basic training principles apply to these situations as well as to more traditional task-focused activities.

◆   **Training Principle 5**—*Training Should Consider the Trainees' Life and Professional Experiences.* Good trainers establish a benchmark of what trainees already know and can do and then build on this foundation of knowledge and skills. This tactic maximizes the worth of training by emphasizing the most important subject matter with which the trainee is unfamiliar. Fortunately, one-on-one training is frequently the training method of choice, and skilled trainers can focus on what the trainee doesn't know instead of repeating what is known.

◆   **Training Principle 6**—*Training Should Be Informal.* The best training is normally personalized and conducted in the workplace with individualized interaction between the trainer and the trainee. It is planned for delivery at a pace that is best for the trainee and addresses the trainee's specific questions and needs as they arise.

◆   **Training Principle 7**—*A Variety of Training Methods Should Be Used.* Do employees learn when a trainer quickly shows them how to do something but doesn't allow them to practice immediately after the training? By contrast, training that allows for demonstration, practice, and comparison of written information with how tasks are actually done is more likely to be effective. Group training that uses case studies, small-group interaction, video followed by discussion, and other interactive techniques will likely be better received by trainees than a lecture-only format.

◆   **Training Principle 8**—*Training Should Focus on Trainees.* Good trainers address trainees' needs. They don't try to impress them with their own personal knowledge or skills, nor do they make training more difficult because everyone should "learn it the hard way." Failure to teach a training point "because everyone should know it" is another error, as is the use of **jargon**. Addressing the question, "How would I like to be trained?" often reveals suggestions about tactics that should (and should not) be used.

Jargon: Terminology used by and commonly known only to people familiar with a topic.

- **Training Principle 9**—*Allow Trainees to Practice.* Hospitality staff in every department and position must have significant knowledge and skills. Few skills can be learned by reading a book, listening to someone "talk through" a task, or by only watching someone else do it. Rather, skills are typically learned by observing how something is done and then by practicing the activity in a step-by-step sequence. After the task is learned, time and repetition are often required to enable the trainee to perform the task at the appropriate speed.

- **Training Principle 10**—*Trainees Require Time to Learn.* This principle, while seemingly obvious, is sometimes violated. Consider that some managers expect a new staff member to learn necessary tasks by "tagging along" with an experienced peer. What happens when these trainers must provide a well-thought-out and organized training program even though they are continually interrupted by the demands of their own position?

- **Training Principle 11**—*The Training Environment Must Be Positive.* The stress created when training principle 10 is violated provides an example of a training environment that is not positive. As another example, consider someone with training responsibilities who does not enjoy the task. These issues can create a hostile environment without the interpersonal respect that is necessary for effective training.

- **Training Principle 12**—*Trainees Need Encouragement and Positive Feedback.* Most trainees appreciate ongoing input about how the trainer evaluates their performance during and, especially, after the training is completed.

- **Training Principle 13**—*Trainees Should Not Compete Against Each Other.* Contests in which, for example, one trainee "wins" and other trainees "lose" do not encourage teamwork. A better alternative is contests in which all trainees that attain specified performance standards can "win."

- **Training Principle 14**—*Teach the Correct Way to Perform a Task.* Showing a trainee how something should not be done does little good, but this happens when, for example, a trainer notes "Here's the wrong way that many employees use. . . ." Instead, use the correct work methods on a step-by-step basis, with trainer presentation followed by trainee demonstration.

- **Training Principle 15**—*Train One Task at a Time.* Tasks should be taught separately, and each should be broken into steps taught in proper sequence.

- **Training Principle 16**—*Train Each Task Using a Step-By-Step Plan.* Consider the task of checking in a hotel guest. Begin by demonstrating how to perform the task for one type of guest, such as an airline crew member. Then, beginning with the task's first step, present correct procedures and encourage the trainee to demonstrate them. Trainer feedback helps the trainee to identify where performance improvements could be helpful. After the trainee demonstrates the step, repeat the process until all steps are presented to and successfully demonstrated by the trainee. The trainer can then demonstrate the correct way to do the entire task again, and the trainee can repeat the correct procedures and practice each step to build the appropriate speed for task performance.

- **Training Principle 17**—*Trainees Should Know Training Requirements.* Experienced trainers often use a "preview, present, and review" sequence. They tell the trainees what they are going to say (preview), they tell them (present), and they tell them once again (review). A preview of the entire training experience is a first step that precedes training.

- **Training Principle 18**—*Consider the Trainees' Attention Span.* Several short training sessions are generally better than one long session. Consider the complete range of subject matter to be presented, then break the total training requirement down into manageable (short) parts for each session.

- **Training Principle 19**—*Learning Should Be Paced.* Learning that is spread out to address one or just a few concepts at a time allows trainees to practice and improve on basic skills in a focused way. They can concentrate on one or several skills rather than on all skills and better learn the correct way to perform all of them.

- **Training Principle 20**—*Learning Speed Varies for Trainees.* Individualized training allows the trainer to incorporate what the trainee doesn't know and exclude what the trainee does know from the training process.

HR Management in Action

The training procedures used in some hospitality operations almost ensure their training efforts are not successful. While HR managers recognize the inadequacy of the procedures, they are sometimes unable to equate the added costs for effective training with the benefits derived from the use of more appropriate training tactics. The result is attitudes that training will never "work" because of reasons such as "untrainable" employees (who, perhaps, should not have been selected!), others who could be trained but don't want to be, and a concern that training is not an investment because trained employees leave and join competitive organizations.

Here are three examples of tactics that almost guarantee training failure:

◆ Assume three employees are needed for a specific shift, and a new person must be trained. Two experienced employees and a trainee are scheduled for the shift. If three productive staff members are needed, how can two experienced staff do the work of three employees and, in addition, train the new person?

◆ A supervisor has been promoted from the ranks of entry-level employees. Among other new responsibilities, he or she must now plan and deliver training activities without knowing how to train. How does this new trainer learn the knowledge and skills necessary for successful training?

◆ Employees with disabilities are selected with the knowledge that "training may be difficult but only because more training time may be needed." In fact, more time may be needed, but so might tactics related to building awareness among employee peers, making task and/ or workplace accommodations, and learning about numerous types of the US Department of Labor and other governmental agency assistance.

Who is responsible for the less-than-successful training in each of the above and numerous other examples? The trainer? The trainee? How about the manager who established the policies related to these practices and didn't recognize that there is significantly more to effective training than just saying, "Go do it"?

❖ FOCUS ON THE TRAINER

LEARNING OBJECTIVE 4. List characteristics important for an effective trainer.

A new maintenance person has just been employed. Who should provide the training? Sometimes this question is answered by asking other questions: Who is available? Who wants to do it? Who has the time? Who will complain least if given the assignment? Who is a good "people person" who can interact with the new staff member? While these factors are relevant, others are more important, including the following characteristics, which are important for good trainers:

◆ **Have the desire to train**—Good trainers want to train for reasons that include helping others, internal recognition for a job well done, and the knowledge that effective trainers are frequently promoted to higher-level positions.

Unfortunately, there are also reasons why training might not be an attractive assignment, including the expectation that the trainer must complete all of his or her regularly assigned tasks and still conduct the training. Also, a trainer might want to do a good job but cannot because he or she has not been taught how to train and/or because there is insufficient time, equipment, money, or other resources required to do so. HR managers know that stress resulting from inadequate training resources is a disincentive for accepting and successfully completing a training assignment.

- **Have the proper attitude about the employer, peers, position, and the training assignment**—Hospitality organizations that emphasize the importance of staff members and that provide quality training opportunities to employees at all levels increase the morale of their trainers. Conversely, when training is just another and not so important responsibility, a less-than-willing attitude is likely to result.

- **Possess the necessary knowledge and skills to do the job for which training is needed**—Effective trainers must be knowledgeable about and have the skills necessary to perform the work tasks for which they will train others.

- **Use effective communication skills**—Trainers are effective communicators when they (1) speak in a language that the trainee understands, (2) recognize that body language is a powerful method of communication, (3) use a questioning process to learn the extent to which a trainee has learned, and (4) speak to communicate rather than to impress.

- **Know how to train**—The importance of train-the-trainer programs should be obvious but often is overlooked.

- **Have patience**—Few trainees learn everything they must know or be able to do during their first exposure to training. Effective trainers understand that training must sometimes be repeated several times in different ways. They know the goal is not to complete training quickly; rather, it is to provide the knowledge and skills the trainee needs to be successful.

- **Exhibit humor**—Use of humor in good taste provides a subtle message to trainees: "I am enjoying the opportunity to provide training, and I hope you enjoy it."

- **Have time to train**—Effective training takes time, and it must be scheduled for the trainer and for the trainees.

- **Show genuine respect for the trainees**—Trainees must be treated as professionals. Trainers know that those whom they respect will also respect them, and mutual respect allows training to be more effective.

- **Be enthusiastic**—Newly employed staff members want reinforcement that their decision to join the organization was a good one. Initial experiences with an enthusiastic trainer help to develop the foundation for successful training and for their long-term commitment. Trainers can reinforce the philosophy of more senior staff: "This is a good place to work; let's make it a better place to work, and this training will help us to do so."

- **Celebrate the trainees' success**—Have you ever heard the saying that, "If a trainee hasn't learned, it is because the trainer hasn't trained"? A successful trainer is one who has successfully trained others. The reverse is also true: Trainers have not been successful when their trainees have not learned. Take time to celebrate when learning occurs.

- **Value diversity**—Most organizations employ workers with a variety of backgrounds and cultures and are strengthened because of the different perspectives that provide decision-making input. An effective trainer accepts the challenge to develop all trainees to the fullest extent possible, even though training tactics might differ based on the trainees' cultural backgrounds. For example, group trainers may need to actively solicit question responses from trainees who don't readily participate in discussions, and trainees from some cultures may be embarrassed to participate in role-playing exercises.

❖ FORMAL PROCESS TO PLAN FOR TRAINING

LEARNING OBJECTIVE 5. Explain procedures used to plan for training activities.

Traditional "tag along" and "shadowing" programs designed for employee training typically do not work because they lack an organized and well-thought-out approach to determining training content and delivery. By contrast, the training model shown in Figure 6.4 identifies activities that better ensure training that attains planned results.

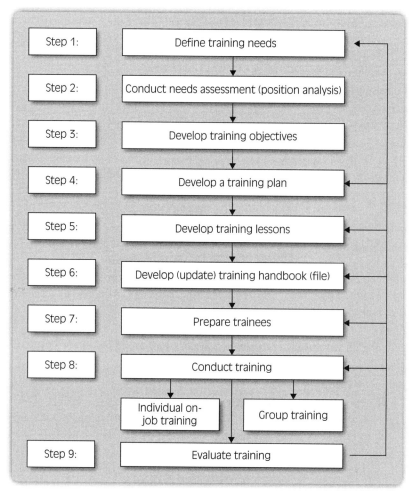

Figure 6.4 Overview of Training Process

The first six steps identified in Figure 6.4 are addressed in the remainder of this chapter. Steps 7 and 8 are addressed in chapter 7. Note that the training steps outlined in Figure 6.4 are universal. They can be used when training recently hired staff members to perform all tasks in their new position, for training experienced employees about revised job tasks, and for ongoing training and problem resolution purposes.

Step 1: Define Training Needs

Ensuring that the time and money budgeted for training is spent on the most important long- and short-term training priorities is important. Examples of the former include the following:

◆ New staff members must be trained to perform all tasks in their new positions. While this seems to be a short-term training need, it is not because training programs must be developed for those being recruited today and in the future.

◆ After planners determine long-range planning goals, the role of training in attaining them can be considered.

◆ Hopefully, the corporate culture of the organization promotes professional development and training opportunities for employees who are proficient in their current position.

There are numerous examples of short-term operating and other concerns that can be addressed by training. New work methods, purchase of new equipment or technology, and/or implementation of cost-reduction processes may be necessary to enable the hospitality operation to "do more with less." As well, there may be need for more or different products and services to meet guests' needs.

If only the "squeaky wheel gets the grease," managers should have little difficulty in knowing about problems that require priority resolution. However, there are also "silent" problems that create difficulties, and many can be addressed with training. Consider opportunities to teach supervisors how to use financial information to identify problems and how to motivate staff as part of the empowerment process.

TACTICS TO IDENTIFY TRAINING NEEDS

Training needs can be determined in several ways.

- ◆ **Observation of work performance**—Those who "manage by walking around" may note work procedures that deviate from standard operating procedures that were taught in applicable training sessions.

- ◆ **Input from guests**—Successful managers attempt to learn about their guests' needs and the extent to which they are met. Surveys can help identify problems, and ongoing personal interactions with guests can also be helpful.

- ◆ **Input from staff members**—Some managers use suggestion boxes, open-door policies, and frank input from performance appraisals and coaching sessions to identify problems that can be resolved by training.

- ◆ **Inspections**—Formal inspections such as those related to safety and informal inspections made by supervisors and others before, during, and after work shifts can suggest work process revisions that lend themselves to training.

- ◆ **Failure to meet performance standards**—Consider unacceptable quality scores achieved during inspections conducted by a franchisor's representatives. Can training help to address these concerns and improve performance?

- ◆ **Analysis of financial data**—Differences between budget plans and actual operating data may suggest negative variances traceable to problems with training implications. After problems are identified, corrective actions, including training, may be implemented.

- ◆ **Performance/skills assessments**—Evaluation after training may suggest that the training provided has not been successful and that additional or different training is needed.

- ◆ **Exit interviews**—Formal or informal discussions with resigning employees may identify training topics to help reduce future turnover rates and improve operations.

Step 2: Define Training Objectives

Training objectives are used for two purposes:

1. To help the trainer connect the purpose(s) of the training program with its content. Specific reasons for training become clear when training needs are defined (step 1), and when, after position analysis (discussed earlier in this chapter) has been completed, the content of the training program is known.

2. To help evaluate training (step 8 in Figure 6.1).

Training objectives specify what trainees should know and be able to do when they have successfully completed the training. Those who plan training programs must know what the training is to accomplish, and training objectives help planners do this. You've learned that effective training is performance-based and must help trainees learn essential tasks. Competent staff are those who have been properly trained and are able to contribute to the achievement of desired results.

Training objectives are critical to training evaluation, and they should describe the expected results of the training rather than the training process itself. Consider the following objectives:

As a result of satisfactory completion of the training session, the trainee will:

Objective 1: Study the process to properly operate a dishwashing machine.

Objective 2: Properly operate a dishwashing machine.

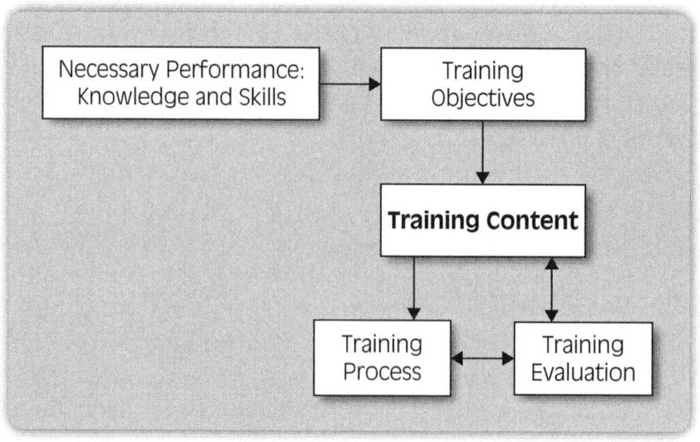

Figure 6.5   Training Objectives Are Important

The first objective is not performance-based because it emphasizes the training process ("study"). The performance expected if the training is successful is described in objective 2 ("properly operate a dishwashing machine"). The skills taught during training can be evaluated because the trainer can compare how the trainee operates a dishwashing machine with the procedures taught during the training. Figure 6.5 illustrates the importance of training objectives.

Figure 6.5 indicates that the knowledge and skills required for effective work performance determine appropriate training objectives. They drive the content of the training program, which impacts the training process that is implemented and the tactics used for training evaluation. Figure 6.5 also suggests that planned training evaluation methods can be used to address the extent to which content was mastered, as well as the usefulness of the training process.

Objectives must be reasonable (attainable), and they must be measurable. Objectives are *not* reasonable when they are too difficult or too easy to attain. For example, the following objective for a supervisory training program is not likely to be attained: "As a result of successful training, there will be a zero turnover rate except for natural attrition, beginning with staff members employed after 1/1/20xx." By contrast, an objective stating, "The turnover rate for the Hightown Restaurant will be reduced by 20% within 12 months of training" may be quite reasonable.

Training objectives should incorporate an element of "stretch." For example, assume that the Anytown Hotel is currently receiving numerous guest complaints each month. Reducing the complaint rate to zero immediately after training is probably an overly optimistic management goal. By contrast, reducing the complaint rate by one per month after a six-month period required for process revision and implementation may not be appropriate for the opposite reason: No or very little significant change in staff performance may be necessary to attain that objective.

A better approach: Managers can assess common reasons for the complaints (step 1 in the training process described in Figure 6.4). Then revised processes resulting from position analysis can be developed to drive training content. Training objectives relating to the trainees' ability to master the revised process to reduce complaints can be developed, and the extent of reduction will be a measure of training effectiveness.

Training objectives must be measurable. The concern that training objectives be measurable relates to the role of the objectives in the training evaluation process. How can training programs be evaluated if success is measured by objectives such as those listed below?

◆   Trainees will *realize* the importance of effective guest service.

◆   Trainees will *understand* the need to use a first-in/first-out (FIFO) inventory rotation system.

◆   Trainees will *recognize* the need to safely operate kitchen equipment.

Contrast the above with measurable objectives for the same topics:

◆   Trainees will demonstrate a six-step method to manage guest complaints.

◆   Trainees will identify poor inventory rotation practices as they review an incorrectly arranged storeroom.

◆ Trainees will operate kitchen equipment according to safe operating instructions in the operating manual.

Training objectives typically use an action verb to tell what the trainee must demonstrate or apply after training. Examples include *operate*, *calculate*, *explain*, and *assemble*. By contrast, unacceptable verbs that cannot be readily measured include *know*, *appreciate*, *believe*, and *understand*.

Step 3: Develop Training Plans

Training plans organize training content and provide an overview of the structure and sequence of the entire training program. They show how individual training lessons should be sequenced to teach required knowledge and skills.

Training plan: A description of the overview and sequence of a complete training program.

Here are suggestions for determining the sequence for subject matter in a training plan:

◆ Begin with an introduction explaining why the training is important and how trainees will benefit.

◆ Provide an overview of training content.

◆ Plan training lessons to progress from simple to complex. Simple information at the beginning allows trainees to quickly feel comfortable in the learning situation. It also provides the confidence needed to master the program.

◆ Build on the trainees' experiences. Combine unfamiliar information with familiar content to allow trainees to build on their experience.

◆ Present basic information before more detailed concepts are discussed.

◆ Progress from general information to specific information. For example, provide an overview of how to set up a dining room and then begin with specific steps.

◆ Consider the necessity of "nice-to-know" and "need-to-know" information. Basics should be presented before other information, and addressing the "whys" before the "hows" is generally best.

◆ Use a logical order and clearly identify what information is prerequisite to other information.

Figure 6.6 illustrates a training plan worksheet.

Training plans allow trainers to (1) plan the dates and times for each training lesson, (2) consider the topic (lesson number and subject), (3) state the training location, (4) indicate the trainer(s) responsible for conducting the training, and (5) determine the trainees for whom specific training lessons are applicable.

Assume a trainer is planning a training program for a new employee who must learn how to correctly perform all tasks in a position. Perhaps some tasks can be taught in one training session. By contrast, several (or more) training sessions may be needed to teach just one other task. The training plan allows planners to think about what must be taught (training lessons) and the sequence and duration of each training lesson.

When a training plan is developed to teach all tasks to a new staff member, training dates and times must only consider the trainer's and employee's availability. If the training impacts several employees, other tactics may be necessary. Perhaps each session will be planned for alternate dates and times to accommodate all affected personnel. The training location could be the same for every session, or it could accommodate group training in a congregate setting and individual training at workstations. The trainees might include all staff members for some sessions and only selected staff members for other sessions.

Step 4: Develop Training Lessons

A **training lesson** provides all information needed to present a single session that is part of a broader training plan. In effect, it is a "turnkey" module that tells about a specific training session:

◆ **Why**—the objective(s) of the training session

◆ **What**—the content of the training session

◆ **How**—the method(s) used to present the training

Training lesson: Information about a single session of a training plan. It contains one or more training objectives and indicates the content and method(s) to enable trainees to master the content.

Training Topic: _____

Date	Time	Training Lesson		Location	Instructor(s)	Trainees
		Lesson No.	Subject			

Figure 6.6   Training Plan Worksheet

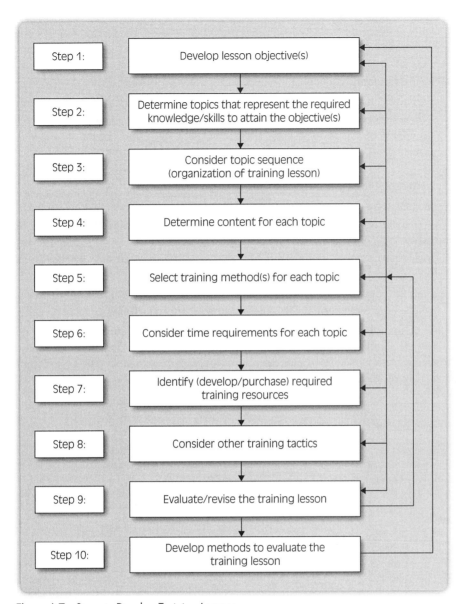

Figure 6.7 Steps to Develop Training Lessons

A training lesson may be needed to teach new staff members how to perform a single task such as operating an oven, or it can be used to teach experienced staff new steps in a single task.

Figure 6.7 reviews steps used to develop training lessons.

Let's assume a training lesson on managing guest complaints has been developed and is shown in Figure 6.8.

Let's see how the steps identified in Figure 6.7 were followed to develop the training lesson:

◆ **Step 1**—*Develop lesson objective(s).* A training objective is stated: "As a result of successfully completing this lesson, trainees will be able to effectively manage guest complaints."

◆ **Step 2**—*Determine topics that represent the required knowledge/skills to attain the objective(s).* The trainer determines that a video will provide most of the subject matter necessary to attain the objective.

◆ **Step 3**—*Consider topic sequence.* The trainer uses an organized topic sequence that begins with an introduction, continues with the video, and then uses a PowerPoint presentation to review the video's learning points. There will also be trainee discussion, a role play exercise, and a review and evaluation.

- ◆ **Step 4**—*Determine content for each topic.* There is only one topic (managing guests' complaints). A review of off-the-shelf training resources reinforces the decision to use a video.

- ◆ **Step 5**—*Select training method(s) for each topic.* A short lecture, video, PowerPoint overheads, trainee discussion, and role play exercise will be used.

- ◆ **Step 6**—*Consider time requirements for each topic.* The trainer knows that 30 minutes will be needed for the introduction, role play, review, and evaluation. The video is eight minutes long. Five minutes is then allocated video review and trainee discussion. The 43 minutes of formal contact time fit well into a planned 50-minute session.

- ◆ **Step 7**—*Identify (develop/purchase) required training resources.* The video and several PowerPoint overheads will be required.

- ◆ **Step 8**—*Consider other training tactics.* The trainer originally planned to facilitate the role play after the video. Instead, he or she will facilitate trainee discussions before the exercise.

- ◆ **Step 9**—*Evaluate/revise the training lesson.* Experience with previous training sessions, including this specific topic if it has previously been taught, help to plan an effective presentation.

- ◆ **Step 10**—*Develop methods to evaluate the training lesson.* A 10-question true/false test will be used to measure the knowledge gained during the training.

Figure 6.7 indicates the cyclical nature of training lesson development because evaluation/revision (step 9) can indicate needed changes in any or all of the earlier steps. In addition, the after-lesson evaluation in step 10 helps the trainer to assess the extent to which the lesson objectives (step 1) were attained.

Training Plan:	Customer Service for Anytown Restaurant Service Staff
Training Topic:	Service Recovery
Training Objective:	As a result of successfully completing this lesson, trainees will be able to manage guest complaints using specific steps presented in the training.
Lesson Duration:	50 minutes
Training Location:	Conference Room

Time	Activity/Method	Materials	Comments
2 minutes	Introduction: ask trainees for examples of customer complaints	None	Ensure examples come from several departments
8 minutes	Show video titled "Customer Service Recovery Tactics"	Laptop, projector, screen, video	Ensure equipment is available and operative
5 minutes	Show PowerPoint slides that review the six-step recovery process	Laptop, projector, screen	Ensure equipment is available and operative
5 minutes	Lead trainee discussion about a complaint from the session introduction and how it could be addressed using video information	Flip chart and pens	Relate discussion to video; note differences between the video and restaurant
15 minutes	Conduct role play exercise and follow-up discussion	None	Review role play procedures
5 minutes	Review service recovery method	None	None
10 minutes	Administer 10-question true/false review	Laptop, projector, and screens (two questions per PowerPoint slide), paper and pencils	Show questions on screen

Figure 6.8 Sample Training Lesson

Trainers can use numerous resources to develop training content, including:

◆ Manufacturers' operating manuals for equipment

◆ Standard operating procedure manuals

◆ Task breakdowns for positions

◆ Applicable books/magazines, including electronic editions

◆ Industry best practices

◆ Training resources from professional associations such as the Education Foundation of the National Restaurant Association and the American Hotel & Lodging Association Educational Institute

◆ Materials available from vendors

◆ Ideas from other hospitality organizations

◆ Trainers' notes from other training sessions

◆ The trainer's own experience

Step 5: Develop Training Handbook

Developing training programs requires time and creativity, and the process is cost-effective when the training plans, lessons, and resource materials are used for more than one training experience. A **training handbook** is a hard copy or electronic manual containing the training plan

Training handbook: A hard copy or electronic manual containing the training plan and associated training lessons for a complete training program.

It's the Law

HR employees are often involved in training the organization's personnel about the Americans with Disabilities Act (ADA). All employees will benefit from some information about the ADA, and more specific information will be needed for managers and supervisors who must implement task and work environment aspects of the law.

Examples of potential training topics include:

◆ Overall knowledge of the ADA

◆ Knowledge specific to ADA employment provisions

◆ ADA-related employment prescreening and applicant interviewing requirements

◆ Medical, drug, and other testing under the ADA

◆ Identifying essential job functions

◆ Writing job descriptions that specify essential job functions

◆ General information regarding specific disabilities and possible accommodations

◆ Job evaluation and compensation information for people with disabilities

◆ Career equity/promotional considerations for people with disabilities

◆ Nondiscriminatory performance appraisals

◆ The role of job coaching and/or supportive employment in the reasonable accommodation process

◆ Guest relations with those with disabilities (because ADA requirements relate to guests and public accommodations as well as to employees)

As suggested above, ADA compliance requires a significant effort involving staff at all organizational levels.

and associated training lessons for a complete training program. A wise trainer maintains this information in an organized fashion that allows easy replication of training, with revision as necessary. It benefits managers because the time and money spent to develop training tools need not be replicated.

A handbook used to train a new person for all tasks in a position may include:

◆ An introduction

◆ A current position description

◆ A copy of the position's task list

◆ Copies of all task breakdowns

◆ Training lessons for each task breakdown, including evaluation processes

◆ Training lessons for generic subject matter such as guest service and safety basics

Step 6: Prepare Trainees

The need to focus on the trainees is an obvious step that is often overlooked and/or done incorrectly. Providing training materials and activities does not necessarily yield more knowledgeable and skilled employees unless the trainees want to learn.

Implementing training programs is easier when trainees have provided input into their development. This occurs when staff members provide suggestions about process revisions and as task lists and task breakdowns are developed.

Trainees can be motivated about training in additional ways:

◆ **Tell trainees what to expect**—The who, what, when, and where of training should be explained, specific questions should be addressed, and opportunities for group discussions about the training should be provided.

◆ **Explain why training is needed**—Whenever possible, tell trainees "what's in it for them" rather than only how the property will benefit.

◆ **Provide training time**—Effective training cannot be rushed and cannot be done during peak business times or "when time is available." Dedicated time must be considered as training schedules are developed.

◆ **Address trainees' concerns**—People with language or reading problems and those wanting to know about the relationship, if any, between training and advancement opportunities have concerns to be addressed before training begins.

◆ **Emphasize the importance of training**—This is easy to accomplish if the property supports training.

◆ **Explain that training will relate to the trainees' work**—Coupled with a discussion about how trainees will benefit from training, this provides a powerful motivator to accept training.

◆ **Stress that the training will be enjoyable**—This tactic is easy to implement when the trainees have enjoyed positive experiences with previous training.

◆ **Tell trainees how they will be evaluated**—New employees want assurance their employment decision was a good one, and positive training feedback focusing on job performance can be very helpful to them. Experienced staff know about their employer's track record relating to training and expect helpful input resulting from training evaluation.

After trainees are prepared for training, the program can be conducted. This topic, along with training evaluation, is addressed in chapter 8.

HR TERMS

The following terms were defined in this chapter:

Training	Warm body syndrome	Quality
Cost-effective	Professional development program	Jargon
Performance-based (training)	Position analysis	Training plan
Morale	Task list	Training lesson
Feedback	Task breakdown	Training handbook
Task	Performance standard	
Off-the-shelf (training materials)	Step (in task)	

FOR YOUR CONSIDERATION

1. List some training activities in which you have participated that were beneficial to you. Why did you enjoy them? How did they help you to learn? What training principles noted in this chapter were incorporated in them?

2. List some training experiences in which you have participated that you did not enjoy. Why did you not like them? How did they hinder your learning experience? What training principles noted in this chapter did they violate?

3. If possible, interview a hospitality manager or supervisor and ask:

   a. What are benefits of training in your operation?

   b. What are significant obstacles to training in the operation?

   c. How, if at all, could training for entry-level employees be improved in the operation?

4. Select a common operating problem such as excessive dish breakage in a restaurant or low scores upon inspection of guest room bath areas in hotels.

   a. Indicate the steps that you would use to develop a task breakdown that addressed the problem.

   b. Explain how you would develop a training lesson for the topic.

5. What types of training assistance might HR personnel in multiunit organizations provide to managers in company-owned and/or franchised units? What types of training may be mandated? Made available on an optional basis?

CASE STUDY

Apply HR Management Principles

Leilani has been a successful manager in quick service restaurants for 10 years. She recently became an area manager for Good Food, a newer company with 35 units, and she reports to one of two regional managers. She accepted the position because of the professional challenges presented by an opportunity to help "grow" this young organization.

The Good Food organization markets to nutrition-conscious guests and offers fresh vegetable and fruit salads, soups, and sandwiches. It is a tough market because the public's expressed interest in nutrition doesn't always translate to parallel dining-out decisions.

Leilani has been with the company three months, and she is impressed with the operating and production support provided by headquarters. There are detailed standard recipes, food purchase specifications, and nutritional information, including a mandatory nutrition training program.

By contrast, Leilani quickly noticed many operating problems including high turnover requiring ongoing recruitment, cost control issues, and opportunities for employee theft of products and money.

Her boss is aware of these concerns and explains the company's owners also know about them. However, the owners consider them to be "part of the business," and there is greater concern about expanding the business than addressing these issues.

"Should we just ignore the problems, should we campaign for change in the organization's emphasis, or should we just dictate policies and procedures to control cost and theft problems?" Leilani asked. "Also, won't we increase our turnover rate if we create a more dictatorial atmosphere?"

"I'm also concerned, Leilani, and I have another option," replied the regional manager. "Another area manager shares your concerns. We all know the correct procedures that should be used, but they are not being implemented. How about a supervisory training program to help them learn how to teach our staff the correct procedures?"

"Let's assume I can talk headquarters into funding a pilot program to train supervisors," he continued. "I know they will want proof that the program is cost-effective, and as professionals we want that as well."

"I came here because I wanted to confront challenges, and this is a big one. Let's do it," replied Leilani.

Dimension: Supervision

1. Review the actions described in the case.
2. What tactics should Leilani use with unit managers and supervisors to reinforce the renewed emphasis on training?

3. How, if at all, should Leilani utilize input from unit managers, supervisors, and employees to develop and implement the new training programs?
4. What, if any, types of rewards/incentives can be used to encourage staff to maximize their participation in the training?

Dimension: Planning for Training

Assume the regional manager, Leilani, and the other area manager meet to determine how to begin the training effort ("who should do what and when"). Develop a list of the most important initial decisions to be made, suggest tasks that are required, and propose a list of intended accomplishments for the first six months. (Recall that these three managers must also run the business.) What, if any, identified tasks might be delegated to unit managers?

Dimension: Strategy

Assume the planning team decides that the project will go more smoothly if a project yielding a "quick and easy" success is implemented. Plan a simple project addressing an issue that can be developed and implemented quickly, such as reducing food cost by portion control or improved inventory management.

Outline the steps you would use to develop and implement a training program to address this simple task. Also, describe how you might provide some quantitative "return on investment" data to help justify the training.

INTERNET ACTIVITIES

1. Many organizations offer off-the-shelf training resources. Enter "hospitality training" into your favorite search engine, review several sites, and answer the following questions:

   a. How would you evaluate the worth of the training resources being advertised relative to their cost?

   b. Do the materials offered seem to address "real-world" and practical training concerns?

   c. What factors would you consider as you evaluate resources from alternative training resource suppliers?

   d. Many hospitality training consultants advertise on the Internet. Type the phrase "hospitality training

   consultants" into your favorite search engine, review some sites, and answer the following questions:

   e. What common themes are noted on the websites?

   f. How do the consultants differentiate their company from competitors?

   g. What services are offered?

   h. How helpful are the testimonials, suggestions, and general information provided?

   i. What factors would be most important if you were considering the use of an external training consultant?

DELIVERING AND EVALUATING TRAINING PROGRAMS

CHAPTER OUTLINE

LEARNING OBJECTIVES

When they complete this chapter, readers will be able to:

1. Prepare an overview of the individual on-job training process.
2. Explain the steps in the four-step individual on-job training method.
3. Explain additional individual training methods.
4. Prepare an overview of the group training process.
5. Identify specific procedures to prepare for group training.
6. Discuss procedures to facilitate group training.
7. Discuss the training evaluation process.

Impact on HR Management

Chapter 6 addressed the benefits of and procedures to plan for training. Carefully planning training does no good if it is not delivered correctly. As well, since all resources, including time and money, are limited, they must be used wisely.

Individual on-job training is widely used throughout the hospitality industry, and this chapter explains a four-step process to implement this method: prepare, present, trainee practice, and coaching. There are also times when group training is the best approach, and this chapter explains when it is best and how to prepare for and facilitate this training strategy.

Training evaluation that occurs before, during, and after training is absolutely critical to ensure the expenditure of training resources represents their best use. Revisions to training identified by evaluation allow the operation to continue on its journey of improvement.

❖ INTRODUCTION TO INDIVIDUAL ON-JOB TRAINING

LEARNING OBJECTIVE 1. Prepare an overview of the individual on-job training process.

On-job training: An individualized training method in which a knowledgeable and skilled trainer teaches a less experienced staff member how to properly perform job tasks.

Figure 7.1 (previously shown in chapter 6) shows the eight-step model we are using to describe the training process. Chapter 6 presented basic information applicable to the first six steps. This chapter begins with step 7, which discusses individual and group training, and concludes with a discussion of step 8: training evaluation.

When **on-job training** is used, the trainer teaches job skills and knowledge to one trainee, primarily at the trainee's workstation. Theoretically, it is the best training method because it incorporates many of the training principles explained in chapter 6. An individual trainee can learn at his or her own pace, and immediate feedback can be provided.

On-Job Training: Not "All or Nothing"

One primary purpose of on-job training is to provide necessary knowledge and skills to new employees. A second purpose can be to teach their experienced peers how to perform an existing task in a different way and to learn new tasks.

On-job training can be supplemented by group training; this tactic is especially useful when several staff members must learn the same thing. For example, assume all cooks must learn how to operate a new piece of equipment. Demonstration is likely to be an important tactic in this training, and on-job training to address some tasks can be supplemented by group training for other tasks.

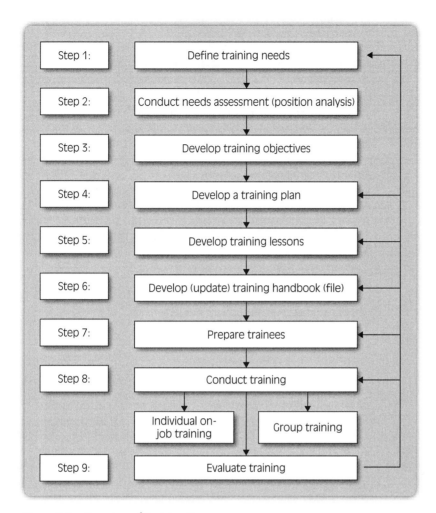

Figure 7.1 Overview of Training Process

In practice, on-job training is frequently not done well. As suggested by other common names ("tag-along" training and "shadow" training), some supervisors erroneously believe trainees can learn simply by watching and helping a more experienced peer. Unfortunately, this approach ignores several training principles. As well, trainers who have not learned how to train, who do so in addition to existing full-time responsibilities, and who have been taught by equally unskilled trainers are not likely to be effective.

There are several advantages to on-job training.

◆ **It incorporates basic training principles**—Training should focus on those being trained. Trainers should consider the trainees' backgrounds, and training should be organized and, when possible, informal. Trainees should be allowed to practice, their individual attention spans and learning speeds should be considered, and appropriate training tactics are needed. One trainee may like to ask questions, another may want to practice before moving to the next step, and still another trainee might attain performance standards without repetitive explanations or demonstrations.

◆ **It provides maximum realism**—Training must focus on real problems, and these are in the workplace.

◆ **It provides immediate feedback**—On-job training allows a trainee to demonstrate (practice) what has been learned as soon as the training is completed. The trainer can observe the trial performance and recognize proper or address improper performance. In both instances, correct performance can be encouraged.

Is On-Job Training Best Because It Is Easy, Fast, and Inexpensive?

S ome supervisors prefer on-job training for the wrong reasons. They believe it is easy, fast, and inexpensive because "All you have to do is allow a trainee to follow along with an experienced staff member who can teach the trainee everything to do the job."

This perception of on-job training is incorrect. The need to define training requirements and develop training objectives, training plans, and training lessons is just as important for individualized training as for group training. As well, trainees must be prepared for the training, and this involves more than just saying, "Tag-along with Joe; he'll show you what to do."

On-job training can be easy because steps involved in its planning and delivery are not complicated. The process does take time, however, and a commitment of financial resources is required to effectively plan and deliver it.

◆ **It can be used to train new and experienced staff**—On-job training can teach new staff members all tasks they must perform and experienced staff about revised work methods for one or a few tasks.

◆ **It is frequently delivered by peers who regularly perform the task**—The trainer can be a role model; in the process, teamwork can be encouraged and a corporate culture that encourages cooperation and mutual assistance can be fostered.

◆ **It is well accepted by trainees**—This is an easy-to-understand advantage because it focuses on the trainee.

Done correctly, there are few disadvantages to on-job training. Practiced the way it is in some hospitality organizations, however, there are several potential disadvantages.

◆ **Experienced staff members who have not learned how to train can make training-related errors.**

◆ **Training can be unorganized**—Effective training requires a step-by-step approach. This is difficult when a trainee follows an experienced peer and instead learns tasks in the sequence they are done. Consider a cook trainee who should sequentially learn each step in a standard recipe. Instead, the experienced staff member (trainer) may perform one or two steps in the recipe, and then do other things before resuming preparation. This is disorganized and may suggest that neither the trainer nor the employer cares about how or what the trainee learns.

◆ **It can ignore correct work procedures**—When task breakdowns are not available or used, the trainer may teach the trainee how he or she does the work. This may be different from how the trainer learned the task from another trainer (who, in turn, modified the task from how he or she learned it). This approach can hinder the attainment of quality and quantity standards.

◆ **It can create inappropriate work attitudes**—Experienced employees who know how and want to do their jobs correctly but who do not know how to train can become frustrated with their training responsibilities. This problem is compounded when the trainer must also perform other work while training.

Improperly planned and delivered training is not cost-effective because the desired result (an employee who can perform tasks meeting performance standards) is not likely to be attained.

Impact on New Team Members

Managers must accept their responsibilities to help employees learn how to correctly perform their jobs. Their role extends far beyond delegating the training task to an employee peer with a request to "show him what to do."

Each training principle discussed in this and the previous chapter is important and plays a role in successful training. Each must be implemented appropriately, and those who train must know how and when to use them. It is always possible that a poor selection decision was made or that a new employee can't or won't be trained. However, these are not always (perhaps not usually) the reasons that training is unsuccessful.

Instead, managers must be committed to the importance of and need for effective training, must train employees to train, and must have defined processes, equipment, tools, and supplies required for the tasks employees must learn.

The impacts of training failure or success are significant. They affect the trainees, the guests, and the hospitality organization. Initial training experiences are part of the on-boarding activities discussed in earlier chapters. Managers must be hospitable to employees; in part, they show the extent to which they respect employees in the way they manage the training process.

There is an old saying that "if the trainee has not been trained, it may be because the trainer was not trained." Managers must objectively consider this possibility when analyzing the reasons for unacceptable employee performance.

It is even less effective if it results in frustrated trainers and trainees who have not received the organizational support they require. This in turn can yield high employee turnover rates and/or disgruntled employees.

❖❖ ON-JOB TRAINING STEPS

LEARNING OBJECTIVE 2. Explain the steps in the four-step individual on-job training method.

As noted in Figure 7.2, there are four steps in the individual on-job training method.

As shown in Figure 7.2, the first step in on-job training involves preparation activities, and the second step is the actual presentation of the training. The third step allows practice and demonstration by the trainee, and a final step involves various **coaching** and related activities that are the trainer's responsibility.

Coaching: A training and supervisory tactic that involves informal on-the-job conversations and demonstrations that encourage proper and discourage improper behavior.

Step 1: Preparation

Several principles are useful when preparing for on-job training. Each will have been addressed if the earlier training steps noted in chapter 6 were implemented.

◆ **State training objectives**—Training objectives for the entire training program must be available in the training plan and for each segment of the training during training lessons. Assume a training lesson addresses how to prepare one dessert of several on a menu. In this example, the trainer will know that the training objective is to "Prepare baked fruit pies according to the applicable standard recipes."

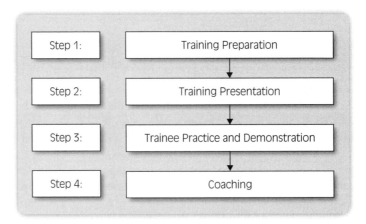

Figure 7.2   Steps in Individual On-Job Training

- ◆ **Use/revise applicable task breakdown**—The trainer who will teach an employee how to prepare a fruit pie should review the applicable task breakdown and recipe because they are important parts of the training content.

- ◆ **Consider the training schedule**—The training plan should indicate the duration of the training activity and where in the overall training dessert preparation activities should occur. Experience may suggest that training for one recipe normally takes 25 minutes. Each recipe can be taught at any time after workplace safety and equipment operation has been taught, so the trainer has flexibility. The best time to conduct training is when production volume is low, when employees normally in the area are working elsewhere or on a break, and when the trainer has adequate time.

- ◆ **Select training location**—When practical, training should occur in the actual workstation where the task will be performed. Training in dessert preparation is planned for the bake shop area.

- ◆ **Assemble training materials/equipment**—The training lesson and supporting standard recipe should be in the training handbook, which should also indicate necessary materials and equipment. The trainer may also duplicate a copy of the standard recipe for the trainee, should ensure all equipment is available, and confirm that all tools, supplies, and ingredients are assembled.

- ◆ **Setup workstation**—The trainer should ensure that the workstation is relatively free of anything that might detract from the training.

- ◆ **Prepare the trainee**—A new employee should know the purpose of initial training: to provide the knowledge and skills required to perform all tasks required for the position. Experienced staff receiving on-job training should understand that the training purpose is to provide the knowledge/skills needed to perform a task in a different way or to learn a task that is not part of the original task list. Trainees should be told how the training they will receive (training lesson) relates to their overall training experience (training plan).

- ◆ **Determine what the trainee already knows**—This is easy when on-job training is used. Assume a specific item of equipment must be operated. If the trainee claims to have this skill, he or she can demonstrate it. If successfully done, that aspect of training is not necessary. If the trainee cannot correctly operate the equipment, training should focus on this task at the appropriate point. Then the trainer can maximize available training time on steps where training is most needed.

Figure 7.3 reviews activities important when preparing individual training programs.

STEP 1: PREPARATION

THE TRAINER SHOULD:

☐   1. Develop a schedule that considers the time allocated for a specific training lesson and the sequence in the training plan when it should be taught.

☐   2. Use a task breakdown to identify how a task should be done.

☐   3. Have all necessary equipment, tools, and materials ready for the training session.

☐   4. Select and properly arrange the appropriate training location.

☐   5. Know *precisely* how to begin the training process.

☐   6. Identify the tasks that the trainee must learn.

☐   7. Put the trainee at ease.

☐   8. Find out what the trainee already knows about the task.

☐   9. Explain what the trainee should expect to learn in the session.

☐ 10. Set a good example for the trainee.

☐ 11. Explain what's in it for the trainee.

Figure 7.3   Checklist for On-Job Training: Preparation

Step 2: Presentation

In addition to developing the training lesson (step 4 in Figure 7.1), the trainer will find the task breakdown completed as part of the position analysis process helpful as the training is presented.

To review appropriate training presentation procedures, let's consider how a trainer might train a new employee to conduct a physical inventory in a restaurant storeroom. The training session begins as the trainer provides the trainee a copy of his or her job description and confirms the inventory task is part of the trainee's position. The trainer then explains the importance of the task: "A physical inventory count helps confirm the accuracy of perpetual inventory records, and we do it monthly."

The training occurs in the storeroom with an overview of the task: "Two people are required. One person physically counts the number of cases, cartons, or bags of each product in inventory. A second person verifies the inventory quantity and enters it onto a worksheet. This process is repeated until all products are counted; it usually takes about one hour in this storage area."

After this explanation, applicable activities are demonstrated. For example, the trainer shows the trainee how the storage area is organized and reviews how the inventory worksheet is completed.

The training lesson used is well developed, so the task is divided into separate and teachable steps. The trainer explains the first step in the task, answers questions posed by the trainee, and then allows the trainee to repeat, practice, and/or demonstrate the step. For example, some products are counted by the purchase unit, some by individual items, and other products that have been issued may (or may not) be counted. Each of these variables is discussed in a separate training step. If necessary, the sequence of steps can be repeated so the trainee can learn all steps.

As the presentation process evolves, trainers follow several principles.

◆   They speak in simple terms and do not use jargon.

◆   When possible, easier tasks are presented before more complex activities are discussed. For example, the trainer teaches how to conduct a physical count before analysis of data from computer printouts is considered.

◆   Tasks are explained and demonstrated slowly and clearly.

STEP 2: PRESENTATION

THE TRAINER SHOULD:

- ☐   1. Explain tasks and steps.
- ☐   2. Demonstrate tasks and steps.
- ☐   3. Ensure the trainee understands each task.
- ☐   4. Encourage the trainee to ask questions.
- ☐   5. Respond appropriately to questions.
- ☐   6. Check for understanding by asking open-ended questions.
- ☐   7. Provide information about and demonstrate only one task or step at a time.
- ☐   8. Follow an orderly sequence using the training lesson as a guide.
- ☐   9. Maintain a patient and appropriate pace throughout the training session.
- ☐ 10. Provide only the amount of information or instruction that can be mastered during one session.
- ☐ 11. Assure the training session is interesting.
- ☐ 12. Ensure that all instruction is clear, concise, complete, and accurate.
- ☐ 13. Provide an applicable task breakdown.

Figure 7.4   Checklist for On-Job Training: Presentation

- ◆ A questioning process is used to help ensure trainee comprehension. The trainer does not use a closed-ended question ("Do you understand what I am doing?"). Instead, an open-ended question is used: "Why do you think full cases are counted before opened cases?"

- ◆ The task breakdown is emphasized during the training. The trainer suggests that the trainee follow the task breakdown provided when the training began.

- ◆ Clear and well-thought-out instructions for each task are provided. The trainer indicates why each step is necessary and should be done in a specific sequence.

- ◆ Questions are asked to help ensure that the trainee understands and to suggest when additional information, practice, or demonstration can be helpful.

Figure 7.4 provides a review of important training points that are helpful when on-job training is presented.

Step 3: Trainee Practice and Demonstration

The third step in on-job training allows the trainee to practice and demonstrate what has been taught. During this step, several principles become important.

- ◆ The trainee should be asked to repeat or explain key points.

- ◆ The trainee should be allowed to demonstrate and/or practice the task. If practical, he or she should practice each step a sufficient number of times to learn its "basics" before training continues. Then the trainer can confirm the trainee can perform the task and that the trainee understands what successful task performance involves. Steps are typically taught by the trainer and practiced/demonstrated by the trainee in the proper sequence.

- ◆ The trainer can coach the trainee to reinforce positive performance ("Joe, you did that task flawlessly") and to correct improper performance ("Andrew, the next item to be counted in the inventory is listed on the inventory sheet according to its storeroom location").

It's the Law

Numerous legal issues could be addressed in on-job training for people in selected positions. Should front-desk staff loudly announce the room number of a check-in guest? Should a housekeeper let a guest who "lost' their key into a guest room? Of course not, and these staff members must be taught about these safety concerns during training.

Should food and beverage servers indicate that there is no monosodium glutamate (MSG) in menu items if they don't know for certain (because this ingredient can be harmful to some guests)? Can a server indicate that a steak is "USDA Grade Prime" when it is not? Of course not, and on-job training should address these and related concerns, which, if not addressed, can lead to lawsuits.

Franchisees sign agreements with franchisors about what they will and will not do. Many organizations require owners and/or managers to attend management training programs when properties become affiliated with the organizations. They may also require that entry-level employees in some positions complete guest relations programs.

Staff members in many positions perform their responsibilities within the restraints of legal considerations all the time. Bar managers must know about safety codes relating to occupancy levels in the lounge, preparation staff must know about health and safety requirements applicable to spraying pesticides in the kitchen, and housekeepers must know what they should and should not do if they suspect the use of controlled substances in guest rooms.

Employees of contract management companies may work in outlets on military bases. They have access to information such as troop movements that is not to be shared with anyone. Vending route drivers must obey traffic laws, and staff members in many organizations must comply with Occupational Safety and Health Act (OSHA) requirements. People in these and numerous other situations must comply with the law at all times, and this is more likely to occur when they acquire the necessary knowledge during formal and documented training sessions.

◆ Trainers should recognize that when the task and/or steps are difficult, initial progress may be slow. Then the trainee may require more repetition to build speed and consistently and correctly perform the task/step.

◆ Trainers must realize that some trainees learn faster than others. This principle is especially easy to incorporate into training when the on-job training approach is used. Within reason, training can be presented at the pace judged "best" for the individual trainee. As well, the time allowed for trainee demonstration can be varied.

◆ Correct performance should be acknowledged before addressing performance problems. Some trainers refer to this as the "sandwich method" of appraisal. Just as a sandwich has two slices of bread with a filling between them, the sandwich method uses an introductory phrase ("Phyllis, you have mastered almost all parts of this task"), followed by problem identification ("Just ensure the scale is set to zero before weighing the products"). This is followed by a concluding phrase ("I'm glad you are learning how to conduct the physical inventory count, and you will do it well").

◆ Trainees should be praised for proper performance. It is probably not possible to say too many good things to a trainee! Everyone likes to be thanked for a job well done, to be told how important and special they are, and to receive immediate input about performance. Trainers should reward trainees for success by noting it and by thanking the trainees for it.

Figure 7.5 reviews some tactics for the practice and demonstration step in on-job training.

STEP 3: PRACTICE AND DEMONSTRATION

THE TRAINER SHOULD:

- ☐ 1. Request that the trainee perform the step after it is presented.
- ☐ 2. Ask the trainee to explain the "hows and whys" of each task or step.
- ☐ 3. Correct all improper (substandard) performance.
- ☐ 4. Assure the trainee understands each step by asking open-ended questions.
- ☐ 5. Complement the trainee when he or she correctly performs a task or step.
- ☐ 6. Point out errors made during practice and demonstration to help the trainee learn from mistakes.
- ☐ 7. Allow the trainee time to practice and build confidence and speed.

Figure 7.5 Checklist for On-Job Training: Practice and Demonstration

Step 4: Coaching

The coaching step includes concluding activities to help ensure the training is effective, that is, that performance-based training objectives are attained. Useful coaching procedures include the following:

- ◆ At the end of the training, the trainee should be asked to perform, in sequence, each step in the task or step.
- ◆ The trainer should encourage, and ask, questions.
- ◆ The trainer should provide ongoing reinforcement about a trainee's positive attitude and when the trainee improves his or her skills and knowledge.
- ◆ Close supervision immediately after training and occasional supervision after a task is mastered can help ensure the trainee consistently performs the task correctly.
- ◆ The trainer may ask the trainee about suggestions for other ways to perform tasks after the staff member has gained experience on the job.
- ◆ Trainees should be asked to retain copies of training materials provided during the session for later referral.

Figure 7.6 reviews principles for effective coaching during on-job training.

STEP 4: COACHING

THE TRAINER SHOULD:

- ☐ 1. Encourage the trainee to seek assistance.
- ☐ 2. Tell the trainee who should be contacted if assistance is needed.
- ☐ 3. Check the trainee's performance frequently but unobtrusively.
- ☐ 4. Reinforce proper performance. Let the trainee know how he or she is doing.
- ☐ 5. Help the trainee to correct mistakes, if any.
- ☐ 6. Ensure that any mistakes are not repeated.
- ☐ 7. Ask the trainee about suggestions for better ways to do the task.
- ☐ 8. Encourage the trainee to improve on previous standards.
- ☐ 9. Compliment the trainee for successful demonstration.

Figure 7.6 Checklist for On-Job Training: Coaching

❖ OTHER INDIVIDUAL TRAINING METHODS

LEARNING OBJECTIVE 3. Explain additional individual training approaches.

The four-step training method just presented is the most frequently used. There are, however, other individualized training processes that can be used alone or with another method, including:

- **Self-study**—Trainees can enroll in **distance education** programs offered by an educational institution or professional association. Self-study in a broader sense also occurs when interested staff members, perhaps with the advice of a supervisor or mentor, enroll in a college course, read a recommended book, or view videos in the HR office.

- **Structured work experiences**—An employee may be assigned a specific project under the guidance of a manager or more experienced staff member to learn and assist the employer, for example, when a hotel designs a new menu, plans a special catered event, or revises procedures for guest room cleaning.

- **Cross-training**—This training method includes activities that allow staff to learn tasks in another position. For example, a dishwasher may learn how to pre-prep vegetables. This may be done at a staff member's request or to help someone gain knowledge and skills that will be helpful when he or she assumes another position.

- **Job enlargement**—Job enlargement occurs when a trainee learns tasks that are traditionally performed at a higher organizational level. As with other individual training methods, this tactic can benefit the trainee and the organization. It can be especially useful when a manager must take on additional responsibilities and, to do so, must delegate some duties.

> **Distance education:** An individual training method in which a staff member enrolls in a for-credit or not-for-credit program offered by an educational facility or a professional association.

> **Cross-training:** A training tactic that allows employees to learn tasks in another position.

> **Job enlargement:** An individual training method that involves adding tasks to a position that are traditionally performed at a higher organizational level.

Online Courses

Technology is rapidly changing how many people participate in self-study courses. Today's generation of new employees are very familiar with technology and use it for many purposes, including e-learning.

Benefits include the advantages of individualized learning and opportunities to provide quality training in both multiunit organizations and in smaller properties without training departments. Trainees can study when and where they desire, and tests, as well as evaluations before and after the course, can assess learning and be electronically tabulated, with results made available to managers. Content can be changed quickly, and updates can be put in place almost immediately.

Some employees have access to computers with Internet connections at their workstation; many others have computers at home. Some properties allow trainees to participate in e-learning activities in a spare office or, for example, at a dedicated desk in an occupied office area.

Programs are typically self-paced, and trainees can learn what is relevant and skip unnecessary and/or already known information. With many alternatives, feedback is possible because employees can e-mail questions to and receive responses from the training facilitator.

E-learning can also be used to pretest employees for placement in on-site training programs and even provide background content/information to expedite traditional training.

To learn more about e-training in hospitality-related topics, enter "hospitality e-learning courses" in your favorite search engine.

Performance Appraisal and Job Enrichment

An employee who is currently performing all tasks in his or her present position might agree to learn a new task in a higher-level position during a performance appraisal session. The extent to which the employee can perform the new task by the next performance appraisal is part of the second evaluation. In turn, additional job enlargement assignments and compensation increases could be based on that performance.

Job enrichment: An individual training method that occurs when additional tasks that are part of a position at the same organizational level are added to another position at the same organizational level.

Job rotation: The temporary assignment of employees to different positions or tasks to provide work variety or experience and to create "backup" expertise within the organization.

◆ **Job enrichment**—This training opportunity occurs when additional tasks that are part of a position at one organizational level are added to another position at the same level. Assume a cook's position is at the same organizational level as that of a baker. Job enrichment could occur as the cook learns baking tasks and as the baker learns cooking tasks.

◆ **Job rotation**—This training method involves the temporary assignment of employees to different tasks to provide work variety or experience. Like other individualized work methods, job rotation benefits the staff member and helps to create backup expertise within the organization.

Each individual training method noted above can help the hospitality organization over the short and longer term. However, each can also be part of a formal effort to provide additional training to staff members who are judged to be proficient in their existing position. There are numerous methods to involve staff in ongoing training, and they are applicable to almost all organizations regardless of size. The most important concerns relate to the interest of managers in providing ongoing learning opportunities for their staff.

HR MANAGEMENT ISSUES 7.1

"Trainers need to be patient," said Bernice, "but I have been so patient that I can't do my own work done while I'm training Lovi." Bernice was in the hotel's employee lunchroom, talking to her supervisor about her experiences with a new staff member.

"What's going on, Bernice?" asked the supervisor. "You've trained lots of people with no problem."

"Well," said Bernice, "first, I haven't trained anyone in the past six months and my duties have expanded during that time. Second, we've had problems with some of our equipment, and it's difficult to teach equipment operation when the equipment doesn't work. Also, we're short two employees since Wilma left and Rita went on sick leave. I haven't been feeling well, and I can't locate some of the training materials I've used in the past. Finally, Lovi wants to do a good job and she is slow to admit that she can do something before we go to the next step."

"There are some problems," responded Bernice's supervisor. "I'd like to help you, but I'm just swamped with other things. Let's just get through this training issue and then we'll have time to improve the training experience for you and the next trainee."

Case Study Questions

1. What is the real problem here, and who might be causing the most trouble?

2. What types of training resources would best help Bernice as she attempts to train Lovi?

3. What can Bernice's supervisor do to provide more time for Bernice to conduct training?

⁙ INTRODUCTION TO GROUP TRAINING

LEARNING OBJECTIVE 4. Prepare an overview of the group training process.

Group training is used to teach the same job-related information to more than one trainee simultaneously, and it can be done at or away from the work site. Advantages include:

◆ It can be time- and cost-effective when more than one staff member must receive the same information, for example, when several dietary assistants must learn how to complete a new dietary intake form.

◆ A large amount of information can be provided in a relatively short amount of time.

Disadvantages of group training typically relate to the difficulty of or inability to consider the individual differences of trainees when training. It is typically not possible to focus on a specific trainee's knowledge and experience, speed of learning, or desire to receive immediate and individualized feedback.

Fortunately, the advantages of both individual and group training can often be incorporated into one training program. For example, all new employees can learn general information in a group orientation program. This can be followed with individualized training so each trainee can learn specific tasks required for the position.

There are two popular group training methods in hospitality organizations:

◆ **Lecture method**—The trainer talks and may use audio/video equipment or handouts to facilitate the session, and question/answer components may be included. This method provides much information quickly but does not typically allow active trainee participation.

◆ **Demonstration method**—The trainer physically shows trainees how to perform position-specific tasks. Trainees can hear and see how something is done, often in the actual work environment. A potential disadvantage is that, without immediate and frequent repetition, trainees may forget all but the basics of the information presented. The best group training methods often include some lecture supplemented with other activities such as demonstrations, question and answer sessions, discussions, role plays, case study analysis, and project assignments. Note that role play and case study activities are discussed later in this chapter.

The best group delivery methods often combine several different techniques. For example:

◆ Lectures can be combined with class discussions, separate break-out discussions, and/or videos or demonstrations followed by discussions.

Group training: A training method that involves presenting the same information to more than one trainee simultaneously.

Use a Variety of Training Methods

Effective trainers consider the best ways to deliver content when developing group training lessons. An on-job training lesson might include demonstration, review of handouts, a question/answer session, and an on-job project. A training lesson for group training might involve the above tactics and exercises, including role plays and case study discussions during the group training. Effective trainers are aware of alternative training delivery methods, know when they are best used, and vary the tactics used to deliver training.

- ◆ Out-of-session projects can be assigned with follow-up presentation/discussion by the trainees.
- ◆ Small-group exercises, including role play and case studies, can be stand-alone sessions or components of broader training programs.

Other combinations of group training methods are possible. Trainers must always consider the best way to deliver training content while maintaining the trainees' interest in the session.

❖❖ PREPARING FOR GROUP TRAINING

LEARNING OBJECTIVE 5. Identify specific procedures to prepare for group training.

Experienced trainers know the best training content does not "automatically" yield the best training program. Problems can occur if the planning process does not address the training environment and any audio/video tools needed to facilitate the training.

Training Room Requirements

Training rooms should be clean, well-vented, free from noisy distractions, and provide controlled room temperature. Meeting facilities such as conference centers and lodging properties with significant meeting business incorporate these environmental factors as meeting spaces are planned. Unfortunately, in many hospitality organizations, these types of spaces are not available. Instead, trainers must use multipurpose space such as meeting rooms or staff dining areas and sometimes must creatively find space in dining rooms or other public access areas.

Proper table/chair arrangements help facilitate training. Figure 7.7 illustrates popular training room setups. In each instance, areas at the front of the room allow space for the trainer's materials and equipment. This can include a table, lectern, flip chart(s), laptop computer, and digital projector and screen (unless mounted on a wall or the ceiling) if PowerPoint slides will be used. Other items include those necessary for demonstrations, handouts, or other needs. Trainers also appreciate ice water or another beverage, so table-top space for this purpose is also required.

Each room setup shown in Figure 7.7 is useful for a specific purpose. The traditional classroom style favors interaction between the trainer and the individual trainees. Hopefully, it is possible for trainees to relocate their chairs for small-group activities. The modified classroom style allows trainers to walk freely between trainee tables, and the style can be used for interactive trainee exercises if chairs are relocated. The boardroom style encourages all trainees to interact with their peers and with the trainer. The large- and small-group discussion room styles allow, respectively, large or small groups of trainees to participate in interactive exercises. Note that in ideal training room setups there may be a traditional classroom setup for lecture and large-group discussion and one or more break-out rooms for small-group discussions.

Other considerations when planning training room setups include the following:

- ◆ There should be good line-of-sight opportunities for all trainees to see the trainer.
- ◆ Window shades or coverings may be required to properly illuminate video-driven sessions and to avoid conditions that distract trainees.
- ◆ While often not available except in dedicated conference or training rooms, modern training technology, including provision for computers and the need to power them and for wireless Internet access, is desirable.
- ◆ Today almost all group training environments are nonsmoking, and special accommodations for this purpose are typically not necessary.

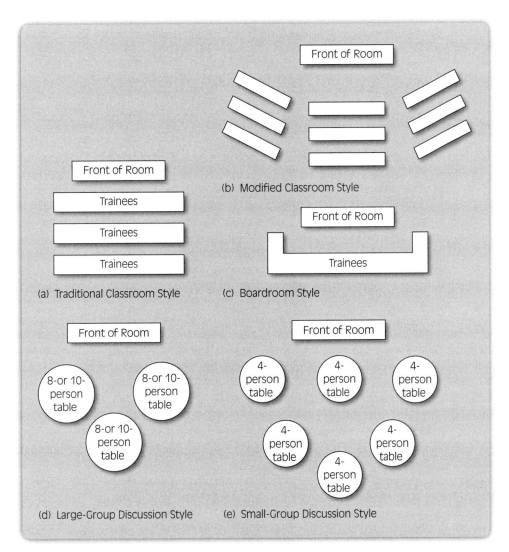

Figure 7.7 Training Room Setups: Traditional Classroom Style (a), Modified Classroom Style (b), Boardroom Style (c), Large-Group Discussion Style (d), and Small-Group Discussion Style (e)

Audio/Video Requirements

Effective trainers use supplemental media to emphasize training points and to maintain the trainees' attention. Among the most popular audio/video tools are flip charts, handouts, videos, and PowerPoint slides.

FLIP CHARTS

Many trainers use flip charts to illustrate training points. If they are used:

- ◆ Ensure the charts are in full view of all trainees.
- ◆ Print (preferably) neatly and in large print.
- ◆ Use different but only dark color felt-tipped pens designed for flip charts.
- ◆ Keep blank sheets between prepared sheets to prevent "bleed through."
- ◆ Don't "talk" to the flip chart; maintain eye contact with trainees.
- ◆ Ensure there is an ample supply of flip chart pages before the session begins.

Sometimes, especially during interactive sessions with trainees, trainers use all space on a flip chart and must continue on a separate page. Trainers should consider where completed pages will be placed and how, if at all, they will be adhered to a wall or other surface to be in full view of trainees. Trainers must ensure that no damage to the wall or other location occurs when the pages are attached.

HANDOUTS

Handouts can supplement and enhance training. They may contain a brief training outline or an exercise to be completed after applicable discussion. Alternatively, the trainer may circulate a worksheet to be completed as a sequence of training points is addressed.

The best use of handouts occurs when trainers:

◆   ensure each handout enhances learning opportunities in a way that is more appropriate than other alternatives;

◆   proofread (more than once) to ensure that there are no word processing or other errors;

◆   ensure that multiple handouts are in proper sequence;

◆   prepare (duplicate) sufficient quantities of handouts;

◆   confirm that handouts are brief, well-organized, and relevant;

◆   confirm that handout information correspond to training points; and

◆   allow space for trainees to take notes, if desired.

Trainers should consider when handouts should be circulated (e.g., before or at the beginning of the training session or when they are discussed). They should also consider when and how much time is required for trainees to read the handouts before they are used.

VIDEOS

Trainers teaching generic topics have an increasingly large variety of off-the-shelf videos available. Those employed by large hospitality organizations may also have customized videos. Ensuring a video is the most appropriate way to deliver training content is important. It is probably rare that an off-the-shelf video explains a training concept exactly as the trainer desires. Instead, some revision in training content may be required or, alternatively, trainers must explain differences between the training points and video content.

Another concern involves the time planned for the video activity. At one extreme, a video may be so short that its excellent quality is marginalized by the cost of renting video equipment. Alternatively, videos that are longer than desired require the trainer to judge whether time should be taken from another training concept or whether only part of the video should be shown. The latter problem becomes more significant when a video must be stopped and restarted to eliminate unnecessary material.

Trainers should preview videos to determine differences, if any, between its content and that desired for training. Further, if discussion materials supplement an off-the-shelf video, they may need revision to fit the trainer's objectives. Trainers should decide whether to show the video from start to finish or to make training points as the video is shown. Some videos have clearly marked stopping points; others don't, and materials must then be prepared accordingly.

Video equipment must be set up before the training begins, and the trainer must know how to use it. If it must be cued to a starting point, this should also be done before the training begins.

POWERPOINT OVERHEADS

PowerPoint overheads are increasingly used today. Technology makes them easy to develop, and they can have a significant visual impact. Their basic purposes are to supplement, emphasize, and facilitate lecture or discussion points. Many tactics are useful, and these include minimizing the number of words, using a font style and size that is easy to read, and including appropriate and interesting graphics.

There are literally thousands of websites providing information about PowerPoint development and presentation techniques. (To view applicable websites , use your favorite search engine and type in "how to use PowerPoints to train.")

Savvy trainers who use PowerPoint allow appropriate time to connect their computer to the projector; different projectors require different start-up procedures. Hospitality operations that generate significant meeting business typically have audio/video technicians to set up the equipment and to manage the technical difficulties that can occur. Unfortunately, trainers in many organizations do not have technical expertise available. The best suggestion is to allow ample time for equipment setup.

Trainers often hand out hard copies of their PowerPoint overheads in formats that include two or three images per page with additional space available for trainees to record notes. This provides an organized way for trainees to take notes, minimizes the number of notes that need to be taken, and provides convenient resources for trainees' use after the training is completed.

❖ FACILITATING GROUP TRAINING

LEARNING OBJECTIVE 6. Discuss procedures to facilitate group training.

Effective trainers must be good communicators. This is important when an on-job training method is used, but it is especially critical for group training. Trainers have fewer opportunities to solicit feedback and determine whether training content is understood.

Trainer Presentation Skills

Many group trainers are excellent public speakers who can keep their trainees' attention. One does not need to be a professional speaker, however, to be an effective group trainer. What is required is a planned, organized, and practiced approach to training delivery that avoids common public speaking mistakes. Trainers who have this foundation of public speaking skills will likely deliver an effective training session.

Effective public speaking begins with a well-planned training lesson or outline that identifies the main points and subpoints to be addressed and the time scheduled for the entire session and for the training points within it. Figure 7.8 shows the three basic steps in presenting a group training session.

Let's discuss the three steps identified in Figure 7.8. Step 1 indicates the need for an introduction.

- ◆ **Use a warm and genuine introduction.** If necessary, the trainer should introduce him- or herself and allow the trainees to introduce themselves. Personal introductions can include information about each trainee's position, years of experience, and personal and professional training goals.

A Note About Public Speaking

Numerous surveys have queried the general public about their fears, and the fear of public speaking is near the top of the list for many survey respondents. While concerns about public speaking might be greatest as one addresses an audience of strangers, it can also be a concern to some trainers who interact with the trainees every day.

Trainers who are competent in the subject matter, who have properly prepared for the session, and who recognize that the goal of training is to improve on-job performance (not to impress the trainees) will likely have reduced anxiety about public speaking. Over time they should be able to speak to large or small groups without stress, and public speaking activities may become an enjoyable part of their experience.

Figure 7.8 Steps in a Successful Group Training Session

◆ **The introduction should focus on "what's in it for me" from the trainees' perspectives**—For example, "Lately we experienced some problems in taking inventory that have caused frustrating rework. Thanks to your input, we've collected some ideas to resolve these problems, and we're going to discuss them today."

◆ **The training session can be previewed**—Training goals can be noted, and trainees can be informed about training tactics. ("We'll view a video and conduct a role play that will be fun and interesting.")

◆ **Establish training requirements,** including those about restroom and coffee breaks, cell phone usage, trainee participation, and related issues.

◆ **Use an ice breaker, if applicable,** to help trainees transition into the session.

◆ **Indicate when questions should be asked**—For example, they can be asked when they arise during the session or they can be held for discussion at its end.

◆ **Gain the trainees' attention**—Ask for trainee anecdotes related to or tell one's own stories about situations related to the training topic.

A note about humor: Many trainers begin a training session with a humorous story. This can gain the trainees' attention and suggest the training will be enjoyable. Inappropriate humor can hinder the training, however, and many topics socially acceptable in the past are inappropriate today. In a workplace that is becoming more culturally diverse, anticipating how a humorous story will be viewed by all trainees is increasingly difficult.

Step 2 in Figure 7.8 addresses training delivery.

◆ **Limit the number of training points**—This is easy when an effectively developed training lesson provides the presentation's outline.

◆ **Discuss topics in the same sequence as noted in the introduction**—If three objectives were previewed at the beginning of the session, they should drive the training sequence that follows.

◆ **Use transitions between main points,** for example, "Now that you know how to assemble the equipment, let's learn how to safely operate it."

◆ **Conclude each main point with a summary, for example,** "To this point, you have learned that the equipment must be operated according to the manufacturer's instructions. Now let's learn how to use it for some specialty items."

◆ **Manage questions effectively** by repeating them, providing a response, or asking other trainees to provide a suggested response. After discussion, requesting that the trainee asking the question respond to an open-ended question can help the trainer to ensure the trainee understands.

◆ **Be aware of nonverbal communication**—Body language can frequently tell the trainees more than the trainer can say. Facial expressions can suggest that the trainer is frustrated with their inability to learn; pacing back and forth may suggest the trainer is bored.

Experienced trainers keep trainees "tuned in" to the session by providing methods for their active involvement and by asking open-ended questions of all trainees (not just those who volunteer). They speak at an appropriate volume and do not speak too quickly or slowly. Effective trainers avoid slang terms and jargon that hinder communication effectiveness. This is frequently a challenge because of the diverse group of employees in many organizations.

The trainees' language fluency can become a significant concern that adds a new dimension to many of the points already made about effective group training presentations. Effective trainers pronounce words correctly, change voice tones, and avoid public speaking errors such as the frequent use of expressions such as, "you know," "let's see," "ahhhhh," and "like, you know."

Step 3 in Figure 7.8 indicates the need for an effective closing. Summarize main points and refer to something noted during the introduction: "When we began the training, I indicated that you would learn how to safely operate the equipment." The closing should also involve a "call to action" about what the trainees should do, for example, "Now that you've learned how to safely operate the equipment, please do so all the time. The right way is the safe way, and this standard should not be compromised."

Group training will not "automatically" be effective if the trainer is a good public speaker; however, training cannot be effective if the trainer is not a good communicator. Fortunately, this skill can be enhanced through experience and when the trainer has an interest in improving communication skills.

Managing Participant Interactions

A lecture-only presentation is often ineffective, and trainers must attempt to get the trainees involved in their own learning process. One way is to ask questions and lead discussions.

Some trainers discuss a training point, ask for questions, and lead a discussion stemming from the questions before continuing to the next point. Others ask questions on a more frequent basis throughout the training session. Both approaches can be effective and depend on the trainer's teaching style. Effective trainers do not lecture extensively, read from lecture notes, stray from an organized sequence of training points, or move on when they sense trainees do not understand concepts being presented.

What should trainers do if it seems that only one or a few trainees understand the material? When redundancy is not necessary for the majority of trainees, it is generally best to continue the training. A general comment such as, "I'd be happy to discuss this concept further with any of you during the break or after the session" may be helpful. Alternatively, especially when the trainer knows the trainees, he or she can initiate a discussion with applicable trainees about troublesome concepts outside of the training session.

Basic principles can help trainers guide discussions.

- ◆ **Have an attitude of openness**—Trainers should not be defensive and have to "sell" a training point. They should solicit questions, consider discussion feedback, and use it as a benchmark for assessing comprehension. Trainees who note, "When I tried that, it didn't work," and "I think there's another way to do that," are providing excellent comments to direct the trainer's responses and improve the training.

- ◆ **Treat trainees as professionals**—Successful hospitality organizations promote teamwork, and this is as important during training as at other times.

- ◆ **Ask clear and direct questions**—The question "Does everyone understand?" is not as helpful as an open-ended question such as, "Why is it important to consider a guest's concern when addressing complaints?"

- ◆ **Invite participants to make comments**—Some trainees like to dominate the training. Others may be passive but able to contribute to it. A question such as "Sally, what do you think?" can help generate new opinions and information.

- ◆ **Allow only one person to talk at one time**—This rule shows respect and is important to control the training environment. Comments such as, "It's important that everyone express an opinion," or the question, "I'd like to learn what you think about this. Who wants to be first?" can often be helpful.

- ◆ **Listen carefully; show respect for all ideas**—Trainers should listen to everyone's comments to understand what is being said. A common mistake—formulating a response while tuning out additional points—must be avoided.

- ◆ **Encourage more than one response**—Effective trainers make trainees feel at ease, and they subtly encourage responses, including questions and comments from everyone. This helps assess comprehension to determine whether and what additional information is necessary.
- ◆ **Don't fear silence**—If there is no response to a question, ask another or use it to guide the next interaction: "Since there's no response, I'd like to repeat what I'm asking another way."
- ◆ **Keep the discussion focused**—Using a training lesson is an excellent way to do this. Trainee discussions can be more difficult to guide, but an effective trainer knows when to steer the discussion back to the applicable topic: "That's an interesting idea, John. It would be great to discuss that, but we should focus on inventory management so we'll have time to cover everything."

Experienced trainers know that more, rather than less, time than planned is often needed to fully address a training concept. To compensate, they try to stay on point. They also evaluate training sessions as they evolve to make time adjustments to focus on the most important training points.

Types of Trainees

There are three different types of trainees in group sessions, and each must be managed differently. Some trainees are passive and less responsive than peers. To include them, trainers can:

- ◆ repeat or restate questions;
- ◆ provide examples of training points and ask trainees for additional examples;
- ◆ break a training point into specific elements and ask a passive trainee how an element relates to a larger concept; and
- ◆ directly question a passive trainee about the topic.

Other trainees try to dominate the session, and tactics to manage them include the following:

- ◆ Don't call on or make eye contact with them.
- ◆ When they speak, wait for a moment, thank them for their input, do not make a comment about that input, and call on another trainee.
- ◆ Ask them to take notes during future training sessions.

Sometimes a trainee may become disruptive, and his or her actions cannot remain unnoticed. Then it is appropriate to:

- ◆ ask the trainee to please make positive contributions;
- ◆ request that all conversations relate to the discussion; and
- ◆ remain enthusiastic and friendly and continue with the training.

During the next training break, the trainer should talk with the disruptive trainee, note the problem(s), and personally request the behavior cease. Note that the trainer should express concern about the trainee's behavior rather than about the trainee him- or herself.

Group Training Exercises

Creative trainers can use role play, case study, and brainstorming exercises to allow trainees to more fully participate in the training.

ROLE PLAY EXERCISES

Role plays are group training exercises in which trainees pretend to be people in situations addressed by the training who apply information presented in the training. These can be very useful because trainees can practice what they have learned in a risk-free situation.

Consider a training session that addresses how to handle guest complaints or how to discuss an unacceptable budget variance with a unit manager. The appropriate techniques could be explained, a question and answer discussion could evolve, and a role play could be initiated.

Trainees might be broken into three-person teams. One trainee could pretend to be the trained staff member applying the principles just taught. A second trainee could role play the individual with whom the trainee is interacting. The third trainee could be an observer. The trainee using proper tactics could respond to comments made by the second trainee, and the trainee observer could note how the situation was managed. At the conclusion of the role play, the trainees could switch roles until each has practiced and demonstrated the skills. Final components of the role play exercise could be to report back to the convened group and reinforcement and a summary by the trainer.

Principles to help trainers manage role plays include the following:

◆ Provide a complete orientation.

◆ Explain the purpose to allow trainees to apply training principles in a risk-free situation.

◆ Stress the need for objective feedback. Trainees critiquing their peers should focus on training points.

◆ Permit participants to develop evaluation factors. Assume the trainer presented five tactics to manage guest complaints. Each trainee team could determine how to assess the extent to which each tactic was addressed.

◆ Allow time for each trainee to consider the strategies to be used when interacting with other trainees during a role play.

CASE STUDY EXERCISES

A case study is a group training activity that allows trainees to study a real-world situation and to use training points to address the case study problem(s). Two examples of training content that could be supplemented with a case study are:

1. The description of an organization with high staff turnover rates to determine what might be causing the problem.

2. A budget and income statement could be shown. Follow-up analysis could allow trainees to determine where financial variances exist and to consider what might be causing them.

Prepared case studies are available from numerous sources. One of the best is contemporary textbooks that address topics covered by the training. Alternatively, trainers can write short (several paragraphs) case studies that focus directly on specific training session topics.

To best manage case studies, trainers should:

◆ ensure cases are realistic;

◆ incorporate training concepts;

◆ allow trainees time to study the case;

◆ serve as a facilitator when leading case discussions; and

◆ summarize each case's learning points.

Some trainers separate trainees into teams, with each team addressing the same or a different case. Each team reads and prepares a response to the case study and reports findings/recommendations to the convened group of trainees. A follow-up discussion then is facilitated by the trainer. When one case study is discussed by different teams, the learning objective typically emphasizes the largest possible number of perspectives. When teams consider different cases, the learning objective may consider a wider range of situations to be addressed with training session content.

BRAINSTORMING

Brainstorming is a group problem-solving method in which all group members suggest possible ideas. A typical use of this tactic in a work setting involves groups of employees who suggest ideas to address a problem.

Training exercises can allow trainees to brainstorm how a training point could be applied in a work situation, alternative solutions to case study or role play issues, or in the development and/or conduct of out-of-session projects.

Trainers should use various brainstorming ground rules:

- ◆ Encourage creative ideas.

- ◆ Request that alternatives generated during a brainstorming session not be evaluated until all alternatives are expressed.

- ◆ Provide an opportunity to "piggyback" on ideas (i.e., to allow one idea to suggest a variation of another).

- ◆ Provide necessary time for trainees to study the ideas presented and then to continue the brainstorming session.

- ◆ Provide an opportunity for the trainer and trainees to organize or categorize ideas and to evaluate them when the brainstorming session is completed.

Trainers and trainees will likely find that brainstorming tactics used during training can be useful opportunities for generating ideas for process improvement when the staff members return to the work environment.

Special Training Issues

Several training issues can impact training outcomes.

- ◆ **Be aware of annoying or distracting mannerisms**—A trainer's body language can distract trainees. Some trainers may not be aware of these expressions and actions and could easily correct them if they were. Trainers can make a presentation to professional colleagues and solicit objective feedback, or they can arrange a videotaping to learn something that might otherwise be overlooked.

- ◆ **Schedule training so applicable procedures can be implemented on a timely basis**—Hopefully, trainees will be enthused about their training and want to immediately begin applying the knowledge and skills they have learned. This may not be possible if, for example, necessary equipment has not been installed or when one phase of an initiative must be implemented before a follow-up phase. Then delaying training and/or providing introductory training followed by detailed training when content can be implemented might be useful.

- ◆ **Effectively manage trainees who don't want training**—Tactics include making a direct request ("Joe, we're looking for input from everyone after this discussion, so you'll need to be prepared for it"). Taking a short training break so the trainer can personally speak with an inattentive trainee may also be useful. There may be other times when many trainees appear unresponsive. Then reconsidering the training approach and implementing efforts to reduce concerns become necessary.

- ◆ **Don't attempt to accomplish too much**—Allow sufficient time for practice (skill training) and discussion (group training). Realize that training often takes longer than the planned time.

- ◆ **Listen to trainees**—Be alert for trainee "overload" and side conversations, blank stares, and a preoccupation with nontraining activities. Remember also that the trainees' body language can "speak" to the trainer.

- ◆ **Be flexible**—Change the training schedule, content, or location or use alternative training delivery formats, when necessary, to make the training more beneficial.

- ◆ **When applicable, field test (pilot) the training**—Assume that new technology will be used to manage inventory data. Should that technology be installed in the quickest manner possible, and should all affected staff members be trained accordingly? Alternatively, is a phased implementation of the new technology with staggered training most appropriate? Experienced trainers talk with operating managers to consider these issues and make decisions based on their analysis.

◆ **Keep the training on track of stated objectives**—This is easily done when training plans and training lessons have been carefully developed and are consistently used. The trainer's role is to facilitate training by pacing it according to a realistic schedule.

◆ **Don't "reinvent the wheel"; if cost-effective materials are available, use them**—A corollary to this principle is also important: Don't rewrite training materials that have been developed in previous sessions. The use of an organized training handbook can ensure that materials can easily be located when needed.

◆ **Rehearse before training**—Just as trainees must practice to learn a task, trainers should also practice to gain experience with their presentation. Be aware of appearance and hygiene. Trainers serve as role models for the trainees with whom they interact.

◆ **Don't develop an inappropriate trainer's ego**—Remember that the objective of training is to improve the trainees' performance, not to impress trainees with the trainer's knowledge, skills, or experience.

◆ **Keep training sessions as short as possible**—It may have been a long since some trainees participated in a training session. Many will feel more at ease on the job than in training. Experienced trainers know that several short training sessions are better than one relatively long one.

◆ **Recognize the importance of the training environment**—Experienced trainers know that the environment of the meeting room is often more detrimental to training effectiveness than is the training content or its delivery.

◆ **Have back-up contingencies for problems**—Training challenges can arise even when the very best training plans and training lessons are available. Some problems, such as inoperative audio/visual equipment and out-of-place training materials, can be anticipated. Others such as building emergencies or trainee health problems may have generated fewer planning considerations. Should these instances occur, however, trainees are likely to look to the trainer for the appropriate reactions.

◆ **Respect the trainees' knowledge and experience**—Wise trainers recognize that adult trainees bring a wide variety of personal experiences, attitudes, core values, and preconceptions to their training experience. They recognize and use them to deliver the best possible training.

◆ **Link training to assessment and performance**—Hopefully, training will create behavioral change, and this will yield results that are beneficial to the trainees and the organization.

◆ **Have fun!**—Trainees cannot learn if they do not enjoy their training. What is pleasurable to one trainee may not be for another. Using a variety of training tactics that involve active trainee participation are preferable to less interactive approaches.

⬩⬩ TRAINING EVALUATION

LEARNING OBJECTIVE 7. Discuss the training evaluation process.

Evaluation is the final step in the training process, and it can indicate the training was successful (goals were attained). Alternatively, the evaluation can suggest the need to repeat the entire planning process or to refocus efforts on specific planning steps.

Consider a training program to improve supervisory skills to reduce turnover. Assume the initial definition of training needs led to a training program to address improvements in how supervisors interact with employees. Also assume that post-training evaluation indicated that the turnover rate was not reduced. Instead, further analysis revealed that the problem was really selection and orientation of staff members. In this example, trainers may need to plan and implement an entirely different training program to properly address turnover.

In a more common situation, post-training evaluation may indicate that the program was less than totally successful. It did focus on the correct problems, but the training plans and/or training lessons didn't provide the best content. In this example, only selected steps rather than the entire training process may need revision to improve training results.

Reasons to Evaluate Training

Time, money, and labor are increasingly in limited supply. Managers must determine whether their commitment of resources to planning and implementing training procedures is a better use than are alternatives. This is one reason training evaluation is important.

More specific reasons to evaluate training include to:

◆ **Assess the extent to which training achieved planned results**—Training objectives identify competencies to be addressed in training and provide a benchmark against which training can be evaluated. Assume one objective of a training program is to help a front-desk agent learn how to register guests using 10 sequential steps in the company's operating manual. This objective drives the training (how to register guests), and it provides a way to evaluate training effectiveness (the extent to which each required step is sequentially used).

◆ **Identify strengths and weaknesses of training**—Few training programs are 100% effective or ineffective. Some training lessons are better than others, some training activities are more useful than their counterparts, and some trainers may be more effective than their peers. Successful evaluation can identify training aspects that should be continued and elements that may require revision.

◆ **Determine the success of individual trainees**—Trainees who are successful (achieve planned results on the job) will not require remedial training. However, others may need revised and/or repeated training. Assessment of individual trainees is relatively easy when an individualized, on-job training method is used, but it is more difficult with group training. The importance of the assessment is, however, equally important.

◆ **Gather information to help justify future programs**—When the success of a training activity is quantified, objective information becomes available to help justify future training efforts. Alternatively, managers can determine whether resources are better invested in other improvement efforts.

◆ **Determine trainees eligible for future training**—Some organizations provide educational or training activities in formalized career development programs that require prerequisite training. Other companies have formal or informal "fast-track" programs in which selected trainees who successfully complete training programs are eligible for additional training opportunities. These, in turn, lead to increased promotional considerations as vacancies occur. In both of these instances, managers must know whether and to what extent individual trainees successfully completed the training.

◆ **Assess costs/benefits of training**—This reason for training evaluation has already been suggested. The expenditure of any resource must generate a return greater than the cost of resources allocated for it. Some benefits of training, including improved morale and increased interest in attaining quality goals, are difficult to quantify. Others, including improved guest service skills and reduced operating costs for a specified task, may be easier to quantify, and both could be assessed by training evaluation.

◆ **Reinforce major points for trainees**—Some training evaluation methods, including objective tests and performance appraisal interviews, allow evaluators to reinforce the most important training points. For example, questions on a written assessment likely address the most important training concepts. If they are self-graded or reviewed by the trainer, reinforcement of these important points becomes possible. Likewise, if performance appraisal interviews address training concepts, additional opportunities for reinforcement arise.

◆ **Assess trainees' reactions to training**—Trainers who are interested in improving training programs want to gain the trainees' perspectives about the programs. Anonymous input gained before, during, and after training can be helpful in this assessment.

HR Management in Action

The importance of teamwork in the success of hospitality management organizations is well known. Traditionally, teams involve people who work together toward a common goal that is defined outside of the team. For example, dining room servers help each other using processes developed by their managers.

Some organizations are now using self-directed teams of employees who work together toward a common goal that is defined by the team members themselves. An example occurs when dining room servers are empowered to define and implement procedures that maximize guest satisfaction.

The use of self-directed teams has significant impact on the HR function, including training activities. For example, if the team defines how tasks are to be done, the members are performing position analysis. The members themselves may be involved in developing, implementing, and evaluating training programs. Other responsibilities with HR implications might include roles in compensation, process improvement, policy development, long-range planning, and evaluating the team's effectiveness.

The widespread use of self-directed teams in the hospitality industry may be years away. However, their implementation does not need to be "all or nothing," and the tactic likely recognizes some of the interests of the changing workforce.

◆ **Assess trainers' reactions to training**—"There's always a better way" is an old saying that applies to training as well as to other management tactics. Trainers who have used a training lesson, for example, may well have ideas about ways to improve it in the future.

Levels of Training Evaluation

Many managers think about training evaluation in the context of an after-training assessment. While training should be evaluated at its completion (and perhaps many months after its completion as well), evaluation can also be helpful before training even begins and while it is conducted.

Any training evaluation method must address at least five assessment concerns:

1. **Valid**—Training evaluation methods must be valid; they must measure what they are supposed to measure. Assume a training objective focuses on the ability of trainees to successfully complete an inventory count using methods taught during training. Trainee demonstration of scanning equipment operation and proper use of inventory counting procedures suggests that the training was successful (at least at the time of the demonstration). In contrast, if training assessment queried trainees about issues such as "Did you like the training?" and "Did the trainer seem enthusiastic?" the trainers could not determine whether training objectives were attained.

2. **Reliable**—Training evaluation methods are reliable when they consistently provide the same results. Training activities that are implemented in the same way by the same trainers using the same training resources and procedures for employees in the same position may be consistent. Will the results be the same or similar each time it is replicated? Trainers do not know unless the same evaluation methods are used.

3. **Objective**—Objective evaluation methods provide quantitative (measurable) training assessments. Acquisition of knowledge can be objectively measured by performance on a well-designed test. Efficiency in a skill might best be assessed by observing the trainee's performance of the task after training. Then performance can be considered "acceptable" if the procedures used are in concert with those taught during training.

4. **Practical**—A training evaluation method is practical when the time and effort required for the assessment are "worth" its results. Knowledge assessments that require trainees to memorize mundane facts and skill demonstrations that are benchmarked against staff with extensive experience and efficiency in performing the task are not practical.

5. **Simple**—An evaluation method is simple when it is easily applied by the trainer, when it is easily understood by the trainees, and when results are easy to assess and analyze by those evaluating the training.

Let's review some methods for use before, during, and after training that incorporate these assessment concerns.

EVALUATION BEFORE TRAINING

Assume a trainee participated in a food safety training session and completed a knowledge assessment at its conclusion. Assume further that the trainee missed only two questions of the 20 that were asked. Many trainers would likely conclude that the training was successful because the participant scored 90% (18 questions correct ÷ 20 questions total = 90%). In fact, the training could really have been a waste of the organization's resources and the trainee's time if the trainee already knew the concepts addressed by the 18 questions that were answered correctly before the session began. In actuality, the after-training evaluation really measured what the trainee knew when the training was completed rather than what he or she learned from the training session.

To address this concern, some trainers use a pretest/post-test evaluation. A trainer can identify key concepts to be addressed during the training. These concepts are addressed in a pretest administered before the training begins. This same measurement tool using the same questions is then administered at the end of training. The improvement in scores between the pre- and post-tests represents a measure of training effectiveness.

There are other advantages of pretest/post-test evaluation:

♦   It provides trainees with an overview (preview) of the training.

♦   It helps trainees identify some of the most important concepts to be addressed during training.

♦   It presents an opportunity for trainers to preview the lesson and suggest priority learning points before training begins.

As is true with other training evaluation methods, administering the post-training assessment several months (or even longer) after training is completed may also be helpful. This tactic can help determine the extent to which training information has been retained and applied in the workplace.

Another pretraining evaluation tactic involves an exercise that requests trainees to answer the following concern: "If this training is ideal, I will learn the following from it:. . . ." This activity can be included in an introductory session that previews subject matter to be addressed in the training. Trainees might be asked to retain their responses to this "ideal training" exercise until the end of training. Then they could undertake a post-training assessment to note their perceptions about the extent to which the training was ideal.

Figure 7.9 illustrates a self-assessment form that could be used.

EVALUATION DURING TRAINING

Effective trainers should indicate in an introductory session that they will ask for feedback during the session. As this feedback is solicited, trainers can obtain a "first-half" reality check to yield helpful information to improve the remainder of the training. Trainers facilitating group sessions can ask trainees to write anonymous responses to statements such as:

♦   I wish you would stop doing (saying) …

♦   I hope we continue to …

♦   I don't understand …

- ◆ I hope you will begin to …
- ◆ A concept that I wish you would discuss further is …
- ◆ A concept I want to learn more about that has yet to be discussed is …

The major point is to learn how to maximize use of the remaining training time. Then revisions to training content and/or delivery methods can better ensure attainment of training objectives.

TRAINING TOPIC: _____

NAME OF TRAINEE (OPTIONAL): _____

TO BE COMPLETED BEFORE TRAINING

If this training program is ideally effective, I will learn the following:

TO BE COMPLETED AFTER TRAINING

To what extent did you learn what you wanted to learn (check one)?

	NOT ALL	SOMEWHAT	VERY MUCH
1. _____ _____ _____	☐	☐	☐
2. _____ _____ _____	☐	☐	☐
3. _____ _____ _____	☐	☐	☐
4. _____ _____ _____	☐	☐	☐
5. _____ _____ _____	☐	☐	☐

COMMENTS:

_____

_____

_____

Figure 7.9 Training Self-Assessment Form

Should Training Evaluations Be Anonymous?

nput from any training evaluation method is not useful unless it is truthful. It is generally easier to obtain anonymous input from group trainees than from those participating in individualized training for an obvious reason: "There is safety in numbers."

The best evaluations are provided by unidentified trainees who do not fear on-job retaliation (especially if they are supervised by the trainer) and those who believe the request for input is genuine and that the results will be used. Hospitality organizations with a culture of respect for employees and a history of utilizing their input for improvements will likely obtain useful feedback. By contrast, organizations that suffer from adversarial relationships between supervisors and staff may have great difficulty in obtaining useful information by any evaluation method.

Given the above, should names of any evaluators be requested? Probably not, unless there is unique and specific reason to do so. As a compromise, some trainers request anonymous input and then seek out trainees to provide more detailed one-on-one input. Mentors in some organizations receive trainee input and summarize this information in reports to HR or other applicable staff members.

EVALUATION AFTER TRAINING

After-training evaluation can help assess whether training achieved its planned results. It may also identify how training sessions might be improved and assess the trainees' success. Numerous evaluation methods can be used. Experienced trainers often use more than one method and analyze the combined results to yield a comprehensive assessment of training results.

Training Evaluation Methods

Several training evaluation methods are in common use. Hopefully, more than one tactic is used. Each can provide anecdotal information that, in total, can suggest training outcomes.

Common assessment methods include:

Objective tests:
Assessment tools such as multiple choice and true/false instruments that have only one correct answer and yield a reduced need for trainers to interpret trainees' responses.

◆   **Objective tests**—These can be written, oral, and/or skill-based and include traditional written exams, oral assessments (hopefully using open-ended questions), and/or after-training demonstrations. Written and oral assessments are typically used to assess after-training knowledge, and skill-based assessments address physical (skill) proficiencies. Written exams can be multiple choice, true/false, fill in the blank, matching, short answer, or essay.

Multiple choice and true/false questions are most often used in hospitality organizations because they are **objective tests**. There is only one correct answer, little or no interpretation is needed, and minimal time is required for trainees to complete the exam and for trainers to score it. Lengthy exams can be computer-scored using optical scan (op-scan) sheets completed by the trainees. Objective measurements should be written after training objectives and instructional materials are developed, and a separate assessment should be used for each performance objective in the training lesson.

◆   **Observation of performance after training**—Managers, supervisors, and trainers can "manage by walking around" and, in the process, note whether knowledge and skills taught during training are being applied. Storeroom personnel can be observed as they receive incoming products, and procedures used can be compared with those presented during training. Note that when proper procedures are used, a "Great job!" compliment is always in order. By contrast, a coaching activity to remind staff members about incorrectly performed procedures may also be needed.

◆ **Records of events (critical incidents)**—Assume there has been theft of food from a storage area after training in appropriate accounting and control procedures has been presented. Subsequent investigation determines that the recommended procedures were not used. The training program would not be considered effective, and staff with responsibilities to double-check as part of the inventory control process must, at the least, be retrained. Alternatively, procedures may need to be revised and followed with updated training in revised procedures.

◆ **Self-reports**—Figures 7.10–7.12 illustrate formats for questioning processes that could provide input for training evaluation. Figure 7.10 illustrates a simple rating scale containing evaluation factors that trainees can rate from very unacceptable to very acceptable. Figure 7.11 lists open-ended questions to which trainees can respond. Finally, Figure 7.12 illustrates the format for and questions that might be applicable to a group training session that involves numerous training lessons.

◆ **Interviews with trainees and/or trainers**—The use of open-ended questions by trainers, managers, mentors, and/or HR personnel may provide useful input about the training. In addition, trainers can be questioned by their supervisor and/or HR staff for the same purpose.

◆ **Trainee surveys**—Trainees can be questioned immediately after training, months after training, and/or during performance evaluation sessions about their training perspectives. General "staff opinion" surveys can, in part, address training issues, as well.

◆ **Third-party opinions**—Feedback from guests can help assess training that addressed aspects of products and service that affect them. The use of **mystery shoppers** in applicable types of hospitality operations is another example. Feedback can also be generated by comment cards, interviews, and/or follow-up surveys with guests.

Mystery shopper: A person posing as a guest who observes and experiences an organization's products and services during a visit and who then reports findings to managers. Also referred to as a "secret shopper."

TRAINING TOPIC: _____

EVALUATION FACTOR	RATING FACTOR		
TIME SPENT ON TOPIC	VERY UNACCEPTABLE	NEUTRAL (NO COMMENT)	VERY ACCEPTABLE
Applicable to job	☐	☐	☐
My interest in topic	☐	☐	☐
Organization of training	☐	☐	☐
Effectiveness of training	☐	☐	☐
Usefulness of training methods	☐	☐	☐
Comfort of training room	☐	☐	☐

My interest in future training sessions: _____

COMMENTS:

_____

_____

Figure 7.10 Trainee Evaluation Rating Scale

Training Topic: _____

1. The three most useful aspects of the training were:

   _____

   _____

   _____

   _____

   _____

2. The three least useful aspects of the training were:

   _____

   _____

   _____

   _____

   _____

3. I will apply the following information learned during the training on the job:

   _____

   _____

   _____

   _____

   _____

4. The best way(s) to improve the training is by:

   _____

   _____

   _____

   _____

   _____

5. What I liked about the program:

   _____

   _____

   _____

   _____

   _____

6. What I disliked about the program:

   _____

   _____

   _____

   _____

   _____

Figure 7.11   Open-Ended Training Evaluation Form

Summary Training Evaluation

Your response to this evaluation will assist us in evaluating different aspects of the program.

Please indicate the extent to which you agree or disagree with the following statements.

| 5 = STRONGLY AGREE | 1 = STRONGLY DISAGREE | (MARK ONE ANSWER ONLY) |

	5	4	3	2	1
The training met my expectations.	5	4	3	2	1
The training challenged my thinking.	5	4	3	2	1
The training held my attention.	5	4	3	2	1
The training appropriately involved the participants.	5	4	3	2	1
The subject matter presented was useful and worthwhile to my career.	5	4	3	2	1
The training was well organized.	5	4	3	2	1
The training matched the description as it was announced.	5	4	3	2	1
The training presented information that was new to me.	5	4	3	2	1
As a result of the training, I am more confident of my knowledge and ability.	5	4	3	2	1
The training environment met my expectations.	5	4	3	2	1

COMMENTS:

_____

_____

Figure 7.12   Training Summary Evaluation Form

- ◆ **Analysis of operating data**—Training that addresses guest service and food costs should yield, respectively, increased guest service scores and lowered food costs (if components of these data can be separated) to determine how they were influenced by training.

- ◆ **Exit interviews**—Formal and informal conversations with employees who are leaving the organization can provide training evaluation input. Unlike their peers, most departing staff will likely have fewer concerns about providing candid and frank responses to queries about training, among other issues. Managers may learn, for example, that inadequate orientation and initial on-job training contributed to frustrations that resulted in turnover.

FOLLOW-UP DOCUMENTATION

Documentation is a final part of training evaluation. Training records to be maintained in the applicable staff member's personnel file include:

- ◆ Name of trainee
- ◆ Training dates
- ◆ Training topics
- ◆ Notes, if any, regarding successful completion
- ◆ Other applicable information

This documentation is useful for planning professional development programs, for considering staff member promotions, and for performance appraisal input. Documentation of training is also helpful when trainers develop long- or short-term plans that address training and professional development opportunities for staff members.

Training and Return on Investment

It's easy to say, "Training should always be worth more than it costs." However, it is not always easy to determine the cost of training or to quantify its benefits. Increasingly, however, and for good reason, HR managers must justify training by confirming that money spent for it cannot be better used for other purposes.

Hopefully, training objectives can assist with return on investment (ROI) assessment. Suggestive selling to increase check averages in the restaurant, up-selling at the front desk to increase hotel room rates, and supervisory training to increase entry-level employee retention rates are examples of activities that can be assessed by studying data before and after training. Costs for trainers' and trainees' time and for materials can be determined, and a comparison of benefits can yield some ROI conclusions.

Some training efforts such as those addressing how to clean a guest room and how to prepare food items can be evaluated (by inspection scores and adherence to standard recipes, respectively). However, these programs are more difficult to assess with an ROI emphasis: While training costs can be calculated, how does one quantify the training benefits?

In today's competitive hospitality industry, a "hunch" that training is "good" can be helpful. Whenever possible, however, more objective measurements are needed.

HR MANAGEMENT ISSUES 7.2

"I don't understand," said Rolando. "Our trainer's formal evaluation ideas seem a waste of time. I work with the people I train everyday. I know if our training is effective because the employees either do their assigned tasks correctly or they don't."

Rolando was talking to Jacelyn, a supervisor peer who worked at the Townson Restaurant. They were attending a one-day train-the-trainer workshop sponsored by the local restaurant association.

"When she first started talking, I thought the same thing, Rolando. But after a few more comments in the follow-up discussion, I began to see her perspectives."

"Well," said Rolando, "it's easy to give a simple example about a cost-benefit assessment for reducing dish breakage. However, I'm trying to teach our staff members how to work safely and be nice to our guests. How can these benefits be quantified?"

"You're giving great examples," said Jacelyn. "However, there must be something you can do to assess the training. After all, you can't closely follow every employee every day.

Our company does spend a lot of money on training. What would we do if you decided your training was effective, and our boss said training for other people was not worthwhile? Do the limited funds go to others to improve training, to you because you say your training works, or to no one who can't justify the funds?"

Case Study Questions

1. What are your thoughts about Jacelyn's responses to Rolando's concern about training evaluation?

2. Do you think that training evaluation must be "all or nothing"? That is, must it totally determine the worth of training or else not be done at all?

3. What advice might you give Rolando as he develops safety and hospitality training programs about what he should do before, during, and after training to provide some assessment of training results?

HR TERMS

The following terms were defined in this chapter:

On-job training

Coaching

Distance education

Cross-training

Job enlargement

Job enrichment

Job rotation

Group training

Objective tests

Mystery shopper

FOR YOUR CONSIDERATION

1. Assume you have been assigned to develop and implement a formalized and organized method of on-job training in your organization.

   a. What are the most important factors you would consider as you identified the experienced staff members who will receive train-the-trainer training?

   b. What training preparation tasks should be the responsibility of the staff member who will be conducting the training?

   c. What training preparation activities should a trainer normally expect to have available in a training handbook or other available resource?

   d. How will you determine the amount of time a trainer will require to present training for a specific task?

2. Develop a checklist to evaluate the public speaking skills of a trainer who will facilitate a group training session.

3. Think about training sessions in which you have participated. Identify special training issues in addition to those discussed in the chapter that should be of concern to trainers.

4. Assume that you are developing a training lesson on the topic of this chapter. Develop 10 true/false and 10 multiple-choice questions that might be used to assess the trainees' knowledge at the completion of the training.

5. This chapter discusses the concept of "managing by walking around." Assume you are a supervisor of entry-level staff who just received training in food safety concerns. Develop a checklist of items that you might formally or informally attempt to observe while you are managing by walking around.

CASE STUDY

Apply HR Management Principles*

Stacey was the food services manager at Global Bank's world headquarters. The bank employed about 2,000 staff members. Average lunch volume was about 800 meals, and daily lunch revenues were approximately $3,800 at the several food services venues. She was unhappy with daily customer counts and revenues, in part because they were lower than expectations based on business at similar accounts operated by her employer.

After a series of meetings with her client's representative (the bank's assistant finance manager), and with input from frequent customers, she devised some creative marketing tactics. One involved use of the bank's intranet system to alert employees about daily specials and to allow them to use the system to place orders for pick-up. Another called for an assistant manager to serve in a catering director role and meet with bank employees in their offices to plan parties for special occasions such as birthdays and retirement parties. In addition, an existing but inactive group of customer "volunteers" (the Food Advisory Committee)

was reactivated to provide advice, sample menu items, and serve as a general "sounding board" about the concerns of their employee peers. Other tactics that were suggested included:

◆ Customer appreciation events

◆ Frequency of purchase (reward) program

◆ Theme events

◆ Guest chef events

◆ Holiday sale events

◆ "Reinvention" of one self-service station to generate excitement

As Stacey reviewed these ideas, she was pleased with their creativity. Then she began to realize that the easiest part of her business "turn around" task was to generate ideas to do so. The more difficult task would be to implement the ideas and keep them going.

CASE STUDY (continued)

Training seemed to be a common element in the ideas. Some involved group training because all staff members needed to know about the renewed emphasis on customer service and about special concerns that would be generated from customer input. Other ideas involved individual training, such as for administrative (secretarial) staff who would be sending and receiving e-mails on the intranet and the assistant manager who would serve as the function planner. Interestingly, other ideas involved "training the customer"—really educating them about food services functions and the services that would be provided.

Stacey did not know which ideas were best, and she knew that not all of these changes could be made at the same time. Perhaps none of them could be implemented quickly. She had to be confident that the best tactics were chosen, that the processes designed were the most appropriate, and that affected staff knew exactly how their job responsibilities and tasks would be changed.

Stacey pondered her plans and thought to herself: "It's easy to decide that efforts to build the business are needed. It is even relatively simple to generate ideas to do so. However, I'm beginning to realize that a much more significant effort will be required to build our business."

Dimension: Strategic

1. Is it important that Stacey do what is necessary to ensure that quality and quantity standards can be attained before these new procedures are put in place? Why or why not?

2. What additional tactics might Stacey have used to generate input about improvement alternatives?

3. What, if any, planning assistance might Stacey request from her regional HR department since the program is managed by a contract management company?

4. How should Stacey and her team evaluate the worth of the tactics that are implemented?

Dimension: Marketing

1. What long-term tactics can Stacey use to generate input about program improvement from potential customers? From her frequent customers?

2. What people/groups of people can assist Stacey in her efforts to "tell the story" about food services?

3. Should a separate public relations campaign be implemented to inform customers about the benefits of the food services program? Why or why not?

4. What process should Stacey and her team use to determine which lunch-building tactics should be implemented?

Dimension: Training

1. What procedures should be used to develop the new processes for using the company's intranet for communication with customers?

2. Assume the intranet communication system is implemented. What specific techniques can be used to train those who are working with it?

3. Assume the tactic of naming a catering director is implemented. Outline the subject matter to be covered in a training lesson to update the assistant manager about his or her staff party planning responsibilities.

4. Who should be responsible for being the point person for interactions with the customer advisory committee? What are the main responsibilities for this task? Which, if any, involve knowledge or additional training?

*This case study was contributed by Curtis Lease, District Manager, ARAMARK Business Services, Houston, Texas.

INTERNET ACTIVITIES

1. Develop a comprehensive list of training principles that are helpful during each step of the four-step individualized on-job training process explained in this chapter. To do so, make a copy of Figures 7.3–7.6. Then enter any or all of the following terms in your favorite search engine, review selected information, and expand the lists of principles noted in the figures cited above:

   a. On-the-job training method

   b. Four-step on-job training method

   c. On-job training principles

   d. Individualized training

   e. Coaching

2. Write an approximately 1,000-word report based on information learned in an Internet search about one of the three following topics:

   a. Planning group training programs

   b. Training program evaluation

   c. Training return on investment

© Jon Feingersh / Getty Images

COMPENSATION PROGRAMS

CHAPTER OUTLINE

LEARNING OBJECTIVES

When they complete this chapter readers will be able to:

1. Describe the differences between extrinsic and intrinsic rewards as they relate to employee compensation programs.

2. Explain how compensation programs are affected by federal, state, and local laws.

3. List and describe the most common forms of direct financial compensation.

4. List and describe the most common forms of indirect financial compensation.

5. List and describe some of the most common forms of nonfinancial compensation.

Impact on HR Management

I n most cases, pay is not the central issue responsible for attracting and retaining good employees. Worker pay is, however, critically important to employees and employers alike because it affects so many other business issues.

In general, if workers feel they are unfairly paid, they will seek jobs they believe more equitably reward their efforts. Alternatively, employers who pay their employees significantly more than other employers may find their operating costs are too high to allow them to stay competitive and achieve the profits they need to stay in business.

Unfortunately, for HR managers, elusive concepts such as fair, equitable, and competitive defy unanimous agreement. As a result, the challenge they face is to design and manage compensation programs that are simultaneously perceived as reasonable by both employees and their employers. The best HR managers actually go one step further and use their compensation programs as an essential tool for both attracting and retaining excellent workers as well as maximizing profits for their employers.

As is true in many other HR areas, managers designing effective compensation programs must understand the law. However, more is at stake than ensuring a program's legality. Managing compensation programs well involves two main issues: controlling costs and using pay to attract and retain the best workers. This can be done by establishing a compensation and benefits program that tracks costs, helps ensure pay equity, is understood by all employees, and recognizes the fundamental, long-term wisdom of justly balancing the financial interests of both employees and their employers.

❖ COMPENSATION MANAGEMENT

LEARNING OBJECTIVE 1. Describe the differences between extrinsic and intrinsic rewards as they relate to employee compensation programs.

The majority of hospitality workers like their jobs and enjoy the rewards they receive from working in the industry. For most of these workers, however, a critically important part of their job satisfaction relates to the compensation they receive for doing their jobs.

Compensation package: The sum total of the money and other valuable items given in exchange for work performed.

While some hospitality workers consider their jobs to be fun, few people have the luxury of working just for the fun of it. In most cases, workers evaluate the entire **compensation package** (see chapter 4) offered by their employer when they assess the value of what they are paid for their work and when they consider whether that pay is adequate and fair. It is important that managers ensure all employees know about their pay, but it is just as important that employees be informed about their entire compensation package, including items such as meals, benefits, and bonuses.

Naturally, most employees would like their compensation package to be as large as possible. It may seem most employers would like employee compensation packages to be as small as possible so profits would be maximized. Experienced business professionals, however, know that it is rarely in the best interest of employers to make compensation packages as small as possible. The reasons are twofold. First, employers who advertise positions offering below-average compensation packages tend to attract workers with lesser skills because those with greater skills seek higher-paying positions. Second, employers who minimize employee pay tend to lose their best workers to organizations willing to pay more.

Consequently, when less-skilled workers are attracted to an organization, and when the best of an organization's workers ultimately seek employment elsewhere, product quality and customer

EXTRINSIC REWARDS

FINANCIAL
Salaries
Hourly pay
Cost-of-Living Adjustments (COLAs)
Tips
Commissions
Bonuses
Merit pay
Incentive pay
Profit sharing
Paid leave
Mandatory benefits
Voluntary benefits

NONFINANCIAL
Preferred office space or work
    station
Preferred personal computer or
    kitchen tools
Preferred meal privileges
Designated parking place
Business cards
Special dress codes
Secretary
Impressive titles
Travel/meal discounts

INTRINSIC REWARDS

Participation in job design
Participation in decision making
Greater job freedom
More interesting work
Opportunities for personal growth
More job security
Empowerment

Figure 8.1 Extrinsic and Intrinsic Employee Rewards

service levels inevitably are below average, resulting in reduced sales and below-average company profits. An optimum compensation program attracts high-quality workers and allows the company to maximize profitability.

When assessing your workers' compensation, you should first consider their salaries, wage paid per hour, and/or tips received during the average shift. When professional HR managers discuss compensation programs, they consider much more than the amount of money paid to their workers. This is so because these managers know a comprehensive compensation program consists of important **extrinsic rewards** as well as **intrinsic rewards**.

For most employees, both extrinsic and intrinsic rewards are important. As a result, you must carefully consider both types when developing your operation's total compensation program. Figure 8.1 lists some of the most common extrinsic and intrinsic rewards used in the hospitality industry.

Not all employees react in the same manner to the rewards offered by their employers. For some workers, intrinsic rewards are critically important. For others, financial rewards may be most important, and for still others, status and nonfinancial extrinsic rewards may be what they like most about their compensation.

All paid employees exchange work for rewards. While not all employees earn the same amount of money, nearly all employees view the amount they are paid as a real indication of their value in the eyes of management. Therefore, an employee who discovers that a coworker makes as little as 5 or 10 cents more per hour than he or she does can become quite upset. For many

Extrinsic rewards: Financial, as well as nonfinancial, compensation granted to a worker by others (usually the employer).

Intrinsic rewards: Self-initiated compensation (e.g., pride in one's work, a sense of professional accomplishment, and/or enjoying being part of a work team).

HR Management in Action

WHAT'S FAIR? WHAT'S LEGAL?

Roberta Jackson, a room attendant with 10 years of experience at the Mayflower Hotel, was clearly angry when she entered the office of Randall Pierce, the Mayflower's HR director. "I just finished talking with Martha, the new housekeeper who started yesterday," said Roberta. "When we were on break Martha told me she was making the same amount per hour as me! And I have been with this hotel for 10 years. I guess employee loyalty doesn't mean much around here."

"Roberta," said Randall, "Martha is an experienced room attendant just like you. She worked for a long time at the Town Center Hotel across town and I think she will do a great job for us. You know we have a confidentiality policy regarding pay, and I simply can't discuss her pay with you. And according to that policy, you shouldn't be talking to her about her pay either!"

This case illustrates several key points, including the impact of a fairly perceived compensation policy on employee satisfaction. In this example, Martha may in fact have as much, or more, experience than Roberta. Thus, if years of experience are a factor the hotel uses in considering employee pay, Martha's pay rate is likely quite appropriate. Roberta, however, clearly views her seniority at the hotel as a factor that should dictate she receive more than new employees doing the same work. In this case, it's fairly easy to recognize the validity of both this employer's and this employee's points of view.

Because the issue of pay among workers is so volatile, many organizations, such as the Mayflower, are tempted to create policies that seek to restrict what workers can and cannot say about their pay rates. While it would clearly be inappropriate for an employer such as Randall to share the confidential pay information of one employee with another, it is also important to recognize that the National Labor Relations Act (see chapter 2) grants workers many rights, including the right to engage in "concerted activity for mutual aid and protection." The National Labor Relations Board has consistently ruled that this includes the rights of workers to discuss their own pay with coworkers. Employers can encourage their employees to exercise discretion regarding the sharing of their pay rates, but Randall needs to recognize he should not, in any way, discipline Roberta or Martha for sharing their own pay information with each other.

Compensation management:
The process of administrating an organization's extrinsic and intrinsic reward system.

workers, the amount of money they make significantly enhances or detracts from their own feelings of status and self-worth. Thus an equitable compensation program that considers pay, as well as all other employee rewards, is critical.

The goal of any effective **compensation management** program should be to attract, motivate, and retain competent employees. To achieve this goal, the program must be perceived by employees as fair and equitable.

Fair pay can be considered only in the context of organizational profitability. Organizations that can pay employees less but still deliver a quality product, will, in the short run, be more profitable than competitors who pay their employees more. This is so because profits are simply computed as revenue minus expenses, and in the hospitality industry employee compensation is one of any operation's largest expenses. You should recognize, however, that an employer whose compensation program is not perceived as fair by employees will not, in the long run, attract and retain the best and most talented workers. This is not to imply that those employers who pay the most money in direct salaries and wages attract the best workers. In fact, HR managers who can clearly show employees the inherent fairness of their company's *complete* compensation program will, in the long run, attract and retain the best workforce. This is so because compensation affects an employee's attitudes about the job. At the same time, highly motivated workers tend to view their company's compensation programs as fair, while those who are less motivated often find fault with the compensation program.

Managing compensation is, to a great degree, the management of employee expectations and perceptions. To do this well, you must devise an effective compensation system. To be of most value, such a system typically includes the following:

1. **Categorization of jobs**—Not all employees do the same work, and the result is that employee pay differences will exist. It is also true that most employees will readily accept this rationale as the reason for pay variations. It is easy for most employees to understand, for example, that a supervisor in a hospital's dietary department would make more money than an hourly wage washer working in the same facility. In a similar manner, employees will undoubtedly understand that a fine-dining operation's executive chef would be paid more than that operation's sous chef. When employees understand real differences in job responsibilities, they can better understand the reasons for differences in pay.

   You can add flexibility and enhance employees' understanding of your compensation programs by creating several categories within the same job, each of which may have its own **pay range**. For example, desk agents at a hotel may be classified as trainee, intermediate, senior, and so on to designate different experience or skill levels. Each classification would, under this system, have its own pay range. Employees can also routinely be made aware of the skills or experience needed to advance to higher levels. They can also be informed about opportunities to help them become trained or eligible for these higher-paid positions.

   Pay range: The lower and upper limits of hourly wages or salary paid for a specific job. For example, the pay range for an entry-level room attendant in a hotel may be between $8.50 and $12.50 per hour to start.

2. **Comparison of employee pay with the local labor market**—Assume that three different hotels offer their employees identical nonwage compensation packages. In such a scenario, would $8.50 be a fair hourly wage to be paid to each hotel's laundry workers? The answer, to some degree, depends on exactly where the hotels are located. Hourly wages paid for laundry workers in New York City will be higher than those paid to similar workers in rural communities in the Midwest United States. International hotel companies operating in China, for example, would likely pay yet a different rate. In each of these cases, however, there is an identifiable **local wage rate**, *which is* based on the individual community and labor market in which the operation is located.

   HR managers can stay abreast of local wage rates by conducting periodic **salary surveys**.

   You can easily conduct your own salary surveys by talking to your counterparts working at other hospitality operations in your area. They will usually be happy to share such information because they want to have the benefit of your data just as much as you desire access to theirs. In addition, managers may be able to purchase commercial salary surveys in some locations.

   Salary surveys can tell you a lot. First, they provide a way to establish pay ranges for various jobs. Second, they can tell how your wages or salaries compare with the labor market. Third, surveys can give you an idea of how many job categories should be established for each job group.

   Managers need not follow the local market conditions by matching the wage rates found in a salary survey. For example, you may pay more aggressively for some jobs than others based on your view of how many qualified workers are available, how critical it is to fill the jobs, and the employee turnover rates you expect.

   Local wage rate: The prevailing pay range for distinct job categories in a specific community or labor market.

   Salary survey: A comprehensive review of local wage rates and pay ranges paid for one or more individual job categories (e.g., the average local wage rate, or range, paid to hotel bartenders, room attendants, or groundskeepers).

3. **Management of internal pay equity**—Most HR managers agree that managing internal pay equity is more important than ensuring external equity. This is so because employees are much more likely to know the hourly pay or salary of the people they work with than the amount paid to a person in another operation. Also, it is difficult to compare, for example, the pay at two different restaurants because each may require differently skilled workers or offer differing benefit packages, and these factors influence pay differences.

   Employees usually feel they can make unbiased comparisons about coworkers within their own operation. Also, employees often have a better foundation for pay comparisons because they have a better idea of what their coworkers actually do on the job and how well they do it. Both of these factors create a much higher potential for morale problems and turnover if pay rates are not seen as equitable.

Internal equity is best achieved by paying people within the pay range established for their jobs and by varying pay for objectively identifiable measures such as rated job performance, full- versus part-time status, shifts worked, assignments completed, or other measurable factors. For example, a hotel may elect to pay a desk agent working the 11:00 p.m. to 7:00 a.m. shift more per hour than a coworker doing identical work on the 7:00 a.m. to 3:00 p.m. shift. In this example, the shift worked, rather than the tasks completed, justifies the pay differential between the two employees.

4. **Linkage of pay to job performance**—Most managers and employees agree that workers who perform their jobs better should receive more pay and larger pay increases than those who do not perform as well. At the same time, they may not believe that their own companies do a good job of rewarding superior effort.

In chapter 9 you will learn more about how you can evaluate employees' contributions to your operation's effectiveness. You'll learn that a quality performance evaluation system is an effective tool for achieving many goals, including improving employee skills and identifying employee efforts worthy of additional pay and responsibility.

Measurable employee effort and other factors, such as difficulty level of the work, shift assignments, and current pay, should play an important role in helping you develop a **merit pay system** that effectively helps to determine appropriate employee pay rates.

5. **Maintenance of open communications**—While some HR managers find talking to employees about pay uncomfortable, it is a topic that every employee talks or thinks about on an ongoing basis. The amount of pay-related communication that is appropriate varies between operations. Many companies do not effectively communicate the mechanics of compensation plans in the organization.

For example, unit managers typically inform employees about their pay, but they may be reluctant to say too much for fear they will have to justify a perceived pay inequity that they may not fully understand or even agree with. When managers say nothing, employees often are required to rely on the rumor mill—an information source well noted for its inaccuracy and exaggeration.

Discussing employee pay is always a delicate situation. What is most critical for all employees (including HR managers) to understand is how their pay or pay increase was determined, why it is that amount, and what, if anything, the employee can do to earn more.

> **Merit pay system:** A compensation program that links increases in pay to measurable job performance. Workers who perform better receive proportionally higher pay.

❖❖ LEGAL ASPECTS OF COMPENSATION MANAGEMENT

LEARNING OBJECTIVE 2. Explain how compensation programs are affected by federal, state, and local laws.

In general, employers may establish wages and salaries as they wish, but they also must comply with federal, state, and local laws that directly affect compensation programs. For example, you learned in chapter 2 that the Equal Pay Act (1963) requires that equal pay must be given to men and women for equal work. In addition to equal pay for equal work, numerous other federal, state, and local laws regulate how you must pay your employees.

Federal Legislation

> **Minimum wage:** The least amount of wages that employees covered by the Fair Labor Standards Act (FLSA), state, or local laws may be paid by their employers.

By the end of the 1800s there were factories in the United States known as sweatshops that employed women, children, and recent immigrants who had no choice but to accept inferior wages and harsh working conditions. Social activists pushed for laws at the state level to pay all workers, regardless of social status or gender, a wage that would allow them to maintain an adequate standard of living.

In 1912 Massachusetts became the first state to enact a law mandating a **minimum wage**. By 1938, 25 states had enacted minimum wage laws. Some states established commissions to determine the minimum wage based on what was perceived to be a fair wage for employees. Eventually, however, a US Supreme Court decision held that state laws regulating wages were unconstitutional.

According to the courts, these laws violated the rights of employers and employees to freely negotiate and form contracts over appropriate wages. Other state courts, following the precedent set by the federal Supreme Court, ruled that their own state statutes were also unconstitutional. President Franklin D. Roosevelt responded by attempting to enact federal legislation granting the president the authority to mandate a minimum wage as part of the federal government's right to regulate interstate commerce. The Supreme Court ruled President Roosevelt's first attempt at such legislation to be unconstitutional, but the Court upheld his second attempt, the 1938 Fair Labor Standards Act (FLSA), as constitutional.

The federal minimum wage, which is established by the FLSA, is periodically reviewed and revised by Congress. You must continually monitor the actions of Congress with regard to changes in the minimum wage because nearly all hospitality employees are covered by the minimum wage, with only a few limited exceptions. For example, the FLSA allows an employer to pay an employee who is younger than 20 years of age a training wage, which is below the standard minimum, for the first 90 consecutive calendar days of employment. Also, tipped employees can be paid a rate below the minimum wage if the reported tips plus the wages received from their employer equal or exceed the minimum hourly rate.

It's the Law

Managing compensation for tipped employees is a challenge in nearly all segments of the hospitality industry. As currently defined, tipped employees are those who customarily and regularly receive more than $30 per month in tips. Tips actually received by tipped employees may be counted (credited) as wages for purposes of the FLSA, but the employer must still pay a minimum amount established by law.

If an employer elects to use the tip credit provision, the employer must (1) inform each tipped employee about the tip credit allowance (including the amount to be credited) before the credit is utilized; (2) be able to show that the employee receives at least the minimum wage when direct wages and the tip credit allowance are combined; and (3) allow tipped employees to retain all tips, unless they participate in a valid tip-pooling arrangement.

If an employee's tips combined with the employer's direct wages do not equal the federal minimum hourly wage, then the employer must make up the difference.

Current law forbids any arrangement between the employer and the tipped employee in which any part of the tip received becomes the property of the employer. A tip is the sole property of the tipped employee. When an employer does not strictly observe the tip credit provisions issued by the FLSA, no tip credit may be claimed, and employees are entitled to receive the full cash minimum wage, plus all of the tips they have received.

The requirement that an employee must retain all tips does not prevent tip-splitting or -pooling arrangements among employees who customarily and regularly receive tips, such as servers, bell-hops, counter personnel, bussers, and bartenders. Tipped employees cannot, however, be forced to share their tips with employees who have not customarily and regularly participated in tip-pooling arrangements, such as dishwashers, cooks, chefs, and janitors. Only those tips that are in excess of tips used for the tip credit may be taken for a tip pool.

When tips are charged on a credit card, and the employer pays the credit card company a percentage on each sale, the employer may pay the employee the tip minus that percentage, but the charge on the tip may not reduce the employee's wage below the required minimum wage. The tip amounts due from payment cards must be paid no later than the employee's regular payday and cannot be held while the employer is awaiting reimbursement from the payment card company.

Among its other provisions, the FLSA established standards for the use of child labor. It also defined the wage rates that must be paid for working overtime. The FLSA does not limit the number of hours in a day or days in a week that an employee over the age of 16 may work. It does allow employers to require employees to work more than 40 hours per week. However, under the FLSA, covered employees must be paid at least one and one-half times their regular rates of pay for all hours worked in excess of 40 in a workweek. Some employees are exempt from the overtime provision of the FLSA. These include salaried professional, administrative, or executive employees.

To enforce federal wage and hour laws, the Wage and Hour Division of the Federal Department of Labor has investigators stationed throughout the country. If they encounter violations, they recommend changes in employment practices to bring the employer into compliance, and they may require the payment of any back wages due to employees. Employers who willfully or repeatedly violate the minimum wage or overtime pay requirements of the FLSA are subject to civil penalties of up to $1,000 per violation. Employees may also choose to bring a lawsuit against their employer for back pay as well as other costs, including attorney's fees and court costs.

State Legislation

Many states continue to maintain their own minimum wage laws. In those states, employees are covered by the law that is most favorable to them (in other words, whichever wage [state or federal] that provides the highest compensation). The differences in state employment laws can be significant, and you must be aware of those that relate to the state(s) in which you do business. To illustrate this fact, consider the very specific differences contained in the sample wage and hour laws of selected states detailed in Figure 8.2. Clearly, individual states have a great deal of latitude in enacting their own wage and overtime laws.

It's the Law

CALCULATING OVERTIME PAY FOR TIPPED EMPLOYEES

Tipped employees are generally subject to the overtime provisions of the FLSA. The computation of the overtime rate for tipped employees when the employer claims a tax credit can be confusing. Consider, for example, a state in which the minimum wage is $8 per hour and the applicable overtime provision dictates payment of one and one-half the normal hourly rate for hours worked in excess of 40 per week. To determine the overtime rate of pay, use the following three-step method:

1. Multiply the prevailing minimum wage rate by 1.5.
2. Compute the allowable tip credit against the standard hourly rate.
3. Subtract the number in step 2 from the result in step 1.

Thus, if the minimum wage were $8 per hour and the allowable tip credit were 50 percent, the overtime rate to be paid would be computed as:

1. $8.00 × 1.5 = $12.00
2. $8.00 × 0.50 = $4.00
3. $12.00 − $4.00 = $8.00 overtime rate

ARKANSAS: Employers of workers who receive board, lodging, apparel, or other items as part of the worker's employment may be entitled to an allowance for such board, lodging, apparel, or other items, not to exceed 30 cents per hour, credited against the minimum wage.

MICHIGAN: Workers younger than age 18 are entitled to a 30-minute meal break after 5 hours of work. Michigan law does not require a meal break for workers older than age 18.

NEW HAMPSHIRE: An employer cannot require a worker to work more than 5 hours without a 30-minute meal break. An employee who reports to work at the employer's request is entitled to be paid a minimum of two hours' wages.

RHODE ISLAND: Time and one-half premium pay for work on Sundays and holidays in retail and certain other businesses is required under two laws that are separate from the minimum wage law.

VERMONT: State minimum wage is increased annually by law.

WASHINGTON: No employer may employ a minor without a work permit from the state along with permission from the minor's parent or guardian and school.

Figure 8.2 Selected State-Enacted Wage and Hour Legislation

The actual hourly minimum wage rates for the individual states vary widely and change often. For an up-to-date listing of the minimum wage and allowable tip credits in each state, go to http://www.dol.gov/whd/state/tipped.htm/.

Local Legislation

In addition to wage and hour legislation passed at the federal and state levels, some wage and hour laws have been passed at the city or county level. In many cases this local legislation takes the form of **living-wage** laws that often directly affect hospitality businesses.

The first living-wage law was passed in Baltimore in 1994. The ordinance there stipulated that businesses holding service contracts with the city pay a minimum of $6.10 per hour, increasing to $7.70 as of July 1998, and thereafter moving in step with inflation. A single mother working full time at $7.70 per hour would (at that time) have been able to live with her child above the federally defined poverty line. Within four years of the Baltimore ordinance, living-wage laws passed in New York, Los Angeles, Chicago, Boston, Milwaukee, Jersey City, Durham, Portland, Oregon, and eight other cities. Today, more than 120 cities and counties have enacted such measures.

The living-wage ordinance in Los Angeles goes further than mandating wages alone. Passed in 1997, the ordinance was only the country's third living-wage law, but it was the first to include a provision for health care benefits. It applies to certain businesses in four categories: those that (1) have service contracts with the city, (2) lease land from the city, (3) require city operating permits, or (4) receive financial assistance from the city. Restaurants, hotels, and bars operate with city permits, so they are covered by the ordinance. Los Angeles is a good example of why you must know and monitor local legislation related to employee pay rates. Seattle, Washington, whose City Council in June 2014 passed legislation to raise that city's minimum wage rate to $15.00 per hour over a seven-year period (the nation's highest mandatory minimum wage rate at the time of its passage), is another such example.

Employers may (voluntarily) commit themselves to the legal responsibility to pay workers a specific amount. Thus, for example, when an employer agrees, in writing, to pay one of its executives $100,000 per year, it is legally obligated to do so. In a similar manner, an organization that agrees to specific wage rates in a union contract must pay those rates to employees covered by the contract.

Living wage: The minimum hourly wage necessary for a person to achieve some subjectively defined standard of living. In the context of developed countries such as the United States, this standard is generally considered to require that a person working 40 hours per week, with no additional income, should be able to afford a specified quality or quantity of housing, food, utilities, transportation, and health care.

❖❖❖❖
HR MANAGEMENT ISSUES 8.1

Sharon Alexander operates The Texas Saloon, an upscale steakhouse restaurant that also serves beer and wine. Sharon's average menu item sold for $20. Employees were allowed to eat one meal during their shift. For those who voluntarily elected to eat this meal, Sharon would deduct 25 cents per hour ($2 per eight-hour shift) from the federal minimum wage rate she paid her entry-level dishwashers, which reflected the reasonable cost of the meal.

Sharon relied on the FLSA Section 3(m), which states that employers can consider, as wages, "reasonable costs ... to the employer of furnishing such employees with board, lodging, or other facilities if such board, lodging, or other facilities are customarily furnished by such employer to his employees." Sharon interpreted this regulation to mean that she could pay the entry-level dishwashers a rate that, when added to the 25-cent–per-hour meal deduction, equaled the federal minimum wage.

One day Sharon was contacted by her state Department of Employment, which charged that she was in violation of the state minimum wage law. That law stated that "total voluntary deductions for meals and uniforms may not decrease an employee's wages below the federal minimum wage on an hourly basis." Sharon maintained that, because she was in compliance with the federal law, she was allowed to take the meal credit against the wages paid to her entry-level dishwashers.

Case Study Questions

1. Is Sharon in compliance with all of the compensation-related laws that affect her?

2. Do federal wage laws take precedence over state wage laws?

3. Do state wage laws take precedence over federal law? Explain your answer.

❖❖ DIRECT FINANCIAL COMPENSATION

LEARNING OBJECTIVE 3. List and describe the most common forms of direct financial compensation.

Although it may take a variety of forms, direct financial compensation for hospitality employees typically consists of one or more of the following:

- ◆ Salaries
- ◆ Wages
- ◆ Incentives and bonuses
- ◆ Tips

Salaries

Salary: Pay calculated on a weekly, monthly, or annual basis rather than at an hourly rate.

Exempt (employee): An employee who is not subject to the minimum wage or overtime provisions of the Fair Labor Standards (FLSA).

Nonexempt (employee): An employee who is subject to the minimum wage or overtime provisions of the Fair Labor Standards (FLSA).

In the hospitality industry, managers and some higher-level supervisors are typically paid a fixed **salary** rather than an hourly rate. The advantage to employees of a salary system is the consistency of their pay. An advantage to employers is that such employees are not subject to the overtime provisions of the FLSA. To illustrate, Jack Lester works as a salaried dining room supervisor. He regularly works between 45 and 65 hours per week, but Jack's employer is not required to pay him overtime for the hours in excess of 40 that he works weekly.

The FLSA requires that most employees in the United States be paid at least the federal minimum wage for all hours worked, as well as overtime pay at one and one-half times the regular rate of pay for all hours over 40 worked in a workweek. Section 13(a)(1) of the FLSA, however, provides an exclusion from both minimum wage and overtime pay for employees employed as verifiable executive, administrative, professional, and outside sales employees. Such employees are termed **exempt** employees (to distinguish them from **nonexempt** employees).

To qualify for exempt status, employees must meet certain tests regarding their job duties and be paid a minimum salary (for current exempt employee status criteria go to http://www.dol.gov/whd/regs/compliance/hrg.htm).

Job titles do not determine exempt status. Therefore, Jack Lester's title (dining room supervisor) does not determine his exempt status. Rather, his specific job duties and salary must meet all of the requirements of the Department of Labor's regulations to qualify for exempt status. In the hospitality industry most exempt jobs fall into either executive, administrative, or (in the case of some hotel sales and marketing positions) outside sales classifications.

In general, to qualify for the executive employee exemption, all of the following tests must be met:

◆ The employee must be compensated with a minimum salary established by federal law.

◆ The employee's primary duty must be managing the operation or managing a customarily recognized department or subdivision of the operation.

◆ The employee must customarily and regularly direct the work of at least two or more other full-time employees or their equivalent.

◆ The employee must have the authority to hire or fire other employees, or the employee's suggestions and recommendations as to the hiring, firing, advancement, promotion, or any other change of status of other employees must be given significant weight.

To qualify for the administrative employee exemption, all of the following tests must be met:

◆ The employee must be compensated with a minimum salary established by federal law.

◆ The employee's primary duty must be the performance of office or nonmanual work directly related to the management or general business operations of the employer or the employer's customers.

◆ The employee's primary duty includes the exercise of discretion and independent judgment with respect to matters of significance.

To qualify for the outside sales employee exemption, all of the following tests must be met:

◆ The employee's primary duty must be making sales (as defined by the FLSA) or obtaining orders or contracts for services or for the use of facilities, for which a payment will be paid by the client or customer.

◆ The employee must be customarily and regularly engaged away from the employer's place or places of business.

The exemptions provided by FLSA Section 13(a)(1) apply only to white-collar employees who meet the salary and duties tests described in their regulations. The exemptions do not apply to manual laborers or other blue-collar workers who perform work involving repetitive operations with their hands, physical skill, and energy. FLSA-covered, nonmanagement employees in production, maintenance, construction, and similar hospitality-related occupations, such as cooks, bakers, carpenters, electricians, mechanics, plumbers, craftspeople, engineers, or general construction workers and laborers, are entitled to minimum wage and overtime premium pay under the FLSA. They are not exempt under the Part 541 regulations no matter how highly they are paid.

There has been some confusion in the hospitality industry regarding when employers may legally deduct pay from salaried (exempt) employees. Generally speaking, exempt employees must receive their full salary for any workweek in which they perform any work, without regard to the number of days or hours worked. However, the following conditions allow employers to deduct wages in daily increments from exempt employees:

◆ Absence for one or more full days for reasons other than illness or disability

◆ Absence for one or more full days for illness or disability provided the deduction is made in accordance with a policy that provides compensation for time lost due to illness (e.g., sick leave)

◆ To offset amounts received for jury duty, witness fees, or military pay

◆ Per diem (per day) payment in the initial and last weeks of employment

◆ Good-faith penalties for violation of major safety regulations

◆ Good-faith unpaid disciplinary suspensions for one or more full days for violation of workplace conduct policies

Several widely publicized lawsuits have been filed against hospitality organizations that violated salary provisions of the FLSA, and it is important to understand the federal provisions related to salary payments. When state laws regarding salary payments differ from the FLSA, an employer must comply with the standard that is most protective (beneficial) to the salaried employee.

For example, in California employers must take into consideration several critical differences when classifying employees. To cite one such difference, the salary threshold in California required to reach exempt employee status requires that employees must earn a monthly salary of no less than two times the state minimum wage (which currently exceeds the per month federal minimum). You can find links to your own state labor department at www.dol.gov/dol/location.htm.

Wages

Hourly wages: Money paid or received for work performed during a one-hour period.

Piecework wages: Money paid or received for completing a certain amount (one piece) of work.

In the hospitality industry, wages paid to workers typically take the form of **hourly wages** or **piecework wages**.

Interestingly, the definition of *wages* can vary greatly, depending on the way the word is used. HR managers must realize, for example, that a taxing authority, such as a state government, may view the term *wages* as including:

- ◆ all remuneration paid for personal service, including salaries, bonuses, and commissions, paid to all workers of all ranks, including officers of a corporation;
- ◆ the cash value of any remuneration paid in any medium other than cash;
- ◆ all tip income;
- ◆ monies paid for time lost due to sickness or accident;
- ◆ expense allowances;
- ◆ dismissal (termination payouts); and
- ◆ money paid to workers for such items as board, lodging, union dues, employee payments to pension or benefit funds, social security tax, and premiums on group insurance policies.

For the purposes of this chapter, *wages* refers only to those monies paid directly to workers based on the number of hours worked (hourly wage) or the amount of work completed (piecework wage).

While most hospitality workers, such as cooks, front-desk agents, clerical staff, and others, are paid an hourly wage in keeping with their position and the area in which their jobs are located, some hotel managers use a piecework wage system (e.g., per guestroom cleaned) when compensating hotel room attendants.

Incentives and Bonuses

Performance-based pay: A compensation system that rewards workers for their on-job accomplishments rather than for time spent on the job.

Incentives: A motivational plan provided to employees based on their work efforts.

Bonuses: A financial reward paid to employees for achieving predetermined performance goals.

In addition to salaries and wages, many hospitality organizations committed to developing compensation systems with **performance-based pay** include **incentives** and **bonuses** in their overall programs.

Incentive or bonus programs may be designed to reward individuals, work teams, departments, or entire operations. Incentive and bonus programs are common in some areas within the hospitality industry because managers believe that they increase their workers' quality and quantity outputs. From a motivational perspective, tying compensation to specific job accomplishments typically focuses employee efforts on tasks that lead directly to increased financial rewards. When designed carefully, performance-based pay components can increase worker income and create improvements in guest service and product quality levels.

Some managers believe that employee bonuses and incentives should be avoided because they are costly. In fact, the opposite is often true. As a cost-saving device, performance-based bonuses and other incentive rewards avoid the fixed expenses of annual and permanent employee pay increases. Bonuses and other financial incentives do not typically become a permanent part of the employee's base (regular) compensation. Therefore, employee pay increases are not computed based on the value of the incentives, and the result can be significant labor cost savings.

Despite the many advantages of including some performance-based components in an operation's compensation system, there can be negative effects. Consider two college students, each of whom has been assigned to read a book with information related to a course in which they are enrolled. One student is told that reading the book will result in extra points being added to the final grade. The other student is given no such assurance. Which student is more likely to read the book?

This example also illustrates that, despite potentially positive results, with this type of grading system, students may choose to do important work only when it leads directly to a payoff. In a hospitality environment, the result may be employees who perform only tasks that lead directly to additional financial compensation, while they ignore other important job components that are not directly tied to performance-based pay. When incentives are tied to specific aspects of job performance, some workers may avoid performing unmeasured, and thus unrewarded, activities in favor of measured and rewarded activities.

Tips

In the hospitality industry, **tips** (and the practice of tipping) are perhaps the most unmistakable example of a performance-based compensation system.

> **Tip:** A gift of money given directly to someone for performing a service or task; also known as a *gratuity*.

Tips are often controversial. They are given to employees by customers and, therefore, if the business did not exist, neither would the employee's tips. As a result of this somewhat unique situation, the laws regarding tips and how they may (or may not) be considered as employer payments to employees are constantly examined at the federal, state, and local levels.

The FLSA defines a tipped employee as one whose monthly tips exceed the minimum established by the Wage and Hour Division of the Department of Labor. Currently, tips received by these employees may be counted (credited) as wages for up to 50 percent of the minimum wage. The Wage and Hour Division also determines the minimum cash wage that employers must actually pay to tipped employees. If an employee's hourly tip earnings (averaged weekly) added to this hourly wage do not equal the minimum wage, then the employer is responsible for paying the difference between the minimum wage and the **tip credit** amount.

> **Tip credit:** The amount of tips employers are allowed to count (credit) toward the wage payments they make to employees.

The value of the tip credit to hospitality employers is significant. Consider the case of Lawson Odde, who is employed in a state with a minimum wage of $8 per hour. Under the law, his employer is allowed to consider Lawson's tips as part of his wages. Therefore, his employer is required to pay Lawson only $4 per hour, and take a tip credit for the other 50 percent of the wages needed to comply with the law.

You should remember that the Department of Labor allows employers whose employees are tipped on a credit (or debit) card to reduce the payment card tips by an amount equal to the handling charges levied by the payment card company. Like the minimum wage and the requirements for overtime pay, state and local laws regarding tipped employees and allowable tip credits vary. Since tips are given to employees (and not to employers), laws carefully regulate the influence that employers have over these funds. In fact, if an employer takes control of the tips an employee receives, that employer will not be allowed to utilize the tip credit provisions of the FLSA.

In general, when a tip is given directly to an employee, management has no control over what that employee ultimately does with it. An exception to this principle is a legitimate **tip-pooling** arrangement. The FLSA does not prohibit tip pooling, but HR managers must approach this area with extreme caution.

> **Tip pooling:** An arrangement in which service providers share their tips with each other on a predetermined basis.

Since a tip is given to an employee, it is different from a **service charge**, which is imposed by management and collected directly from the guest. This is common, for example, when a menu states that a service charge (sometimes labeled on the menu as a *gratuity*) will be added to all dining parties larger than a predetermined size (for example, tables larger than eight guests). In this case, the employer collects the mandatory service charge and is then free to distribute all, part, or none of it to individual workers.

> **Service charge:** An amount added to a guest's bill in exchange for services provided.

Not surprisingly, tip-pooling and sharing is a complex area because the logistics of providing hospitality services is itself complex. When a server clears a table, resets it, serves guests by him- or herself, and then again clears the table, the question of who should benefit from customers' tips is straightforward. When, however, a hostess seats a guest, a busser—who has previously set the table—provides water and bread, a bartender provides drinks, and a server delivers drinks

Stephen was hired as a busser by the Sportsman's Fishing Club. This private club served its members lunch and dinner, as well as alcoholic beverages. Stephen's duties were to clear tables, replenish water glasses, and reset tables for the servers when members finished their meals. Stephen's employer paid a wage rate below the minimum wage because they used the tip credit portion of the FLSA minimum wage law.

Before being hired, Stephen read the tip-pooling policy in place at the club, signed a document stating that he understood it, and voluntarily agreed to participate in it. The policy stated that "All food and beverage tips are to be combined at the end of each meal period and then distributed, with bussers receiving 15 percent of all tip income."

John Granberry, an attorney, was a club member and a guest who enjoyed dining in Stephen's assigned section because Stephen was attentive and quick to respond to every member's needs. Mr. Granberry tipped well, and the dining room staff was aware that Mr. Granberry always requested to be seated in Stephen's section.

One day, after Mr. Granberry had finished his meal and had added a generous tip to his member charge slip, he stopped Stephen in the club lobby and gave him a $20 bill, with the words, "This is just for you. Keep up the good work." A club bartender observed the exchange. Stephen did not place Mr. Granberry's tip into the tip pool. When confronted by his supervisor, Stephen stated that Mr. Granberry's $20 tip was clearly meant for him alone. Stephen's supervisor demanded that Stephen contribute the tip to the pool, but Stephen refused.

Case Study Questions

1. Do you think Stephen is obligated to place Mr. Granberry's tip into the tip pool?

2. If Stephen continues to refuse to relinquish the tip, how would his employer determine what steps, if any, it could legally take to resolve this issue?

3. Do you feel it would be fair if Stephen was allowed to voluntarily withdraw from the tip pool arrangement and still maintain his current employment? Why?

---

and food to the table, the question of who deserves a portion of the tip can become perplexing. Employers are legally allowed to assist employees in developing a written tip-pooling arrangement that is fair: one based on the specific duties of each service position. This participation should be documented in the employee's personal file.

By law, employees in a tip-pooling arrangement cannot be required to share tips with their peers who do not customarily receive tips, including those in positions such as janitor, dishwasher, and cook. Even well-constructed, voluntary tip-pooling arrangements can be a source of employee conflict and litigation. In addition, state laws in this area vary, so it is a good idea to check with legal counsel and/or the local Wage and Hour Division regulator in your state to determine the tip-pooling or sharing regulations applicable in your specific operation.

❖❖ INDIRECT FINANCIAL COMPENSATION

Benefits (employee): Indirect financial compensation offered to attract and keep employees or to comply with legal mandates.

LEARNING OBJECTIVE 4. List and describe the most common forms of indirect financial compensation.

While many employees tend to focus primarily on the amount of direct financial compensation paid as salary or wages, HR managers know that the cost of employee **benefits** accounts for 20 to 40 percent of the total amount their operations actually spend on employee compensation.

Mandatory benefits (employee): Indirect financial compensation that must, by law, be offered to employees.

In most countries, an employer's compensation program must include more than just the salaries or wages owed to employees. As a result, employers must provide their workers with more than just money. In the United States, federal, state, and local legislators have passed laws that require employers to provide their workers a variety of **mandatory benefits**. In addition, many companies seek to enhance their ability to attract and retain the best possible workforce by providing additional **voluntary benefits**.

Voluntary benefits (employee): Indirect financial compensation a company elects to offer its workers in an effort to attract and keep the best possible employees.

Mandatory Benefits

The amount of money employers are required by law to spend on employee benefits is significant. Most experts estimate that government-mandated benefits such as social security, workers' compensation, and unemployment insurance represent approximately 10 percent or more of an employer's total payroll cost.

At the federal level, the government's mandatory social security program is an insurance program funded through a dedicated payroll tax. It is formally known as the Federal Old-Age and Survivors Insurance Trust Fund and the Federal Disability Insurance Trust Fund program (OASDI), in reference to its three components (OA for old-age retirement, S for survivor's [widow/widower] income, and DI for disability income). When initially signed into law by President Franklin D. Roosevelt in 1935, the term *social security* covered unemployment insurance as well. The term *social security* now is used to mean only benefits paid out for retirement, disability, or death. In this program, an employer's contributions are matched by a mandatory, equal contribution from the employee.

At the state level, workers' compensation now provides medical and disability benefits for work-related injuries and illnesses. In addition, all states mandate an employer's participation in a workers' unemployment insurance program. Unemployment insurance specifics vary by state. All states provide those who have lost their jobs some amount of replacement income for a temporary period of time if the job loss was not the fault of the employee. Under this insurance program, the employer pays the insurance premiums, while the employee is the recipient of any payments.

Health insurance is a popular employee benefit, but even after passage of the Affordable Care Act (ACA) federal law does not require businesses employing fewer than 50 workers to provide health insurance coverage for their employees. It does, however, impose a penalty on businesses if:

◆ the business employs more than 50 workers, provides coverage to at least one full-time worker (usually the owner or manager), but does not also provide employee coverage; and

◆ provides coverage that is either unaffordable or inadequate, resulting in one or more full-time employees receiving a government subsidy to purchase health insurance.

Small employers with fewer than 50 employees are exempt from any penalties and, in some cases, they can qualify for significant tax credits if they offer their employees health care coverage.

The Consolidated Omnibus Budget Reconciliation Act (COBRA) mandates requirements for the continuation of health care benefits in the event of an employee's job loss or a business closing. These provisions cover group health plans of employers with 20 or more employees. Essentially, COBRA gives workers who were covered by health insurance, but who are no longer employed, the ability to maintain their insurance coverage under the employer's health plan at their own expense for a limited period of time (currently 18 months).

Voluntary Benefits

When you design your overall compensation program, a crucial area of concern relates to the voluntary benefits you provide. All employers must provide those benefits required by law. Today's workers, however, expect more than just a salary or hourly wage and mandatory benefits; they increasingly seek additional considerations that will enrich their lives and assist them financially. Employers understand that their employees desire these benefits. Each organization must determine what it feels is the best set of benefits to offer. In many cases the answer to this question is determined by the type of worker employed, the profitability of the company, and the operational philosophy of the employer.

Employees often are allowed to choose from a variety of voluntarily offered benefits based on their own life needs. These popular "cafeteria-style" benefit programs recognize that, for example, the benefits sought by a single mother working full time may be vastly different from those desired by a semiretired employee working only a few hours per week. In this case, it is unlikely that an identical benefit package would be best for either employee.

Name of Law: Consolidated Omnibus Budget Reconciliation Act (COBRA)

Applicable to: Employers with 20 or more employees

Requirements of the Law	Key Facts About the Law
Employers with 20 or more employees on more than 50 percent of its typical business days in the previous calendar year are subject to COBRA and must notify their employees of the availability of such coverage. Affected employees have the right to continue their health care insurance coverage at their cost for a period of up to 18 months. COBRA coverage can be the result of qualifying events including the voluntary or involuntary termination of employment for reasons other than gross misconduct or the reduction in the number of hours of employment. For detailed information on the law's requirements go to: www.dol.gov/ebsa/cobra.html/.	Congress passed the COBRA health benefit provisions in 1986. The law amends the Employee Retirement Income Security Act, the Internal Revenue Code, and the Public Health Service Act to provide continuation of group health coverage that otherwise might be terminated. In certain cases, a retired employee, the retired employee's spouse, and the retired employee's dependent children may be covered under COBRA. The federal government's departments of labor and treasury have jurisdiction over private-sector health group health plans affected by COBRA.

You may choose to voluntarily offer a variety of employee benefits. Some of the most popular include:

◆ Medical insurance

◆ Prescription drug plans

◆ Dental plans

◆ Vision care plans

AD&D insurance: Short for Accidental Death and Dismemberment, a form of life and income replacement insurance.

In addition to health-related insurance, many employers offer their employees life and accident insurance policies. In the most common cases, life insurance equal to two or three times the employee's annual pay and **AD&D insurance** equal to two times the employee's annual pay are provided. Supplemental life insurance plans are also offered by many companies. These plans allow employees to purchase additional life insurance coverage through a **payroll deduction** at little or no cost to the employer.

Payroll deduction: A payment method in which the employer deducts money from an individual employee's paycheck and submits it directly to a program (e.g., insurance, savings, or retirement) in which the employee participates. These deductions may be made from an employee's after-tax or pretax wages.

An additional and popular income protection plan is a short-term disability, or pay continuance, program. Typically, these plans offer income continuance that provides the employee with full pay for the first month of disability and then provides a benefit that ranges from 50 to 75 percent of the employee's pay for up to three more months of disability. At some companies, long-term disability policies that continue the employee's pay beyond that provided by the short-term disability policy are also offered.

Other Voluntary Benefits

While health insurance–related insurance programs and life and disability insurance are the most widely offered voluntary employee benefits, others offered by many hospitality organizations include:

◆ **Paid time-off**—Companies spend approximately 10 percent of payroll on paid time-off plans. This is usually money well spent by the organization because paid time-off is highly valued, especially with today's time pressures on employees and their families. Paid time-off typically takes one of three forms:

  • **Holidays**—The paid holidays that virtually every company provides are New Year's Day, Memorial Day, Independence Day (July 4), Labor Day, Thanksgiving Day, and Christmas Day. In the hospitality industry, most businesses are open on these days. Then employers may offer employees additional wages to work on these days.

  • **Vacation days**—Paid vacation is usually granted only to full-time employees. In the United States, employees are typically granted 10 days of vacation per year upon hire, with the number of days granted increasing as the number of years worked increases.

  • **Sick pay**—Sick or personal days are paid time-off for employee illness. Most companies also allow employees to use these days for the illness of a family member.

◆ **Retirement programs—401(k) Retirement plans** are increasingly popular in the hospitality industry. As a result, many companies offer employees the opportunity to contribute their own pretax money to a 401(k). These plans have several popular features, including the fact that they are portable: If employees leave the company, they can take the full value of the 401(k) account with them. Furthermore, employees can typically choose where to invest their funds from among several investment options. These programs are relatively easy for companies to administer. Some hospitality companies match a portion of their employees' 401(k) retirement contributions.

401(k) Retirement plans: A retirement plan that allows employees to make contributions of pretax dollars to a company pool of funds that is then invested for the employee in stocks, bonds, or money market accounts.

◆ **Employee Assistance Plans (EAPs)**—These programs provide counseling for employees encountering a variety of life issues related to:

  • Alcohol
  • Drugs
  • Health
  • Legal
  • Financial
  • Housing
  • Mental health
  • Child care
  • Elder care
  • Grief
  • Spousal/child/parent abuse
  • Career planning
  • Retirement

◆ **Health Care Reimbursement Accounts (HCRAs) and Dependent Care Reimbursement Accounts (DCRAs)**—These programs allow certain medical expenses, deductibles, and child care costs for employees and their families to be paid by employees on a pretax basis.

◆ **Hospitality organization–specific benefits**—By the very nature of their businesses, some hospitality companies can offer their employees benefits such as reduced-cost meal programs, hotel stays, or travel. Discounted dining, guest rooms, and transportation offered at greatly reduced employee rates are popular employee benefits and can usually be offered by employers at a relatively low cost.

HR Management: Impact on New Team Members

New employees are understandably concerned about the compensation they will receive as they start in their new positions. It is your job to ensure your new employees know important aspects of their total compensation package, including:

- ◆ Their rate of pay (hourly or salary pay)
- ◆ What day of the week or month they will receive their first paycheck
- ◆ What deductions will be made from the checks, including:
  - • The amount
  - • The reason for the deductions
- ◆ Benefits for which they will immediately qualify, such as:
  - • Employee meals
  - • Sick days
  - • Vacation days
  - • Health insurance (if applicable)
- ◆ Other mandatory or voluntary benefits available to new hires

New employees may be hesitant to ask detailed questions about their compensation packages, but they will be keenly interested in them. Experienced HR managers know that part of the process of starting employees off in a positive manner is the careful explanation of all financial and nonfinancial benefits included in each new employee's total compensation package.

❖ NONFINANCIAL COMPENSATION

LEARNING OBJECTIVE 5. List and describe some of the most common forms of nonfinancial compensation.

Intrinsic rewards can be powerful employee motivators. In addition to mandatory and voluntary benefits and other financial incentives, many companies complete their compensation programs by including intrinsic rewards designed to enhance workers' positive feelings about themselves and their jobs. While these rewards may not include direct financial payments to employees, they are certainly an integral part of a company's overall compensation program. Some of the most common and effective of the intrinsic motivators used in the hospitality industry provide employees with:

- ◆ Increased participation in decision making
- ◆ Greater job freedom
- ◆ More responsibility
- ◆ Flexible work hours
- ◆ Opportunities for personal growth
- ◆ Diverse tasks

Perhaps the most critical part of an effective intrinsic compensation package is provided simply by giving employees more responsibility in their work assignments. Effective HR managers determine their employees' suggestions about changes that can yield efficiency, productivity, customer service, or other improvements and then determine whether it is possible to make these changes.

It is important to remember that recognition of their efforts is valued by most employees nearly as much as the size of their paycheck. You must recognize that pay plus praise is a better motivator than pay alone. A variety of low-cost but effective techniques can be used to demonstrate appreciation of employee efforts. Examples include:

◆ Simple thank you notes that show appreciation for good work. Awards or plaques for good performance, preferably presented in front of peers or management, are also highly valued.

◆ Employee outings arranged by employees and designed to increase camaraderie. Outings of these types can include picnics, visits to skating rinks or bowling lanes, golfing, or another activity desired by employees.

◆ Paid time-off certificates (given, for example, to reward perfect attendance).

◆ Baseball caps, hats, shirts, jackets, and the like, embossed with the company name or logo.

◆ More job freedom and autonomy.

◆ A change in job title.

Regardless of the components of the specific compensation program you institute, your employees must know exactly how and why that system was developed. Failing to keep your employees informed about how the program was created and, when it changes, the reason for the changes, will likely yield employee dissatisfaction and conflict.

Many experienced HR managers believe that an organization's ability to communicate the rationale behind its compensation programs is just as important as the quality of the programs. Organizations that maximize the effectiveness of their overall compensation programs find that clear communication of the program's processes and objectives helps them to achieve their employee recruitment and retention goals and consistently maintain a highly motivated workforce.

HR TERMS

The following terms were defined in this chapter:

Compensation package	Salary	Tip pooling
Extrinsic rewards	Exempt (employee)	Service charge
Intrinsic rewards	Nonexempt (employee)	Benefits
Compensation management	Hourly wages	Mandatory benefits
Pay range	Piecework wages	Voluntary benefits
Local wage rate	Performance-based pay	AD&D insurance
Salary survey	Incentive	Payroll deduction
Merit pay system	Bonus	401(k) Retirement plan
Minimum wage	Tip	
Living wage	Tip credit	

FOR YOUR CONSIDERATION

1. In this chapter you learned about different forms of direct, indirect, and nonfinancial compensation. Consider your own career. Which of these types of compensation is most important to you? Do you believe the same form(s) of compensation would be most important to those you will directly manage? Explain your answer.

2. Insurance benefits have traditionally been offered to employees and their immediate families. Today's employees, however, often define *family* in a much different manner than did previous generations of workers. The increase in the acceptance of gay marriage and of same-sex living arrangements has resulted in more employees seeking insurance benefits for their domestic (live-in) partners, regardless of their marriage status or their partner's gender. Some companies now offer insurance benefits to domestic partners, but others do not. Do you think companies should offer benefits to domestic partners? Why or not?

3. Finding affordable, quality day care is a challenge for many hospitality employees. In some cases, progressive hospitality employers have done a good job of securing reduced-cost services of this type, or even providing on-site day care at no or low cost to their employees. Assume you were an HR manager in such a progressive facility. How would you respond to a group of older employees who questioned the fairness of the company's use of significant resources directed only at a targeted subcategory of workers (those with young children)?

4. Some HR managers believe that their younger workers are increasingly aware that a company's care for the environment is often reflected in its care for its employees. As a result, companies espousing genuine commitment to sustainable, or "green," practices tend to attract a more committed and, as a result, higher-quality staff. Would you agree with these managers? Explain your answer.

5. The number one complaint among hospitality customers is not poor product quality; rather, it is poor service quality. How do you think the features of an operation's overall compensation program could affect its employees' commitment to providing high-quality customer service?

CASE STUDY

Apply HR Management Principles

"Look," said Adrian, "I really like it here. It's great. But the Downtown Inn is paying three dollars more per hour. I have a family. I have to take it for them."

"It" was a banquet manager's job that had been offered to Adrian, a young and talented banquet manager at the Uptown Inn. Adrian was meeting with LeeAnn Krenshaw, his boss and the director of banquet services at the hotel where he had worked for two years.

"Are you sure the tips will be the same?" asked LeeAnn.

:::::CASE STUDY (continued)

"They said their service charge was 20 percent, same as ours," replied Adrian.

LeeAnn thought about the situation before she approached Tim Thatcher, the hotel's HR director. She told Tim about Adrian's pending resignation.

"That's really unfortunate," replied Tim. "Adrian is a great worker, and we really don't have anyone on staff ready to move up to his position. Do you have any active applicants for the job?"

"No, but I do know the banquet supervisor at another local property," replied LeeAnn. "She's good, and makes about the same money there as Adrian does here."

"Do you think she would want to work here?" asked Tim.

"If the money was right, I think she would," replied LeeAnn.

"How much do you think it would take to make her consider the move?" asked Tim.

"Well, she wouldn't likely move for the exact same pay," replied LeeAnn. "She'll want a raise to move. I think it would need to be in the three-dollar range or so per hour to make it worthwhile for her."

Dimension: Employee Perspective

Review the scenario described in the case study, and then address the following questions:

1. Why (in addition to money) do you think Adrian seems prepared to accept the job offer from the Downtown Inn?

2. Assume you are Adrian. What, if anything, could your current employer do to convince you to stay?

3. As a tipped hotel employee, Adrian's income could vary based on the tip-pooling policy in place at the Downtown Inn. Identify at least three additional areas in which the compensation program at the prospective employer might vary significantly from the Uptown Inn's program.

Dimension: Company Perspective

Review the conversation described in the case:

1. What, in addition to a pay increase, do you believe is the primary cause of workers seeking alternative employment opportunities?

2. What are the specific real, and potential, disadvantages to your organization of losing an employee such as Adrian?

3. Assume Adrian is one of several talented banquet managers on the hotel's staff. Also assume LeeAnn's colleague Sara is hired at a pay rate $3 per hour higher than the average pay of these employees. What are the likely outcomes that would occur if and when Sara's pay becomes common knowledge in the food and beverage department?

Dimension: Compensation Program Assessment

1. If you were Tim, would you advise LeeAnn to pursue Sara as a potential employee? Why or why not?

2. Assume you are LeeAnn. What specific problems within your departmental compensation program does this situation illustrate?

3. Assume you are the general manager of this hotel. Who on your management team is responsible for ensuring that your property does not lose talented employees such as Adrian to your direct competitors? Explain your answer.

INTERNET ACTIVITIES

1. For many managers, the issue of tipped employee pay is important because many of their employees receive tips. Requirements for how tipped employees can be paid vary by state. To see requirements for paying tipped employees, enter "tipped employee pay rates *<your state's name>*" in your favorite search engine. Choose the appropriate state agency website, then answer the following questions.

    a. What is the minimum wage rate that must be paid to tipped employees in your state?

    b. How is the overtime pay rate for tipped employees in the state to be calculated?

2. Because it is still relatively new, many managers are unsure about the provisions of the Affordable Care Act (ACA), especially its requirement that states provide their residents access to health care exchanges (marketplaces). To see how the marketplace is operating in your state, enter "health care marketplace *<your state's name>*" in your favorite search engine. Choose the appropriate state agency website, then answer the following questions.

    a. Is your state operating a health care marketplace, is the marketplace operated by the federal government, or is it operated through a partnership between the state and federal government?

    b. If your state is not operating its own marketplace, who in the state would employers contact to find further information about the impact of available marketplace options for their own hospitality employees?

© Eric Audras / Getty Images

CHAPTER

9

PERFORMANCE MANAGEMENT AND APPRAISAL

CHAPTER OUTLINE

LEARNING OBJECTIVES

When they complete this chapter, readers will be able to:

1. Identify the benefits of a formal employee performance appraisal program.

2. Explain the rationale for each of the four steps in a progressive disciplinary program.

3. Describe the role of employee improvement efforts as an integral part of the performance management process.

4. Differentiate between a voluntary and a nonvoluntary employee separation and explain the function of an exit interview.

5. Identify major legal issues related to performance management and appraisal.

Impact on HR Management

I n previous chapters you learned how hospitality managers recruit, select, orient, and train their employees to help ensure the best possible staff. These are continual processes because workers' jobs continually evolve as guests' needs and desires change and new work methods are implemented.

HR managers' efforts to improve their employees' job performance must be ongoing; fortunately, these efforts most often are successful. Sometimes, however, problems with the quality or quantity of an employee's work arise. In other cases an employee's work may be acceptable, but difficulties about compliance with workplace rules and procedures arise. Managers must fairly evaluate the quality of their employees' efforts and, if necessary, correct and improve their performance.

Most staff members want to do a good job, but concerned and enlightened managers can often help them to do better. Knowing how to objectively evaluate and improve worker performance and, if necessary, to properly terminate employees are important aspects of an HR manager's job. Actions taken are important because laws related to how and why employees are disciplined and/or terminated are complex. Violation of these laws may cause managers to spend excessive amounts of time defending their actions. Violations can also create substantial financial hardship if fines or penalties are levied. And, if widely publicized, violations can even result in significant adverse publicity that negatively affects a business's profits.

❖ PERFORMANCE MANAGEMENT

LEARNING OBJECTIVE 1. Identify the benefits of a formal employee performance appraisal program.

Effective HR managers provide ongoing performance feedback to their employees. This process is integral to maximizing the effectiveness of an operation's workforce. Documenting performance appraisal efforts is often an HR responsibility, but those who directly supervise the worker and have firsthand knowledge of their performance often can best perform the evaluation, and they are most often the ones best able to help employees improve performance levels.

Performance management and **performance appraisals**, when properly implemented, can help employees do their best.

Performance appraisal is not a new concept, but performance management has only recently become integral to HR management. As shown in Figure 9.1, performance management is ongoing and includes:

- ◆ **Planning** work and setting expectations
- ◆ **Monitoring** performance continually
- ◆ **Developing** employee skills
- ◆ **Appraising** performance periodically in an objective manner
- ◆ **Rewarding** good performance

Performance management: A systematic process by which managers can help employees improve their ability to achieve goals.

Performance appraisal (employee): An objective and comprehensive evaluation of employee effectiveness.

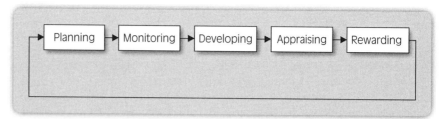

Figure 9.1   The Performance Management Process

The distinguishing characteristic of an effective performance management program is its focus on achieving results. It addresses the effectiveness of employees, as well as work processes and output quality. To illustrate, consider a skilled food service employee who chops cabbage quickly and produces a high-quality product. Traditional performance appraisal systems might rate the employee highly because of his or her hard work and efficiency. A performance management system, however, would involve the worker in an objective assessment of effectiveness. Perhaps the cabbage chopping process should be mechanized (new equipment should be purchased) or prechopped cabbage should be purchased. Then the employee's knowledge and skills might be better utilized doing other important tasks. A properly designed performance management system emphasizes goal attainment over employee effort (output).

Traditional performance appraisal systems frequently emphasize employees' negative characteristics. While performance management systems are designed to identify and correct employee weaknesses, they also recognize, reinforce, and reward employees' strengths.

Performance appraisal is the employee evaluation component of a performance management process. An effective process yields clear employee goals and an objective assessment of goal attainment.

HR Management in Action

ARE WE ACTUALLY TALKING ABOUT THE SAME PERSON?

James Cramer is the HR Director at the Bartello Palms resort hotel. And he is confused. He is reading an employee performance appraisal report written by Ron Dukes. The employee Mr. Dukes evaluated was Sandy Rinaldo. Sandy had worked at the resort for over 10 years, but Ron had only recently been appointed as her supervisor, and this was his first formal evaluation of Sandy.

In all of her prior positions within the hotel Sandy had consistently received outstanding performance appraisals. But the report James was now reading indicated that Sandy's current performance was far below average and that her attitude was poor. In fact, Ron was actually recommending immediate disciplinary action for Sandy's failure to meet his performance expectations.

This case illustrates the fact that HR managers must play an important role as an advocate for both their employer and the employees for whom they are responsible. In this scenario, the integrity of the hotel's entire employee performance system is at issue. In the best employee performance appraisal systems the ratings given to an individual employee are dependent only on an employee's performance, not the personal opinions of the supervisor assessing the employee.

Perhaps Sandy's performance has in fact declined. This is certainly something James would want to investigate. It is also possible, however, that the problem lies not with Sandy, but with Ron Dukes—and with the ability of the hotel's performance appraisal system to be consistently and reliably applied regardless of who is doing the appraisal.

Overview of Performance Appraisal

The most successful performance appraisal programs typically combine four critical characteristics. You can apply these characteristics as you design your own appraisal program.

1. **Performance goals set by supervisors and employees**—Goals can be short-term or long-term and address numerous issues. They should be specific and measurable where possible (e.g., completion of a specific task within a defined period of time and at an established quality level). Employees may require additional training or other support to meet their goals. As workplace changes occur, goals should be reviewed and modified, if needed, with employee input.

2. **Regular, informal feedback from supervisors**—Traditional annual formal appraisals alone do not allow employees to assess progress toward goal attainment. More frequent input is needed, which occurs as supervisors work closely with employees and provide them with ongoing coaching.

3. **A formal method to address performance or disciplinary problems**—Methods used to correct inadequate job performance should be known, be fair, and be applied equally to all employees. From a legal perspective, this means using a formal method that details, in writing, the procedures and policies to be followed by all managers. Performance problems should be identified as they occur, and a course of action for improvement should be agreed on. Written procedures should require that managers document problems and agreed-on resolution plans.

4. **Regular and formal appraisal**—Formal reviews that accurately document each staff member's performance should be conducted regularly. In addition to pinpointing improvement concerns, appraisals should identify specific steps for employees to enhance their long-term position with the organization.

Each of these performance appraisal characteristics may seem obvious, but busy supervisors may not receive training in the methods required to address them. At large properties HR specialists typically work with department heads, managers, and supervisors to develop property-wide procedures. In small organizations, the unit manager and other personnel with HR-related duties must make sure these characteristics are incorporated into their operations' performance appraisal systems.

A properly implemented formal performance appraisal system yields many benefits:

◆ **Recognition of outstanding performance**—In the best appraisal systems, employees learn about the areas in which they excel. This increases their morale and helps reduce turnover. Unless a termination decision will be made, managers should praise desired employee behaviors. Every employee likely has positive personal work characteristics, such as attendance, punctuality, neatness, adherence to dress code, friendliness, or other traits. You should be sure to emphasize these because positive reinforcement of employee strengths often makes it easier to achieve improvements in other areas.

◆ **Identification of necessary improvements**—When an employee can excel in a position, it becomes more enjoyable. Few employees want a job that they do not understand, nor one in which they perform poorly. Some employees may not know about necessary improvements. When an unbiased supervisor conducts a regularly scheduled appraisal, employees will learn how their performance can be improved. The result is positive for both the employee and the operation.

◆ **Clarification of work standards**—Well-designed performance appraisal systems emphasize how well employees have attained goals. Sometimes this is simple. For example, a room attendant's guest room cleaning times can be assessed. In other cases performance is more difficult to measure. For example, while most hospitality managers agree that helpfulness is an important characteristic of a good hotel concierge, an objective evaluation of this trait is more complex than a timed measurement of task completion. In fact, a more subjective assessment approach, such as the results of guest surveys, may be useful in such cases.

Regardless of measurement difficulty, if friendliness will be evaluated, an employee should understand its importance, how the trait should be displayed, and the expected end results of displaying it. Guest comments, observation by management, and mystery shopper services (see chapter 7) can provide input for the appraisal. If a friendliness concept is not communicated clearly, whether managers can evaluate employee efforts to display it is questionable. Performance appraisal includes the responsibility for HR managers to clearly define and communicate job expectations.

◆ **Provide an opportunity to analyze and redesign jobs**—An effective performance appraisal program can identify the need for job redesign. Consider a situation in which a better way to perform an inventory is suggested by an employee who is responding to concerns that his or her performance of this task is below standards. In this case the employee's ideas on how to do the job better may result in real benefits to the worker and the operation.

◆ **Identify specific training and development needs**—A performance appraisal system that identifies deficiencies but does not address them is a poor one because it creates frustration. Specific steps that an employee and the operation should take to improve the employee's skill levels are needed. Opportunities to discuss professional development activities can be part of this dialogue.

◆ **Determine professional development activities**—Information discussed during a performance appraisal session establishes a foundation to help plan an employee's career. If career goals are known, beneficial educational or training activities can be considered, agreed on, and used as a benchmark for subsequent performance appraisal. For example, an agreement might be made that an employee will complete an online course offered by a community college, and the hospitality organization will reimburse the employee if the course is successfully completed. This can be a factor in a subsequent appraisal session because the manager and the employee agreed that successful completion of the course would be a priority.

◆ **Validate screening and selection processes**—In chapter 4 you learned about the importance of proper employee selection. Performance appraisal sessions allow managers to evaluate the effectiveness of these procedures. If employees consistently do not meet expectations, the screening and selection procedures in use may be the cause. Well-managed appraisal systems help managers to pinpoint potential employee selection shortcomings.

◆ **Provide an opportunity for employee feedback and suggestions**—The best managers use appraisal sessions to learn about issues that affect guest satisfaction from the employees who actually interact with customers. Remember that employees at all levels of the organization serve either **internal customers** or **external customers**. Most employees are eager to share beliefs about how their jobs could be improved and how service to customers can be enhanced.

◆ **Use an objective method to identify candidates for pay increases and promotion**—Performance appraisal systems commonly yield decisions about which employees receive pay increases and promotions. It is a workplace reality that scarce organizational resources must be allocated rationally, and properly designed appraisal systems help with this task.

Internal customers: Employees of a hospitality operation.

External customers: Guests served by a hospitality operation.

Performance Management and Performance Appraisal

Performance management systems can help managers deal with changes affecting their employees. Globalization, quality initiatives, changing franchise brand standards, changes in consumer preferences, new product market forms of foods and beverages, and the increased importance of teamwork are some factors continually changing in the hospitality industry's world. Recurring performance appraisal sessions are opportunities for regular examination about how these and other important factors affect employee performance. Professional, respectful, and two-way conversations during appraisal sessions are important and can yield significant benefits.

Performance Appraisal Systems Must Be Consistent

Basic procedures should be used to evaluate the performance of all employees at the same organizational level regardless of their functional department. HR managers can develop policies and procedures that address concerns, such as:

◆ Specific goals of the appraisal process

◆ Mechanics of the system

◆ Frequency of appraisal

◆ The process, if any, by which performance assessment comments are provided to employees before the formal session

◆ Suggested length of time for the appraisal session

◆ Documentation of appraisal information (e.g., a copy provided to the employee and included in the staff member's permanent personal file)

Those responsible for conducting appraisal sessions will likely require training. HR managers should design and implement this training for all new supervisors and managers with appraisal responsibility. Training updates may also become necessary as policies and procedures change and as new laws and regulations impact the performance appraisal process.

As an HR manager, what will be your role in the performance appraisal process? Figure 9.2 addresses this question.

As noted in Figure 9.2, HR managers play three primary roles in performance appraisal: (1) advocate for effective appraisal, (2) coordinate process planning and implementation, and (3) determine legal requirements. In efforts to coordinate the planning process, they should evaluate alternative processes. Should an in-house-developed system or an externally purchased system be used? HR personnel can assist with the selection decision by providing specialized input and interacting with legal counsel.

What About Money?

Wage and salary increases are often based on performance and thus are discussed during performance review sessions. When should this financial discussion occur? Industry observers make three suggestions. Some say that financial discussions should occur at the beginning of the performance appraisal session. Then employees can focus their attention on the discussion that follows. Others believe that approach is out of sequence because the compensation decision should be based on performance, so the appraisal review should occur before discussing any wage/salary adjustments. A third view is to discuss compensation matters during a separate session that can occur before or after the actual performance appraisal session.

There are pros and cons to each of these alternatives. However, the timing of wage and salary adjustments is important, and it illustrates the types of issues that must be considered as performance appraisal procedures are developed.

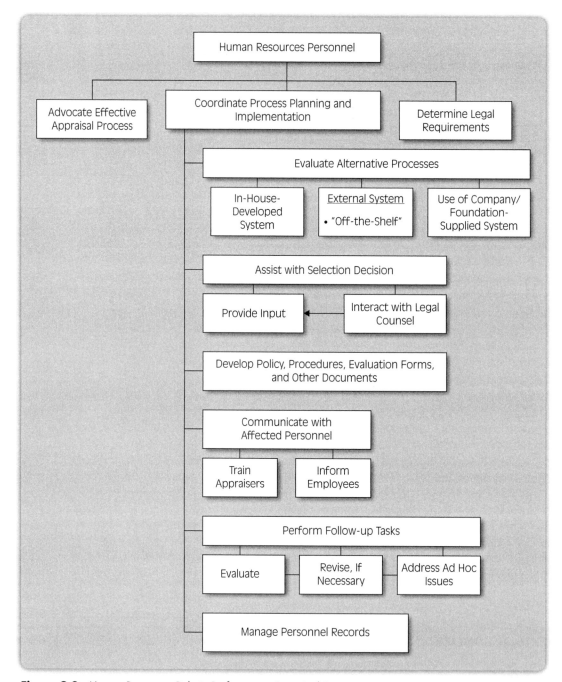

Figure 9.2   Human Resources Role in Performance Appraisal Process

After the performance appraisal system is established, the HR manager's role continues as policies, procedures, evaluation forms, and other documents are developed. Implementation involves communication with affected personnel. Those who will conduct performance appraisals must be trained, and employees must learn about the system. Follow-up tasks, including process evaluation, revision (if necessary), and management of the process, are required. Also, because appraisal information will become part of the employees' personal records, information must be collected and managed.

This brief description of steps in the process of developing and implementing a performance appraisal system suggests that it is complex (many steps are required), and it must be equally applied to all personnel. HR managers are usually in the best position to assume this coordinating responsibility.

Popular Performance Appraisal Methods

Hospitality organizations can use several approaches to and methods of performance appraisal, and HR managers play a role in their selection. Three popular approaches involve the use of absolute standards, relative standards, and targeted outcomes.

ABSOLUTE STANDARDS

When an **absolute standard appraisal** method is used, employee performance is compared with an established productivity standard not related to any other employee. Examples of absolute standard evaluation methods include:

Absolute standard appraisal (performance appraisal method): Measuring an employee's performance against an established standard.

Critical Incident

Critical incidents are those specific behaviors needed to do a job successfully. With this approach, behavioral traits that employees exhibit on the job (the critical incidents) are documented in writing. For example, an observation about Li Min, a bartender, might be: "Li Min showed poise, maturity, and patience with an agitated guest after she could no longer serve him alcoholic beverages. She calmed him down, and he ordered coffee."

Note that the incident report focuses on Li Min's behaviors and their results, rather than on Li Min's personal traits. One advantage of this method is that, during a formal appraisal session, the discussion can address specific positive and negative critical incidents to help support an objective evaluation of the employee's performance. A disadvantage is that frequent documentation of critical incidents can be time-consuming.

Checklist Appraisal

As shown in Figure 9.3, yes or no responses are used to address behavioral factors related to the successful completion of tasks identified in a job description. While the checklist can be modified to apply to specific positions, this can become a disadvantage if individualized checklists must be prepared for a large number of job categories and positions.

Continuum Appraisal

This approach uses a scale to measure employee performance relative to specific factors. The point on the scale that best represents the employee's performance is selected. Figure 9.4 shows a sample of continuum appraisal questions that address two factors: work quantity and dependability. Note that each performance factor is carefully defined to maximize consistency among those conducting the appraisals.

	YES	NO
1. Laundry supervisor's instructions consistently followed	_____	_____
2. Quantity of work performed is consistently acceptable	_____	_____
3. Quality of work performed is consistently acceptable	_____	_____
4. Work area is consistently kept clean	_____	_____
5. Dryer maintenance (lint filters cleaned) consistently performed	_____	_____
6. Responds willingly to special linen and terry products cleaning requests	_____	_____

Figure 9.3 Partial Laundry Worker Checklist Evaluation

PERFORMANCE FACTOR: Quantity of work (the volume of work done in a normal workday)
PERFORMANCE RATING (check one):

Consistently unsatisfactory	Occasionally unsatisfactory	Consistently satisfactory	Sometimes excellent	Consistently excellent
_____	_____	_____	_____	_____

PERFORMANCE FACTOR: Dependability (following directions and company policies without supervision)
PERFORMANCE RATING (check one):

Requires constant supervision	Requires occasional supervision	Usually can be counted on to perform	Requires very little supervision	Requires minimum supervision
_____	_____	_____	_____	_____

Figure 9.4 Sample Continuum Appraisal Questions

The number of alternative rating choices in a continuum appraisal system usually ranges between four and eight. In Figure 9.4, each of the five rating response categories, like all continuum scales, represents an ordinal (ranked) level of measurement. While the categories represent an inherent order (e.g., more to less, stronger to weaker, or very unsatisfactory to highly satisfactory), the categories do not indicate the magnitude (extent of differences) between each level. While the system lacks the depth of analysis found in, for example, a critical incident appraisal system, an advantage of continuum appraisal is its ease of use.

Forced-Choice Appraisal

This appraisal method is a special checklist approach in which the evaluator must choose between two (or more) alternative statements that describe two (or more) opposing choices. Alternative statements may be favorable or unfavorable, and the appraiser selects the statement that is most descriptive of the employee being evaluated. An example of this approach is:

> *Which of the following tasks is best performed by the employee? (check one)*
>
> ____ *Those involving detailed guest-service interaction*
>
> ____ *Those involving detailed non-guest-service duties*

Because there is no right answer associated with questions of this type, these appraisal systems can only be properly scored by professionals who are familiar with the system's specific design and intent.

RELATIVE STANDARDS

When HR managers use a **relative standard** of performance appraisal, they compare one employee's actions with those of another employee.

The two most common approaches to this appraisal alternative are group order ranking and individual ranking.

Group Order Ranking

Group order ranking requires the evaluator to place the employee into a specific classification, such as the top 10 percent or lowest 50 percent. This approach is often used when evaluating employees for possible promotion or pay increase.

Relative standard (performance appraisal method): Measuring one employee's performance against another employee's performance.

To illustrate, assume that Julia is the dining room supervisor at a restaurant and she supervises 20 servers. She must rank (compare with each other) all 20 employees. For example, if the system asks Julia to identify her top 10 percent of employees, she must identify only her top two employees (10 percent of 20 employees = 2 employees).

One advantage of this appraisal system is that raters cannot inflate evaluations, resulting in everyone being rated above average, nor can they rate nearly all employees as average or below average. A disadvantage, especially with small groups of employees, is that some individual or individuals must always be rated in the below-average group, regardless of their actual talent level. A second disadvantage is that a supervisor with clearly inferior workers will still generate groups of *best* and *worst* staff members (although the best employees may simply be the best of the worst). Conversely, a supervisor with a group of outstanding employees must still rank some of them in a below-average group.

Individual Order

This method requires supervisors to rank employees in order from highest to lowest. Only one employee can be rated as the very best, and ties are typically unacceptable. This system tends to work best with smaller groups of workers. However, because this system also represents an ordinal level of measurement, the rank achieved does not indicate the magnitude (extent) of differences between the ranks. For example, if 10 employees are ranked, there is no real rationale for believing that the difference between the first- and second-ranked employees is equal to the difference between the ninth- and tenth-ranked workers. The system is simple, but it is subjective, not objective.

TARGETED OUTCOMES

A third approach to employee evaluation involves the identification of **targeted (achieved) outcomes**. Employees are evaluated based on how well they accomplished a specific set of objectives critical to successful job completion. For example, restaurant managers might be evaluated primarily on whether they did (or did not) achieve preestablished food and/or labor cost percentages and profit targets.

Among increasingly popular targeted outcome appraisal systems are those using rating scales designed to award employees for exhibiting specific behaviors. **Behaviorally anchored rating scales (BARS)** and **behavioral observation scales (BOS)** both rate employees along a continuum; however, the points on the continuum represent examples of actual behaviors on a specific job, rather than general descriptions or traits.

HR managers should establish and communicate work targets or goals to employees, whether the targets are of a financial, attitudinal, or behavioral nature. An inherent advantage of this approach is that employees who know their goals—especially those who have participated in establishing them—will more likely work diligently to achieve the goals. Note that goal setting and goal achievement measurements and rewards are not new concepts. **Management by objectives (MBO)**, the concept of using identifiable objectives to measure performance and to assign employee rewards, is decades old.

Essentially, a targeted outcome appraisal system requires four components:

1. Identification of potential performance targets
2. Employee input in final target selection
3. A defined time period for target completion or achievement
4. Performance feedback (appraisal)

Properly managed, targeted outcome appraisal systems can be successfully implemented at all levels of a hospitality operation.

Additional Performance Appraisal Methods and Issues

Several other methods can be used for performance appraisal or, more typically, can be used in conjunction with other approaches. For example, while performance appraisal is primarily a manager's task, employees can play a valuable role in their own performance evaluations. While many employees believe their input would be helpful, some managers refuse to seriously consider

Targeted outcome (performance appraisal method): Measuring the extent to which specified goals were achieved. Also referred to as "achieved outcome."

BARS: Short for behaviorally anchored rating scale, an appraisal system in which employees are evaluated based on their display of definitive, observable, and measurable behaviors.

BOS: Short for behavioral observation scale, a type of appraisal system in which judgments about employee performance are related to a series of statements describing specific examples of observable behaviors.

Management by objectives (MBO): A plan developed by an employee and his or her supervisor that defines specific goals, tactics to achieve them, and corrective actions, if needed.

self-evaluation information. This is often a mistake because valuable information can be lost. Consider a current or previous job you have held, then think about the self-appraisal questions in Figure 9.5. How much would a manager learn about your work performance if you could address such questions?

Guests can provide additional information helpful for performance appraisal. Consider, for example, comments that guests might make on guest comment cards or in online surveys in response to questions designed to solicit this input. In addition, some hospitality organizations utilize **peer evaluation** information to generate the perspectives of those at the same organizational level and **upward assessments** that involve feedback from a worker's subordinates. These methods can be combined with a traditional appraisal approach involving the perspectives of a worker's own supervisor to create a **360-degree appraisal** method.

Many industry observers think the role of employee teams will increase in importance in the future. As this occurs, teams may be involved in determining work responsibilities, work schedules, and performance standards and may even play an increased role in compensation and team peer evaluations. Team members might use factors such as initiative, creativity, teamwork, communication skills, and collegiality to evaluate their peers.

HR managers may purchase performance appraisal tools from companies that specialize in their development or create them. In either case the goal should be to develop a system that is fair to employees, that benefits the organization, and that meets legal requirements.

Any tool used for performance appraisal must be reliable and valid. Recall that reliability (see chapter 4) refers to the degree to which a measurement tool delivers consistent and dependable measurements. A performance appraisal instrument is reliable if it consistently measures the employee trait being evaluated. Assume you are preparing a recipe for a dessert, and exactly one tablespoon of flour is needed. A reliable measuring device (a one-tablespoon measure), if properly used, will consistently (reliably) measure exactly one tablespoon of flour. Contrast that situation with the use of a one-cup measuring device, in which you must guess the amount to put into the cup to yield one tablespoon. A reliable measurement device is available in the first example, but not in the second case.

Reliable appraisal tools must also possess validity. Validity is the ability of a measuring tool to evaluate (measure) what it is actually supposed to evaluate. Even with use of a reliable measuring device, a cook could accurately and dependably measure the wrong thing. Consider the previous example: Assume a one-tablespoon measure was used to measure salt instead of flour. While the measuring device was reliable, it would consistently measure the wrong ingredient if salt, not flour, were added to the recipe. In this case, the recipe results would not be good, despite the reliability (but not validity) of the measuring device.

To better understand the concept of validity in performance appraisal, assume that a supervisor is evaluating a front-desk agent relative to the employee's speed when guests are being checked out of the hotel. On a personal level, this employee seems not to care for the supervisor very much and thus rarely engages the supervisor in general conversation (e.g., "How are you today?," "How was your weekend?," and other general comments of that nature).

Peer evaluation: An appraisal system that utilizes the opinions of coworkers to evaluate an employee's performance.

Upward assessment: An appraisal system that utilizes input from those staff members who are directly supervised by the staff member being evaluated.

360-Degree appraisal: A method of performance appraisal that utilizes input from supervisors, peers, subordinates, and even guests and others to provide a comprehensive evaluation of a staff member's performance.

◆ What skills and knowledge do you possess that our work team would find difficult to replace?

◆ What have you done, on your own, in the past six months to enhance your job knowledge or skills?

◆ Identify specific instances when, in the past six months, you have gone beyond what persons in your position are expected to do to directly benefit your coworkers or help the company achieve its goals?

◆ In one sentence, describe the main reason you contribute to our team's long-term success?

◆ What specific traits make you better than average at what you are assigned to do?

Figure 9.5 Sample Employee Self-Evaluation Questions

Threat	Example
1. Basing evaluation scores on the employee's most recent behavior rather than evaluating the entire performance period	Rating a usually outstanding employee negatively based on a recent argument
2. Allowing irrelevant or non-job-related factors to influence the evaluation	Evaluating physical appearance or disabilities, race, social standing, participation in employee assistance programs, or use of excused time-off instead of actual performance
3. Failing to include unfavorable comments on the evaluation, even when justified	Not wishing to offend an employee by not discussing undesirable traits, such as poor personal grooming or consistent display of a negative attitude
4. Rating all subordinates at about the same point on a ranking scale, usually in the middle	The tendency of supervisors, because they want to be liked by all employees, to avoid strong negative (or even positive) statements about their employees
5. Judging all employees too leniently or too harshly	The tendency of some supervisors, wanting to enhance their own credibility, to unfairly criticize (or praise) the performance of those they are evaluating
6. Permitting personal feelings to bias the evaluation process	The tendency of some supervisors to rate employees they like very highly, while rating employees they dislike much lower
7. Allowing one very good (or very bad) trait to affect all of the other ratings of the employee (the **halo effect** and the **pitchfork effect**)	Rating an employee with one exceptional (or unfavorable) trait as equally exceptional (or unfavorable) in all other measured criteria

Halo effect: The tendency to let the positive assessment of one individual trait influence the evaluation of other, nonrelated traits.

Pitchfork effect: The tendency to let the negative assessment of one individual trait influence the evaluation of other, nonrelated traits.

Figure 9.6 Threats to Fair Performance Appraisals

If the supervisor can ignore this less-than-friendly (to the supervisor) trait and focus solely on evaluating the speed of the employee when checking out guests, that measurement will be valid. If, however, the supervisor (because of the employee's lack of sociable conversation) subconsciously reduces the worker's "speed of check-out score," then the supervisor is actually assessing "friendliness to the supervisor" rather than speed. As a result the "speed of check-out" score given would not be valid.

Reliability and validity can be complex concepts. Some companies use sophisticated procedures to calculate the reliability and validity scores of the performance appraisal devices they use, but others do not. Those using the results of unreliable and/or invalid assessment devices to make decisions about employee promotion, discipline, and/or termination risk significant legal liability.

You should know about some additional challenges you may face related to the legitimate measurement of employee performance. Some evaluation actions, if taken, can threaten and even invalidate the results. Figure 9.6 presents seven significant threats to legitimate appraisal and specific examples of their occurrence.

❖ PROGRESSIVE DISCIPLINE

LEARNING OBJECTIVE 2. Explain the rationale for each of the four steps in a progressive disciplinary program.

Discipline is often thought of as management's response to an employee's improper behavior. While this is partially true, a broader view recognizes that discipline is any effort designed to change an employee's behavior. Managers should reinforce desired behavior and discourage

Discipline: Any effort designed to influence an employee's behavior.

Disciplined (workforce description): The situation in which employees conduct themselves according to accepted rules and standards of conduct.

Positive discipline: Any action designed to encourage proper behavior.

Negative discipline: Any action designed to correct undesirable employee behavior.

Progressive discipline: A program designed to modify employee behavior through a series of increasingly severe punishments for unacceptable behavior.

undesirable actions. The term **disciplined**, as used in the military (e.g., a disciplined squad or platoon is one in which soldiers follow orders and perform in a way that enhances the ability of the unit to achieve its objectives), is also appropriate to the hospitality industry. Disciplined staff members follow an organization's established set of rules and regulations, and thus a disciplined workforce in any organization is highly desirable.

Positive discipline is used to encourage desired behavior. **Negative discipline** is used to discourage improper behavior. Both HR and supervisory personnel should be concerned about the proper use of a property's discipline efforts.

Managers use direct instruction, written directions, employee manuals, role modeling, and often company traditions to relay their expectations about employee behavior. Most employees will adhere to specific behavioral standards when they know what is expected of them.

Unintended mistakes and occasional errors do occur, however, and coaching activities can typically correct these actions. However, intentional and repetitive noncompliance with standards should result in preestablished consequences that are identified in a **progressive discipline** program.

A consistently applied progressive discipline program lets employees know, in advance, the consequences of unacceptable behavior, which become more serious as the behavior is repeated. For this approach to be effective, the subordinate must view the consequences of repeated behavior to be undesirable. If they are not, behavior is unlikely to change.

Figure 9.7 reviews the role of HR in the progressive discipline process. Similar to that required to develop and maintain the performance appraisal process (Figure 9.2), HR managers typically perform coordination, communication, and administration responsibilities.

As you review Figure 9.7, note the role of HR personnel in advocating for an effective progressive discipline process and determining the basic legal requirements to be incorporated into it. Coordinating efforts include soliciting input from top-level property leaders, managers, and supervisors and, perhaps, the employees themselves.

Proposed disciplinary procedures must be developed, reviewed, and revised, and input from legal counsel is required as a final step before they are adopted. Then, policies, procedures, and necessary documents must be developed and used in communicating with employees. Follow-up tasks include evaluation, revision (if necessary), and the possibility of addressing unanticipated issues. Finally, information from the progressive discipline process must be managed as it is entered and maintained in workers' personnel records.

A commonly used four-step progressive discipline program includes (1) documented oral warning, (2) written warning, (3) suspension, and (4) dismissal. Coaching to correct behavior may come before the documented oral warning, especially if a one-time occurrence does not create significant difficulties (e.g., an initial violation of a policy regarding use of solid-toed shoes in the kitchen).

Documented Oral Warning

Documented oral warning: The first step in a progressive discipline process: a written record of an oral reprimand given to an employee is made.

Reprimand: A formal criticism delivered as a result of a wrongdoing.

The first (mildest) step in this form of employee discipline is the **documented oral warning**.

The written record of an oral warning should include the employee action that caused the warning, the date of the incident and of the oral warning, and the name of the supervisor issuing the **reprimand**. Figure 9.8 illustrates the format for an oral reprimand record.

Some managers believe that an initial discipline activity should not become part of the employee's permanent personal file but, instead, should be maintained in a separate manager's file. Other managers document the issuance of an oral warning but do not include the actual reprimand in the employee's permanent file. The property's progressive discipline program should explain how oral warnings must be documented so all employees receive identical treatment.

To illustrate this initial progressive discipline step, assume that Sam, a new cook in a hospital, has been late twice in the past week and has been coached about the problem by Ajay, his supervisor. When the problem next occurs, Ajay meets privately with Sam to explain why punctuality is important. Ajay should then allow Sam to respond. Ajay may discover that Sam did not understand some aspect of the expected behavior or learn that a legitimate reason for the late arrival existed.

Ajay and Sam should mutually develop and agree on an appropriate solution, and Ajay should tell Sam about the consequences of further late arrivals. An oral reprimand record can be completed and signed by Ajay and Sam to finalize the oral warning process. Hopefully, this will resolve the problem. If not, the next step in the progressive disciplinary process will be necessary.

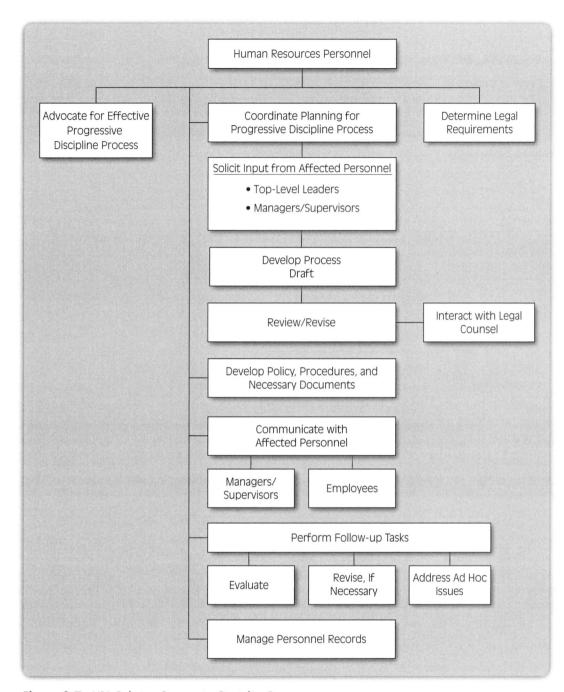

Figure 9.7 HR's Role in a Progressive Discipline Process

Written Warning

A **written warning** is a document that becomes part of an employee's permanent file. The content of a written warning is similar to that of the oral written warning (see Figure 9.8). It should include the employee's name, date of the incident, the name of the supervisor issuing the written warning, and the plan to prevent further occurrences. It also typically permits the employee to provide his or her own version of the incident. Signatures of the supervisor and the affected employee are required.

The written warning step must be done correctly to protect the organization if the employee later challenges the legality of the progressive disciplinary process. The employee behavior leading to this step should relate to that exhibited in the first step. Managers should remember that the courts generally view the term *progressive discipline* as discipline "related to the same issue."

Written warning: The second step in a progressive discipline process that alerts an employee that further inappropriate behavior will lead to suspension.

DISCUSSION RECORD

Name of Employee: _____

Discussion Date: _____ Time: _____

Incident Date: _____

Incident Description: _____

_____

_____

_____

Follow-up Action(s): _____

_____

_____

Employee's Signature: _____ Date: _____

Supervisor's Signature: _____ Date: _____

Note: A copy of this discussion record will be included in the personnel file and is available for the employee upon request.

Figure 9.8 Oral Reprimand Record

HR MANAGEMENT ISSUES 9.1

"Let me see if I understand," said Allisha, the F&B Director at Foxwoods Country Club, as she reviewed the employee file of Lani Meier, a dining room server. "Lani has worked here for five years with no write-ups. Now, in the two weeks since you have become her supervisor, Lani is at stage three of our four-stage progressive discipline process, and your recommendation is suspension."

"She did it to herself, Allisha," replied Michelle, a former dining room server and Lani's new boss. "Lani never liked me. I think she is jealous of me, but I played it straight up. Every write-up I give is legitimate. She needs to be suspended or fired because I don't think she'll ever change."

Allisha reviewed Lani's file one more time. Lani's first written oral warning, dated 10 days ago, was for returning from her unpaid lunch period 10 minutes late. Lani stated that she had gone to the bank and was caught at a train crossing returning to work, which delayed her timely return.

The written warning followed two days later, when Lani was reprimanded for being out of uniform. In fact, in the written report, Lani admitted that she was working and had forgotten to put on her nametag when she clocked in, but that she had been clocked in for only five minutes and was on her way back to the locker room to put on her name tag, when a club member asked her some questions. While Lani was responding to the member, Michelle walked by and noticed Lani was "working while out of uniform." Michelle then verified that Lani had already punched in, and, as a result, wrote her up.

The suspension that Michelle was now proposing was the result of an incident yesterday when, as required by the employee handbook, Lani failed to notify her supervisor four hours before her shift began that she would not be at work as assigned on the schedule. On that day Lani was scheduled to work at 7:00 a.m., but at 3:00 a.m. had to take her 2-year-old son to the emergency room for a condition diagnosed as a severe ear infection. At 5:00 a.m. Lani had left a voice mail on Michelle's office phone stating she was still at the hospital and would not be in that day. That 5:00 a.m. call was placed two hours later, Michele now pointed out, than the four-hour notice required by the employee manual, and so it justified the suspension.

Case Study Questions

1. Do you think Allisha should support Michelle's recommendation that Lani be suspended? Why or why not?

2. Do you believe Michele is following a progressive disciplinary process? Why or why not?

3. What do you think is happening in this situation? How would you address it if you were Allisha?

Returning to the example of Ajay and Sam, assume that Sam neglected to properly label and date a pan of food before placing it in the cooler and that this action resulted in loss of the product. It would not be appropriate to issue a written warning to Sam for this behavior, because it does not relate to his late arrivals. Because this is a first offense, a documented oral warning would be appropriate. Sometimes it is not so clear whether an incident is one in a series or the beginning of a new series of incidents. When that is the case, this sometimes difficult question must be carefully answered to determine the appropriate management action.

While it is generally a good rule to praise in public and to reprimand in private, many progressive discipline processes require an observer to be present at the second and later steps in the process. Comanagers, supervisors, or others can monitor the discussion and serve as an eyewitness.

Suspension

Suspension is the third step in the progressive discipline process, and it should be undertaken if the previous steps have not resolved the performance problem. A suspension may be for any period deemed appropriate by management. Suspensions, however, should be applied consistently: If one employee is suspended for a specific period for a particular behavior, then all other employees suspended for the same behavior should be suspended for the same length of time.

> **Suspension:** The third step in a progressive discipline process; a period off from work resulting from ongoing inappropriate behavior.

An action to suspend an employee must be documented, and the information should be placed in the employee's permanent file. Some employees may refuse to sign the suspension document. Despite an employee's view that an unsigned document will somehow invalidate it, this refusal carries virtually no legal meaning if the employee was given the opportunity to sign it. If an employee refuses to sign a discipline report, then the observer should sign the document and note the employee's refusal to sign.

An employee's suspension, with or without pay, is a serious step. It should signal that the employee's behavior is clearly not acceptable and that he or she is in danger of losing the job. If the employee's behavior is not corrected after this step, dismissal is likely.

Dismissal

Dismissal is the final step in the progressive discipline process and should be implemented only for continued serious infractions. Unfortunately, in some cases this step may be management's only alternative. Later in this chapter you'll learn more about the specific issues related to employer-initiated dismissals. In the context of a progressive disciplinary program, dismissal represents not only a final step in the process but also a failure on the part of both the employee and the employer. This is so because an effective progressive discipline program should modify and improve employee behavior.

> **Dismissal:** An employer-initiated separation of employment.

From an employee's perspective, dismissal means that, even after repeated warnings, the organization's behavioral expectations were not met. From the employer's perspective, dismissal means that the manager was unable to persuade the employee to modify his or her behavior sufficiently to maintain the job.

⋮⋮ BEHAVIOR IMPROVEMENT TACTICS

LEARNING OBJECTIVE 3. Describe the role of employee improvement efforts as an integral part of the performance management process.

Discipline was defined earlier as the efforts used to reinforce acceptable behavior and to eliminate unacceptable behavior. These are the topics of this section.

Reinforce Acceptable Good Behavior

When managers encourage employees to perform in specific ways and the employees can do so, desired behaviors are reinforced, and they will occur more frequently. Even when the employee cannot perform a task perfectly, enthusiastic encouragement can cause performance to improve.

Most staff members, like all people, respond to praise and encouragement. It feeds their self-esteem and ego and pushes them to achieve more and to try harder. However, many managers focus on poor performance and ignore the employee's internal and fundamental motivators. Recognizing employee efforts (not just results) can elevate a manager to a position of greater leadership.

Here are examples of specific tactics to reinforce positive behavior:

- **Saying more than "thank you" or "good job"**—The best managers encourage specific behaviors. For instance, assume you are a hotel manager, and Carol, your director of sales, has just completed a phone conversation with a difficult customer. You could say: "Carol, I heard your conversation, and I really liked how you handled it. You kept calm and focused on resolving the complaint, and you paraphrased the client to show you were listening to her concerns." Note that Carol will be encouraged with specific mention of actions that you want to affirm and see her repeat in the future.

- **Praising on the spot**—The best managers do not wait to encourage employees until it is less hectic. Encouragement only takes an extra moment, and busy, chaotic times are when employees typically most need encouragement. When managers praise employees only during formal performance reviews, the employees may feel cheated the rest of the year.

- **Telling them directly**—Managers may tell those around them how much they appreciate a specific employee, but they sometimes feel uncomfortable telling that employee directly. Employees will not get inflated egos or expect an immediate raise just because they are complimented. The more likely case is that they will be pleased when their effort is noticed, and they will work even harder to justify their manager's continued appreciation.

- **Meaning what is said**—A manager's tone of voice, eye contact, and body language can enhance or detract from a message. Managers must be sincere, make eye contact, and take the time to stop and look at the employee when conversing. Insincere praise is often worse than no praise at all!

- **Putting it in writing**—Encouraging words need not be typed and formal. A short, handwritten note is fast and easy. A complimentary note from one's boss can be shared proudly with family members and friends. A written compliment is a source of pride to nearly every employee and demonstrates the power of recognition.

Eliminate Unacceptable Behavior

When employees exhibit unwanted behavior, it is usually because they don't know the desired behavior, know it but do not know how to perform it, or know it and do not want to perform it.

In the first case, improving behavior may involve careful explanation about the performance standard. In the second case, skills training is likely required (see chapter 6). In the third case, a progressive discipline process is likely the appropriate response, and **counseling** is an important tactic in the process.

Counseling: A process used to assist employees in overcoming performance problems.

Effective employee counseling assists workers in making their own good decisions from among available choices. To plan counseling to overcome employee performance problems, you should prepare a list of concerns about your employee's performance, including times, dates, and other information about unsatisfactory behavior. Time when uninterrupted conversation with the employee is possible should be arranged. The employee should receive sufficient notice about the meeting and subject matter to properly prepare for it.

During the counseling session, you should focus on behavior, not the person or his or her attitudes. For example, you should not say: "Jerome, you are totally irresponsible. You arrive late nearly every day!" Rather, the comment could be: "Jerome, you have been arriving at work late nearly every day, and this causes a problem for our operation. What is the reason for your lateness?"

Listening to the employee helps him or her feel valued and understood. Employees should be encouraged to talk and to explain their behavior. Hopefully, options can be considered and a realistic solution to the performance problem can be proposed. Then clear objectives can be developed, specific action plans can be identified, and the manager will commit to supporting the employee's improvement efforts.

In some cases, undesirable employee performance may result from forces beyond his or her control. Financial difficulties, marital trauma, family emergencies, death of parent, spouse, or child, substance abuse, and legal issues are examples of factors that can negatively affect performance. Despite management's admonitions that employees must leave their personal problems at home, employees cannot always readily do so. Notwithstanding the desire of caring managers to want to help in difficult personal situations such as marital difficulties, substance abuse by other family members, or financial difficulties, comments should be limited to the employee's performance.

Some off-job factors affecting employees may be the result of poor lifestyle choices, whereas others are caused by circumstances the employees cannot control. In all cases, when external factors are the prime reasons for unsatisfactory performance, the best course of action is to refer the employee to an effective internal or external employee assistance program (EAP; see chapter 10).

❖❖ EMPLOYEE SEPARATION

LEARNING OBJECTIVE 4. Differentiate between a voluntary and a nonvoluntary employee separation and explain the function of an exit interview.

Despite the costs and disruption that occur when an employee leaves a job, in some segments of the hospitality industry employee **turnover**, as measured by the business's turnover rate, is exceptionally high.

Turnover: The replacement of one employee by another.

The inevitable result of turnover is an increase in managerial time and other real financial costs. A survey conducted by the Center for American Progress estimates that for those jobs paying $50,000 or less per year, the cost of job turnover is approximately 20% of the employee's salary, or $10,000.[1] For those jobs paying less than $30,000 per year, the study found the cost of turnover was 15%, or approximately $4,500 per employee. Regardless of the exact amounts, experienced HR managers agree that costs associated with replacing employees who do not remain with the organization are high, and they should be avoided when possible. Then HR managers will not need to continually recruit new staff members and move them through the expensive and time-consuming orientation and training processes.

Some turnover is inevitable and is good for a business because, in many cases, new staff members with diverse attitudes and ideas can be recruited. However, excessive employee separations and the high turnover rates that result are detrimental to an operation's ability to maintain quality standards and costs and, sometimes, to remain financially viable. Employee separations can be viewed as voluntary or involuntary.

Voluntary Separation

Voluntary employment separations are often inevitable. Employees graduate from school, retire, move away, or, for numerous other reasons, elect to resign from a job.

Voluntary (separation): An employee-initiated termination of employment.

While these employee-initiated separations are often inconvenient, they rarely cause significant replacement issues. In the best-case scenario, employees will inform managers about their pending departures in enough time that replacements can be recruited and trained.

Involuntary Separation

Involuntary employment separations are frequently caused by poor employee performance. However, management may also have failed to properly select, orient, train, or direct the work of these employees.

Involuntary (separation): An employer-initiated termination of employment.

Involuntary employee separations affect more than just immediate employee replacement and training costs. In most states employees who are involuntarily separated qualify for

HR Management: Impact on New Team Members

In most cases, new employees are excited to get started in their new jobs, want to do high-quality work, and hope to learn that their decision to join a new organization was a good one. But experienced HR managers know that even with the best of intentions new employees are likely to make some errors as they begin their jobs.

For this reason all new employees should be assured that an operation's disciplinary program has been designed to help them succeed, not simply to catch them in their mistakes. When new employees are convinced management's performance appraisal system has been designed to increase their chances of long-term success, it's a win–win situation for both!

unemployment compensation payments. While there are exceptions (e.g., for employees dismissed for theft, assault, or other illegal activities), significant increases in payments to employees who are involuntarily separated result in an increase in the amount the employer must pay into their state's unemployment compensation accounts.

We have examined employment separation from the perspectives of employees who leave the organization for good reason and those who are asked to leave. A third case, however, is the employee who leaves voluntarily but does so involuntarily! In other words, the employee decides to leave the job, but the reason relates directly to a negative aspect of the job.

Consider Stella, a good employee who likes her job but who is leaving for another job doing the same work at the same rate of pay. She currently feels her manager does not appreciate her, and recognition of a job well-done is important to her (as it is to many employees). Because Stella does not receive the recognition she seeks, she is leaving the organization. Often, the motivations of employees like Stella remain unknown. In other cases exit interviews can help uncover reasons for the involuntary/voluntary separation of employees.

Exit Interviews

Exit interview: A meeting between a representative of the organization and a departing employee.

Exit interviews are typically used when an employee voluntarily resigns. Then HR managers ask questions while taking notes or request that the employee complete a questionnaire or a short survey.

Exit interviews can yield vital information about the workplace and sometimes can prevent the loss of employees who really want to remain at the job but feel they cannot. Figure 9.9 lists examples of questions that may be asked of separating employees during a well-planned exit interview.

⁘ LEGAL CONSIDERATIONS OF PERFORMANCE MANAGEMENT AND APPRAISAL

LEARNING OBJECTIVE 5. Identify major legal issues related to performance management and appraisal.

As you have learned, employers have much freedom in how they design and administer their performance management and appraisal systems. They are not, however, free to terminate employees in violation of the laws specifically enacted to ensure fairness in these systems. While the laws related to termination may vary depending upon the country or state or city in which the business operates, in the United States several laws directly affect performance appraisal and termination systems.

- ◆ What is your primary reason for leaving?
- ◆ Did any specific event or thing make you decide to leave?
- ◆ What did you like best about working here?
- ◆ What did you like least about working here?
- ◆ Were your job duties the same as you anticipated when you were hired? (If not, how were they different?)
- ◆ Did you receive enough training?
- ◆ Did you receive enough feedback about your performance from your supervisor?
- ◆ Did this job help you advance in your long-term career goals?
- ◆ Are there any current employees you feel would perform well in your job?
- ◆ Do you have any tips to help us find your replacement?
- ◆ What would you do to improve our operation?
- ◆ Were the pay, benefits, and other incentives in our operation fairly administered?
- ◆ What was the quality of your supervision?
- ◆ Based on your experience with us, what does it take to succeed at this company?
- ◆ Did any company policies or procedures (or any other problem) make your job unusually difficult?
- ◆ Would you be leaving this job if your pay was higher?
- ◆ Would you consider working for our company in the future (or at another location)?
- ◆ Would you recommend working for this company to your family and friends?
- ◆ What does your new job offer that this job does not?
- ◆ Can this company do anything to encourage you to stay?
- ◆ Did anyone in this company discriminate against you, harass you, or cause you to feel hostility in your working conditions?
- ◆ Is there anything you would like the owners (managers) of this operation to know about their business that they may not currently know?

Figure 9.9 Sample Exit Interview Questions

Title VII of the Civil Rights Act

Title VII of the Civil Rights Act specifically prohibits employers from using non-job-related factors for employee evaluation, promotion, or termination. While most of today's hospitality employers would not knowingly use individual characteristics such as race, religion, or gender when evaluating or terminating employees, HR managers should be alert for some signals that informal discrimination practices are in place:

1. The underrepresentation of workers in specific **protected classes** in highly desired jobs
2. Variations in performance appraisal scores based on a worker's membership in a protected class
3. Variations in employee pay based on a worker's membership in a protected class
4. Variations in employee promotions based on a worker's membership in a protected class

Protected class: A group of workers with a characteristic specifically identified by an employment-related law or ordinance as protected.

For example, under Title VII, the characteristics of age, color, disability, national origin, race, religion, and sex designate protected classes of workers. Employees in protected classes cannot be treated differently from other employees, discriminated against, fired, or laid off because of their protected class status.

Equal Pay Act

The Equal Pay Act requires equal pay for men and women doing equal work; if the jobs performed require equal skill, effort, and responsibility; and if they are performed under similar working conditions. Surprisingly, a few hospitality managers still perceive some jobs to be best suited for men while they believe other jobs are best suited for women. Women working in these managers' operations are often evaluated in a way that disallows them from qualifying for the higher-paying

It's the Law

In many cases employers justify the involuntary separation of their employees based on the at-will employment doctrine discussed in chapter 4. At-will employment laws usually allow employers great latitude to terminate employees with or without cause. There are at least five exceptions to this, however, and if evidence of any one of these exceptions is documented in the appraisal process or elsewhere, the affected employee will likely win a wrongful termination lawsuit.

◆ **Contractual relationship**—Employees may not be terminated at will if there is a contractual relationship. A contractual relationship exists when employers and employees have a legal agreement regarding how employee issues are handled. Under such contracts, discharge may occur only if it is based on just cause.

◆ **Implied contractual relationship**—An implied contract is any verbal or written statement made by members of the organization that suggests organizational guarantees or promises about continued employment. These statements are most often found in employee handbooks that have not been carefully reviewed to ensure there is, in fact, no implied contractual relationship.

◆ **Public policy violation**—An employee cannot be terminated for refusing to obey an order from an employer that is considered an illegal activity (e.g., being asked to bribe a public food safety inspector to receive a higher kitchen inspection score). Furthermore, employees cannot be terminated for exercising their individual legal rights, such as agreeing to serve on jury duty or filing a complaint against an employer with a governmental entity, even if that complaint ultimately is dismissed because it was unfounded.

◆ **Statutory considerations**—Employees may not be terminated if doing so would result in a direct violation of a federal or state statute. For example, an employer may not terminate an employee for reasons that would violate either the Civil Rights or Age Discrimination Acts. Thus an employer who terminates a female employee in preference of a male employee is in violation of a federal mandate that such gender-based employment decisions are not permitted.

Good faith: The honest intent to act without taking an unfair advantage over another person.

◆ **Breach of good faith**—While it is difficult for employees to prove breach of **good faith** on the part of an employer, the courts have determined that the at-will employment concept does not allow employers total freedom to terminate. For example, if the national director of sales for a large hotel company secures a contract with a large organization, the employer may not terminate that person's employment to avoid paying the legitimately earned but significantly large bonus that is rightly due to the salesperson. In such a case the courts would take the position that the employee worked on the sale in good faith (expecting to earn the commission), and the employer cannot use the at-will employment doctrine to avoid paying the commissions because doing so would not be acting in good faith.

jobs considered best suited for men. In nearly all cases this approach to employment is a clear violation of the law and is typically accompanied by compensation and performance appraisal systems that violate the Equal Pay Act. Enlightened HR managers should be constantly aware of signs that might indicate the existence of hidden gender bias in their operations.

Americans with Disabilities Act

The Americans with Disabilities Act (ADA) affects the hiring of workers in this protected class, and it also directly affects the manner in which managers evaluate workers with disabilities. The act prohibits managers from considering disability when evaluating worker performance. For

HR MANAGEMENT ISSUES 9.2

"We need to reduce payroll during the holidays, when our business drops off," said Penny, the Landmark Restaurant's manager. Mark, the kitchen manager, was discussing staffing in his department.

"Well," he said, "the two people I could lay off are Tina and Nate. They both are in the pre-prep area, and when it gets slow, I really only need one of them."

"Which one will you keep?" asked Penny.

"They both are equally good," replied Mark, "but Nate has a wife and family to support and Tina lives at home with her folks. She'll be okay with the layoff; Nate would have more problems getting by."

Case Study Questions

1. Do you think Mark's proposed decision is a violation of the Civil Rights Act, the Equal Pay Act, or both? Why?

2. Do you believe Penny should allow Mark to go forward with his layoff plan? Why or why not?

3. As an HR manager what would you advise Penny to tell Mark?

---

example, a worker possessing limited hearing who is hired for a job in which hearing level is immaterial to success may not be evaluated lower than his or her coworkers based solely on their hearing limitation.

An employer can, however, hold employees with disabilities to the same standards of performance as other employees without disabilities for performing essential job functions with or without reasonable accommodation (see chapter 2). More complex, however, are issues related to employee evaluations that consider employee behaviors that may in fact be disability-based but are unacceptable. For example, assume a manager first learns during an appraisal review that an employee believes his disability is the cause of his poor performance or misconduct. Must the manager excuse the poor performance? The answer is no. As long as managers treat these employees in exactly the same manner as they would any other employee who performed poorly or violated conduct rules, they are not in violation of the ADA, even if the employee has a disability.

If a performance appraisal system uncovers a previously undisclosed disability, however, management action may be required. To illustrate, assume that Shondra cleans floors and bathrooms for a large restaurant. She did not disclose any disability when she was hired. During her appraisal review, however, her supervisor discusses performance problems. Shondra states that she has a learning disability and does not always understand written instructions. She asks that instructions be given to her both orally and in writing so she can review them carefully. Her manager may legally address her current poor performance through the regular appraisal process, but the manager must now consider providing a reasonable accommodation to enable Shondra to meet performance standards in the future. Before providing an accommodation, the manager may require Shondra to provide medical documentation to establish that she in fact has a disability and needs a reasonable accommodation.

Here's a final example of how the ADA should be considered when evaluating and terminating (if necessary) a disabled employee. Assume that Nestor, a hotel's swimming pool attendant, is observed by several other employees and his manager to be smoking marijuana in the employee locker room. When he originally applied for his job, Nestor disclosed that he was recovering from a drug addiction, so he was covered by ADA provisions. However, Nestor may be terminated because any person currently engaging in the illegal use of drugs is specifically excluded from the definition of a "qualified individual with a disability" protected by the ADA. Nestor's employer can take action against him based on his confirmed illegal drug use. In fact, under the circumstances in this example, *failure* to terminate Nestor for illegal drug use could, because of the nature of his job, subject the employer to charges of negligent retention (see chapter 4) if an accident that Nestor should have prevented resulted in serious injury to or the death of a guest.

Age Discrimination in Employment Act

Recall from chapter 2 that the Age Discrimination in Employment Act (ADEA) prohibits affected organizations from treating workers aged 40 and older differently (including in the areas of appraisal and performance management) from other workers based on their age. The Equal Employment Opportunity Commission (EEOC) is responsible for ADEA enforcement. The following situations illustrate activities that, if discovered, could lead the EEOC to conclude that age discrimination is present in a hospitality operation:

◆ The boss wanted younger-looking, more attractive women (or men) for front-of-house positions, so older workers were not hired.

◆ The boss selected workers for advanced training based on his view of which employees would be with the company for a long time and were therefore worth the significant investment required. As a result, older workers closer to retirement age were not selected for the training.

◆ Money was tight, so the boss fired older, higher paid workers to keep younger workers who are paid less.

◆ The boss intentionally gave older workers lower employee evaluation scores and then used the record of these employees' allegedly poor performance to justify terminating them.

In these cases it is possible (and probable) that bosses engaging in such activities are practicing illegal age discrimination and should be prohibited from doing so by their own supervisors.

HR TERMS

The following terms were defined in this chapter:

Performance management

Performance appraisal (employee)

Internal customer

External customer

Absolute standard appraisal

Relative standard (performance appraisal method)

Targeted (achieved) outcome (performance appraisal method)

BARS (behaviorally anchored rating scales)

BOS (behavioral observation scale)

Management by objectives (MBO)

Peer evaluation

Upward assessment (performance appraisal method)

360-Degree appraisal (performance appraisal method)

Halo effect

Pitchfork effect

Discipline (management action)

Disciplined (workforce description)

Positive discipline

Negative discipline

Progressive discipline

Documented oral warning

Reprimand

Written warning

Suspension

Dismissal

Counseling (employee)

Turnover

Voluntary separation

Involuntary separation

Exit interview

Protected class

Good faith

FOR YOUR CONSIDERATION

1. Some managers maintain that employee rating and appraisal systems must include the evaluation of subjective employee characteristics such as personality, attitude, appearance, demeanor, friendliness, and social behavior. Other managers maintain that these characteristics most often do not reflect a worker's ability to successfully perform a job. In addition, they point out that an overreliance on subjective factors can undermine employee morale and lead to perceptions of unfairness. What role do you believe subjective factors should play in evaluating hospitality employees?

2. Some forms of undesirable employee behavior are so serious that they warrant immediate termination, despite the existence of a progressive disciplinary program. Examples include on-the-job fighting or intoxication. Consider the case of theft by an employee. Should such behavior result in the use of progressive discipline, or should it always result in immediate termination? Would the item or dollar amount taken by the employee affect your decision? Why or why not?

3. When being evaluated by their bosses, most employees say they prefer a system that treats each employee in exactly the same manner. Interestingly, however, these same employees believe bosses should consider the individual

circumstances of an incident when evaluating objectionable behavior. As an employee, which system would you prefer your boss to use? Explain your answer.

4. Alcoholism is a disability covered by the ADA. Assume a bartender was caught drinking on the job. Assume further that the bartender had disclosed he was a recovering alcoholic at the time of his hiring. As an HR manager what specific steps would you take to determine and document whether this employee could in fact be fired for violating your company's strict policy against drinking on the job or whether the employee, as a member of a protected class, is protected by the ADA?

5. In an effort to curb their escalating health care costs, some businesses have implemented policies that ban smoking off duty. Employees of these businesses must agree to submit to random nicotine testing and are terminated if they test positively. This practice is legal in some states but prohibited in others. Are there other currently legal off-work activities such as overeating or engaging in risky behavior such as skydiving or rock climbing that you feel employers may seek to restrict in the future? Would you support such efforts? Explain your answers.

CASE STUDY

Apply HR Management Principles

"The problem, I'm afraid, may just be her age," Lisa Oliver, the executive housekeeper, said to Ashley Austin, the hotel's general manager.

"What do you mean?" asked Ashley.

"Well, Paula Cooper has worked as a housekeeper in this hotel for more than 25 years and has always done an excellent job. Recently, she has had trouble cleaning her rooms in the time allowed. Some room attendants are complaining because,

::::::CASE STUDY *(continued)* :::::::

after they finish their own rooms, they must help Paula. They think it's unfair to make them do her job."

"She tries hard," continued Lisa, "but as you know, room cleaning is a tough, physically demanding job. With our chain's new bedding standards, even lots of the younger room attendants are challenged. In Paula's case, she knows what to do, but she cannot do it as fast as she used to. The room inspectors find her work acceptable; it's the quantity that is the problem. She almost never meets the 30-minute-per-room standard anymore. I just wonder how long we can keep her."

Dimension: Performance Appraisals

Review the conversation described in the case.

1. What do you believe is the most likely cause of Paula's substandard work performance?

2. Assume you are the hotel's general manager. Do you believe your executive housekeeper is evaluating Paula's work performance any differently than that of other room attendants based on her age? Why or why not?

3. What would you, as the hotel's general manager, advise Lisa to do about Paula? Explain the intended goal of each recommended step.

Dimension: Responsibility to the Team

Review the conversation described in the case.

1. What obligation does Lisa have to be fair to the other employees in her department? Justify your answer.

2. Is the fact that Paula now works slower than her peers inherently unfair to the other employees? Explain your position.

3. Many hotels and restaurants utilize a work system that essentially requires all team members to complete the tasks assigned to its members (e.g., cleaning up at the end of a shift, cleaning all guest rooms, and preparing all menu items) before any person leaves work. Other managers allow individual team members who complete their work ahead of their teammates to leave when they are finished. Identify at least one advantage and one disadvantage of each approach.

Dimension: Responsibility to the Individual

1. Should Paula's length of employment affect the manner in which her current work performance is evaluated? Explain your position.

2. Assume you operate a business in which there are some jobs that most younger workers can do more easily than older workers. Should your employee compensation programs reflect such differences? Would such an approach be "fair"? Explain.

3. Identify at least two legal issues inherent in the HR challenge identified in this case.

INTERNET ACTIVITIES

1. The assessment and management of employee performance is important in all organizations. Complete programs designed to assist in the process are readily available for purchase. Enter "employee performance assessment programs" in your favorite search engine, then review the details of two or three currently available products.

   a. Based on your review, what would be the advantages of purchasing a generic "off-the-shelf" employee performance assessment/management system?

   b. Based on your review, what would be the advantages of developing your own operation-specific employee performance assessment program?

2. The use of secret (mystery) shopper services is an increasingly common way to evaluate employees and the service levels they provide in the hospitality industry. To review some of the most commonly offered services of such companies enter "secret shopper service" in your favorite search engine. Review the services offered by two or three companies.

   a. Based on your review, would you consider hiring such a company to assess hourly staff performance in an operation for which you were responsible? What factors might cause you to do so?

   b. Would you consider hiring such a company to assess the performance of managers in an operation you owned? What factors might cause you to do so?

ENDNOTE

1. Suzanne Lucas. "How much does it cost companies to lose employees?" November 21, 2012. Accessed June 22, 2013. http://www.cbsnews.com/8301-505125_162-57552899/how-much-does-it-cost-companies-to-lose-employees/.

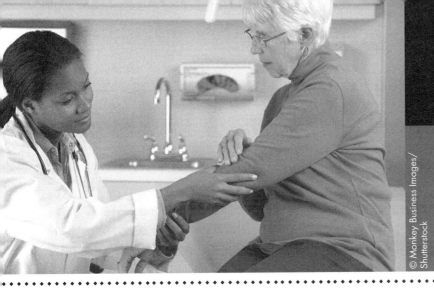

EMPLOYEE HEALTH AND SAFETY

CHAPTER OUTLINE

LEARNING OBJECTIVES

When they complete this chapter readers will be able to:

1. Explain the roles of the two most important federal agencies responsible for ensuring employees are safe and secure at work.

2. Explain the advantages enjoyed by employers who provide healthy worksites for their employees.

3. Describe the differences and similarities between employee assistance programs and employee wellness programs.

4. Describe the legal and moral responsibilities employers have to ensure a safe and secure worksite for their employees.

5. List and describe specific steps employers can take to help prevent workplace violence.

Impact on HR Management

mployees are keys to the success of any hospitality business. In fact, most managers would agree that their employees are the most important asset, and their protection must receive the highest priority. Effective hospitality managers carefully enact programs designed to help ensure the long-term care and protection of physical assets, such as their buildings, equipment, and cash. In a similar manner, it makes good sense for these managers to just as carefully design and implement programs that help ensure the safety and protection of their workers.

While it is certainly good business for managers to help ensure the health and safety of workers, it is also a legal requirement that they do so. The hospitality industry includes job positions that, if not properly structured, can be quite dangerous. Legislation has been enacted to guide managers in addressing these concerns. It is the responsibility of HR managers to prevent employees from working in unhealthy or threatening environments because healthy workers are more productive than those who are not. In addition, from an ethical perspective, all employers should want to ensure the safety of their workers simply because it is the right thing to do.

Despite the best efforts of concerned employers to make their worksites safe and secure, good workers can still encounter personal difficulties that negatively affect their performance. Those organizations with designated employee assistance programs can help minimize the effects of the personal difficulties faced by employees and, in many cases, can assist these workers in completely overcoming their challenges. Employers that have implemented employee wellness programs also often find that performance-affecting challenges faced by their employees can be prevented, minimized, or even eliminated before they cause a significant negative impact at work.

Despite their best programs and planning, HR managers can encounter situations that directly threaten employee safety and security. While unavoidable crises of these types may not be preventable, they can be managed. Experienced HR managers know that well-planned and frequently practiced emergency response programs, as well as crisis management preplanning, can make the difference in successfully surviving an unavoidable catastrophic event.

Unavoidable crises are unfortunate, but even more unfortunate are those crises that, with proper preplanning, could have been prevented. Experienced HR managers know that security programs designed to eliminate threatening and violent behavior at work are important—and critical to the protection and productivity of their employees.

❖ LEGAL ASPECTS OF EMPLOYEE PROTECTION

LEARNING OBJECTIVE 1. Explain the roles of the two most important federal agencies responsible for ensuring employees are safe and secure at work.

Most HR managers and the organizations for which they work would agree that they have a moral obligation to ensure their workplaces are free from unnecessary hazards and that conditions in the workplace are safe for employees' physical and mental health. All HR managers must recognize their legal responsibilities to maintain a healthy workplace. In the United States, the federal government has enacted two pieces of legislation that directly influence what hospitality organizations must do to ensure an appropriately safe and secure workplace.

Before examining those two pieces of legislation and their impact in detail, it is important to remember that most members of society must work to maintain the lifestyle they desire for themselves and their families. Because that is so, it is not surprising that society maintains a legitimate interest in requiring employers to take reasonable steps designed to ensure worker safety. While some business owners and managers might find legislation related to worker safety time-consuming or cumbersome to implement, it is certainly in the best interest of all businesses to minimize on-job accidents, especially when reasonable management action could prevent worker accidents or even worker deaths.

Despite the importance to society (as well as businesses) of protecting its members who must work, the first legislation specifically designed to address workplace safety was not enacted in the United States until 1970. In that year Congress passed the Occupational Safety and Health Act and in doing so created the Occupational Safety and Health Administration (**OSHA**).

Occupational Safety and Health Act

The passage of the Occupational Safety and Health Act dramatically changed the way HR managers in hospitality and other industries viewed their role in ensuring that the physical working conditions in their operations meet subscribed standards. Just as the Civil Rights Act of 1964 significantly altered the manner in which employees were to be selected and treated while at work, passage of the Occupational Safety and Health Act ultimately altered the physical conditions in which workers would do their jobs.

HISTORY AND ENFORCEMENT

Concerned about worker safety and health, the US Congress passed the Occupational Safety and Health Act in 1970. The act established, for the first time, a nationwide, federal program to protect almost the entire workforce from job-related death, injury, and illness. After its passage the secretary of labor established within the Labor Department a special agency (OSHA) to administer and enforce the act.

As initially created, OSHA's stated mission was to prevent work-related injuries, illnesses, and deaths. OSHA's current role is to ensure the safety and health of America's workers by setting and enforcing standards; providing training, outreach, and education; establishing partnerships; and encouraging continual improvement in workplace safety and health.

The work of OSHA has been a tremendous success. Since 1970, workplace fatalities have been reduced by more than 65 percent and occupational injury and illness rates have declined by 67 percent. At the same time, US employment has almost doubled.[1]

The safety and health standards administered by OSHA are quite complex. They include standards related to noise levels, air quality, personal protective equipment, and even the proper size for ladders, to name but a few. Regardless of one's view of the detail with which OSHA involves itself, hospitality managers are responsible for knowing and following the act's provisions. From a practical perspective, you will most often interact with OSHA in the areas of compliance and recordkeeping.

COMPLIANCE AND RECORDKEEPING REQUIREMENTS

The Occupational Safety and Health Act applies to nearly all hospitality employers. It requires employers to keep detailed records regarding employee illnesses and accidents related to work, as well as to calculate on-job accident rates.

OSHA monitors workplace safety with a large staff of inspectors called compliance officers. Compliance officers visit workplaces during regular business hours and have the right to perform unannounced inspections to ensure that employers are operating in compliance with all OSHA health and safety regulations. In addition, the officers are required to investigate any complaints of unsafe business practices. Managers can accompany OSHA compliance officers during an inspection, and they should do so for two reasons: (1) the manager may be able to answer questions or clarify procedures for the compliance officer; and (2) the manager should know what transpires during the inspection. Afterward, the manager should discuss the results of the inspection with the compliance officer and request a copy of any inspection reports filed.

In the hospitality industry, some of the most commonly cited safety violations and penalties relate to an employee's "right to know" about potential threats to their safety. Early in 1984, OSHA put in place the Federal Hazard Communication Standard that has come to be known as the "right-to-know" law. Originally, the law affected primarily chemical manufacturing facilities. In 1985, however, the courts decided that these regulations should apply to all facilities. The right-to-know law is designed to protect workers from potentially hazardous chemicals. The requirements

OSHA: Short for Occupational Safety and Health Administration; the agency responsible for enforcing the Occupational Safety and Health Act.

Material Safety Data Sheets (MSDSs): Documents designed to provide workers with information about the safe handling and use of hazardous chemicals.

and regulations concerning the right to know include the mandatory use of **Material Safety Data Sheets (MSDSs)**. MSDSs must be distributed to hazardous chemical buyers at the time of the first shipment of the product. Employers must share the information contained in MSDSs with employees who will use the hazardous chemicals. Employers must also ensure the written MSDS materials are readily accessible to the employees in their work area throughout each work shift.

The Occupational Safety and Health Act also requires that the secretary of labor produce regulations that ensure employers keep records of occupational deaths, injuries, and illnesses. Recording or reporting a work-related injury, illness, or fatality does not mean that the employer or employee was at fault, that an OSHA rule has been violated, or that the employee is eligible for workers' compensation or other benefits. Instead, the records are used for a variety of purposes.

Injury and illness statistics are used by OSHA to help direct its programs and measure its own performance. Inspectors use the data during inspections to help direct their efforts at the hazards that are hurting workers. The records also are used by employers and employees to implement safety and health programs at individual workplaces. Analysis of the data is a widely recognized method for discovering workplace safety and health problems and for tracking progress in solving them. The records employers submit to OSHA also provide the base data for the Annual Survey of Occupational Injuries and Illnesses, the country's primary source of occupational injury and illness data.

Currently, the major areas of OSHA-mandated record keeping related to the hospitality industry include:

◆　**Log and summary of all recordable injuries and illnesses**—All OSHA-recordable injuries and illnesses that occur in the workplace or during the course of an employee's duties must be entered in a log approved by OSHA within six working days after the employer is notified that a recordable injury or illness has occurred. A summary of the reported accidents or illnesses must be signed by a responsible company official and posted in regular work areas each year from February 1 through March 1. If no recordable injuries or illnesses were reported during the previous year, zeros must be written in the required spaces, and the blank form still must be posted. OSHA-approved injury and illness reporting forms are available at www.osha.gov/recordkeeping/RKforms.html.

◆　**Personal protective equipment (assessment and training)**—The Personal Protective Equipment (PPE) Standard specifically addresses an employer's responsibility to identify any potential threat to an employee's eyes, face, head, and extremities and to allow for the necessary clothing or gear required to protect employees from harm. If potential hazards, such as chemical or radiological hazards or mechanical irritants, are identified, issues related to those substances must be assessed. The assessment must be written, certified by a responsible official, and be work area and job specific. Employers must train employees on the use of any necessary PPE. The facility's policy on PPE and training must be documented in the employer's records and retained for at least five years.

◆　**Control of hazardous energy (lock out/tag out)**—The Lock Out/Tag Out Standard applies to activities related to servicing and/or maintenance of machines and equipment. It is intended to protect employees from the unexpected movement or start-up of machines and equipment. OSHA requires that employers develop a written plan that identifies specific equipment and activities that would require lock out or tag out of the equipment when broken or under repair and include an employee training element about them. The program must include specific lock out/tag out procedures for each affected piece of equipment. Employees must be trained on the company's lock out/tag out policy and procedures, and the record of this training must be documented and maintained in the employer's files for at least five years.

◆　**Hazard communication standards**—The Hazard Communication Standard is intended to address the issue of potentially hazardous chemicals in the workplace and informing employees of the specific hazards and protective measures that must be undertaken when using, handling, and/or storing these products. Some recordkeeping requirements of this standard include (1) developing and maintaining a written hazard communication program, including lists of hazardous chemicals in the workplace; (2) providing employees with access to MSDSs; (3) employee training (including documentation) about the hazards of the chemicals they are or may be exposed to and protective measures that must be taken; and (4) labeling of chemical containers in the workplace.

It's the Law

The Hazard Communication Standard adopted by OSHA requires that MSDS labels be provided for all hazardous chemicals used by a business. The labels must show health, fire, and reactive hazards associated with each chemical, as well as what personal protective equipment must be used to handle the chemical. In addition, definitive information about the chemical must be provided to employees, based on the Material Safety Data Sheets (MSDSs) provided by manufacturers that provide detailed information about the specific chemical, its use, and any potential danger. Employers must also train and educate their employees about:

a. their rights under Hazard Communication Standard legislation;

b. what hazardous chemicals are used by the facility (especially those the employee might come in contact with); and

c. how the chemicals will be labeled.

The general uses of the chemical, protective clothing required, and accident response procedures associated with the chemical must also be communicated.

◆ **Emergency action plans and fire prevention plans**—Any facility that employs more than 10 people must develop a written Emergency Action and Fire Prevention Plan. Facilities that employ fewer than 10 people do not have to develop a written plan, but they are required to orally communicate emergency action procedures to each employee.

Additional examples of recordkeeping requirements that may or may not directly apply to a specific hospitality organization include those related to the respiratory protection of workers, asbestos exposure, hepatitis B, and blood-borne pathogens. HR managers can remain current about recordkeeping requirements by regularly logging into the OSHA website (www.osha.gov).

HR MANAGEMENT ISSUES 10.1

Carlos Magana was a non-English-speaking custodian working in a health care facility's kitchen. Bert LaColle was the new F&B Director. Mr. LaColle, who spoke only English, instructed Mr. Magana to clean the grout between the red quarry kitchen tiles with a powerful cleaner that Mr. LaColle had purchased from a chemical cleaning supply vendor. Mr. LaColle demonstrated to Mr. Magana (who spoke only Spanish) how Carlos should pour the chemical directly from the bottle onto the grout, and then brush the grout with a wire brush until it was white.

Because the cleaner was so strong, and because Mr. Magana did not wear protective gloves, his hands were seriously irritated by the chemicals in the cleaner. In an effort to lessen the irritation to his hands, Mr. Magana decided, on his own, to dilute the chemical. He added water to the bottle of cleaner, not realizing that the addition of water would cause toxic fumes. Mr. Magana inhaled the fumes while he continued cleaning and because of that later suffered serious lung damage.

Mr. LaColle was subsequently contacted by OSHA, which cited and heavily fined the facility for a safety (MSDS) violation despite the fact that Mr. LaColle's employer maintained that MSDS statements, including the one for the cleaner in question, were, in fact, available for inspection by employees.

Case Study Questions

1. Assume MSDSs were, in fact, available in English only, to the facility's employees. Do you think the facility fulfilled its obligation to provide a safe working environment for Mr. Magana?

2. Do you believe the facility has an obligation to provide safety information to Mr. Magana in his primary language (Spanish)?

3. Based on your knowledge of HR management, if you were Mr. LaColle, what specific steps would you take to avoid future OSHA violations of this type?

Name of Law: Occupational Safety and Health Act

Applicable to: All nonfarm employers

Requirements of the Law	Key Facts About the Law
This law authorized the secretary of labor to set mandatory occupational safety and health standards applicable to businesses affecting interstate commerce by creating an Occupational Safety and Health Review Commission for carrying out the act.	The act was passed by Congress to ensure safe and healthful working conditions for working men and women by authorizing enforcement of the standards developed under the act.
Requires employers to furnish to each of their employees employment and a place of employment that are free from recognized hazards that are causing or are likely to cause death or serious physical harm to the employees.	The act does not cover the self-employed or farm workers. The act resulted in the formation of the Occupational Safety and Health Administration (OSHA).
Requires employers to provide to workers information about the safe use and handling of hazardous chemicals.	To carry out the act, inspectors, upon presenting appropriate credentials to the person in charge, are authorized to enter without delay and at reasonable times any factory, plant, establishment, construction site, or other area, workplace, or environment where work is performed by an employed worker.
For detailed information on the law's current requirements go to: www.osha.gov	

Harassment per the Civil Rights Act of 1964

In chapter 2 you learned that Title VII of the Civil Rights Act of 1964 outlaws discrimination in employment on the basis of race, color, religion, sex, or national origin. It is also important to recall that, in 1972, the passage of the Equal Employment Opportunity Act, a revision to

HR Management in Action

CAN AN EMPLOYEE'S ACT BE LEGAL AND ILLEGAL AT THE SAME TIME?

Employers enforce drug-free workplace policies to help ensure employee and guest safety. But consider an employee living and working in one of the growing number of states that allows the medical use of marijuana. In such states the use of marijuana for medical purposes is considered a legal activity. But in those same states, employers retain the right to enforce drug-free workplace policies. Can an employee who tests positive for marijuana in a state in which it is legal to use it be fired for the use of illegal drugs?

This case illustrates why HR managers must continually monitor labor-related legislation that affects their employees. Regardless of the action of some states, marijuana possession and use is still illegal at the federal level. Thus far, employees who have been terminated for testing positive for marijuana use have not been able to appeal to the courts to have them reinstated in their positions, even though many states prohibit employers from firing an employee for engaging in a lawful activity off the premises of the employer during nonwork hours.

Currently, the position of the courts seems to be that for an activity to be lawful, it must be lawful under both state and federal law. So an activity that violates federal law but complies with state law still isn't lawful in that state.

Societal views on medical marijuana use are changing, and it is possible that the position of the courts will change in the future as well. HR managers should stay tuned for continuing developments in this unique and evolving area of the law.

the Civil Rights Act of 1964, resulted in the formation of the Equal Employment Opportunity Commission (EEOC).

In 1980 the EEOC issued regulations defining sexual harassment, stating that it is a form of discrimination prohibited by the Civil Rights Act. In 1986 the US Supreme Court ruled that sexual harassment was a form of job discrimination—and held it to be illegal.

Today there is greater understanding among managers that the Civil Rights Act prohibits sexual (and other types of) harassment at work, even when the harassment occurs among people of the same gender. In addition, most states have their own laws regarding fair employment practices that prohibit harassment based on a variety of factors; as a result, many state harassment laws are more strict than the federal law.

Employees can face a variety of harassment forms. These include:

◆ **Bullying**—Harassment that can occur on the playground, in the workforce, or any other place. Usually, physical and psychological harassing behavior is perpetrated against an individual by one or more persons.

◆ **Psychological harassment**—Humiliating or abusive behavior that lowers a person's self-esteem or causes them torment. This can take the form of verbal comments, actions, or gestures.

◆ **Racial harassment**—The targeting of an individual because of his or her race or ethnicity. The harassment includes words, deeds, and actions that are specifically designed to make the target feel degraded because of his or her race, origin, or ethnicity.

◆ **Religious harassment**—Verbal, psychological, or physical harassment used against targets because they choose to practice a specific religion, or no religion at all.

◆ **Stalking**—The unauthorized following and surveillance of an individual to the extent that the person's privacy is unacceptably intruded upon and the victim fears for his or her safety. In the workplace, those who know, but do not necessarily work with, the victim most commonly exhibit this form of harassment.

◆ **Sexual harassment**—This harassment can happen anywhere but is most common in the workplace (and schools). It involves unwelcome words, deeds, actions, gestures, symbols, or behaviors of a sexual nature that make the target feel uncomfortable. Gender and sexual orientation harassment fall into this form of harassment.

In US legal terms sexual harassment is any unwelcome sexual advance or conduct on the job that creates an intimidating, hostile, or offensive working environment. Such environments are unsafe for employees both physically and mentally. In real-life terms, harassing behavior ranges from repeated offensive or belittling jokes to outright physical assault. In the hospitality industry workers can be subject to extreme forms of harassment by coworkers and customers.

Workers can be required to follow company policies regarding harassment, but employers can also be held directly responsible for the acts of customers and vendors who are not subject to the company's disciplinary procedures. Therefore, the effective management of a **zero-tolerance** sexual (and other forms of) harassment policy should be implemented, should apply to all individuals with whom employees come into contact, and should be designed to help ensure the safety and security of all employees. Because they are so important, zero-tolerance programs are addressed in greater detail in the Employee Safety and Security section of his chapter.

Zero-tolerance: A policy that permits no amount of leniency regarding harassing behavior.

❖ EMPLOYEE HEALTH

LEARNING OBJECTIVE 2. Explain the advantages enjoyed by employers who provide healthy worksites for their employees.

Unhealthy workplaces should be of concern to you and all HR managers. If your workers' productivity is reduced because they cannot function properly at their jobs due to constant headaches, watering eyes, nausea, or fear of exposure to elements that can cause long-term health problems, then your guests and the entire industry will suffer. Consequently, maintaining a healthy work environment benefits all hospitality organizations, their workers, and their customers.

Although the specifics of exactly what constitutes a healthy work environment vary based on an individual hospitality business, in general, as an HR manager concerned about the health of your workers, you should always ensure your workplace:

1. **Provides sufficient quantities of fresh air**—In the hospitality industry, air quality concerns in work areas can be significant. Ventilation hoods in cooking and other food production areas should provide workers with enough fresh air to do their jobs comfortably. In most cases, the cost of providing an increased number of air exchanges per hour (to reduce heat levels) is minimal.

2. **Keeps air ducts clean and dry**—Water and grease in air ducts is a fertile breeding ground for mold and fungi. Regularly cleaning air and grease filters can prevent air quality problems such as mold and mildew before they start.

3. **Maintains effective equipment inspection programs**—The frequent and thorough inspection of restaurant equipment, especially those pieces using gas as their energy source (e.g., hot water heaters, boilers, ovens, ranges, and broilers), can help detect gas or carbon monoxide leaks before they endanger staff or guests.

4. **Monitors repetitive movement injuries**—Whenever workers must do repetitive tasks, they risk the potential for headaches, swollen feet, back pain, or nerve damage. The most frequent site of repetitive movement injury is the wrist due to carpal tunnel syndrome. Properly designed work areas can help minimize or eliminate repetitive stress injuries of this type.

5. **Monitors stress levels**—Stress can be caused by a variety of factors, but an in-depth discussion of stress, various means of reducing it, and the many methods of channeling stress in a positive direction is beyond the scope of this text. You should be aware, however, that in the fast-paced hospitality industry, stress can be job-related or it can be brought to the job. Employees often arrive at work concerned about personal matters such as troubling family issues, personal economic problems, and even their individual personality characteristics (e.g., prone or not prone to have high stress levels). When the stress levels at work are excessive, absenteeism, burnout, and turnover typically increase.

6. **Provides first aid training**—OSHA requirements mandate that, in the absence of a health care facility in near proximity to the workplace that is used for the treatment of all injured employees, a person or persons shall be adequately trained to render first aid. In addition, many operations ensure they have one or more employees trained to administer cardiopulmonary resuscitation (CPR) to fellow workers or guests. The American Red Cross provides this type of CPR training.

7. **Pays attention to workers' complaints**—Dates, events, and employee concerns should be recorded to detect any potential patterns that indicate continued threats to employee safety.

⠕⠕ EMPLOYEE ASSISTANCE PROGRAMS (EAPS)

LEARNING OBJECTIVE 3. Describe the differences and similarities between employee assistance programs and employee wellness programs.

Even if hospitality employers work hard to provide healthy worksites, employees will occasionally have personal problems. Whether the problem relates to job stress or to marital, relationship, legal, financial, or health issues, the common feature of such issues is simply this: The issue will likely eventually be reflected at the workplace in terms of lowered productivity levels and increased absenteeism or turnover.

To help employees address problem areas in their lives, more companies are implementing employee assistance programs (EAPs). An EAP (see chapter 3) relates to a variety of employer-initiated efforts to assist their employees with family concerns, legal issues, financial matters, and health maintenance. The identifiable goal of these programs benefits both employee and employer because they aim at getting employees back to work in a productive manner as quickly as possible.

To illustrate the importance of EAPs, consider the case of Mike Edgar. Assume Mike is in the maintenance department at the hotel where you are the HR manager. Mike is a talented worker and has performed very well during his 15 years of employment with the property. He is respected by his fellow employees, his department head, and the hotel's other managers. In addition, he has been selected as employee of the month several times during his tenure with the property. Most recently, however, Mike's performance has not been so good. He has been late three times in the past five weeks and, just yesterday, called in sick to work only 15 minutes before the beginning of his scheduled shift. The rumor in the hotel is that Mike is having significant marital problems and that his wife and children are now living in a town several hours away.

Mike's boss approaches you to discuss disciplinary action to be taken against Mike. Certainly, your hotel has every right to discipline Mike for his performance shortcomings. Ultimately terminating Mike, however, will likely result in the implementation of a new employee search involving significant expenditure of time and money and an extended period of training to bring the new employee up to Mike's level of experience and productivity. In this case you would likely want to help Mike through this difficult personal period and, if at all possible, help retain him as a high-quality employee. Effective EAPs are designed and implemented for cases such as Mike's.

Today some hospitality employers provide their workers help in nontraditional areas of support such as adoption counseling, legal assistance, and bereavement counseling, as well as mental health and substance abuse counseling. Such programs can be very cost-effective if an operation's employees view them positively. For employees, the biggest concern about utilizing their employer-provided EAP relates to confidentiality. Simply put, employees must be assured that if they voluntarily enroll in an EAP, their participation will be kept strictly confidential. In quality EAPs the administrators of the programs ensure that the confidentiality of its participants is scrupulously maintained.

Employee Wellness Programs

Some progressive companies take the position that it is best to help employees eliminate lifestyle factors that can lead to personal problems and, as a result, can help prevent some difficulties before they begin. To do so, some employers implement employee **wellness programs**.

Typical examples of employer-initiated wellness programs include the topics of smoking cessation, nutrition, weight loss and management, high blood pressure control, self-defense, exercise, and stress management. Employers who provide these programs often find that their employees stay healthier and that the business's health insurance providers offer discounts for implementing these type programs. In addition, some companies find that employee participation in wellness programs increases when the employee's family members participate because the rules allow them to do so. Thus, for example, employees who are interested in participating in a company-sponsored weight loss program may be more inclined to regularly attend sessions if their spouse (or significant other) is also allowed to join in.

Wellness program (employee): An employer-sponsored initiative designed to promote the good health of employees.

❖ EMPLOYEE SAFETY AND SECURITY

LEARNING OBJECTIVE 4. Describe the legal and moral responsibilities employers have to ensure a safe and secure worksite for their employees.

In most English-language thesauruses you would find the words *safety* and *security* listed as synonyms. However, in the context in which we examine these terms, each designates a distinct concept related to HR management.

From the perspective of an HR manager working in hospitality, **safety** can be considered a condition that minimizes the risk of harm to workers, whereas **security** relates to employees' feelings of fear and anxiety. Thus an individual employee at work might be very safe but still not feel secure. Alternatively, employees might feel they are secure when they are, in reality, quite unsafe.

You should seek to ensure your employees are as safe as possible at work and, as a result, that they feel a high degree of security. You can do so by implementing well-designed programs that

Safety: Freedom from conditions that cause personal harm.

Security: Freedom from fear and anxiety related to personal harm.

Vandalism
Fire/arson
Bomb threats
Robbery
Looting
Severe storms, including:
◆ Hurricanes
◆ Tornadoes
◆ Floods
◆ Snow
◆ Ice
Accident/injury
Drug overdose
Medical emergency
Rescue breathing/cardiopulmonary resuscitation (CPR)
Death/suicide of guest or employee
Civil disturbance
Terrorist attack
Foodborne illnesses

Figure 10.1 Additional Types of Crises

Crises: Situations that have the potential to negatively affect the health, safety, or security of employees.

enhance worker safety and security. For example, you can implement fire safety programs designed to minimize the risk of fire-related harm to employees. Figure 10.1 details additional types of **crises** for which you might consider designing specialized employee safety and/or security programs.

While believing that employees can be insulated from all potential threats to their safety or security is not realistic, you must take steps to help minimize these threats. From a moral perspective, employers certainly have a responsibility to provide workers with a worksite that is as free from threatening conditions as it can reasonably be. From a legal perspective, the Occupational Safety and Health Act of 1970 (PL 91–596) requires that employers address safe and healthful working conditions. Specifically, the law requires employers to provide their employees with a place of employment that is *"Free from recognizable hazards that are causing or are likely to cause death or serious physical harm to employees,"* as well as *"the exposures at which no worker will suffer diminished health, functional capacity, or life expectancy as a result of his or her work experience."*

Employee Safety Programs

Because the safety and security needs of different hospitality organizations vary so widely, providing one all-purpose, step-by-step list of activities that should be implemented to minimize the chances of employee accidents or injury is difficult. From a legal perspective, a hospitality operation's basic obligation is to act responsibly in the face of threats. One way to analyze and respond to those responsibilities is illustrated by the four-step system presented in Figure 10.2.

Step 1: Recognize the safety threat. Safety programs generally start with recognizing a need; that is, realizing that a threat to people (or property) exists. Some of the most common threats to employee safety in the hospitality industry include those related to natural disasters, coworkers, guests (in dining rooms, bars, lounges, guest rooms, and the like), the worksite, and even the employees themselves.

Step 2: Develop a program in response to the threat. Once a threat to safety or security has been identified, you can develop an appropriate response to address it. The proper response to an identified threat may take the form of any one or more of the following:

• Employee training for threat prevention

• Increasing surveillance and/or patrol of facilities (for external threats)

Step 1	Recognize the safety threat
Step 2	Develop a program in response to the threat
Step 3	Implement the program
Step 4	Evaluate the program

Figure 10.2 Four-Step Safety Management System

- Systematic inspections
- Modifying physical facilities to reduce the threat
- Establishing standard operating procedures

Step 3: Implement the program. When your hospitality operation has identified a threat and designed a safety and security program that directly addresses the threat, you must put the program into action. A large hospitality facility may have a safety and security department. Its head ordinarily reports to the general manager of the facility. Staff members in the department are responsible for routine duties, such as patrolling the facility for unauthorized people or suspicious activity, performing inspections, assisting the police with crime reports, and serving as a liaison with insurance carriers.

In a smaller facility, a property safety committee can play a valuable role in identifying and correcting safety and security problem areas. Ideally, a safety committee should consist of members from each of an operation's departments. For example, a restaurant might have members from the preproduction, production, and cleanup areas in the back of the house and bartenders, servers, and hosts from the front of the house. A hotel's safety committee might include one or more members from housekeeping, laundry, maintenance, food and beverage, front desk, guest services, and the administrative offices. In the smallest of hospitality facilities, the operations manager assumes the primary responsibility for ensuring the implementation of appropriate safety-related training.

Step 4: Evaluate the program. If a safety program is not working (i.e., if it is not reducing or eliminating the threats to people or property you have identified), then the program must be reviewed for modification. If it was legally necessary, you will be in a much stronger position to defend your safety-related activities if you can document not only that you have a safety program but also that the program is effective. There are a variety of ways to measure your safety program's effectiveness. Some tangible measurements managers may use include:

- Number of facility inspections performed
- Inspection or quality scores
- Number of safety-related incidents reported
- Dollar amount of losses sustained
- Number of insurance claims filed
- Number of lawsuits filed
- Number of serious or minor accidents
- Number of workdays lost by employees
- Number of employees disabled
- Number of drills or training exercises properly performed

The important point to remember is that a safety-related program can be said to have been successfully implemented only after an appropriate evaluation component has been developed and implemented. Unless you know a program has made a measurable difference, you may easily be lured into a false sense of confidence about the program's effectiveness in reducing safety threats.

Crisis Management Programs

Just as the safety needs of hospitality organizations vary widely, so too do their crisis management needs. For example, a hotel would more likely face challenges associated with evacuating employees and guests during a weather-related crisis than would a take-out restaurant. Geographic location is also a factor in crisis preparations. Hospitality managers in the midwestern United States, for example, do not have to worry about preparing for a typhoon, but they do have to be ready for snow and ice storms that can be just as disruptive and threatening.

Planning for such contingencies is an activity that affects all managers, not just those with HR responsibilities. Because guests, as well as facilities, are typically affected in a crisis, hospitality managers in all functional areas should develop plans to deal with the potential for calamities they cannot prevent. As previously pointed out, in many small hospitality operations the general manager may be responsible for a crisis response and for anticipating and managing the ways it will directly affect employees.

Recall that *crisis* was defined earlier in this chapter as a situation with the potential to negatively affect someone's health, safety, or security. Even though some types of crises cannot be prevented by management (e.g., floods, severe weather storms, and robberies), effective HR managers still seek to manage crises to the greatest possible degree. Essentially, precrisis management consists of two distinct activities:

1. Precrisis planning
2. Emergency plan practice

PRECRISIS PLANNING

It is too late to prepare for a crisis when your operation is experiencing one. If you are unprepared and, as a result, respond poorly, you may not only increase the severity of the crisis, but also may be held legally responsible by guests or employees for your lack of planning. To prepare effectively for a crisis, HR managers should develop and practice **emergency plans**. An emergency plan identifies a likely crisis situation and then details how the operation will respond to it. After it is developed, an emergency plan must be practiced so all employees know what they should do during the crisis and when they should do it.

Experienced managers know that many crises actually require similar responses. For example, training employees in the proper procedures for handling general medical emergencies will likely prepare them for responding to slips and falls, employee accidents, guest injuries, and other threats to safety that could require medical attention. Similarly, preparing a facility **evacuation plan** will be helpful not only in case of a fire but also during a weather-related disaster or power outage.

By developing responses to a relatively small number of circumstances, you and your staff will be well equipped to address a wide variety of potential crises since all crises have some characteristics in common, including:

- Urgent danger
- Halt of normal operations
- Human suffering
- Financial loss

It is important to commit emergency plans to writing. This is crucial for two reasons. (1) A written plan clarifies precisely what is expected of management, as well as employees, in times of crisis. (2) If the operation is involved in a lawsuit, the written emergency plan can serve as evidence to support its defense. A judge or jury would readily acknowledge that an operation's emergency plan was in place, indicating a level of reasonable care.

An effective emergency plan need not be complicated. In fact, it is best if it is not. A crisis is a stressful time, during which confusion is a real threat. Thus any planned response to an emergency should be clear and simple, regardless of the number of steps required. In its simplest form, a written emergency plan should address

- the nature of the crisis;
- who is to be informed when the crisis occurs;

Emergency plan: The specific actions to be taken by managers and staff in response to a crisis.

Evacuation plan: The specific actions to be taken by managers and staff when vacating a building in response to a crisis.

HR Management: Impact on New Team Members

I n many hospitality operations the hiring of new employees is a common occurrence. In their first few days of work these new employees must learn many things. One of the most important is what to do in emergency situations. For that reason, experienced HR managers know that frequently practicing emergency plans is a good idea. That way, employees will rapidly become aware of their responsibilities in crisis situations.

As part of an effective orientation program, HR managers can ensure that even an operation's newest employees have the minimum required knowledge of what to do in the event of a crisis. This information can be shared on an employee's first day of work. An individual worker's responsibilities during a crisis vary based on the employee's specific position in the operation. For that reason, it is critical that HR managers work with supervisors and managers to make sure these key management team members understand their own responsibility for ensuring that their newest employees perform properly in the event of an unexpected crisis or emergency.

♦ what each employee is to do in response to the crisis; and

♦ when they are to take the required action.

When emergency plans have been finalized, each manager and affected employee should be given copies or have immediate access. Subsequently, it is important to review and practice the emergency plans regularly.

EMERGENCY PLAN PRACTICE

Once your emergency plan has been developed, the next step is to practice the procedures included in it. Obviously, it is not possible to create, for example, an actual snowstorm to practice your staff's response to it, but you can still practice your response. Practicing an emergency plan may include verbal plan review or an actual emergency plan run-through. The question of which emergency plans to practice (and how often) vary by the individual operation's needs. Management can, however, write and follow an emergency plan practice schedule. The objective in developing a schedule for practicing emergency plans is to emphasize the most likely and serious threats and to allow each staff member with responsibilities during the crisis to fully understand his or her role.

Crises affect employees both in the short and long term. Experiencing a crisis, especially one that entails injury or loss of life, can be very stressful. Negative effects on employees can include anxiety, depression, nightmares, flashbacks, and even physical effects such as insomnia, loss of appetite, and headaches. Collectively, these and related symptoms are known as **post-traumatic stress disorder (PTSD)**. Employers have increasingly been called on to recognize and respond to the PTSD symptoms among employees following their exposure to a crisis.

Post-traumatic stress disorder (PTSD): A severe reaction to an event that caused a threat to an individual's physical or emotional health.

⸭ EMPLOYEE SECURITY PROGRAMS

LEARNING OBJECTIVE 5. List and describe specific steps employers can take to help prevent workplace violence.

It would be nice to believe that groups of employees, all united toward achieving the same goals, are able to work with a high degree of peace, harmony, and security. Unfortunately, sometimes that simply is not the case. Although hospitality workplaces are generally peaceful, HR managers must ensure, to the greatest degree possible, that they stay that way.

As you have seen, employers should take a variety of steps to help ensure that their employees enjoy a high degree of safety while at work. These workers deserve management's best efforts to ensure their security, as well. In most cases these security-related efforts take the form of protecting workers from harassment of all types, as well as from physical aggression, cruelty, and bodily harm.

Zero-Tolerance Harassment Programs

If employees are to enjoy security (freedom from fear and anxiety) at work, it follows that they must work in a harassment-free environment. While in the past most media attention has focused on sexual harassment (see chapter 2), eliminating all forms of harassment (e.g., racial, gender, sexual orientation, religion, and the like) from the workplace will be one of your most important jobs. Because there is more established case law about how the courts view sexual harassment, and because of its common occurrence in the hospitality industry, the major focus of this section is on preventing sexual harassment. Many of the prevention principles addressed, however, also apply to other forms of harassment.

The US Supreme Court first ruled that unwelcome sexual conduct creating a hostile and offensive work environment violates Title VII of the Civil Rights Act in *Meritor Savings Bank, FSB v. Vinson* (1986). Since then, the EEOC and the courts have expanded the definition of a hostile and offensive work environment to prohibit harassment based on race, color, sex, religion, national origin, age, and disability. The EEOC is the federal agency that enforces Title VII of the Civil Rights Act. The regulations issued by the EEOC on sexual harassment provide that

> [a]n employer should take all steps necessary to prevent sexual harassment from occurring, such as affirmatively raising the subject, expressing strong disapproval, developing appropriate sanctions, informing employees of their right to raise and how to raise the issue of harassment under Title VII, and developing methods to sensitize all concerned.[2]

The EEOC expects employers to affirmatively act to prevent all types of harassment. HR managers need to understand that the *Meritor Savings Bank* case ruling by the Supreme Court also addressed different standards for determining liability in cases of **hostile work environments** and **quid pro quo** sexual harassment.

From a legal perspective, if harassment is established under the quid pro quo version, the employer automatically is liable and will be held accountable for whether or not steps were taken to correct the situation. By contrast, an employer's liability in a hostile work environment case must be established by showing not only that the harassment occurred but also that the employer did not take appropriate action to stop it.

Sexual (and other forms of) harassment policies and the training procedures required to fully comply with the law can be quite complex and should be thoroughly reviewed by legal counsel before their implementation. For general guidelines in preventing harassment of all types, all HR managers should understand:

Hostile work environment (sexual harassment): A workplace infused with intimidation, ridicule, and insult that is severe or pervasive enough to create a seriously uncomfortable or abusive working environment with conduct severe enough to create a work environment that a reasonable person would find intimidating (hostile).

Quid pro quo (sexual harassment): Quid pro quo literally means "something for something." Harassment that occurs when a supervisor behaves in a way or demands actions from an employee that force the employee to decide between giving in to sexual demands or losing her or his job, losing job benefits or promotion, or otherwise suffering negative consequences.

◆ **What is, and isn't, a hostile work environment**—A hostile work environment can exist even if no employees have yet complained. HR managers and supervisors have a legal duty to stop anything that could generate charges of harassment.

◆ **The company policy**—The company's harassment policy should be as familiar to supervisors as their own work schedules. Sometimes supervisors know there is a policy but have little idea of what it entails. If the operation is sued and supervisors cannot display a good understanding of the company policy, then it will likely be viewed by the courts as not having been enforced.

◆ **The impact on unions**—If your employees are unionized, how supervisors deal with harassment can have a lot to do with how well management gets along with the union and the number of grievances filed. If you are not unionized, failure to address harassment creates a workplace that can be ripe for union organization.

◆ **The effect of speech**—Just about everyone who works has heard coworkers or customers use language that could be considered inappropriate, hostile, sexist, racist, ethnically charged, crude, gross, insensitive, age-based, or derogatory. HR managers need to know and inform their supervisors about the specific types of language that will likely lead to charges of harassment in their own operation.

◆ **Proper investigations**—Properly conducted harassment investigations are essential to limiting an operation's legal liability. An operation's harassment policy should make clear who investigates claims, what should be done if a supervisor is the target of the investigation, at what point legal counsel should be involved, and whether, when applicable, a specific supervisor can continue to oversee the complaining employee during the investigation.

◆ **Personal liability**—When a harassment case results in a lawsuit, the operation is sued, but in many cases so is the supervisor and/or HR manager. If you are the individual in charge of the operation, this can be the case even though you weren't the harasser, did not know about the situation, and the employee allegedly being harassed did not report directly to you.

Earlier in this chapter you learned about the concept of zero-tolerance (harassment) policies. A legitimate question for workers who will be disciplined or fired if they violate their company's zero-tolerance policy is: *When exactly does the language used or action displayed constitute harassment?*

This question can be difficult to answer because not all employees would find the same behavior offensive. For example, some culinary employees (male and female) might consider hearing coworkers swearing while working the entrée station in the kitchen during a busy Saturday night rush as very offensive and thus potentially harassing, whereas others may not find it to be so.

The courts have addressed this question and have instituted a **reasonable person** standard. Thus, when determining whether conduct is considered hostile environment harassment, the courts, as well as the EEOC, typically evaluate the objectionable conduct from the standpoint of a "reasonable person" under similar circumstances. Under this standard, complaining employees must establish not only that they personally perceived their work environment to be hostile but also that a reasonable person would have perceived it to be hostile as well.

> **Reasonable person (standard):** The typical, or average, person (and their behavior and beliefs) placed in a specific environmental setting.

HR managers must also understand the implications of the court's increasing acceptance of a "reasonable woman" standard to use instead of the reasonable person standard for sexual harassment cases. In *Ellison v. Brady* (1991), the US Ninth Circuit Court concluded that offensive conduct must be evaluated from the perspective of a reasonable person of the same gender as the victim. That court rejected the non-gender-specific reasonable person standard because it does not take into consideration the different perspectives of men and women. In its ruling the court wrote, "A complete understanding of the victim's view requires, among other things, an analysis of the different perspectives of men and women. Conduct that many men consider unobjectionable may offend many women."[3]

In all cases, a company will be held liable for a hostile work environment created by its workers if it knew (or should have known) that the harassment was occurring and it did not take reasonable action to stop it. Thus a swift and appropriate resolution of harassment complaints is the best way to ensure a secure work environment and to protect your company from liability. For example, in *Tutman v. WBBM-TV* (2000), the US Seventh Circuit Court held that the employer in the case was not liable for a racially hostile work environment because it took "prompt and appropriate" action to remedy the harassment, including reporting the incidents to supervisors, conducting an immediate investigation, and taking appropriate disciplinary actions.

Managers should use zero-tolerance harassment policies to take action even for offensive conduct that does not meet the legal standard of a harassing environment. The reason why is that even mild forms of harassment that go unchecked can disrupt an operation through decreased morale and productivity and increased employee turnover.

For example, HR managers can take disciplinary action against employees who occasionally use obscene language or tell off-color jokes, even if that conduct would not generally constitute illegal harassment unless the employees engaged in it on an ongoing basis. Using this approach goes well beyond the legal standard for harassment, and it emphasizes the expectation of respectful and professional behavior in the workplace at all times. When implemented, such policies should apply to customers, guests, and vendors as well.

Before concluding our examination of zero-tolerance harassment policies, it is important to note that use of such policies is not devoid of its own legal issues. In fact, their use can create unique litigation issues of their own. If, for example, you are taking disciplinary actions against the perpetrators of harassment, the question of appropriate punishment is often legitimate.

It's the Law

Everyone would agree that harassment of any type has no place in a work environment. Managers should understand, however, that a *charge* of sexual harassment is not synonymous with an incident of sexual harassment any more than being accused of a crime means the accused is automatically guilty of it. Because of perceived abuses by some who have charged harassment, and the response of some employers, the state and federal courts are increasingly defining the rights of the accused in sexual harassment cases. The rights of accused individuals vary by state. In Ohio, for example, state law requires that the accused have the right:

1. **To be free from discrimination**—For example, a member of a minority group may not be treated differently from whites when assessing whether harassment occurred or how it will be dealt with.

2. **To a thorough investigation**—An employer cannot conduct a "kangaroo court" (i.e., a mock or unauthorized justice proceeding) without risking a jury second-guessing what the employer might have found if it had looked at all of the facts. It is simply naïve to believe that there have never been unfounded charges of harassment.

3. **To a good-faith basis for believing that the allegations are true before taking adverse employment action**—This is especially true if the employee can point to a "just cause" employment contract. In Ohio the employer's policies and conduct can create such a contract.

4. **To be free from defamation**—An employer should not share information about an investigation with anyone other than those who need to know the results.

Employers have a clearer duty to protect employees from harassment, which carries far greater penalties if it is breached, than to protect the rights of the accused. Therefore, in cases that are not clear-cut, employers are well advised to continue to err on the side of protecting the victim in a harassment case. Increasingly, however, employers are legally required to keep the rights of the accused in mind as well, especially as the number of same-sex harassment cases wind their way through the court systems.

The term *zero tolerance* could actually make it more difficult to defend a case on appeal because a third party (judge or jury) could conclude, however mistakenly and inappropriately, that you did not impose a penalty appropriate for the particular harassment offense.

For example, consider a woman who had worked for a company for 10 years, had a stellar record, and who admitted to telling a single off-color joke to a longtime friend and coworker (but within earshot of other employees). If that employee were reported and treated (under the zero-tolerance policy) in exactly the same manner as a supervisor in the same operation who was found to have traded choice work assignments for sexual favors, one might argue that the policy would have resulted in a punishment that did not fit the crime.

There are other possible consequences. The term *zero tolerance* might seem to eliminate any flexibility you have in dealing with highly complex and difficult situations, even when that is not the policy's intent. Consider the case of two coworkers who date for several years, then break up, with the immediate result that one of these workers charges the other with harassment because of continued pestering designed to continue the dating relationship.

Last, another potentially undesirable side effect is that the appearance of inflexibility can in some cases actually discourage employees from reporting incidents because they do not want to get their coworker fired; they simply want the behavior to stop. This may discourage generally collegial coworkers from reporting the actual occurrence of harassing behavior. As a result, some companies have changed wording in their harassment policies from

To ensure a quality workplace, this company has a policy of "zero" (no) tolerance of any objectionable harassing behavior.

to wording such as:

To ensure a quality workplace, this company simply will not tolerate harassing behavior; as a result, all reports of harassing incidents will be taken seriously and dealt with appropriately.

Preventing Workplace Violence

While harassment is most often considered verbal abuse at work, HR managers must increasingly concern themselves with **workplace violence**, a concept that includes harassment, physical assault, and even homicide.

Just as some managers think of harassment as a verbal attack, some managers think of violence only in terms of a physical assault. However, workplace violence is a much broader problem. It occurs any time a worker is abused, threatened, intimidated, or assaulted in his or her place of employment. Workplace violence includes:

◆ **Threatening behavior**—Includes actions such as shaking fists, destroying property, or throwing objects.

◆ **Verbal threats**—Include **implicit threats** or **explicit threats** made in person or left on answering machines, as cell phone messages or texts.

◆ **Written threats**—Consist of everything from Post-It notes to e-mails, texts, tweets, and even long letters.

◆ **Harassing activities**—Include a wide range of behaviors that demean, embarrass, humiliate, annoy, alarm, or verbally abuse a person and that are known to be, or would reasonably be expected to be, unwelcome (including sexual harassment), including words, gestures, intimidation, bullying, or other inappropriate activities.

◆ **Verbal abuse**—Includes swearing, insults, or condescending language.

◆ **Physical attacks**—Include hitting, shoving, pushing or kicking, rape, or homicide.

Spreading rumors, playing pranks, and inflicting property damage, vandalism, sabotage, armed robbery, theft, physical assaults, psychological trauma, anger-related incidents, rape, arson, and murder are all examples of workplace violence. Managers must understand that workplace violence is not limited to incidents that occur within a traditional workplace. Work-related violence can occur at off-site business-related functions such as conferences and trade shows, at social events related to work, and in clients' offices or away from work but resulting from work (e.g., a threatening telephone call from an employee to another employee's home or cell phone).

Workplace violence threatens both male and female workers. According to the Bureau of Labor Statistics' in 2011, 21 percent of fatal work injuries among women were homicides. In 40 percent of these female workplace homicides, the perpetrators were relatives—almost all a spouse or a domestic partner.[4] In 30.3 percent of all attacks on men in the workplace and in 49.4 percent of all attacks on women, friends, acquaintances, and relatives are the perpetrators.[5]

Every hospitality workplace must be protected from disgruntled workers and customers, but, as the events of 9/11 clearly demonstrated, workplaces must now be prepared to face both traditional internal workplace threats and the external threat of terrorism. Certainly, effective HR managers should take reasonable steps to protect their workers from violence. In the hospitality industry, these steps can include concrete activities such as the following:

◆ Install bulletproof glass and limited-access barriers for drive-thru windows (restaurants) and front-desk areas accessible late at night (hotels).

◆ Increase workplace security by installing video surveillance, alarm systems, and door detectors.

◆ Increase lighting in dimly lit areas such as parking lots and around trash dumpsters.

◆ Trim bushes and shrubs that could provide hiding places for would-be thieves and attackers.

Workplace violence: Any act in which a person is abused, threatened, intimidated, or assaulted in his or her place of employment.

Implicit threat: A threatening act that is implied rather than expressly stated, for example, the statement "I'd watch my back if I were you!" said in a menacing voice by one employee to another.

Explicit threat: A threatening act that is fully and clearly expressed or demonstrated, leaving nothing merely implied, for example, the statement "If I see you in my work area again, I'll personally throw you out of it!" said in a menacing voice by one employee to another.

- ◆ Locate drive-thru windows (restaurants) within the same building as the restaurant, rather than in the parking lot by themselves.
- ◆ Implement effective alcohol server training programs to prevent and discourage excessive alcohol consumption (bars and restaurants).
- ◆ Train room attendants to keep guest room doors open when cleaning occupied rooms (hotels).
- ◆ Minimize the amount of cash available to cashiers (all businesses).

Specific actions that can be taken to help deter workplace violence are important, but it is also important to understand that in most cases workplace violence is committed by a business's current and former employees. Because that is true, it is equally critical that HR managers in hospitality implement written workplace violence policies for current employees.

At the very least, an effective workplace violence policy details:

- ◆ What specific behaviors (e.g., swearing, intimidation, bullying, harassment, and the like) management considers inappropriate and unacceptable in the workplace
- ◆ What employees should do when incidents covered by the policy occur
- ◆ Who should be contacted when reporting workplace violence incidents (including a venue for reporting violent activity by one's immediate supervisor)
- ◆ That threats or assaults that require immediate attention should be reported to the property's security department (if applicable) or directly to the police at 911

While these points cover the basic minimum of a workplace violence policy, the best workplace violence prevention policies:

- ◆ are developed by management and employee representatives.
- ◆ apply to management, employees, customers, clients, independent contractors, and anyone who has a relationship with the operation.
- ◆ define exactly what is meant by "workplace violence" in precise, concrete language.
- ◆ provide clear examples of unacceptable behavior.
- ◆ state in clear terms the operation's view toward and its commitment to preventing workplace violence.
- ◆ precisely state the consequences of making threats or committing violent acts.
- ◆ encourage the reporting of all incidents of violence.
- ◆ outline the confidential process by which employees can report incidents and to whom.
- ◆ ensure that no reprisals are made against those employees reporting workplace violence.
- ◆ outline the procedures for investigating and resolving complaints.
- ◆ describe how information about potential risks of violence is communicated to employees.
- ◆ commit to providing support services to victims of violence.
- ◆ describe an active and effective employee assistance program (EAP) to allow employees with personal problems to seek help.
- ◆ demonstrate a commitment to monitor and regularly review the policy.
- ◆ describe any regulatory or union-related requirements related to the policy (if applicable).

Unfortunately, no matter how carefully an operation is managed or what attempts at prevention are made, workplace violence will continue to occur. When it does, hospitality managers must be well-prepared to deal with its effects and the aftermath of these crisis events.

HR MANAGEMENT ISSUES 10.2

Charles Lapinski is the district manager for a franchised quick-service, Mexican-style restaurant in a large city. On a Friday night at 11:30 p.m., just after the restaurant locked its front doors to the general public, three masked men entered the store through the unlocked back kitchen door. They demanded that the assistant manager on duty at the time turn over all of the restaurant's cash. Nervously, the 19-year-old assistant manager explained that all of the cash had been deposited in a safe in the manager's office and that he had no ability to open it.

Angry at their inability to rob the restaurant, the gunmen, one of whom was a former employee, shot two of the restaurant workers, including the assistant manager, as they fled the restaurant. The assistant manager later died from his wounds. The attempted robbery and shooting made that night's local television news.

A lawsuit filed by the assistant manager's parents charged that the restaurant lacked proper alarms and locks on the back door. In addition, they charged that the restaurant owners and the franchise company failed to provide any training to its staff regarding the proper response to an armed robbery. The lawsuit was reported in a front-page article in the local paper.

An investigative reporter from another television station in the city called the restaurant's general manager to request an on-air interview regarding the training related to robberies that the restaurant's employees receive. The restaurant manager referred the call to Mr. Lapinski.

Case Study Questions

1. What issues do you think the courts and a jury would likely consider as they evaluate the legitimacy of the parents' lawsuit?

2. What is the likely outcome if Mr. Lapinski refuses to meet with the investigative reporter? What if Mr. Lapinski has not been properly trained to do so?

3. Assume you were the HR manager assigned to Mr. Lapinski's district. What would you advise him to do regarding this investigative reporter's request?

HR TERMS

The following terms were defined in this chapter:

OSHA	Crises	Quid pro quo (sexual harassment)
Material Safety Data Sheets (MSDSs)	Emergency plan	Reasonable person (standard)
Zero tolerance	Evacuation plan	Workplace violence
Wellness programs (employee)	Post-traumatic stress disorder (PTSD)	Implicit threat
Safety	Hostile work environment (sexual harassment)	Explicit threat
Security		

FOR YOUR CONSIDERATION

1. Some business owners believe that OSHA has too much power in its ability to dictate the manner in which employers operate their business. In your opinion, what limits, if any, should apply to OSHA's ability to dictate employee-related safety and security activities on the job? Defend your answer.

2. Assume you are a unit manager in a hospitality organization and that a talented young assistant manager reporting to you approached you and confessed that he was struggling with a substance abuse problem. The employee also states that he wants help from the company's EAP to overcome it. Also assume that, before this, your evaluation of the employee was that he was ready to assume responsibility for his own unit. Would the fact that the employee was seeking to enroll in your company's EAP affect your assessment of his readiness for promotion? Explain the reason for your answer.

3. Some companies have gone as far as refusing to employ (or continuing to employ) workers who these companies know engage in legal but unhealthy activities (such as drinking or smoking) while off the job. To ensure that the employees do not engage in such behavior, the workers in such companies must agree to submit to random testing. Do you think employers have a right to force employees to conform to such random testing?

4. Assume that a testing company approached you and indicated they had developed a test to predict, with a high degree of (but not perfect) accuracy, the likelihood that individuals you employ would be prone to commit an act of workplace violence. Also assume that the cost of implementing such an employee testing program was quite reasonable. Would you purchase such a test for use in your operation? Would you terminate a current employee who tested poorly (i.e., tested as likely to commit an act of workplace violence)? Explain why or why not.

5. The constant flow of large numbers of people in and out of hotels during daily business hours makes them especially vulnerable to terrorist attacks. What special steps do you think hotel operators in locations prone to such attacks should undertake to protect their guests? To protect their workers?

CASE STUDY

Apply HR Management Principles

"If he touches me again, I'm going to deck him," said Angela Larson, a cocktail server at the Windmere Casino, as she walked into Peggy Richards's office. "He's creepy."

"He" was Roger Sheets, corporate vice president of operations for Jennus Casino Management, the operator of the casino, as well as the immediate supervisor of Peggy Richards, the casino's general manager.

Angela was an attractive, single mother of two who had worked at the casino for three years. Her coworkers considered her to be very friendly, and her attendance was excellent.

Tom Delaney, the casino's HR manager, had brought Angela to Peggy's office. Tom had called Peggy to give her a heads-up about the meeting's purpose. The day before, Angela had approached Tom regarding Roger's latest visit to the casino. According to Angela, this was not the first time Roger had gotten close or brushed up against Angela while talking to her on the casino floor.

But during Roger's most recent visit to the casino, he had put his hand on Angela's back while he asked her about her future career goals and indicated that, if she really wanted to advance, he would be glad to discuss her future career goals over dinner, away from the casino. This he said as, according to Angela, his hand trailed a good bit lower than her back.

"When I first met Roger, he seemed really nice, and we had really friendly conversations about me, my kids, and my ex. But now, well, I can handle the normal flirting of customers," said Angela to Peggy. "I'm pretty touchy-feely myself. You know, patting a customer's arm when I deliver a drink—that kind of thing. I know most of my customers are harmless, and I can deal with the ones who aren't, but this is different. Ms. Richards, you know I really need this job, and I think Roger was implying that if I didn't have dinner with him, well, I don't know for sure. But I do know he needs to keep his hands off my backside!

"I talked to a lawyer friend, who I'm dating now," Angela continued, "and he said it's definitely sexual harassment and that I needed to report it. My lawyer friend said the company needs to fire him or I should sue, and I'd win. A lot of money. So I'm officially reporting him."

Dimension: Employee Protection

Review the scenario described in the case study, and then address the following questions.

1. What evidence is there of a hostile work environment in this case?

2. What evidence is there of *quid pro quo* harassment in this case?

3. Discuss the specific advantages and disadvantages to Angela Larson if she initiates an EEOC sexual harassment charge (or lawsuit) in this case.

Dimension: Management Response

Review the conversation described in the case. Assume that the Windmere Casino has a zero-tolerance harassment policy.

1. What are the most important rights of Angela Larson that must be protected?

2. What are the most important rights of Roger Sheets that must be protected?

3. If you were Peggy Richards, how would you advise Tom Delaney to proceed?

Dimension: Company Protection

Assume that you are the CEO of Jennus Casino Management, and Roger Sheets was hired by and reports to you. In your best-case scenario:

1. What would you like to see Peggy Richards and her HR director do next?

2. Assume that, when approached, Roger Sheets denies that the conversations and actions reported by Angela Larson ever took place. Would you instruct your corporate attorneys to defend, at company expense, him and your corporation in any forthcoming legal action brought by Angela Larson?

3. What specific steps would you instruct your corporate-level HR director take to minimize the chances that a problem such as this would occur again?

INTERNET ACTIVITIES

1. Healthy worksites are not only important to employees; they also often directly affect the safety of guests. In the hospitality industry one of the most devastating events that can affect a food service operation is a foodborne illness outbreak. Even if your area of hospitality specialization is not food production, you should understand the sources of foodborne illnesses. The federal government provides information on food poisoning and its prevention. To review information about food-related illness caused by bacteria and viruses, parasites, allergens, and molds and toxins, go to www.foodsafety.gov. Select "Food Poisoning" and review the posted information. After you have read the information presented, answer the following questions:

   a. What similarities exist between how each of these threats can be controlled?

   b. What specifically would you do if you found out that your operation's efforts at foodborne illness prevention were deficient?

2. OSHA provides to employers information about how to minimize the chances of workplace violence in operations (such as restaurants and hotels) that are open late at night or all night. To review this information go to http://www.osha.gov/Publications/osha3153.pdf. After you have read the information presented, answer the following questions:

   a. What special responsibilities related to workplace violence do those who own or manage retail establishments open late at night have?

   b. What should HR managers do to help ensure steps are taken to address these special responsibilities?

ENDNOTES

1. Occupational Safety and Health Administration, US Department of Labor. "Commonly used statistics." Accessed July 30, 2013. www.osha.gov/oshstats/commonstats.html.

2. Equal Employment Opportunity Commission. "Guidelines on discrimination because of sex." Accessed November 11, 2014. http://www.gpo.gov/fdsys/pkg/CFR-2014-title29-vol4/xml/CFR-2014-title29-vol4-sec1604-11.xml.

3. *Kelly Ellison v. Nicholas F. Brady*, 924 F.2d 872 (9th Cir. 1991). Accessed July 15, 2013. http://www2.law.columbia.edu/faculty_franke/Torts/ellison.pdf.

4. Bureau of Labor Statistics, US Department of Labor. Economic news release. "Census of fatal occupational injuries news release." September 11, 2014. Accessed July 15, 2013. http://www.bls.gov/news.release/cfoi.htm.

5. BLine Security Training. "The most common myths of workplace violence." Accessed July 15, 2013. http://www.blinesecuritytraining.com/blog/the-most-common-myths-of-workplace-violence/.

© michaeljung / Shutterstock

CHAPTER

11

CRITICAL ISSUES IN HUMAN RESOURCES MANAGEMENT

CHAPTER OUTLINE

LEARNING OBJECTIVES

When they complete this chapter, readers will be able to:

1. Explain how the responsibilities of HR managers are affected in unionized operations.

2. Explain guidelines that are helpful when hospitality operations are downsized.

3. Identify planning and implementation alternatives for outsourcing.

4. Describe benefits of and procedures to implement diversity initiatives.

5. Explain how HR activities can reduce employee turnover.

6. Discuss why and how a hospitality organization contributes to its community.

Impact on HR Management

Most hospitality organizations in the United States are not unionized; however some, especially large operations in metropolitan areas, do negotiate and administer agreements with one or more labor unions. This chapter addresses why employees are attracted to unions, how bargaining agreements affect management responsibilities, and procedures for collective bargaining.

The strategy of doing more with less while attaining performance standards is a concern of managers in every type of hospitality operation, as is effective business operations during tough economic times. Managers should recognize when downsizing (often called "rightsizing") is appropriate. They should also understand the role of HR managers in the process and the impact of its potential effects on the organization. Another tactic—outsourcing HR functions—is also sometimes implemented, and the best hospitality leaders know the "whys and hows" of the outsourcing alternatives available to managers in the hospitality industry.

The benefits of a diverse hospitality workforce are well known, and this chapter reviews these benefits and suggests tactics useful in implementing a successful diversity program. In addition, HR personnel play an important role in managing turnover as they develop (or don't develop) policies and procedures that define the roles and expectations of employees in the organization.

Finally, successful hospitality organizations are an integral part of their communities. They give back to their community and its environment in numerous ways. Benefits of and opportunities to assume an important role in the local society are addressed in this chapter.

❖❖ UNIONIZATION IN THE HOSPITALITY INDUSTRY

LEARNING OBJECTIVE 1. Explain how the responsibilities of HR managers are affected in unionized operations.

Union (employee):
An organization comprising employees who act together to promote and protect their mutual interests through collective bargaining; see *collective bargaining.*

Labor contract: A written agreement, covering a specific period of time, that explains management's expectations for employees and limits to management's authority; also called a collective bargaining agreement.

Employee **unions** represent some workers in hospitality organizations in metropolitan areas. HR practices in these operations must comply with the terms of the applicable **labor contract**, and managers work with other top-level officials, including those with HR responsibilities, to negotiate and administer these agreements. Those with line-operating responsibilities may spend a significant amount of time ensuring contract compliance.

Strategies to deal with employee unions from the time their representatives make initial contact with employees during the unionization process through labor contract negotiation are developed by top-level managers, including those with HR responsibilities. Because supervisors likely have more direct contact with union employees than higher-level managers, they must learn about allowable interactions. Top-level managers must provide this union relations training to their supervisors.

Reasons for Union Affiliation

One reason why some employees want to unionize relates to perceptions that their employer is unfair and, for example, shows disrespect, disciplines unjustly, and/or does not correct problems in a reasonable or consistent manner. In other cases workers may believe that business owners' profits are high relative to employee wages, and their unions can help to spread financial rewards more equitably.

In many cases unions can increase employees' bargaining power through unified demands and opportunities to communicate and interact with higher-level managers in ways not otherwise possible. For example, the **grievance process** detailed in union contracts formalizes how managers are required to communicate with employees when problems arise.

Equal treatment based on **seniority** replaces decisions based on personal relationships. Higher compensation levels, more control over work rules, and greater job security are additional factors some employees believe are better addressed with union affiliation. Still other employees join unions because of peer influences and **union shop** provisions in some contracts which state that if all employees in a department are unionized, new employees must join and pay dues to the union.

Interestingly, union affiliations enhance business for some hospitality organizations. For example, some large meeting groups may use only unionized hotel and resort properties, or will not do business with properties having union problems.

Grievance process:
A process explained in union contracts and designed to resolve employee complaints.

Seniority: Employee status based on length of employment with an organization.

Union shop: The requirement that nonunion workers must join and pay dues to the union.

A Brief History of Unions in the United States

The historical purpose of labor legislation has been to maintain a balance of power between labor and management. Until the 1930s, unions were discouraged by court rulings as conspiracies in restraint of trade out of concern that employee groups interfered with employers' rights to run their businesses as they desired. Most employees were hired with the understanding they would not join a union or engage in union activities.

During the Great Depression (1929 through most of the 1930s), many politicians began to believe that poor treatment of low-paid workers contributed to the nation's economic woes. To achieve a balance of power between labor and management, the National Labor Relations Act (also called the Wagner Act) was passed in 1935; it prompted the growth of employee unions (see chapter 2). Employees could affiliate with unions, union activities could be promoted, and union agreement violations could be reported without reprisal. Also, employers had to undertake good-faith collective bargaining about wages, hours, and employment terms and conditions.

Some Employees Dislike Unions

Many hospitality employees are not union members, and unions do not generally attempt to unionize organizations with relatively few employees. Some employees are disinterested in unions because of:

◆ **Cultural and social reasons**—Some employees believe that professionals should not join unions.

◆ **Individual reasons**—Some staff want to negotiate their own responsibilities and compensation and control their own futures. Basic human needs involving esteem and ego may contribute to this emphasis on individualism.

◆ **Promotional considerations**—Some staff members develop antiunion views because of career goals. While union membership typically results in increases in members' wages, benefits, and security, rarely do rank-and-file members achieve the same levels of advancement and income within their companies as do talented individuals in nonunion operations.

The Taft-Hartley Act (1947) amended the Wagner Act and removed some power given to unions by the earlier act. For example, unions could no longer:

- force workers to join unions;

- mandate that employers select specific grievance or bargaining representatives;

- refuse to bargain in good faith with employers;

- authorize strikes or boycotts for purposes the act considered illegal;

- charge inappropriate dues to employees under union shop contracts; or

- operate closed shops. When employees joined a union they were trained by union personnel. Then, when employers needed employees, they were requested from the union.

Unions Affect Hospitality Managers

When employees are represented by a union, managers can no longer make unilateral decisions, and the decisions they do make are applicable to all rather than specific union employees. All staff members must be treated equally if they are in the same or similar positions, regardless of their knowledge, experience, or skills. Seniority is frequently the most important factor in personnel decisions.

There may be company benefits to unionization. For example, managers develop and/or improve policies or procedures that affect relationships with line personnel, and use of these personnel management tools likely benefits the organization. Managers deal with one representative of unionized employees rather than with individual staff members. Top levels of management may need to recover some decision-making responsibilities delegated to supervisors. This can sometimes be beneficial because more centralized decision making can result in decisions that more closely align with the organization's overall goals.

A local union is typically affiliated with a national-level union. It can represent all unionized hospitality employees performing specific functions in a single community, or it may only represent members within a specific property. Local unions elect officers by a democratic vote of its members.

Union steward: A union member elected by other union members to represent the unionized employees within a work unit.

Grievance: An allegation that a work requirement or management action violates the union contract.

Full-time union officers are generally only found in large unions. Small employee unions have a president whose responsibilities may include part-time union duties. Union members elect **union stewards** who represent unionized employees. Both the president and union stewards hold full-time jobs with the employer and are paid by the employer, and they typically use some job-related time as well as their own time for union activities. Local union officials have numerous responsibilities, including the negotiation of labor contracts, filing **grievances**, ensuring the bargaining agreement is complied with, and calling for work actions such as slowdowns or strikes, if necessary.

Some unions have regional organizations that coordinate affiliated local unions. They establish basic policies, provide necessary services, collect information, and administer strike and retirement funds. These organizations may employ staff specialists such as attorneys with key responsibilities.

Authorization card (union): A card signed by prospective union members specifying their interest in having a designated union represent them.

Voluntary recognition (union): This occurs when an employer agrees that signed authorization cards have been received from a majority of employees.

The Unionization Process

Employees join unions in a several-step process.

1. Initial contacts are made by employees to union representatives, or union representatives may begin a membership drive within an organization.

2. A campaign is undertaken to secure signed **authorization cards** from at least 30 percent of applicable employees requesting that a specific union represent them.

3. After the union receives signed authorization cards, the union or employees can request **voluntary recognition** of the union. The employer may comply or, alternatively, request that cards be verified by a neutral third party. If voluntary recognition is granted, contract bargaining can begin.

4. If the employer refuses voluntary recognition, a petition is made to the **National Labor Relations Board (NLRB)** requesting an election to determine whether the majority of eligible voting employees want the union to become their certified bargaining unit.

5. A union drive is conducted in which union advocates and management must comply with strict requirements as they make their cases about why employees should or should not affiliate with the union.

6. If the union receives a majority vote, the NLRB certifies and recognizes the union as the exclusive bargaining unit for the employer. If this occurs, there is **mandatory recognition**.

National Labor Relations Board (NLRB): The organization that conducts union representation elections.

What should (can) hospitality managers do during a union-organizing drive? Labor laws allow them to properly defend themselves against a unionizing campaign. Tactics include:

◆ Remaining neutral if employees ask their position about unionization

◆ Allowing union-organizing activities during work hours if they do not interfere with ongoing operations

◆ Refusing to let nonemployee organizers distribute union information on the property

◆ Allowing employees to distribute union information during breaks

◆ Avoiding opportunities to question staff members in public or private about union-organizing activities.

◆ Not spying on employees' unionizing activities

◆ Not making threats or promises about unionization

◆ Refusing to discriminate against employees involved in unionization efforts

◆ Keeping alert to union efforts to coerce employees to join or commit otherwise unfair labor practices

Mandatory recognition (union): Union recognition that occurs after the National Labor Relations Board conducts a secret ballot election and confirms a majority of employees want to be represented by the union.

Sometimes union members become dissatisfied with their union and want to join another union or return to a nonunionized status. When this is the case, union members petition the NLRB for a decertification election, and decertification occurs if a majority of the members vote to disaffiliate with the union.

The Collective Bargaining Process

Collective bargaining involves negotiating and administering written agreements between union and management officials. A common stereotype of the contract negotiation process is one of labor and management attempting to win **concessions** from each other in an "I win, you lose" strategy. This approach is used, for example, when a union bargains for increased compensation packages when the organization cannot afford it. Management concessions negotiated during good economic times are infrequently given up during periods when profits are lower. Unfortunately, hospitality organizations often move through almost predictable profitability cycles tied to the nation's economy, and higher levels of compensation can become very troublesome during down periods in the economy.

Collective bargaining: The process of negotiating and administering written agreements between union and management officials.

Concession (collective bargaining): The act of conceding (yielding) something as a labor contract is negotiated.

Hopefully, the collective bargaining process involves a cooperative effort focusing on each party's interests, including those that are mutual, rather than positions that must be defended. The premise that a hospitality organization must survive to benefit both parties becomes a foundation on which labor and management can work to "make the pie bigger," rather than to merely divide it up.

Significant time and effort is required by union and management personnel to negotiate agreements, and it is common for contracts to span several years. Both parties are interested in current compensation rates and the organization's current and projected financial positions. Details about the current contract must be assessed, if applicable, and issues of concern to both parties must be considered before negotiations. Union and organization representatives must consider going-in and fallback positions about their priority concerns.

Recall that the Wagner Act required employers to bargain in good faith about three issues: wages, hours, and employment terms/conditions. In addition, grievance procedures are addressed in almost all labor contracts.

Must Employees Join Unions?

Right-to-work law: A state law that prohibits a requirement that employees join a union.

Agency shop: A labor agreement provision requiring employees to pay union dues and fees even if they do not join the union.

Open shop: A labor agreement provision in which employees are not required to join the union and do not need to pay union dues and fees if they are not union members.

Dues check-off: A process by which employers withhold union dues from the paychecks of union members.

Many labor agreements contain security arrangements to attract and retain dues-paying members. Under the most stringent arrangement (union shop), all employees hired for unionized positions must join the union or quit their jobs after a specified probationary period. However, many states have **right-to-work laws** that do not usually permit union agreements in which employees are required to join or pay dues to a union. Under these laws, employees may resign from union membership at any time.

An **agency shop** arrangement requires nonunion employees to pay the union the equivalent of applicable fees and dues as a condition of continuing employment. With this plan, the union represents all employees regardless of whether they are union members.

The least desirable union arrangement (from the unions' perspective) is the **open shop**. With this arrangement, union membership is voluntary, and those who do not join do not pay dues or fees.

When a **dues check-off** system is used, the employer withholds union dues and fees from members' paychecks in the same way other payments such as taxes are withheld.

It's the Law

A state's Right to Work law guarantees that no person can be compelled, as a condition of employment, to join or not to join, nor to pay dues to, a labor union. Currently, 24 states have enacted right-to-work laws (see Figure 11.1).

Those supporting right-to-work laws maintain that every individual should have the right, but must not be compelled, to join a labor union. Those opposing right-to-work laws typically counter that it is not "fair" for an employee to enjoy the benefits negotiated for them by a union without paying dues to support the union's bargaining efforts.

The legality of the states to establish right-to-work laws is specified in section 14b of the Taft-Hartley Act (see chapter 2), which states:

> Nothing in this subchapter shall be construed as authorizing the execution or application of agreements requiring membership in a labor organization as a condition of employment in any State or Territory in which such execution or application is prohibited by State or Territorial law.

While it is unlikely that states currently operating as right-to-work states will eliminate that legislation in the future, increasing numbers of states that do not have such laws are now considering or implementing this type of legislation. For example, Indiana enacted its right-to-work law in 2012 and Michigan in 2013. In both cases proponents of the law cited their belief that such laws attract businesses and thus spur economic activity.

Regardless of their personal positions relative to right-to-work laws, hospitality managers must know whether the state in which they are operating has a right-to-work law and, if necessary, must take appropriate steps to stay abreast of any efforts to enact such laws in their own states.

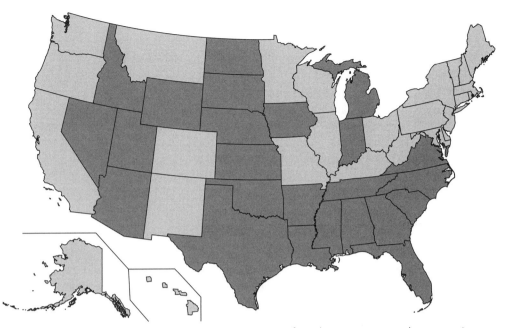

Figure 11.1 Right to Work States (Shaded). (Image courtesy of Panda Pros.; www.pandapros.com.)

Labor contracts typically address concerns that unions make on behalf of their membership. Those typically most important relate to compensation, benefits, and job security. Bargaining issues generally concern one of two types. **Mandatory items** include those about which labor and management must negotiate if either party desires to do so, including wages, working hours, and benefits. **Permissible items** are those that can be negotiated if labor and management agree to do so, such as union veto power over a restaurant's hours of operation.

Employee unions are concerned about current and future compensation for their employees. They typically negotiate **cost-of-living adjustments (COLAs)** that tie wage increases to changes in consumer purchasing power.

Other typical union concerns relate to employee benefits, including retirement, paid holidays, and working conditions. Unions typically negotiate for employer payment of all or most employee insurance costs. Job security is another typical collective bargaining priority, and seniority is integral to this discussion. Other union-initiated issues include working hours, overtime pay policies, rest periods, differential pay for employees on different shifts, and use of part-time and temporary employees.

What if the union and management negotiators cannot agree on one or more contract clauses? One typically thinks about strikes; unfortunately, these do occur, and they can cause significant disruption to hospitality operations and their guests. Other legal labor actions that unions can use to deal with labor disputes include **picketing**, **boycotts**, and **work slowdowns**.

Typical union agreements contain clauses addressing:

◆ Recognition of the union
◆ Wages and benefits
◆ Vacation and holidays
◆ Working conditions
◆ Layoffs
◆ Management rights
◆ Working hours
◆ Employee seniority
◆ Arbitration
◆ Union renewal clause

Mandatory items (collective bargaining): Concerns over which labor and management must negotiate if either party wants to do so.

Permissible items (collective bargaining): Concerns that may be negotiated if both parties agree to do so.

Cost-of-living adjustment (COLA): An arrangement in which future wage increases are tied to the consumer price index that reflects changes in consumer purchasing power.

Picketing: A legal labor action in which union employees promote grievances at the entrance to the employer's property.

Boycott: A legal labor action in which employees refuse to purchase the products or services of a specific employer.

Work slowdown: A legal labor action in which employees work at a slower-than-normal pace.

Three conflict resolution tactics may be used when negotiations reach an impasse.

Voluntary arbitration:
An action in which both
parties submit a dispute to
an external, disinterested
third party for binding or
nonbinding resolution after
the presentation of evidence
and related discussion.

◆ **Voluntary arbitration**—An action in which both parties submit a dispute to an external, disinterested third party for binding or nonbinding resolution after presentation of evidence and related discussion.

◆ **Compulsory arbitration**—An action in which an arbitrator is appointed by the government to make a binding decision for the parties negotiating the contract. Note that this contract resolution tactic is not typically used to settle labor disputes in commercial hospitality operations.

Compulsory arbitration: An
action in which an arbitrator is
appointed by the government
to make a binding decision
for the parties negotiating the
contract.

◆ **Mediation**—A nonbinding but structured process in which a third party helps management and a union to reach an agreement.

Contract Administration

Mediation: A nonbinding,
structured process in which a
third party assists management
and union negotiators to reach
an agreement. Advice, not
a final, mandated decision,
results.

After union and hospitality organization representatives agree to contract provisions and the contract is ratified (approved) by union members, communication and coordination efforts are required to ensure the contract is understood by all parties. Even if changes are minor, significant communication, training and education, and meetings may be necessary so both parties understand all contractual terms. Changes involving work rules and hours, for example, can involve significant details that require focused explanation.

The union steward represents union employees, and managers represent the organization's interests. They must both consider each other's rights to work together cooperatively. If approved by the union steward, an employee may attempt to resolve a complaint through a formal grievance process that often includes the following steps if resolution is not forthcoming at an earlier step:

1. The union steward and affected employee meet with the supervisor.
2. The employee, union steward, and chief steward meet with the supervisor and the organization's labor relations (HR) specialist.
3. The employee, steward, and union grievance committee meet with labor relations (HR) and the property's top management personnel.
4. National union representatives or other top union officials meet with top-level organization management.

If this grievance resolution procedure is unsuccessful, a final step will likely be arbitration. Note that in small organizations, the grievance process is often abbreviated. After step 1, the property's senior manager or owner may become involved and, if still unresolved, the grievance may then move to arbitration.

The labor agreement should effectively spell out management's and employees' rights. The identification of management's rights is important because they directly impact the ability of managers to operate the business. Those negotiating labor agreements and participating in grievance procedures should ensure contractual terms are properly worded and understood. Some rights managers should never negotiate away include:

◆ Terms and conditions for employee performance reviews
◆ The ability to develop schedules managing overtime
◆ Employee assignment, reassignment, and promotion decisions
◆ Use of tests to assess employment qualifications
◆ Length of probationary periods
◆ Expected on-job conduct
◆ Discretion to administer work rules, policies, standard operating procedures, and performance standards
◆ Modification of job description tasks
◆ Implementation of tactics to increase productivity

- ◆ Decisions about staff members qualified for specific positions, merit increases, and promotions
- ◆ Property reorganization including closure of departments or properties (in multiunit organizations)

Basic management rights are important, and employees should be informed about them during orientation sessions.

Union agreements affect other aspects of employee relations that should be addressed during orientation, including:

- ◆ Employees', managers', and supervisors' rights and responsibilities
- ◆ Relations with supervisors and union stewards
- ◆ Union contract provisions and company policies
- ◆ Discipline and reprimands
- ◆ Grievance procedures
- ◆ Employment termination

Many employee and management rights and responsibilities may not differ significantly between unionized operations and their nonunionized counterparts. These special concerns relate to most employees, should be addressed during orientation, and should be administered equitably and consistently in all hospitality organizations regardless of union affiliation.

While total union membership has been decreasing in the United States since the mid-1940s, renewed efforts have yielded some expansion of union membership in the hospitality industry (e.g., in Las Vegas and New York City). While the future is unknown, economic and/or organizational changes may increase the interest of hospitality industry employees in union membership. If this occurs, managers and supervisors with HR responsibilities will be challenged to manage according to the labor agreement while addressing the needs of the guests being served.

HR Management: Impact on New Team Members

You are learning how unions can impact the management of hospitality operations. Many details about how managers and employees interact in "routine" day-to-day situations can create difficulty, and there may be significant differences between how things work in a unionized and nonunionized operation.

For example, a union contract may specify that only people in specific banquet positions can "legally" (according to the labor agreement) set up tables at a meeting room entrance. If a guest desires an additional table, no other employees can perform that task, even if they are willing to do so, without a monetary penalty, which typically consists of additional wages for department employees working during that shift.

The frustration these kinds of concessions present to managers should be obvious, and many guests as well as new employees will likely also think such requirements are unusual.

Hopefully, managers recognize that these and related challenges are not created by the employees. In fact, clauses such as these are agreed to by the hospitality organization's top-level managers, and they, not entry-level employees, are responsible for the operating procedures that must be implemented.

It is especially important that new entry-level employees complete orientation programs with a clear understanding of the organization's top-level managers' and supervisors' positions about usual and somewhat unusual contract-related circumstances that may arise in the new employee's job.

⚡ DOWNSIZING HOSPITALITY OPERATIONS

LEARNING OBJECTIVE 2. Explain guidelines that are helpful when hospitality operations are downsized.

Managers in hospitality organizations, like their counterparts in other industries, consistently try to increase productivity without sacrificing quality and quantity standards. Often, productivity increases yield some time savings that can efficiently be used for other purposes. By contrast, new work methods that reduce the need for one or more employees may sometimes be implemented. At still other times, unfortunately, economic conditions may require a larger-scale reduction in the workforce.

Outsourcing: The transfer of responsibility to perform services that have been (or could be) undertaken by the organization's employees to an external service provider.

Managers may also decide to use the services of external contractors for work that would otherwise be done by the organization's employees in a process called **outsourcing**. For example, should windows in a restaurant be washed by employees or an external vendor? Should a hotel's housekeeping staff be employees or should tasks related to cleaning rooms be outsourced to a third-party employment service?

In each instance above, HR managers must use downsizing principles. This section explains important dimensions of downsizing decisions.

Overview of Downsizing

Downsizing: The reduction of staff or labor hours to create greater operating efficiencies.

Downsizing refers to the reduction of staff or labor hours to create greater operating efficiencies.

Downsizing is not an all-or-nothing decision. An organization that is downsizing in specific positions may also be hiring other employees with required skills to implement new strategies. In addition, some properties in a multiunit organization may downsize or even close while others in the chain expand or are newly built.

Downsizing Myths

Downsizing, like many other HR strategies, does not always accomplish its objectives. Here are some examples:

- Profitability is always improved after downsizing. **Fact:** Profitability does not necessarily improve, especially if the underlying causes of the higher costs and/or lowered revenue that prompted the downsizing are not addressed.
- Downsizing does not impact the quality of product or services. **Fact:** Downsizing does not always lead to long-term improvements in output quality unless changes that specifically consider quality standards are successfully implemented.
- Downsizing is a one-time event. **Fact:** Many organizations that downsize do so more than once.
- There are no negative effects on staff members who remain after downsizing. **Fact:** The morale of remaining employees is frequently affected.
- Stress-related disorders are most likely for terminated employees. **Fact:** Many employees who survive downsizing also report increased job stress and burnout.

Downsizing decisions are significant because they affect the employees whose work hours are reduced or who are terminated and those employees who remain. These decisions also affect the organization's financial success and reputation. All downsizing alternatives have critical HR implications, and managers with these responsibilities must be concerned about the human factor as they deliberate these options.

Top-level managers, including those with HR responsibilities, must be involved in downsizing decisions. They can help to plan and defend this strategy to all employees and to help remaining personnel adapt to the change. This is especially important because perceptions of remaining staff members about their careers with the organization often cause them to begin job searches, and the best employees are typically among the first to leave.

HR managers must consider numerous **attrition** estimates, assess the skills needed by the organization, and determine whether remaining employees have or can attain these skills. The involvement of top-level managers is critical as downsizing is considered. However, affected employees interact most closely with managers and supervisors at lower levels. Therefore, these staff members must be committed to communicating and helping affected employees, and this requires ongoing communication about the status of downsizing plans.

Attrition: The reduction in an organization's workforce because of voluntary or involuntary employee separation.

Honest and ongoing communication is critical when downsizing is considered and implemented. Employees must know what, why, and when, and employers should advise employees about their rights and what will be done to assist them. Careful planning is important to create a better vision for the organization. Careful analysis of perceived benefits and potential problems is also important, and input from employees is helpful (and is likely required in unionized organizations).

Planning for Downsizing

Much internal and some external information is required for successful downsizing. Unfortunately, some of this information may not be available or easily collected because it is not used for day-to-day operating decisions.

For example, managers require information to plan for and monitor the downsizing process. This includes demographic data about the existing workforce and information about employee skills and staff members covered by federal, state, or other laws. Note that minorities, women, disabled persons, and older employees may be disproportionally affected, and the impact of downsizing on these groups should be projected and monitored. Employees require information to help them plan their futures, and in multiunit organizations information including employee-related data may be helpful as transfer assignments are considered.

Departmental plans should be developed to suggest how each unit can operate effectively after downsizing. Department managers can identify unnecessary work processes to target affected positions for elimination.

The impact of downsizing is difficult to reverse, at least in the short term, so several alternatives should be considered, depending on the challenges being confronted. These include:

- Careful review of alternative opportunities to reduce costs and/or to increase revenues
- Cross-training
- Transfer within the organization (if a multiunit organization)
- Reduced employee hours and/or wages
- Attrition, including the use of early retirement and/or employee buyout incentives and leaves of absence
- Involuntary separation (Note that organizations bound by collective bargaining agreements must typically use seniority-based factors when deciding which employees to terminate.)
- Leaves without pay
- Flexible work arrangements including part-time, flexible work hours, variable work-weeks, and job-sharing

Transitional Services

A wide range of useful activities can help staff members who are to be laid off. Examples of transitional services include:

- ◆ Career counseling to help affected employees identify competencies and assess skills necessary for future careers
- ◆ Personal counseling to help reduce stress and improve the affected employees' self-esteem
- ◆ Career transition training so employees know what to expect during the downsizing process
- ◆ Assistance to help staff find other jobs or enhance their skills for doing so
- ◆ Relocation assistance if staff can obtain employment in other locations where the organization has properties
- ◆ Use of a career transition center as a clearinghouse of information, services, and resources for affected staff members
- ◆ **Outplacement assistance** to help employees secure new employment (e.g., resume writing assistance and information about job placement websites)
- ◆ Paid time off and/or child care assistance for staff while they search for new positions
- ◆ Personal financial counseling

Results of downsizing are of obvious concern. Because cost reduction and productivity issues are typically among the primary reasons for downsizing, these factors must be addressed; this can be done by considering and measuring, if possible, the following:

- ◆ Reduced number of **full-time equivalent (FTE)** employees and associated labor costs
- ◆ Impact on diversity goals
- ◆ Extent to which revised budget goals are met
- ◆ Compliance with legal/regulatory-mandated programs
- ◆ Payback periods to pay for early retirement or other incentive programs
- ◆ Number of appeals (grievances) in union operations
- ◆ Impact of guest service ratings

Those who remain (survive) in an organization after downsizing require special consideration. They should receive ongoing communication from top-level leaders to learn that the separated employees were treated equitably and that those employees are being helped to find new positions.

Outplacement assistance:
The process of helping employees secure new employment.

Full-time equivalent (FTE): The number of an organization's employees if all employees worked full time. Full-time equivalent is calculated as the total labor hours utilized divided by the average number of labor hours in a workweek. For example, if three part-time employees worked a total of 60 hours during a workweek in which full-time work consisted of 40 hours, the three workers represent 1.5 full-time equivalent employees (60 hours worked ÷ 40 hours = 1.5 FTE). Full-time equivalent is often abbreviated as FTE.

Annual Downsizing Activities

Many people think of downsizing as a one-time event. However, for some hospitality properties, downsizing occurs annually. Consider private clubs in Florida and other southern states that lose members during the hot summer months and regain them in the fall when it begins to get cold in the northern United States. The reverse is also true; consider hotels, resorts, and restaurants in northern locations, which enjoy high volumes of business during the summer but have significantly reduced revenues during the winter.

Employees in these properties are aware of their short-term employment opportunities, and some move north and south according to the seasons. However, HR personnel at these properties face unique challenges as business slows and as recruitment, orientation, and training activities are required for new staff members when business volumes increase.

Other tactics to minimize negative downsizing experiences include the following:

◆ Top-level leaders must be visible and involved, and they must continually reemphasize the organization's vision, mission, and goals after layoffs are completed.

◆ The remaining employees must know where they fit in the reorganized structure and should be given assistance in planning their continued careers with the organization.

◆ Appropriate rewards and recognition for the remaining employees should be provided.

The Law and Downsizing

The Worker Adjustment and Retraining Notification (WARN) offers protection to workers by requiring employers to provide notice 60 days in advance of the closing of an employment site or in the event of a mass layoff. This notice must be provided either directly to the affected workers or their representatives (labor union) or to the appropriate unit of local government.

One intent of the law is to allow workers to seek alternative employment options when their employer is committed to closing their employment sites. In most cases, employers are covered by WARN if they have 100 or more employees, excluding those who have worked less than 6 months in the past 12 months, and those who work an average of less than 20 hours per week. Private, for-profit employers and private, nonprofit employers are covered. Employees entitled to notice under WARN include hourly and salaried workers, as well as managerial and supervisory employees. Business partners such as vendors are not entitled to notice under the act.

An employer must give notice if an employment site will be shut down and result in employment loss for 50 or more employees during any 30-day period. Note that an "employment loss" relates to termination other than a discharge for cause, voluntary departure, or retirement, a layoff exceeding six months, or a work hour reduction of more than 50 percent in each month of any six-month period.

Many restaurants and limited-service hotels employ too few workers to be covered by WARN. An exception, however, is common when larger, full-service hotels are sold and there is a partial

Name of Law: Worker Adjustment and Retraining Notification Act (WARN)

Applicable to Employers with 100 or more employees, excluding those who worked less than 6 months in the past 12 months and those working an average of less than 20 hours per week

Requirements of the Law	Key Facts About the Law
WARN requires covered employers to provide notice 60 days in advance of the closing of an employment site or in the event of a mass layoff.	WARN became effective in 1989.
The employer must give this notice if there will be employment loss for 50 or more employees during any 30-day period.	Exceptions to the 60-day notification rule apply to faltering companies, unforeseen business circumstances, and natural disasters.
Many hospitality organizations employ too few workers to be covered. However, WARN requirements do apply when larger, full-service hotels are sold with a partial or full closure to rebrand the hotel with a new franchisor.	The law allows workers to seek alternative employment options when their employer is committed to closing their employment sites.
	An "employment loss" relates to termination other than a discharge for cause, voluntary departure, or retirement; a layoff exceeding six months; or a work hour reduction of more than 50 percent in each month of any six-month period.
For detailed information on the law's requirements go to: www.dol.gov/compliance/laws/comp-warn.htm/	Employees entitled to the WARN notice include hourly and salaried workers and managerial and supervisory employees.

✦✦✦✦✦
HR MANAGEMENT ISSUES 11.1

Tom, the regional manager of a chain of barbecue restaurants, just explained to Travis that the restaurant Travis had managed for three years would be closed in eight weeks.

"You've done a great job, Travis," said Tom. "And when our new store opens in Crossville, you can manage it. Bigger store, more money—but you must keep this unit operating well until the end of the month when our lease ends."

Travis was troubled after the meeting with Tom because he knew his employees were the major reason his boss was so pleased. They were a great team, but the Crossville store was 100 miles away. Travis also knew if he told his current employees about the restaurant's closing, they would immediately start looking for and find other jobs. Then he would have problems keeping the store open in the final weeks.

Case Study Questions

1. Assume Travis's restaurant is too small to be covered by the Worker Adjustment and Retraining Notification Act (WARN). Does he have a legal obligation to inform his employees of the impending restaurant closing?

2. Consider the following statement: "An action can be legal but still not be ethical." Do you agree? Does it apply in this case? Why or why not?

3. Assume that you are Travis, and you know the restaurant is large enough to be covered by WARN. Assume also that your boss instructs you not to announce the closing to your employees. What would you do?

or full closure to rebrand the hotel with a new franchisor. In such a case the following requirements apply:

1. In each situation either the buyer or the seller is, at all times, the employer responsible for giving notice.

2. If the property sale results in a covered employment site closing or a mass layoff, employees must receive at least 60 days' notice.

3. The seller must provide notice of any covered employment sites closing or a mass layoff that occurs up to and including the date/time of the sale.

4. The buyer must provide notice of any covered employment sites closing or a mass layoff that occurs after the date/time of the sale.

5. No notice is required if the sale does not result in a covered employment site closing or a mass layoff.

6. On the date of the sale employees of the seller become, for purposes of WARN, employees of the buyer immediately upon completion of the sale. This provision preserves the notice rights of the employees of a business that has been sold.

There are some exceptions to the 60-day notification rule noted above:

◆ **Faltering company**—Situations where a company has sought new capital or business contracts to stay open and where giving notice would ruin the opportunity to obtain new capital or business. Note that this applies only to property closings.

◆ **Unforeseeable business circumstances**—Closings and layoffs caused by business circumstances not reasonably foreseeable at the time notice would otherwise have been required.

◆ **Natural disaster**—Closing or layoff that is the direct result of a natural disaster such as a flood, earthquake, drought, or storm.

✦ OUTSOURCING

LEARNING OBJECTIVE 3. Identify planning and implementation alternatives for outsourcing.

Outsourcing is frequently discussed in the context of procurement and the purchase of services. However, it has an HR dimension because its alternative (use employees to perform the affected activity) involves personnel.

Outsourcing can refer to the transfer of jobs only out of the organization as well as out of the country; to some, *outsourcing* and **offshoring** mean the same thing. Some hospitality jobs have been moved out of the country. Examples include centralized hotel reservation operations for some hotel organizations and even quick-service restaurant companies that relocate the taking of drive-through guest orders to international locations. However, these terms do not generally have the same meaning for most hospitality organizations.

Offshoring: The transfer of jobs from an organization in one country to an organization in another country.

Overview of Outsourcing

What jobs that are frequently outsourced could be done by a hospitality organization's own employees? Examples are numerous and include HR functions that are addressed later in this chapter. Other examples include accounting and bookkeeping activities, permanent or temporary security services, and technology applications. Operations-related services such as cleaning kitchen exhaust systems, window cleaning, landscaping, maintenance, and pest control and janitorial services may be outsourced. Some lodging operations outsource some or all of their housekeeping needs, and many health care, educational, business and industry, and other organizations outsource their entire food service operations to contract management companies.

Priority reasons to consider and implement outsourcing alternatives typically relate to cost concerns and often to an inability to attract and retain qualified personnel to perform the necessary work. Some small properties, for example, contract for outside cleaning services. Their service providers employ many staff members and can obtain and provide medical and other benefits at lower costs than can the property using its own employees. This enables the service provider to attract and retain staff members, whereas their counterparts (small properties) must continually recruit to fill these high-turnover positions. The excessive time needed for recruitment, selection, and training of personnel, along with problems that frequently arise when cleaning duties are not effectively completed, prompts many organizations to consider outsourcing alternatives.

Outsourcing decisions must consider the organization's mission and **core business strategies**. What is it trying to accomplish? What are the most important things it does? Management goals must focus on core business strategies, and some organizations then transfer noncore business functions to specialized service providers to provide required products and services at specified quality levels.

Core business strategies: The highest-priority activities required to address an organization's mission.

Those with HR responsibilities should be part of the team that considers outsourcing alternatives to address questions, including:

◆ Can outsourcing help the business by reducing costs, improving performance, and/or improving guest value?

◆ What internal expertise is available or must be acquired to select potential vendors, negotiate agreements, and manage vendor relationships if outsourcing is used?

◆ How can we identify and control costs, assess the accuracy of financial projections, and consider the financial and nonfinancial costs and benefits of an outsourcing relationship?

◆ What is the impact on existing employees? Note that this issue is especially critical when existing personnel will be eliminated if outsourcing is implemented.

◆ What type of **escape clause** is needed? The hospitality organization may want to terminate the contract without significant harm if the products and services provided under the contract are unacceptable. It also needs to manage (perform) the function while the decision to use internal employees or external organizations for the service is reassessed.

Escape clause: A contract provision that permits one party to terminate the agreement when one or more specified events occur.

When should potential outsourcing solutions be considered? It depends on the severity of concerns prompting consideration of an existing outsourcing alternative. Factors typically prompting an analysis include personnel issues, including unqualified/unwilling staff members, high turnover rates, and loss of key personnel. Other factors include an inability to meet standards using in-house personnel, the need to focus on core business strategies, and the belief that outsourcing will improve financial results.

Making an outsourcing decision typically involves the following steps:

1. Determine exactly what is needed.
2. Review resources available in-house relative to those available externally.
3. Identify and evaluate potential bidders.
4. Develop and issue a **request for proposal (RFP)**.
5. Evaluate proposal responses.
6. Select a service provider and negotiate the contract.
7. Administer the service agreement.
8. Renegotiate or terminate the agreement on its expiration date.

Request for proposal (RFP):
A document that requests price quotations for and suggestions and other information about the provision of products and/or services from vendors considered eligible to supply them.

Managers must consider the HR impact of the outsourcing process when it affects employees. Examples include the following:

◆ when announcing an outsourcing alternative will be considered
◆ when evaluating outsourcing alternatives. Input from existing employees may be helpful, for example, as RFPs are developed and as proposal responses are considered.
◆ when announcing the outsourcing decision
◆ when transitioning to a service provider
◆ when administering a service agreement
◆ when continuing to use a provider as an escape clause is being considered or when the contract will expire

Many principles for communicating and interacting with staff members during downsizing activities explained in the previous section apply when outsourcing decisions are made. In both instances, managers must consider employees whose jobs will be eliminated and their counterparts who will remain with the organization.

Much of the decision-making process involves cost and process analysis, legal issues, and delivering services. However, the HR dimension is important because the organization relies on employees to perform core service functions. Their interest in effectively doing so is affected by the extent to which their perspectives are considered as decisions are made.

Outsourcing HR Functions

Hospitality organizations may outsource some of their HR functions. Small-volume organizations often consider this alternative as HR responsibilities become more complex. Attracting and retaining qualified HR professionals to address specialized concerns such as employee benefits management, payroll and administration, and employment law and regulatory compliance is also increasingly difficult. Outsourcing allows hospitality managers to focus on the core business strategies and delegate HR tasks to specialists.

HR outsourcing began with payroll processing companies in the 1990s. Today, numerous organizations can provide comprehensive or limited services on an ongoing basis or an as-needed basis or for special projects such as developing employee handbooks.

ADVANTAGES AND DISADVANTAGES

For some businesses, HR functions are too complex to maintain in-house, and they note the following advantages of outsourcing:

◆ **Risk management**—Employment laws change regularly and remaining current on regulations can be difficult. Outsourcing firms employ HR professionals, often attorneys, who keep up with changes and inform their clients. This compliance can help the business avoid employee lawsuits. These HR firms also maintain and audit company policies and practices to protect the organization.

◆ **Cost**—An HR department requires office space and knowledgeable HR staff. It may be more cost-effective to outsource HR functions. In addition, these costs are variable and can be reduced if necessary.

◆ **Efficiency**—Advanced HR technology used by service providers minimizes the time needed to manage payroll, benefit administration, and compliance.

◆ **Employee development**—Outsourced service providers can monitor employee performance plans to ensure employees comply with company policies and meet their business goals. They can also develop and/or deliver training and education programs to employees and reduce workloads that must otherwise be done by managers.

Outsourcing HR functions may create some disadvantages for hospitality organizations:

◆ **Poor performance**—Many companies outsource HR responsibilities to limit costs; however, decreased costs (accepting the lowest bid) may yield a decrease in the quality of services provided.

◆ **Distance**—Use of an offsite location can make HR personnel seem to be inaccessible. Employees may feel unimportant and morale problems may result.

◆ **Recruitment problems**—Outsourced HR employees may not experience the company culture. If they in turn are involved in employee recruitment, the outsourced provider may recruit employees who are not the right fit for the company.

◆ **Information leaks**—Some sensitive information might be needed to perform HR functions, and an information leak to competitors is a possibility.

◆ **Dependency**—Hospitality executives may become dependent on the HR provider, and they may find that the service provider seems to have complete power over employee benefits and the advice received on legal matters, among other concerns. This can be a challenge if the outsourcing alternative is no longer desired or if the provider desires to change contract terms. Note that hospitality managers should understand that if they do not receive the quality of kind of services they require, their HR needs can be rebid when their current outside services contract expires.

COMMONLY OUTSOURCED HR FUNCTIONS

Some small businesses outsource many or most of their HR functions; however, many companies outsource one or just a few functions. Common HR functions that are outsourced generally involve recruitment, compliance, compensation, and professional development activities. Numerous hospitality organizations, for example, use executive search firms (recruitment), have attorneys on retainer (compliance), utilize payroll services (compensation), and provide education programs presented by topic experts (professional development).

Specific HR responsibilities that may be outsourced include:

◆ Payroll
◆ Background checks
◆ Employee assistance programs (EAPs)
◆ Flexible spending account (FSA) administration
◆ Consolidated Omnibus Budget Reconciliation Act (COBRA) administration
◆ Health care benefits administration
◆ Pension benefits administration
◆ Temporary staffing
◆ Retirement benefits administration
◆ Software services
◆ Recruiting, staffing, and searching
◆ Employee relocation
◆ Training and development
◆ Incentives
◆ HR (Web-based) services
◆ Reference checks
◆ Expatriate services

❖ DIVERSITY IN THE HOSPITALITY INDUSTRY

LEARNING OBJECTIVE 4. Describe benefits of and procedures to implement diversity initiatives.

Diversity: The range of human characteristics and dimensions that impact employees' values, opportunities, and perceptions of themselves and others at work.

To some, **diversity** means providing equal opportunities to people of selected characteristics such as age, gender, mental/physical abilities, sexual orientation, race, or ethnic heritage. To others the concept implies responses to legal concerns such as equal employment opportunities. To still others it connotes equalizing the percentage of employees (and sometimes an organization's vendors) with selected demographics of the general population in which the operation is located.

Overview of Diversity

Hospitality organizations have historically employed many minorities seeking short-term jobs, and these organizations compete with potential employers in other industries for people without specialized knowledge or skills to work at beginning wage rates in entry-level positions. This has led to a commonly held but incorrect stereotype that industry employees can only work in low-paying and "dead-end" positions. Increasingly, the industry in general, and many organizations in particular, have invested significant time, money, and creativity into efforts to offer career opportunities to all interested people.[1]

Increasingly, then, the definition of *diversity* is evolving and being revised. It is now being defined in broad terms so all employees in an organization are included and so everyone's diversity is valued because of the contributions they make.

A reasonable definition of *diversity* might separate the entire population into the six characteristics noted above: age, gender, mental/physical abilities, sexual orientation, race, and ethnic heritage. These factors do influence how one experiences the world. In addition, however, there are other dimensions that shape one's values, expectations, and experiences. These include education, family status, organizational role and level, religion, first language, income, and geographic location. Every person is unique and brings to the job special qualities that influence his or her attitudes about it and opportunities to contribute to it.

Equal Employment Opportunity Laws and Affirmative Action Programs Differ from Valuing Diversity Efforts

Equal employment opportunity laws (see chapter 2) address the prevention and/or correction of employment practices that discriminate against individuals based on age, color, disability, Vietnam-era veteran status, national origin, race, religion, and gender. Affirmative action programs are implemented to address these types of discrimination. Their goal is to close gaps by establishing targets and time frames to modify race and gender profiles in organizations. Many organizations that are exempt from these requirements also implement programs to better match their employee profiles to that of the labor pool.

Hospitality organizations that implement valuing diversity efforts move beyond race and gender concerns and attempt to provide a welcoming and rewarding environment to all employees. The goal is to move beyond satisfying legal requirements to addressing environmental concerns, improving productivity, and increasing morale. Doing so creates a corporate culture in which diversity is desired because it allows the full utilization of diverse talents of every staff member.

Many people argue that a diversity effort should be implemented and maintained because "it is the right thing to do." However, a strong business case can also be made, and several benefits of a diversity emphasis affect HR concerns:

◆ A welcoming and rewarding work environment encourages excellent job performance.

◆ The changing makeup of the US labor force increasingly requires the employment of those with diverse personal dimensions.

◆ When all employees are valued, turnover and absenteeism are minimized and associated costs are reduced.

◆ A culture of understanding, respect, and cooperation encourages teamwork.

◆ Diverse backgrounds create more creative alternatives as decisions are made.

◆ Many consumers are attracted to businesses that employ staff members who reflect the diversity of those consumers. This improves the financial viability of the organization.

Implementing Diversity Initiatives

Diversity efforts do not occur simply because top-level officials require it, because HR specialists have been asked to "make it happen," or because a manager in a specific department desires it. In addition, it is not a "program" in which a committee decides what to do and an employee training effort follows. Instead, valuing diversity represents a significant change in organizational culture that must have the ongoing commitment from those just mentioned. It must also have buy-in from employees in every department throughout the organization.

Basic changes in management strategies may well be required. People typically respond to new ideas in predictable ways based on how they tolerate perceived risks. Those who perceive little or no risk in valuing diversity view it as a creative opportunity and will be among the first to endorse it. Those who are more cautious about new ideas may view diversity as desirable only after it has been proven beneficial. Employees with the highest level of perceived risk will see diversity as changing the status quo, will mistrust it, and will want to keep things as they are.

Strategies to implement an effort to value diversity should begin by involving those who see its value; it should also recognize that anxious or mistrusting employees are not likely to change their attitudes quickly. There are no "quick fix" implementation plans; instead, it involves life-long learning, personal commitment, and ongoing self-improvement—in other words, a change in attitude.

Hospitality employees who value diversity have some basic beliefs:

◆ Valuing diversity requires a change in corporate culture, and these change efforts never end.

◆ When diversity is valued, benefits accrue to employees and to the organization.

◆ Efforts to implement diversity efforts should include everyone because every staff member brings diverse attitudes, backgrounds, and experiences to the job.

A leadership team of people throughout the organization who believe in the concept, who have some knowledge about multicultural issues, and who desire and have the time to become involved should be brought together. This group must:

◆ obtain input from numerous internal and external sources;

◆ identify and consider cultural diversity implementation concerns;

◆ arrive at objective conclusions about the readiness of the organization to adapt to cultural change;

◆ develop specific and useful plans;

◆ assign tasks and monitor their completion;

◆ communicate effectively with leaders about diversity issues; and

◆ plan ongoing activities to promote diversity and its benefits.

It typically takes longer than some diversity advocates believe to change an organization's culture. Attitudes that have built up over many years must be changed. Even when it is an accepted organizational goal, it may take a long time for many employees to value diversity, and some are unlikely to ever accept it.

Diversity goals recognize simple issues. Those who support the concept believe that all staff members want to:

◆ be recognized for whom they are and appreciated for what they do;

◆ feel comfortable with others with whom they work; and

◆ believe their input is valued and that they can have some impact on the decisions that affect them.

As the importance of diversity is better recognized and addressed in the hospitality workplace, the basic human needs of all staff members will be better recognized.

⋰ HR AND TURNOVER MANAGEMENT

LEARNING OBJECTIVE 5. Explain how HR activities can reduce employee turnover.

Employee turnover rates are high in many hospitality organizations. Some reasons are readily explainable, such as the need to work at undesirable times and the interest of many employees to seek only temporary employment. Unfortunately, other reasons involve the inconsistent or incorrect practice of basic supervisory principles that encourage high retention rates. Managers and supervisors have significantly more contact time with other employees than do those with HR responsibilities. As a result, these important team members most directly affect an organization's turnover rate.

There are three basic strategies managers can use to address labor shortages, and each has overt HR implications.

1. **Keep the people currently employed; reduce the turnover rate**—Selecting the "right" people and using tactics to retain staff members are examples of ways to accomplish this.

2. **Increase productivity**—When increased output that meets required standards is achieved using the same or a reduced number of labor hours, fewer personnel are needed. Again, selecting the "right" employees is helpful, as is providing well-thought-out orientation, training, and professional development programs for interested staff members.

HR Management in Action

What makes an employee want to quit his or her job? Many times it is a long series of little things that, when combined, create an unacceptable work environment. One of these "little things" may be policies and rules that seem to make no sense. Note that a policy is a guiding principle to explain how things are done. By contrast, a rule is an informal statement about what one should do—or not do—in a specific situation. For example, a policy may state an employee will receive one week's vacation after a specified time from the employment date, and a rule may indicate that a vacation day cannot be taken if there is no other employee available to cover the position.

Rules should be considered from the affected employees' perspectives. Use of cell phones and social media on the job, specified times for restroom breaks, and exact scripts to follow when answering the telephone may make sense to managers developing the rules; however, they may make no sense to employees, especially if they are explained improperly.

Hopefully, HR personnel help develop policies and rules and at that time consider the employee's perspectives. They can also be involved in disseminating and explaining reasons for these requirements and can provide feedback to appropriate managers.

Will the introduction of one new policy or rule encourage staff members to quit? Perhaps not, but it can be one of the little things among many that negatively affect morale and contribute to higher-than-necessary turnover rates.

3. **Recruit from nontraditional labor markets**—Many hospitality managers enjoy great success when they employ "empty nesters" (parents of grown children), older workers seeking part-time employment to complement retirement income, and other people with physical and mental challenges who can become proficient at performing many important tasks.

What role can HR personnel play in reducing turnover rates? First, they can advise managers about effective recruitment tactics to bring the best applicants to the job. Examples include ensuring that job descriptions are current, providing training as necessary to help managers conduct effective job interviews, and managing other on-boarding activities (see chapters 4 and 5).

Many hospitality managers indicate that their most significant challenge is recruiting qualified employees. Much of a manager's time is often spent recruiting and training new employees. Time is also needed to correct defects caused by employees who no longer care because they are only working until they find a new position and by newly hired personnel who want to do a good job but have not yet completed their training. It should be obvious that keeping the employees you have is the best tactic to reduce employee recruitment challenges. HR professionals can assist with this tactic as they emphasize the need for supervisory training programs that teach effective leadership skills.

When applicable, HR personnel can also ensure that compensation plans, training and professional development activities, and performance appraisal systems are fair and reasonable and address employee concerns identified during exit interviews. They can also advocate for employees when policies and procedures are developed and when employee recognition and incentive programs are planned and implemented.

It is important that those with HR responsibilities role model their concerns about employees. They can do this as they show genuine respect during interactions with staff members and as they participate in later steps in progressive discipline programs.

❖ THE ORGANIZATION AS COMMUNITY CITIZEN

LEARNING OBJECTIVE 6. Discuss why and how a hospitality organization contributes to its community.

The concept of **corporate (social) responsibility** relates to the hospitality organization and commitments to its constituencies including guests, employees, other businesses including suppliers and investors, and society and the community at large. These groups, also called **stakeholders**, are directly affected by the organization's action.

It is obvious that a hospitality organization must satisfactorily address its commitments to its guests, employees, and investors. However, interactions with other businesses including suppliers should be managed carefully. It is also important that organizations act as good "citizens" in their specific communities and in society as a whole.

Corporate (social) responsibility: Relates to an organization's efforts to address its commitments to its constituencies including guests, employees, other businesses including suppliers and investors, and society and the community at large.

Stakeholders: Groups, individuals, and organizations that are directly affected by an organization.

HR MANAGEMENT ISSUES 11.2

"Our GM couldn't be more clear, could she?" asked Hemal in a meeting with his two HR staff specialists. "Our employee turnover rate is the highest in the region, and she is calling a special Executive Committee meeting in two weeks. Each department head, including me, is to make a report on what specifically will be done within each department to reduce turnover.

"My report is to focus on what we in HR can do to help the department heads with their assignment. I want to brainstorm an extensive list of suggestions that represent our best ideas for helping each department to increase their retention rates. Let's get started."

Develop the list that Hemal will present that indicates the HR department's suggested role in helping to reduce turnover at the hotel.

At this point, careful readers might be thinking, "While this is true, how exactly does corporate responsibility relate to the management of hospitality human resources?" The answer addresses two issues:

1. **Cultural consistency**—Can an organization and its leaders be concerned about three constituencies (guests, employees, and investors) without being concerned about others? Doesn't the concept of business ethics apply beyond the organization itself? Those who shape an organization's culture in ways that attract and retain the most qualified staff members (the primary goal of HR) will likely treat others in ways that mirror their concern for their staff members.

2. **Employer of choice concerns**—Applicants are attracted to organizations within their community that have favorable reputations. In perhaps the simplest example, networks of young people at high schools and colleges provide answers to questions for their peers, such as, "What's it like to work at specific restaurants, hotels, and/or other hospitality organizations?" However, an organization's reputation is influenced by, and is known to, many people beyond the pool of current potential employees. Consider, for example, the impact of positive publicity that arises as organizations participate in community activities and assist with or lead in addressing broad societal concerns.

Everyone benefits when hospitality organizations assume corporate (social) responsibility for their actions. Is this factor the primary concern of a young person applying for an entry-level position in a hospitality organization? Probably not, although it might prompt an employment recommendation from a concerned parent. Do those employed by an organization feel good when they hear and/or read positive things about their organization? Probably so. Would employees of a hospitality operation like to contribute their time and even money to worthwhile causes sponsored or coordinated by their employer? Many would. You can recognize, then, that the extent of an organization's corporate responsibility can have an impact on the management of its human resources.

Today's society increasingly emphasizes that organizations be good corporate citizens, and businesses do so as they:

◆ assume a responsibility toward the environment by controlling (minimizing) the pollution of air, water, and land; and

◆ accept a responsibility of concern toward guests by staying clear of unethical and irresponsible business practices relating to consumers' rights, unfair pricing, and being honest with advertising messages.

Some Examples of Corporate (Social) Responsibility

It makes good business sense for hospitality operations to help improve their communities. They can do so in numerous ways:

◆ Contributing time and money to worthwhile community projects and charitable causes

◆ Providing products and services during times of disasters and other emergencies

◆ Participating in environmentally friendly initiatives such as recycling, conserving energy, and using environmentally friendly packaging

◆ Coordinating activities for employees who provide volunteer services for the community

◆ Investigating and correcting supplier abuses of employees in international locations

◆ Recognizing animal welfare concerns in agreements with food suppliers

◆ Avoiding, when possible, publically taking controversial positions on issues that have the potential to divide local communities

HR TERMS

The following terms were defined in this chapter:

Union (employee)	Right-to-work law	Outsourcing
Labor contract	Agency shop	Downsizing
Grievance process	Open shop	Attrition
Seniority	Dues check-off	Outplacement assistance
Union shop	Mandatory items (collective bargaining)	Full-time equivalent (FTE)
Union steward	Permissible items (collective bargaining)	Offshoring
Grievance	Cost-of-living adjustment (COLA)	Core business strategies
Authorization card (union)	Picketing	Escape clause
Voluntary recognition (union)	Boycott	Request for proposal (RFP)
National Labor Relations Board (NLRB)	Work slowdown	Diversity
Mandatory recognition (union)	Voluntary arbitration	Corporate (social) responsibility
Collective bargaining	Compulsory arbitration	Stakeholders
Concession (collective bargaining)	Mediation	

FOR YOUR CONSIDERATION

1. Assume you were beginning a supervisory position in a unionized hospitality organization. How might your initial work experiences be different than if your initial employment was with a nonunionized property? Which type of beginning management position would you most like? Why?

2. How do you think employees' perspectives about an organization would be affected if they heard rumors about the possibility of downsizing? What facts would you want to know about the situation? What would be your priority concerns if you were to be terminated? If you were a survivor?

3. Managers sometimes blame HR personnel for employee turnover problems. They think, for example, "If the HR department gave me good job applicants, I could train and supervise them to be good employees." What can HR personnel do to best ensure they have an excellent working relationship with managers and supervisors?

4. What are some practical tactics a department manager can use to help his or her organization achieve diversity goals?

5. The last section of this chapter notes some activities hospitality organizations can undertake in efforts to be a good community citizen. Brainstorm with your classmates about specific things that restaurants and hotels can do.

CASE STUDY

Apply HR Management Principles

"Last night wasn't a good night?" asked Maureen, the food services director for the school district in an affluent suburb of a large city.

She was meeting with Francine, the business manager, who replied, "No, it was a disaster!" The two were discussing the results of a school board meeting in which the local union representing the food services workers obtained a collective bargaining concession that, in their opinion, went too far.

"I can't believe it," said Francine. "Now we cannot increase productivity because the labor contract specifies a required number of union employee labor hours for every 100 meals we serve. It even defines our á la carte operations to ensure that the mandated productivity level is controlled."

"Yes, that is the most significant challenge," replied Maureen. "In addition, isn't it ironic that we just spent $80,000 for trash compactors because our payback analysis indicated equipment costs would be recovered in only 11 months because of reduced waste pick-up fees? Now the labor agreement specifies workers can't lift more than 35 pounds, so the compactors can't be used to their capacity. Another example relates to employee breaks. A 10 o'clock break cannot be given at 5 minutes to 10 or 5 minutes after 10 according to work task completion."

"One thing I know is that, even while the school board wants us to increase the quantity and quality of our outputs, they have really limited our ability to do so," said Francine.

Dimension: Collective Bargaining Process

1. Assume the union had represented the employees for the past several years. What kind of financial- and employee-related information should the food services management team have provided to the school board committee negotiating with union representatives?

2. What are the most important management rights that remain and, hopefully, will not be lost by the school district?

3. What impact do you think the results of this bargaining process will have when the agreement is next negotiated?

Dimension: Supervision

1. What procedures should Maureen use to educate her supervisors and managers about the terms of the new agreement?

2. What are the most serious consequences of the new contractual clause that ties input (labor hours) to output (number of meals/meal equivalents served)?

3. What, if any, employee scheduling tactics can be used when specified employees must take breaks at specified times?

Dimension: Financial Management Concerns

1. What tactics are available to Maureen to manage labor costs given the contractual clause relating to productivity restraints?

2. What are the priority alternatives available to Maureen as she develops future operating budgets and attempts to manage future operating costs?

3. What can Maureen do to help reduce the stress and anxiety of the food service managers in each school as they attempt to cope with the new operational and financial constraints?

INTERNET ACTIVITIES

1. The Internet can provide a wealth of information about labor unions. Enter "hospitality industry and labor unions" into your favorite search engine and answer the following questions:

    a. To what extent are hospitality organizations unionized?

    b. What recent work stoppages have occurred? What concerns prompted the work stoppages?

    c. For what reasons do labor unions suggest hospitality employees should join them?

2. Managers in the hospitality industry may be involved in many more outsourcing alternatives than you might have initially imagined. Enter "outsourcing in the hospitality industry" into a search engine and answer the following questions:

    a. What are cited advantages to outsourcing HR functions?

    b. What are cited disadvantages to outsourcing HR functions?

    c. What types of HR functions are often outsourced?

ENDNOTE

1. Portions of this section were adapted from Marilyn Loden. *Implementing Diversity* (Boston: McGraw-Hill, 1996).

HUMAN RESOURCES IN EVOLVING HOSPITALITY ORGANIZATIONS

LEARNING OBJECTIVES

When they complete this chapter, readers will be able to:

1. Identify factors that influence organizational change and discuss how HR professionals can address them.

2. Discuss guidelines that are helpful in facilitating the efforts of staff members belonging to the various generations that make up today's workforce.

3. Identify key concerns that should be addressed as employee mentoring programs are planned and implemented.

4. List procedures that are useful in the succession planning process.

5. List the reasons HR managers develop and assist staff members with their career planning activities.

Impact on HR Management

All hospitality organizations change as they evolve. Some of the change may be gradual, whereas other changes may occur quickly. In some instances an organization's evolution means expanded business opportunities and the addition of new operating units. In other cases an organization's evolution may entail changing menu offerings, production procedures, service delivery styles, or physical locations. While change is constant, it is also true that some workers in an organization resist change. When that happens, HR managers can play an important role in helping the organization's staff adapt to needed changes.

In addition to managing change, HR professionals assist organizations when they help owners, managers, and supervisors understand that today's workers are exceptionally diverse. Gender, race, and ethnicity are some of the areas in which workforce diversity is expanding. An additional, and essential, area for HR professionals to recognize is that of generational diversity. Experts agree that the factors that motivate and inspire individual workers are dependent, to some degree, on the worker's age. When HR professionals recognize the characteristics of multigenerational workforces they can better respond to these characteristics. As HR professionals seek to prepare their organizations for change and manage their multigenerational workforces, they can use three effective tools: mentoring programs, succession planning activities, and career development programs. When these tools are applied properly, evolving hospitality organizations can be well prepared for the future.

❖ HR AND ORGANIZATIONAL CHANGE

LEARNING OBJECTIVE 1. Identify factors that influence organizational change and discuss how HR professionals can address them.

Hospitality organizations are dynamic; they cannot stay the same. If they do so, they essentially go backward. Line-operating supervisors and managers are confronted by internally directed changes of all types. Many are driven by an evolution in guests' preferences. For example, restaurant managers modify a menu and hotel managers change a guest room's décor to modernize it. Entry-level employees are affected when, in the first case, cooks must learn to prepare new menu items and, in the second instance, housekeeping personnel alter guest room cleaning procedures. **Organizational change** is ongoing, and it must be effectively managed to the greatest extent possible.

Organizational change: The process by which an organization moves away from what it is currently doing toward some desirable future status.

Causes and Types of Change

Both external and internal factors can result in the need for organizational change. Some common causes of change in the hospitality industry include:

- ◆ **Legislation**—Labor-related laws and other regulations directly impact what a hospitality organization must and cannot do. Sometimes changing governmental regulations directly affect a business's operating procedures or how it must manage its employees.

- ◆ **Competition**—Some hospitality operators react to their competitors in a (seemingly) never-ending effort to stay one step ahead to enhance the perceived value of their products or services and attract additional guests. Others try to lead the pack by being early innovators. Still other organizations consider the competition but try to develop or improve core business strategies to distinguish their business in the marketplace.

Regardless of the strategy, all hospitality operators must consider their competitors and, when necessary, initiate change in response to actions taken by the competition.

◆ **Consumer preferences**—All businesses must meet the needs of their **target markets**. As these needs evolve, businesses must respond or risk losing their target market to other businesses that are more responsive. As a result, changes in menu offerings, cooking methods, and presentation styles are continually evolving in the food service business. In the lodging industry, changing customer preferences include the desire for additional services (e.g., free Internet access), an increased ability to book online, and enhanced in-room amenities.

◆ **Economy**—The financial health of the country, state, or local economy within which a hospitality operation is located directly impacts its operating decisions. In addition, increased operating costs resulting from inflation mandate the need for careful cost analysis, which often leads to revised work procedures.

◆ **Advancements in technology**—As hospitality industry-related technology continues to advance, the manner in which needed products are purchased, the way operational revenues are recorded, and how guest reservations and bill payments are accepted are just a few examples of technological advances that have resulted in direct changes to how hospitality organizations must operate.

◆ **Global issues**—Disruptions in the supply of critically needed foods or supplies and rising oil prices can dramatically increase product costs, including their transportation costs. Concerns related to international terrorism are additional examples of global factors that can change the way a hospitality organization does business and thus can result in the need for change.

Because a variety of factors can result in the need for change, HR managers spend a significant amount of time and effort addressing the challenges of both **gradual change**, intermediate change, and **dynamic change**. Figure 12.1 provides specific examples of each of these types of change and typical organizational reactions to them. A review of this figure can help you to see how typical reactions intensify as the factors prompting change become more significant and as change, in turn, moves from gradual to dynamic.

Target market: The specific types of customers a business seeks to attract.

Gradual change: Organizational change that is simple and narrowly focused on a specific department or management function and that has an incremental impact on the hospitality organization.

Dynamic change: Organizational change that is complex and broadly focused and that impacts the entire hospitality organization as it creates a significant difference in its operation.

HR Management in Action

TERRORIST TARGETS

The early morning hours of November 26, 2008, were uneventful at the Taj Mahal Palace and Tower Hotel in Mumbai, India, the five-star property that had once hosted such notable guests as the Beatles, Mick Jagger, Bill Clinton, Angelina Jolie, and Brad Pitt.

That calm was shattered, however, when terrorists attacked that hotel and other sites in this city of over 20 million people. Hostages were taken and, over the next three days, more than 150 people were killed, including many foreign tourists. Mumbai authorities ultimately stormed the hotel and killed the attackers. The damage to the hotel, and the impact on its staff and management, was immense.

Because they are open 24 hours a day and typically have many points of entry, hotels are increasingly targets of worldwide terrorism. While HR managers are not typically responsible for hotel security, they are responsible for training employees in what to do, and not to do, in the event of such an attack.

The attack in Mumbai, as well as other more recent events across the globe, illustrates well the fact that HR managers in both the United States and abroad must be proactive as they develop and train their employees to be ready for a wide variety of events, including those with real life-and-death consequences.

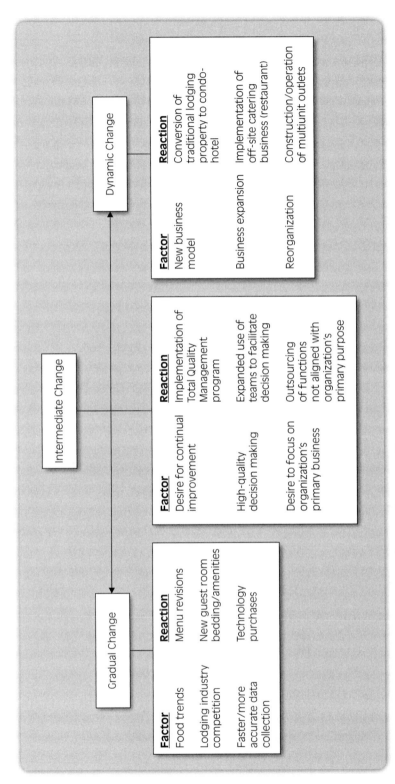

Figure 12.1 Examples of Gradual, Intermediate, and Dynamic Change

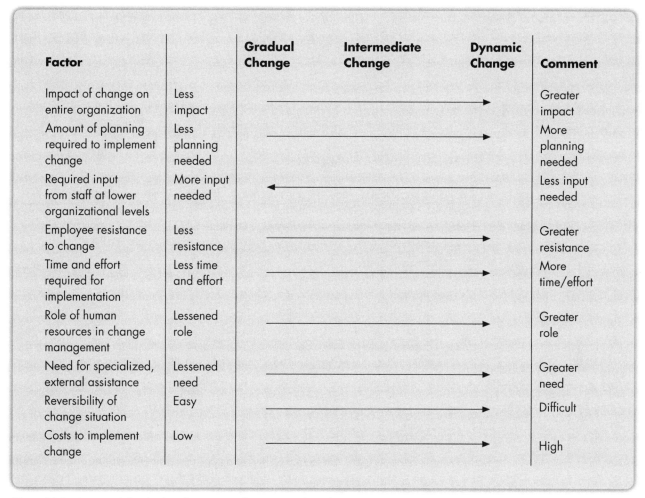

Factor	Gradual Change	Intermediate Change	Dynamic Change	Comment
Impact of change on entire organization	Less impact			Greater impact
Amount of planning required to implement change	Less planning needed			More planning needed
Required input from staff at lower organizational levels	More input needed			Less input needed
Employee resistance to change	Less resistance			Greater resistance
Time and effort required for implementation	Less time and effort			More time/effort
Role of human resources in change management	Lessened role			Greater role
Need for specialized, external assistance	Lessened need			Greater need
Reversibility of change situation	Easy			Difficult
Costs to implement change	Low			High

Figure 12.2   Impact of Gradual and Dynamic Change on Selected Factors

As one might expect, there are significant differences in how these different types of changes are managed. Figure 12.2 reviews several of these differences. As noted in Figure 12.2, the impact on the total organization, the amount of planning required, the level of employee resistance, and the amount of time and effort needed for implementation are likely to increase as the change process moves from gradual to dynamic.

Resistance to Organizational Change

Numerous factors can influence the need for organizational change, and those with HR management responsibilities should be involved in decisions about how the hospitality organization anticipates and/or reacts to the changes. One might think that a well-thought-out response to pressure for organizational change would prompt everyone to unite and work together to promote meaningful change. In fact this desired result of the planning process does not always occur. There are numerous reasons why employees at all organizational levels might resist change efforts.

One common concern relates to honest differences of opinion about the factor(s) suggesting the need for a change (or if there is even the need for a change), as well as the best approach to address the change. Consider the problem of declining profitability in a hotel. Accounting records indicate that occupancy rates have been decreasing steadily. What is the reason? Top-level managers may **brainstorm** potential issues that have created the problem.

Assume potential reasons for the decline include inadequate marketing messages, improper employee service attitudes, and untrained staff members who fail to meet performance standards. Before change can be implemented, determining what must be changed (e.g., marketing, service, employee performance) is necessary. Without a consensus of all top-level decision makers,

Brainstorm: A decision-making approach in which group members suggest alternative potential causes and/or solutions to problems for group consideration.

Role of HR Personnel in Problem Solutions

How can those with HR responsibilities help resolve problems? The answer is that it depends on the specific problem. Let's consider three problems: inadequate marketing, improper service, and performance failures due to inadequate training.

◆ If the problem solution involves marketing issues, there may be little, if any, HR input that can be helpful, assuming marketing staff are competent. However, if the decision to hire an external marketing consultant is made, HR staff may help to develop a Request for Proposal (RFP). If a resolution tactic involves securing the services of hospitality students or other part-time personnel to make cold calls to community businesses, then HR personnel (in a large organization) can assist in these efforts. In a small property, marketing managers may assume these duties.

◆ If the problem is judged to be service-related, HR managers might assist by developing (selecting) and implementing guest service training programs. They might also deliver leadership training to supervisors. The goal is to modify the relationship between supervisors and their employees in an effort to improve staff members' attitudes about their jobs.

◆ If the problem relates to widespread job performance problems, this is a significant HR concern. It begins when employees are selected, and it continues through orientation and training; again, it relates to the manner in which supervisors facilitate the work of their employees.

resistance to any change is likely. For example, marketing personnel believe renting guest rooms in a hotel that fails to deliver what guests desire is difficult. Some department managers believe that service is a problem, but not in their own departments. They may also concede that some performance standards are not attained in their own departments. However, they allege that the reason relates to staffing reductions required because of decreased revenues that make it almost impossible to deliver training designed to increase output standards. In this example, without a consensus about the real problem, a unified effort to respond is not likely to occur.

There are numerous reasons why good employees may resist needed change. They include:

◆ **Concerns about the change or the change process**—Top-level decision makers may question the need for change and may be defensive about making changes because of concerns that to do so would question the relevance of their earlier judgments. Changed work responsibilities, effect on budgets, and the need to relearn and/or to significantly modify work practices are among the concerns that can prohibit buy-in to problem resolution ideas that alter how the organization currently does things.

◆ **Fear and uncertainty about one's professional future**—"Will I still be needed?" and "How will I fit in?" are two obvious questions that can arise when significant organizational change is proposed because this type of change will likely impact staff members at all organizational levels, including those at the top. "Why must I relearn everything if I will be retiring soon?" and "I don't think I can do things any other way" are two additional examples of concerns that can affect employees at any organizational level as change is proposed and implemented.

◆ **Conflict between departments**—The process of change may benefit some departments and staff members and negatively affect others. Outsourcing housekeeping responsibilities may ease the pressure on the accounting staff that must develop payroll reports and process employee paychecks. At the same time, stress is likely to increase for housekeeping and HR managers, who may need to terminate staff and secure the services of and administer the contract for an external service provider. If the power struggles that may result from conflicting interests and impacts are not effectively managed, change will not occur or, at least, will not happen without significant offsetting problems.

- **The organization itself**—Organizations with many management levels typically require a longer time to make decisions than do their flatter organizational counterparts. Some observers say this is good because decisions are more likely to be considered and carefully analyzed as they flow down through the organization's management layers. Other observers counter by noting that decision makers in small entrepreneurial businesses are much more able to quickly respond to and take advantage of changes that impact the organization because there are fewer layers of management. With today's emphasis on less is better and doing more with less, many organizations are becoming less centralized and push decision making to the lowest possible level.

- **The organization's culture**—Consider the cultural values of an organization that emphasize its reputation, history, respect for the contributions of employees, and quality and guest value. Contrast these values with others that emphasize "We go slow and don't make mistakes" or "The best approach is to be conservative and follow everyone else." While change for the sake of change is not always a virtue, an organizational culture striving to be its long-term best is certainly influenced by values that are very different from those in organizations where the status quo and a dislike of change are emphasized.

- **Unfamiliarity with details about the change**—Groups of employees (teams) and specific individuals within departments may resist change when reasons have not been explained and justified and if the impact on them is not carefully explained.

Human Resources Managers Must Have Change Management Skills

Human resources and other managers who are most effective at helping their organizations confront and benefit from changes use numerous skills to do so.

- **Business skills**—An organization must be carefully managed before, during, and after changes are made. Revenues must be generated, costs must be controlled, product and service development efforts must continue, and the work of an organization's staff members must be facilitated. Effective change managers are good business managers.

- **Political skills**—Interpersonal relationships can become strained when, for example, managers compete for priorities, limited resources, and job security as the change process evolves. The organization's social systems must be understood, and judgments must consider the relationships with and personalities of those involved in the change process. Effective change managers are effective politicians.

- **Analytical skills**—One must be able to undertake an objective analysis of the conditions before and after change, and considering financial implications of change alternatives is especially necessary. Effective change managers are effective change analysts.

- **System skills**—Change managers know how employees in the organization's work sections, departments, and divisions, if applicable, affect and interact with each other. Those making change-related decisions in multiunit organizations further understand the relationship between individual properties and other levels in the organization. They consider how change impacts each element in the total system and how each component can be made better as a result of the change. Effective change managers are effective system managers.

- **People skills**—The types of communication and interpersonal skills required for successful change management are addressed throughout this chapter. Those managing change must be able to minimize resistance to it, resolve conflicts as they occur, and, as the process evolves, use the best input from those affected by the change. Effective change managers are effective people managers.

Role of HR in Change Management

Figure 12.2 indicates that the role of HR in change management increases as change moves from gradual to dynamic. Gradual change is often accomplished with relatively simple changes in operating procedures and work methods, revisions to policies, and modifications to service standards. Equipment and supplies may need to be purchased, staff may need to be trained, and new vendors may be required. Work schedule changes, new supervisory methods, and new performance evaluation concerns may also become important. The list of changes needed to implement gradual changes can be extensive. However, the primary point is that most gradual changes can be planned and implemented by managers and staff members in the departments directly affected by the change.

The assistance HR professionals can give an organization increases as the organization addresses intermediate-level changes. Those with HR management training and responsibilities are among the likely choices to determine company-wide or property-wide training needs, select training vendors and/or develop and modify existing training materials, and conduct train-the-trainer sessions on applicable topics. In large organizations some or all of these responsibilities likely are centralized in an HR department because of the HR focus required when planning and implementing significant change.

When a hospitality organization is confronted with dynamic change, it can become a significant challenge just to continue day-to-day operations. Managers at higher organizational levels will likely be involved in numerous planning activities and in the implementation of a variety of actions dictated by their new plans.

Each of the examples of dynamic change noted in Figure 12.2 (i.e., a new business model, business expansion, and reorganization) requires significant management expertise and time necessary for careful planning and follow-up actions. HR managers must address these tasks while doing their fair share of the assignments applicable to preparing for the change. Meetings with staff at all organizational levels as they represent top-level leaders and the implementation of specific change-related activities become priority responsibilities for HR managers. Determining reporting relationships so organizational charts can be revised, working with higher-level managers to

HR MANAGEMENT ISSUES 12.1

"It just can't be done; it will never work. What does Susan think she is doing?" said Tamara, the head cook at the Grayville Widget Company, an account managed by the Good Times Food Service Management Company. She was talking to Abhijit, the assistant cook.

Good Times had won the food service management account for the Grayville Widget Company about two years ago. It had successfully negotiated the contract by emphasizing high-quality food at reasonable prices for employees with no required company subsidy. In fact many of the menu items were high quality, but they were also convenience foods, and that was alleged to be the reason for a slow but steady decline in the employee participation rate.

Susan, the unit manager, analyzed responses from numerous surveys, focus groups, and suggestion box memos and conducted many face-to-face conversations with employees. The conclusion was almost unanimous: The employees wanted freshly prepared foods or, at least, a lot more of them than were now available.

The head cook was responding to Susan's announcement about fresh food preparation at the meeting earlier in the day:

"We don't have the staff, we don't have the time, we don't have the necessary storage and preparation equipment, we don't have the recipes, and many of our staff members don't have the skill. We just can't do it!"

"If I was neutral about this," said Abhijit, "I would say that I could see both sides of the situation. The guests want what they want, and we want what we think we can do. I'm glad I'm not Susan as she figures this out."

Case Study Questions

1. What role, if any, do you think that Susan's production staff played in the situation that has caused the present marketing challenge?

2. List actions that Susan, as her facility's HR manager, should take now to involve her production staff in the decision-making process.

3. What are alternative ways that Susan can now work to minimize the production staff members' resistance to change?

develop job descriptions, planning recruitment activities, and participating in selection decisions are examples of HR-related tasks that become important at this time.

Is the property unionized? If so, collective bargaining agreements may be affected and may result in contract renegotiations. Labor staffing levels and schedules may be affected, and a need for additional training efforts may be required.

An organization's employees are affected by any type of change, and they must be considered as an integral part of the change process. Someone (HR specialists in large organizations and managers with these responsibilities in smaller organizations) must undertake these tasks along with their other ongoing duties.

⠋ MANAGING A MULTIGENERATIONAL WORKFORCE

LEARNING OBJECTIVE 2. Discuss guidelines that are helpful in facilitating the work of staff members belonging to the various generations that make up today's workforce.

For those in HR management, change directly initiated by the characteristics of the workforce itself is especially important to address. The specific racial, gender, and ethnic makeup of a hospitality organization's work staff often varies depending on the type of organization and where it is located. But people of all ages enjoy stimulating and interesting careers in the widely diverse hospitality industry. That means that within any organization workers of a variety of ages are typically employed. Experts from numerous disciplines have suggested that people are fundamentally different because of their life experiences, which are affected by the era during which they grew up, matured, and entered the workforce. These experts further suggest that these differences result in continual changes in work attitude and thus should be considered as people are managed at work. This section discusses how HR professionals can best manage in the large majority of organizations employing a multigenerational workforce.

Overview of Generations in the Workforce

Workers can be grouped in a variety of ways, including their position title, assigned tasks, and length of time on the job. Figure 12.3 presents basic demographics about workers categorized by their date of birth.

While the exact beginning and ending birth years, and even the most popular names, for the various generations identified in Figure 12.3 vary somewhat among observers, there is general agreement about some of the specific characteristics that can be associated with the members of each generation. For example, because of their length of time on the job, **Baby Boomers** occupy a large number of senior management positions in hospitality organizations. Many of the oldest of these (i.e.,

Baby Boomers (workforce generation): People born between approximately 1946 and 1964.

Name of Generation	Dates of Birth	Age Range (in 2016)
Baby Boomers	1946–1964	53–70
Generation X	1965–1979	51–37
Generation Y (Millennials)	1980–2000	36–16
Generation Z	After 2000	Younger than 16

Figure 12.3 Four Generations That Comprise the Majority of Today's Workforce

Generation X (workforce generation): People born between approximately 1965 and 1979.

Generation Y (workforce generation): People born between approximately 1980 and 2000. Also known as "Millennials."

Generation Z (workforce generation): People born after 2000.

those older than 65) and even some members of the generation that came before them frequently supplement their retirement incomes by holding part-time jobs in the hospitality industry.

Generation X employees, especially those on the fast track, are also likely to be in the senior management ranks of hospitality organizations. Even some **Generation Y** staff members, especially those with new and highly specialized skills, are now advancing to middle-management positions. Other Generation Y employees make up a large number of those in entry-level jobs, whereas the oldest of **Generation Z** are just reaching the age at which they can begin working.

Just as it can be a mistake to generalize about (stereotype) people based on nationality, ethnicity, and other factors, developing generalizations applicable to all people in a given age group is also inappropriate. Some observers, however, have identified advantages to modifying leadership styles to accommodate different groups of individuals based on those factors that motivate them to be effective performers. This reasoning may be applied to the suggestion about modifying leadership styles based on employees' ages. This might be an appropriate tactic, and it is relatively easy to do, when, for example, most staff members belong to a specific generation (e.g., think about quick-service restaurants and the majority of teenagers/young adults who are employed by them).

However, changing one's leadership style based on employee age is much more difficult to implement in other operations with many employees of differing ages. For example, consider a restaurant with a high check average with Baby Boomer senior managers, Generation X production and service staff, and younger (Generation Y or Z) employees in assistant production, server, and clean-up positions.

Wise HR managers should be aware that employees may have different perceptions about work, its meaning, and their interest in it based on their age and other factors. Supervisory training sessions can address these topics, and analyses of personnel-related challenges can consider these issues. Also, if possible, management–employee interactions can address the potential impact of generational differences in employees' attitudes.

Managing the Generations

It is difficult for some managers to interact with different generations because doing so can challenge their own beliefs and values, force them to consider the impact of change and conflict, and create the need to modify their communication skills. Let's review some basic information about the work beliefs and characteristics of the four workforce generations in today's hospitality industry: Baby Boomers, Generation X, Generation Y, and Generation Z. Figure 12.4 suggests general beliefs, characteristics applicable to work ethics, view of work, and personal and work traits of these workforce generations.

Even a brief review of the generational characteristics noted in Figure 12.4 identifies some very interesting factors that differentiate members of each generation. Note that these differences often become much more noticeable when one considers people at the midpoint of each generation. For example, when you think about differences between Generations X and Y, think about people in their mid-40s (Generation X) versus those in their mid-20s (Generation Y). Don't think about those who are the youngest people in Generation X and the oldest people in Generation Y because their ages are relatively similar.

When reviewing the work characteristics of Baby Boomers, recognize that they have often been called the "me generation." They are also the largest generational group. Their work incentives include money, position titles, and recognition for the work they do. When they entered the workforce, Baby Boomers wanted to build a significant career to enhance their reputation. They challenged the status quo, and those in this generation are responsible for many of the opportunities now taken for granted in the workplace. They became the first workaholics, and they believe that hard work and loyalty are a good way to get ahead. Many Baby Boomers sense that who they are as individuals is directly connected to their work and career achievements.

Generation X employees are motivated by job satisfaction. They don't anticipate remaining in one job or with one company throughout their careers. They know they can jump from one job to another in their efforts to attain desired compensation and other benefits and to receive increased opportunities for growth and personal fulfillment. They desire to provide input to their

Work Characteristics	Baby Boomers (1946–1964)	Generation X (1965–1979)	Generation Y (1980–2000)	Generation Z (2001 and beyond)
Work ethic (view of work)	Driven (work is exciting)	Balanced (work is a challenge)	Eager (work is done to make a difference)	Yet to be fully determined
Personal traits	Idealistic, not enough time	Practical, flexible, individualistic, entrepreneurial, interested in quality of life	Politically conscious, high self-expectations, team builders, tolerant of differences, confident, desire challenges	Comfortable multitasking; advanced technology skills; globally connected to their peers via social media
Work traits	The first workaholics Want to climb ladder of success Want to be politically correct Compete with peers Performance measured by time in the office Respect top-down authority Casual attire means unprofessional	Don't like office politics Have less loyalty to employers Multitask workers Like collegial work environment Like to do projects Are concerned more about job responsibilities than job titles Performance measured by output Do not like power structures Flexible with authority Casual attire is comfortable	Want to know why Desire public praise Enjoy a fun workplace Money is not a motivation; they can get it anywhere Want immediate responsibility Want small goals with tight deadlines Work–life balance is important Do not seek longevity with a company High expectations of employers Confident in their abilities	Very accustomed to working in groups and collaborating with others Seek technology-based solutions to problems Want to make a difference in the world through their own eco-efforts and the efforts of their employers May be a more sedentary generation than those that have gone before them

Figure 12.4 Work Beliefs and Characteristics of the Generations

Workforce Generations Are Different!

HR managers should learn about the generations and their differences because:

◆ there are now at least four generations of employees working side by side in the hospitality industry.

◆ the industry is labor-intensive and will continue to need employees, regardless of their age, to staff the many available positions.

◆ the range of differences between the oldest employees (Baby Boomers) and the youngest staff members (Generation Z) is very wide.

◆ differing values, experiences, lifestyles, and attitudes toward the future and life in general can create significant misunderstandings and frustrations.

◆ those who better understand and appreciate each generation may gain ideas about how to motivate and retain people within these generations and will be better able to consistently work with individuals of differing ages.

employers, and they have an interest in understanding how the company works because they know this will influence their growth opportunities. Personal acknowledgment and job satisfaction are very important for this generation.

Generation Y employees want to know the why of what they are being asked to do; they want to know what's in it for them. They enjoy a fun workplace, and money is not a motivator because they think they have numerous employment opportunities. They are also quick to speak their opinions and are not responsive to the do-it-or-else supervisory tactics that some hospitality managers frequently use.

While members of Generation Z are just now entering the workforce—and, as a result, their work-related values and beliefs are just becoming known—there is information related to this group that is very well known:[1]

◆ In 2006 there were a record number of births in the United States, and 49% of those born were Hispanic. Since the early 1700s the most common last name in the United States has been Smith; now it is Rodriguez.

◆ The number of births in 2006 far outnumbered the start of the Baby Boomer generation; thus the size of this generation will eventually exceed that of Baby Boomers.

◆ Members of this generation have never known a world without cell phones and computers. They take for granted the amount of data they have access to and the speed with which they can access it.

◆ Social media use readily connects them to their global peers, and they are the generation most accepting of those with significant cultural differences.

◆ They likely will not be as loyal to their employers as past generations because they have witnessed lack of corporate loyalty when they experienced how their parents' jobs were affected by the economic downturns of 2001 and 2009.

◆ They are very comfortable with Web-based learning, and multitasking is second nature to them.

Should Managers Dwell on Generational Differences?

There are diverse opinions about how people should be managed. Some say that everyone should be treated the same. Others say it is important to emphasize—or at least consider—generational differences. Still others suggest that employees should be treated as individuals.

One industry observer suggested several tactics that work equally well for employees in every generation, in every organization, at any time:[2]

◆ Show employees that what they do matters.
◆ Tell employees the truth.
◆ Explain to staff members why they are being asked to do something.
◆ Learn the employee's language.
◆ Provide rewarding opportunities.
◆ Praise staff members in public.
◆ Make the workplace fun.
◆ Model the desired behavior.
◆ Give staff members the tools required to do their jobs.

While different generations may appreciate different leadership tactics, these best-practice techniques work with all staff members.

⁂ MENTORING PROGRAMS

LEARNING OBJECTIVE 3. Identify key concerns that should be addressed as employee mentoring programs are planned and implemented.

One way an organization can help many of its multigenerational staff members do their best work is by mentoring them. In a business, **mentoring** is a relationship in which an experienced staff member provides professional advice to a less experienced staff member. These activities can arise informally when a relatively inexperienced person solicits advice from an "old-timer" about how the organization works. Mentoring relationships can also be more formal, such as when experienced volunteers receive training in mentoring activities and then interact with staff selected for participation in "fast-track" career development programs. Sometimes a mentoring relationship lasts for a short while or it can last for many years.

Mentoring: A formal or informal relationship in which an experienced staff member provides advice and counsel to a less experienced staff member.

Several advantages can accrue to your organization when you implement an effective mentoring program:

- ◆ **Rapid assimilation**—Junior staff can more quickly learn about the organization's culture and how to act within it.
- ◆ **Enhanced commitment**—Mentorees may have increased commitment to the organization because they are better assimilated into the corporate culture.
- ◆ **Increased satisfaction levels**—Higher levels of job satisfaction can occur, with a decreased chance that those being mentored will leave the organization.
- ◆ **Early intervention**—Problems that hinder the mentoree's current performance can be more rapidly addressed.

Advantages can also accrue to those who serve as mentors:

- ◆ **Enhanced self-esteem**—A mentor will likely feel good about the opportunity to provide advice and to make a difference.
- ◆ **Increased knowledge**—Mentors learn as they interact with mentorees.
- ◆ **Seen as good citizens**—Mentors may receive special consideration as their own careers are evaluated.
- ◆ **Helps to train successors**—Sometimes mentors cannot be promoted until someone is available to assume their position, and this can be the mentoree.

An effective mentor can serve several roles in interactions with mentorees:

- ◆ **Trainer**—Mentors who are queried about specific on-job performance issues can provide applicable assistance and serve as an informal trainer.
- ◆ **Coach**—Mentors can provide positive reinforcement about desired performance, and they may advise against actions that may lead to on-job difficulties, just as a supervisor does when coaching a staff member.
- ◆ **Counselor**—Counselors do not make decisions for another person. Rather, they discuss the pros and cons of a situation. They ask open-ended questions to learn what the other person is thinking and, in the process, allow the other person to more clearly think things through. A counselor provides benchmark information that can help one to evaluate personal perspectives.
- ◆ **Guide**—Just as a guide safely leads someone who is unfamiliar with a geographic area to a destination, so can a mentor help a mentoree to move on to interim locations on the way to a longer-term destination (career).
- ◆ **Role model**—The old saying "actions speak louder than words" suggests that mentorees can learn much from their mentors just by observing them as they interact with others in the organization.
- ◆ **Advocate**—A mentor in a senior position can emphasize the strengths and abilities of a mentoree to those at higher organizational levels.

Phases of a Mentoring Relationship

It is not typical that a senior staff member begins to interact with a less experienced counterpart and immediately gives free advice. Instead, time is required for a relationship of mutual respect to evolve and for the mentoree to appreciate and trust the mentor's judgment. The relationship between a mentor and mentoree can involve the same steps as building a friendship:

◆ **Introduction**—A mentoring relationship can begin by chance as two persons meet on the job, or it can begin more formally when a senior staff member is paired with a less experienced person in a planned career development program.

◆ **Cultivation**—Time is needed for both individuals to get to know each other, to understand each other's position, and for the mentor to understand the context within which the mentoree is soliciting advice.

◆ **Redefinition**—Few relationships on the job remain the same. They typically grow stronger or weaker, and they sometimes end. At some point, the junior staff member may not require or desire advice and counseling. Conversely, mentors may have a lessened desire to continue in the mentoring role. By contrast, relationships can become stronger and evolve into lifelong (or at least career-long) opportunities to share information and to enjoy a mutually rewarding relationship.

How exactly can a mentor assist a mentoree? Examples of mentoring activities include:

◆ Helping the mentoree to develop a **career ladder**

◆ Advising about development activities that can assist the mentoree in moving toward career ladder goals

◆ Evaluating alternative education and training programs and courses of action to address on-job concerns

◆ Providing applicable reading materials

◆ Suggesting alternative courses of action that address on-job problems

◆ Making special assignments and arranging for special training, if applicable

◆ Providing ongoing counseling

HR managers can use 10 steps when implementing a formal mentoring program, as outlined in Figure 12.5. Let's look at each of these steps more closely:

◆ **Step 1: Obtain support of top-level managers**—HR personnel, managers, supervisors, and others who support the need for a formal mentoring program should serve as its advocates to top-level officials. A discussion of the benefits noted earlier may help the program gain approval.

◆ **Step 2: Determine goals of the mentoring program**—Numerous goals, including the benefits to the organization, the mentors, and mentorees noted previously, are likely to be among desired results.

◆ **Step 3: Appoint key planning staff**—Those interested in developing a mentoring program are likely candidates. The project could also be appropriate for consideration by a **cross-functional team** of people who could bring differing perspectives to the planning process.

◆ **Step 4: Plan the mentoring program**—Decisions about how mentors and mentorees will be selected and paired, their responsibilities, the mechanics of how and when the

Career ladder: A progression of positions with increasingly more responsibilities within an organization or an industry.

Cross-functional team: A group of staff members comprising representatives from different departments (functional areas) that address a common concern.

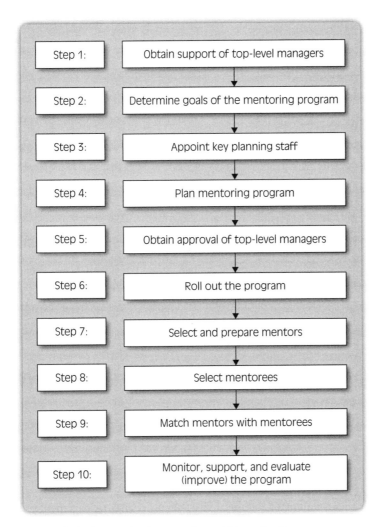

Figure 12.5   Steps to Implement a Formal Mentoring Program

parties will interact, topics for which mentoring discussions are appropriate, and how the program will be announced, administered, and evaluated are required.

◆   **Step 5: Obtain approval of top-level managers**—Interim input from these officials may have been provided; if so, approval is likely to be easier and faster. The mentoring program should be seen as beneficial, inexpensive to implement, and with few disadvantages that require consideration as an approval decision is given.

◆   **Step 6: Roll out the program**—Program announcements, staff meetings, organizational newsletters, information during orientation programs for new staff, and conversations among managers, supervisors, and staff members are among promotion possibilities. The availability of and procedures for the mentoring program should also be an integral aspect of applicable career development programs.

◆   **Step 7: Select and prepare mentors**—Effective mentors are usually successful, high-performing staff members. They have a track record of successful performance over many years and in probably several positions. However, they may need to learn basic mentoring skills. The knowledge, skills, and abilities of effective mentors most frequently include:

- the desire to assist mentorees

- an ability to think creatively and to suggest problem-solving alternatives to mentorees

- the ability to motivate mentorees

- effective oral communication skills, including the ability to present, explain, organize, and defend suggestions

Ground Rules for a Mentoring Relationship

The environment within which an effective mentoring relationship exists is one of mutual respect and trust, productivity, and safety (comfort). Ground rules for managing the mentoring partnership can help ensure that this environment continues. Examples of mentor and mentoree agreements can include:

◆ How and when meeting times are established

◆ How discussion topics are determined

◆ How disagreements, if any, should be resolved

◆ What, if any, contact should occur between scheduled meetings

◆ Statement of confidentiality: Neither the mentor nor the mentoree should share each other's confidences without mutual approval

◆ Meetings are treated as a priority, and each person's full attention is concentrated on them.

◆ Honesty is important

◆ Humor, if used, is respectful and appropriate

◆ Anecdotes of past mentoring and learning experiences are shared

◆ The mentor is supportive, not controlling

- an interest in assisting the organization and the mentoree
- an understanding of and the ability to apply change management principles
- an understanding of the organization's culture and the ability to use this knowledge to explain, defend, and justify suggestions
- detailed knowledge of business and operating principles applicable to the organization

How should mentors be prepared for their role? Topics to be addressed in training sessions can include a discussion of:

- mentoring goals of the organization and for the mentor and mentoree
- critical attributes of the mentoring relationship
- suggestions for determining the mentoree's needs and for generating alternatives that address them
- training and career development opportunities within the organization. If applicable, a special emphasis should be placed on fast-track and other programs that include a formal mentoring component.
- training in communication skills, including active listening techniques
- relationship skills
- effective coaching tactics
- problem-solving and conflict resolution suggestions

◆ **Step 8: Select mentorees**—In informal mentoring programs, less experienced staff may simply request that a more experienced counterpart discuss issues of concern. Some organizations have mentor open-door policies, where any staff member with a question or concern can seek out a more experienced person on an ad hoc or continuing basis. In a more formal model, fast-track staff are assigned a mentor, and this input is an integral part of their planned career development program.

◆ **Step 9: Match mentors with mentorees**—Considerations in matching mentors and mentorees can include close proximity (same location) and the extent to which the mentor has held positions similar to that of the mentoree. In some instances, matching gender and/or a common ethnic, racial, class culture, or class background may be judged to reduce barriers that hinder trust. In addition, observers typically suggest that mentors not be a staff member's immediate supervisor or trainer.

◆ **Step 10: Monitor, support, and evaluate (improve) the program**—Once implemented, mentoring efforts should be evaluated to ensure that they are cost-effective and that they are achieving planned results. Also, like many other programs, continuous quality improvement efforts are helpful to ensure that the mentoring effort best meets the needs of the organization, the mentors, and the mentorees as it evolves.

❖❖ SUCCESSION PLANNING ACTIVITIES

LEARNING OBJECTIVE 4. List procedures that are useful in the succession planning process.

One area in which organizations continually evolve is that of staffing. Position vacancies can occur for a variety of planned and unplanned reasons including promotions, retirements, and other forms of voluntary or involuntary separation. When vacancies occur they must be filled. **Succession planning** is the process used by HR managers to help ensure that they continue to have the key professional and other staff needed to support their planned growth and to replace key employees who leave their position or the organization.

As with any type of planning, succession planning is easier when it is done for the short term rather than for longer time periods. However, organization executives, HR staff, and operations managers do well to think about the future and to consider how their HR needs are likely to change over time.

Figure 12.6 identifies steps that you can use in the succession planning process.

◆ **Step 1: Identify priority positions for succession planning**—While all positions in the organization are critical (they should not exist if they are not), some positions require more specialized training, experience, and/or skills than do others. These are among those requiring special attention as future HR needs are considered. Examples may include positions in which incumbents are responsible for specific multiunit locations in relatively small companies and others in which incumbents have district, area, regional, or other responsibilities in larger organizations. Top-level executives and staff advisory

Succession planning: The process of considering the organization's future needs for key professional and other staff and developing plans to select and/or to prepare individuals for these positions.

Staff Members Have Different Career Goals

Not every person in a hospitality organization wants to advance to positions with more responsibilities and higher compensation levels. While some employees do, others do not and are content with their present responsibilities. A primary goal of every manager should be to provide the education and/or training necessary for staff members to become proficient to consistently attain performance standards in their existing position. Then managers should have another concern: to help interested staff members attain competencies that allow them to assume new positions to further benefit themselves and their organizations.

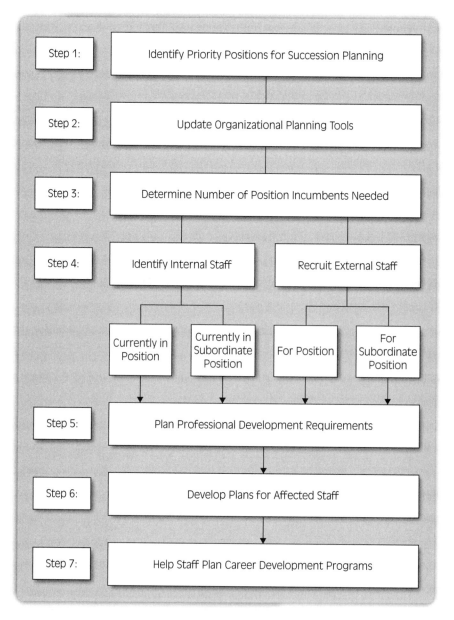

Figure 12.6   Steps in the Succession Planning Process

specialists with human relations, accounting, purchasing, and other responsibilities in small or large organizations may also occupy hard-to-fill positions that require specialized expertise for which succession planning can be helpful.

◆   **Step 2: Update organizational planning tools**—Sometimes the urgency of ongoing business hinders opportunities to keep organizational charts, job descriptions, and job specifications current. HR managers must consider three key issues: (1) What is the relationship between the high-priority positions identified in step 1 and others in the organization? A current organizational chart indicates this relationship. (2) What are the current tasks in the priority positions? Current job descriptions answer this question. (3) What experience, skills, knowledge, and educational and/or other personal requirements are judged necessary for an incumbent in the position to be successful? Current job specifications provide this information.

Each of these issues must be carefully assessed because they drive much of the succession planning process that follows. For example, will business volume and/or organizational structure change so that more, the same number, or fewer area managers are required? How, if at all, will responsibilities of position incumbents change? Will responsibilities become more generalized or, alternatively, will positions become more focused, with one or more of the current tasks being assigned to someone else?

◆ **Step 3: Determine the number of position incumbents needed**—Assume, for example, that a regional quick-service restaurant organization currently has four area managers and that top-level managers are using a succession planning process to identify critical needs over the next five years. How many area managers will then be required? Concerns about anticipated organizational changes and business volume noted previously affect this decision. The increased role, if any, of technology and other means to increase productivity of those working in the positions, and to fulfill the communication needs of the organization, should also be considered as the number of future position incumbents is addressed.

Planners must also think about the number of vacancies likely to occur that will need to be filled. In this example, the organization currently has four area managers. Assume that planners (1) anticipate the need for six area manager positions in five years; (2) believe that one current incumbent will be retiring; and (3) plan to promote another area manager to a regional position within that time frame. Four area manager positions must be filled during the next years (i.e., four current managers – two managers leaving = two managers available; six managers needed – two managers available = four new managers needed).

◆ **Step 4: Identify internal staff and/or recruit external staff**—Some current employees may fill higher-level positions in the future because they possess the necessary traits and have expressed a desire to be promoted. Alternatively, they may be competent in their current position but are not believed to be qualified for the position for which succession is being planned. Other staff members who are considered eligible for promotion to these key positions may currently occupy positions at a variety of subordinate (lower) organizational levels. The difference between the number of position incumbents needed (step 3) and those currently in the position or who can be prepared for it (step 4) represent the number of external staff to be recruited. External staff might be recruited for key positions as they become vacant, or they can be immediately recruited for a subordinate position with the assumption that they can be trained now to assume key positions in the future.

◆ **Step 5: Plan professional development requirements**—Current position tasks and education and training requirements for those in the key positions should already be known based on their positions' job descriptions and job specifications. HR managers must address how currently employed workers holding lower-level skills can learn new skills. They consider what additional tasks or responsibilities are likely to be of concern in the future. Finally, they must consider how those selected as part of the succession plan can be become competent to perform in the future. The answers to these and related issues help identify the specific professional development activities needed to prepare an employee for a future position.

◆ **Step 6: Develop plans for affected staff**—Fortunately, incumbents currently in a position and external staff recruited for it will be competent in many (or even all) of the required tasks. Currently employed staff and their externally recruited counterparts will likely have some time to prepare themselves for their next position. In many cases HR professionals prepare a specific development plan for each staff member. Part of this plan may include participation in an effective mentoring program. Staff members identified for advanced positions should also be encouraged to participate in job enlargement and job enrichment programs. Special projects might be delegated to them to simultaneously assist the hospitality organization and prepare the staff members for their future positions.

◆ **Step 7: Help staff plan career development programs**—Ideally, staff members identified in the succession planning process are interested in long-term positions within

HR Management: Impact on New Team Members

I n the majority of cases an organization's new employees hope that their new job choice was a good one and that it will lead to a high level of job satisfaction and future earning potential. While some employees certainly take a job with the expectation of staying only a few weeks or a few months, HR managers often find they are orienting new employees who have long-term job aspirations. In some cases assuming that new employees will be able to advance much beyond the position for which they were initially hired may not be realistic. For many employees, however, one of the appealing aspects of the hospitality industry is their ability to advance in the specific areas chosen for their careers. Advancements such as these are beneficial to the individual and to the organization for which they work. Skilled production workers may become production supervisors. Skilled servers may become dining room managers. Supervisors at all levels may become unit managers, and unit managers may become multiunit managers.

HR managers have an opportunity to influence a new employee's current performance by discussing in realistic terms the worker's potential for future advancement in an organization. This may occur during the interviewing process or be included as a part of the organization's employee orientation program. While no guarantees of advancement should be made, it is good for new employees to know that if they work hard and are receptive to learning new skills, they have good prospects for achieving higher levels of responsibility, status, and pay.

the organization. Those identified for advancement will require a specific career development program. Procedures helpful in training for, implementing, and monitoring individualized personal career development programs are discussed in the next section.

Every hospitality organization should be concerned about its future. While top-level managers can never predict the future with certainty, they can and should use their knowledge of the present to influence likely occurrences. They can do so by:

◆ carefully considering a succession planning program that addresses anticipated HR needs;

◆ identifying existing employees with the potential for advancement; and

◆ assessing how deficiencies in employee knowledge and skills can be addressed by professional development plans and activities.

∴ CAREER DEVELOPMENT PROGRAMS

LEARNING OBJECTIVE 5. List the reasons HR managers develop and assist staff members with their career planning activities.

Career development program: A planning strategy in which one identifies career goals and then plans education and training activities designed to attain them.

A **career development program** (also called a professional development program) identifies training and educational opportunities to help staff members become more proficient in their current positions and to prepare them for career advancement. Much of the effort required to attain these objectives will have been expanded as basic training and education requirements applicable to each position were developed (see chapter 6) and as the succession planning process (see the previous section) is completed.

Advantages that can accrue to your hospitality organization when you emphasize career development opportunities for your staff include:

- **Reducing absenteeism and turnover**—Managers who help staff members prepare for the future show human relations concerns. These efforts can improve morale, which helps reduce absentee levels and turnover rates. While labor and other costs associated with absenteeism and turnover are difficult to quantify, they are real and significant. Organizations that improve their staff's morale do much to improve service to their guests and, in the process, to increase their bottom line.

- **Assisting with productivity increases**—Staff who are prepared for a new position can reduce the learning curve and be useful immediately when they assume the new position. The necessary transitional period before quality and quantity outputs reach desired performance standards will likely be reduced. Also, costs to provide necessary education and training programs today will likely be less than those in the future.

- **Emphasizing managers' concerns about their staff**—Showing respect for staff members, exhibiting a genuine desire to assist them, and providing open lines of communication are additional examples of ways that management concerns can be actualized through professional development programs.

- **Preparing for future challenges**—Training alternatives such as cross-training, job enlargement, job enrichment, and job rotation programs have already been noted. Organizations are better prepared for challenges that can arise when the range of job tasks that staff members can correctly perform is expanded. Professional development activities undertaken to improve performance in existing positions help improve product and service quality, reduce costs, and increase profits.

- **Addressing future labor needs**—As suggested in the previous section, succession planning tactics can help managers identify general education and work experience requirements that likely are required for future successful performance. In the process professional development opportunities needed by existing staff will be better known.

In addition to helping the hospitality organization, career development activities are of direct benefit to those who undertake them.

- **They allow staff members to learn and gain the experience necessary for promotional opportunitie**s—Many organizations use and many staff members appreciate promotion-from-within programs that recognize the potential for future contributions of existing staff and in the process help reduce turnover rates.

- **They reinforce the employment decisions made by new staff**—Corporate cultures that emphasize professional development opportunities allow staff members to enjoy on-job success and to feel positive about their employer.

You've learned that career development enables employees to plan for their futures within an organization or industry by identifying career goals and then developing plans to attain them. At the same time, it helps the organization to reduce turnover and related expenses because of the increased morale that typically occurs when affected staff members are given opportunities for career growth.

For many employees, career decisions are influenced by factors such as personal interests, likes and dislikes, and being at the right place at the right time. However, a staff member's career plans can also be influenced by opportunities presented by the employer. The mentoring, counseling, and encouragement provided by those at higher organizational levels can significantly influence staff members' plans, aspirations, and the energy levels required for career advancement within the organization. You've also learned that opportunities to acquire greater levels of knowledge and skill can be addressed during performance appraisal sessions, as ongoing work responsibilities are assigned, and even as simple coaching conversations evolve.

Many staff members will not require significant encouragement to become involved in professional development programs, but others will. Employees benefit from their employer's efforts to encourage them to prepare for promotions, and they can do so by participating in well-planned education and training activities.

Professional Associations Assist with Career Development

Professional associations exist to assist their members with numerous needs, including the provision of continuing education opportunities. Examples include conducting national conferences and developing and providing training resources and services. Continuing education opportunities for group and/or individual study and the coordination of regional or other chapters that provide educational opportunities in local areas are additional examples.

In some cases separate foundations or institutes have been established for the specific purpose of developing and administering continuing education programs. Examples include the National Restaurant Association, which operates the National Restaurant Association Educational Foundation, and the American Hotel & Lodging Association, which operates the American Hotel & Lodging Educational Institute.

Professional associations charge membership dues and fees to support their services. Typically, a significant percentage of the revenues generated are used to develop educational and training resources to improve the organization's members and the industry served by the association. To review educational resources available from selected hospitality associations, enter the association name in your favorite browser and review their websites.

Professional Association	Membership
National Restaurant Association	Restaurant and food service professionals
American Hotel & Lodging Association	Hotel owners, managers, and suppliers
Asian American Hotel Owners Association	Hotel owners, managers, and suppliers
Club Managers Association of America	Managers of private membership clubs
American Culinary Federation	Culinary artists
School Nutrition Association	Managers of school food service operations
National Association of College & University Food Services	Colleges and universities operating student dining programs, as well as their suppliers
Academy of Nutrition and Dietetics	Dietitians and nutrition specialists
Association of Nutrition & Foodservice Professionals	Nutritional care specialists
Association for Healthcare Foodservice	Managers of self-operated health care food service facilities
International Flight Services Association	Airline and railroad onboard services providers
National Association for Catering and Events	Catering and event management professionals
The Council of Hotel and Restaurant Trainers	Training professionals in the hospitality industry

HR MANAGEMENT ISSUES 12.2

"I have an idea that will benefit our business and our employees and that has no downside to it," said Joshua. He is the HR manager for the food services operation at the Metropolitan Bank, one of the largest banks on the East Coast, and the largest bank in the United States with a self-operating food services program. Joshua is attending a meeting of department heads and has just returned from a national conference of hospitality HR managers.

"I would call the program, 'We Care About You.' We would make an offer to all of our staff members: First, become proficient in your existing position—and we could tie this to results of our performance appraisal procedures. Then we would assist them with career planning activities and provide them with ongoing professional development experiences. This would result in increased job skills and help prepare them for promotions to positions with greater responsibilities and more compensation."

"Joshua, that's sounds like a great idea and I would personally support it in theory," replied Suzanne, the department manager. "I think we've emphasized this philosophy as we encouraged employees to do better and to learn more. However, we've never formalized a process, communicated it consistently and effectively, or really worked hard to encourage and help our employees to be better performers and stay with us."

"I guess it sounds like a good idea," said Raoul, the food production manager, "but I have two concerns. First, it sure wouldn't look good if we make a big deal out of this now as we rolled out the program and then deemphasized it later. Also, do we really have time to do everything necessary to help all of our staff given the million and one things we must all do every day to keep the operation running?"

"I do like the general idea of the program, and I'm certain it will encourage spirited discussion as we consider it further," said Suzanne. "My suggestion is that we table the conversation for now, and let's all consider it over the next two weeks and then make it a primary agenda item at our next staff meeting."

Case Study Questions

1. What are the benefits to the Metropolitan Bank food services department if the "We Care About You" program can be implemented? The potential disadvantages?

2. What is the employees' likely reaction to the program?

3. What suggestions would you make to Suzanne, Joshua, and the management team as they consider implementing the program?

Documentation of career development plans and accomplishments can help workers further prepare for their future advancement. Figure 12.7 shows specifics that can be identified when creating an individual employee's career development plan.

Figure 12.8 illustrates a worksheet that can be used to indicate the planned methods by which the required competencies identified in Figure 12.7 can be obtained. It also allows the career planner to indicate scheduled and actual completion dates.

Figure 12.9 provides a detailed summary of information about how and when the required competencies identified in Figure 12.7 were actually acquired.

As a final example, Figure 12.10 shows a format for a career progression record that comprises the experience portion of one's professional resume.

Activities that relate to one's career comprise a significant part of the waking hours of many people. Those who enjoy their careers are therefore very fortunate. Organizations with a culture that allows and encourages staff members to enjoy what they do while working provide a win–win situation for all constituents. Managers in these organizations plan professional development programs to help their staff members become competent in future positions. The personal career development programs HR professionals put in place benefit guests, the hospitality organization, and its staff members.

Name: _____   Date: _____

Employer: _____

Position: _____

Time in current position: Years _____   Months: _____

Current Supervisor: _____

_____

Personal/Professional Interests: _____

_____

_____

_____

Education: High School Graduate or GED: YES _____   NO _____

College: YES _____   NO _____
If yes, circle one: GRADUATE   ATTENDING   ATTENDED

Other Formal Education: _____

CAREER GOALS:

To what position do you aspire: New competencies needed to attain this
                                             career goal:

In one year: _____   _____

_____   _____

_____   _____

In five years: _____   _____

_____   _____

_____   _____

In ten years: _____   _____

_____   _____

_____   _____

Figure 12.7   Career Development Plan

EDUCATION LEARNING METHOD

Required Competencies	On-Job Training	Ongoing Staff Meetings	Independent Learning Course	Group Study Course	Local Chapter Program	College Course	Other (Indicate)	Completion Date	
								Planned	Actual

Other Education/Training Plans:

Figure 12.8 Training and Education Planning Worksheet

Name: _____

Intermediate Career Goal: _____

_____

New Competency: _____

_____

_____

Date Completed: _____

Name of Institution/Training Organization: _____

_____

Certificate Awarded: YES   NO   Type: _____

_____

Other Details: _____

_____

_____

Figure 12.9 Competency Score Card

Name: _____

Career Goal: _____

Starting Date	Ending Date	Position	Name of Organization	General Position Responsibilities

Figure 12.10 Career Progression Record

HR MANAGEMENT ISSUES 12.3

Charles has recently relocated to the Republic of the Fiji Islands (Fiji) from a major city in the eastern United States to manage a resort for a West Coast hotel chain that is just beginning an international expansion. His company had the best intentions of adequately preparing him for his new assignment. His background and motivations were considered, and personal assessment tools used by the company suggested that he and his family would adjust well to the new culture.

Before departing, Charles and his family learned background information about the culture of the islands and knew what to expect about personal issues such as housing, education, and access to medical services. Charles also received some general information about conducting business in Fiji. He had not, however, learned details about hotel management protocols in the country because his company was not able to locate people with this background who could or would provide basic information for a reasonable fee. The consensus was that this was not a major problem because, in its most general sense, the hotel would be managed and operated in the same way as any other hotel in the company.

Charles and his family arrived in Fiji and were pleased to learn that their prearrival preparation was good and there were only a few minor surprises to which they were able to adapt without significant hardship.

Charles's experiences on the job, however, were different. All of the employees spoke English (as he knew they would), and communication did not seem to be a significant issue. However, there were two concerns that he did not expect. One involved the fact that most of his staff members lived in the same tribal village. Numerous awkward situations arose when people of different tribal rank and/or familial relationships were required to supervise, or to be supervised by, each other. Problems arose when, for example, a family patriarch in the village was supervised on the job by a junior nephew.

The second concern was one that he wished he could have experienced in his domestic positions: entry-level staff members wanted (almost excessively) ongoing training. Charles liked this request, wanted to provide the training, and realized its long-term benefit to the organization. However, he was concerned about the time needed for these staff members to learn tasks required for their current positions. The time available for additional training for future positions was minimal because of the significant amount of start-up work that was necessary.

Charles wished that he would have been prepared for these issues so he would have known how to deal with them better.

Case Study Questions

1. How can Charles deal with these issues in a way that is acceptable for both the organization and the employees?

2. What, if any, general assistance can his organization, headquartered in the United States, likely give him as he addresses these concerns?

3. Assume you were the HR manager of Charles's company. Based on Charles's experiences, what specific recommendations would you have for better preparing employees selected for international assignments?

HR TERMS

The following terms were defined in this chapter:

Organizational change
Target market
Gradual change
Dynamic change
Brainstorm

Baby Boomers
Generation X
Generation Y
Generation Z
Mentoring

Career ladder
Cross-functional team
Succession planning
Career development program

FOR YOUR CONSIDERATION

1. Consumer preferences for food, beverage, and lodging products are continually evolving. The operational changes that result from these evolving consumer preferences can directly affect the efforts of HR managers.

   a. What are some specific consumer-driven changes you believe are directly affecting the menu items produced and sold by food service operations today? How will these changes affect HR management?

   b. What are some specific consumer-driven changes you believe directly affect the manner and locations in which food service items are sold today? How will these changes affect HR management?

   c. What are some specific consumer-driven changes in the desires of today's travelers for lodging products and services that directly affect how hotel managers and supervisors operate their facilities? How will these changes affect HR management?

2. The characteristics of Generation Z employees are currently being evaluated and analyzed. Clearly, however, one of the most significant characteristics of this generation is their tremendous ability to use and apply technology in their personal lives.

   a. What specific challenges are likely to occur within hospitality organizations as these employees enter the workforce in increasing numbers?

   b. What are some specific ways HR managers can utilize the technology-related skills of this generation to help improve customer service and product delivery in hospitality settings?

3. Consider one of the jobs you have held personally. Were there one or more members of your employing organization that you would have, if given the opportunity, selected to become your mentor? What specific personal characteristics did these individuals display that makes you feel they would have been a good mentor? Do you think you will likely display similar characteristics in your future career? Explain your answer.

4. Succession planning can be a challenge for any organization. It is especially challenging for hospitality organizations that are rapidly expanding internationally. What specific steps would you recommend an organization take to identify and develop managers who are being considered for job placement in international assignments of significant responsibility?

5. How would a career development process such as that described in this chapter benefit you if you were just beginning your hospitality management career? If you were in an entry-level (nonmanagement) position in an operation? If you were in a middle-management position with an organization?

CASE STUDY

Apply HR Management Principles

Mindy and Rachel grew up in the lodging business. Their family owned a franchised property in an area that attracted family vacationers during the summer months. Over the years, occupancy rates during these months were always very high, even though more properties were (seemingly) always being built.

They and their families took over the operation of the property after their father retired, and he has since passed away. During the intervening years, they perceived a decreased number of advantages to their property's franchisee affiliation. Mandated upgrades, many of which did not seem to be worth their cost, were an ongoing concern. The hotel did generate significant room nights through the centralized reservation system, but they also had a good base of repeat visitors. Also, they thought they could attract many more travelers with a marketing and advertising budget that could be funded from monies saved because franchise fees would no longer be necessary.

"I think we should just go ahead and do it; the franchise agreement will be up within the next two years,' said Mindy. "We can make more money, we won't have to endure so many hassles, and we can be successful by using lots of our own ideas instead of those of the franchisor, which don't always work."

"You might be right, Mindy," said Rachel. "We've talked about this a lot, and we have undertaken some feasibility studies that defend your position. Many people are coming through this area during the summer months, and I don't think we need to rely on our franchisor's reservation systems anymore. With all the Internet booking sites available to us, we can market directly to target customers. Also, we talked about adding an indoor water park with features that might attract people from within the region during our slow months. If we do this, it will mean changing a lot of things in our current operation."

Dimension: Change Management

1. Mindy and Rachel are considering taking steps that will require significant change in their operation. What factors do you think have generated their sense that change is necessary? What additional factors would you recommend they consider?

2. The decisions Mindy and Rachel are about to make will have a significant impact on their staff. What role, if any, do you think existing managers and the operation's employees should play in Mindy and Rachel's decision-making process?

3. The changes Mindy and Rachel are considering are substantial. If they elect to drop their franchise affiliation and create an on-site water park, what dynamic changes do you think they will immediately encounter? What intermediate changes should they anticipate? What are some gradual changes they are likely to experience?

Dimension: Employee Resistance to Change

1. When, if at all, do you recommend that Mindy and Rachel inform the employees of their existing lodging property about the decision to eliminate the franchise relationship, if this decision is made? What about their interest in considering an indoor water park?

2. Do you think Mindy and Rachel's employees are likely to become stressed and anxious about these pending decisions? Why? Defend your response.

3. What types of similar concerns, if any, might the hotel's front-office managers and its food and beverage managers have as these changes are made?

Dimension: HR Management

1. If they are no longer affiliated with the chain organization, what difference do you think this will make in the way Mindy and Rachel recruit new staff members for their property?

2. What changes relating to staff training will occur if the franchisor–franchisee affiliation ends?

3. What longer-term changes in HR management might occur if the lodging property becomes independent?

INTERNET ACTIVITIES

1. One of an HR manager's most important challenges is that of ensuring the continued employment of their very best employees. Talented individuals are in high demand in the hospitality industry. Because that is true, an organization's best workers will continually find they have many alternative employment opportunities. Effective HR managers help an organization retain its best workers in the face of significant competition for these workers' services.

   To review employee retention–related resources available to HR managers, enter "tips for retaining quality employees" in your favorite search engine and review the results.

   a. Based on your review, what are specific actions HR managers can take to help ensure the best of their managerial and professional staff are highly satisfied at work?

   b. Based on your review, what are specific actions HR managers can take to help ensure the best of their hourly paid staff are highly satisfied at work?

2. One of the significant advantages of membership in a professional association is that of low-cost access to the association's professional development programs. Consider your own career aspirations and

a professional association (or two) of which you would likely be a member. Visit these associations' websites and search for information directly related to their continuing education and professional development programs.

    a. Based on your review, what types of professional development activities are offered by this association on an ongoing basis? Do you think these pro-

grams would be of interest to you as a professional in this field? Explain your answer.

    b. Based on your review, what types of professional development activities are offered during the association's annual and/or quarterly meetings and conferences? Do you think these programs would be of interest to you as a professional in this field? Explain your answer.

ENDNOTES

1. Jill Novak. "The Six Living Generations in America." MarketingTeacher.com. Accessed July 30, 2013. http://www.marketingteacher.com/lesson-store/lesson-six-living-generations.html.

2. Carol Verret. "Generation Y: Motivating and Training a New Generation of Employees." Ideas & Trends, Hotel Online. November 2000. Accessed July 30, 2013. http://www.hotel-online.com/Trends/CarolVerret/GenerationY_Nov2000.html.

INDEX